Secular Societies, Spirit

CW00493261

Secular Societies, Spiritual Selves? is the first volume to address the gendered intersections of religion, spirituality and the secular through an ethnographic approach.

The book examines how 'spirituality' has emerged as a relatively 'silent' category with which people often signal that they are looking for a way to navigate between the categories of the religious and the secular, and considers how this is related to gendered ways of being and relating. Using a lived religion approach the contributors analyse the intersections between spirituality, religion and secularism in different geographical areas, ranging from the Netherlands, Portugal and Italy to Canada, the United States and Mexico. The chapters explore the spiritual experiences of women and their struggle for a more gender equal way of approaching the divine, as well as the experience of men and of those who challenge binary sexual identities advocating for a queer spirituality.

This volume will be of interest to anthropologists and sociologists as well as scholars in other disciplines who seek to understand the role of spirituality in creating the complex gendered dynamics of modern societies.

Anna Fedele is Senior Researcher at the CRIA-Instituto Universitário de Lisboa (ISCTE-IUL), Portugal. Her research focuses on the intersections of gender and religion with a particular interest for ritual creativity and pilgrimage. She has done fieldwork in Southern Europe and Latin America about holistic spiritualities and Catholicism.

Kim E. Knibbe is Associate Professor of Anthropology and Sociology of Religion at Groningen University, the Netherlands. She is currently directing the project 'Sexuality, Religion and Secularism' (funded by the Netherlands Foundation for Research, NWO). Previous research focused on Catholicism and spirituality in the Netherlands and on Nigerian Pentecostalism in Europe and the Netherlands.

Gendering the Study of Religion in the Social Sciences

Titles Include

Secular Societies, Spiritual Selves?
The Gendered Triangle of Religion, Secularity and Spirituality
Edited by Anna Fedele and Kim E. Knibbe

For more information about the series, please visit:
https://www.routledge.com/anthropology/series/GSRSS

Secular Societies, Spiritual Selves?

The Gendered Triangle of Religion, Secularity and Spirituality

Edited by
Anna Fedele and Kim E. Knibbe

Routledge
Taylor & Francis Group
LONDON AND NEW YORK

First published 2020 by Routledge

2 Park Square, Milton Park, Abingdon, Oxon OX14 4RN
605 Third Avenue, New York, NY 10017

Routledge is an imprint of the Taylor & Francis Group, an informa business

First issued in paperback 2022

British Library Cataloguing-in-Publication Data
A catalogue record for this book is available from the British Library

Library of Congress Cataloging-in-Publication Data
A catalog record has been requested for this book

ISBN: 978-0-815-34975-4 (hbk)
ISBN: 978-1-03-233615-2 (pbk)
DOI: 10.4324/9780429456923

Typeset in Times New Roman
by Taylor & Francis Books

To all those who struggle to combine care (including self-care) with the demands of academic careers

To the memory of Gianfranco Fedele (1931–2020). Per aspera ad astra.

Contents

Figures

Contributors

Kristin Aune is Professor of Sociology of Religion at the Centre for Trust, Peace and Social Relations, Coventry University, and Vice President of the International Association for the Study of Religion and Gender. Her research focuses on religion, gender and higher education, and she has published widely, including in the journals *Men and Masculinities, Gender & Society, Religions* and *Social Compass* (a 2017 special issue on 'Is secularism bad for women?'). Her books include (with Sharma and Vincett) *Women and Religion in the West: Challenging Secularization* (Ashgate, 2008) and (with Redfern) *Reclaiming the F Word: Feminism Today* (Zed, 2013). Her current research projects are on modest fashion in UK women's working lives (funded by the UK's Arts and Humanities Research Council) and tackling religion-based hate crime on the multi-faith campus (funded by the UK government's Office for Students).

Irene Becci has been a professor at the Institute for the Social Scientific Study of Contemporary Religion, University of Lausanne since 2012. She has studied in Lausanne, Rome, Florence and New York, and holds a PhD in social and political sciences from the European University Institute. In her post-doctoral years she has been doing research and teaching at the Max-Planck Institute for Social Anthropology in Halle/S., at Bielefeld and Potsdam University, Germany. In her research she focuses on religious diversity and new spiritual practices in particular settings, such as prisons, urban spaces and ecological activism, with a particular attention given to gender. Together with Olivier Roy she has published *Religious Diversity in European Prisons – Challenges and Implications for Rehabilitation* (Springer, 2015). Her publications can be found among others in *Archives des sciences sociales contemporaines, Critique internationale, Social Compass, Tsantsa, Journal of Religion in Europe* and *Women's Studies*.

Renée de la Torre has been Professor of Anthropology at the CIESAS Occidente, in Guadalajara, Mexico, since 1993. She is a member of the National Research System (SNI-level III) and the Academy of Science in Mexico. She has a PhD in social science, with a speciality in social anthropology. She has specialized in the study of religious change in

Mexico, the changes in Catholicism, spiritual movements, religious pluralism and secularism, the transnationalization of Aztec dance. Her recent publication include *New Age in Latin America: Popular Variations and Ethnic Appropriations* (Brill, 2016) and *Mismos pasos y nuevos caminos: Transnacionalización de la danza conchero azteca* (CIESAS, 2017–2018).

Manéli Farahmand holds a PhD in Anthropology of Religions, specialized in Central America religious phenomena, transnational studies and contemporary religious movements. She completed a joint PhD (University of Lausanne/University of Ottawa), based on a multi-sited ethnography project, investigating the encounter between Maya revival movements and New Age spiritualities. She was the 2017 local coordinator for the International Society for the Sociology of Religion (ISSR) in Lausanne, as well as the 2019 Programme Chair for the ISSR Conference on "The Politics of Religion and Spirituality" in Barcelona. She is now preparing her postdoctoral research and habilitation on the dynamics of ritual and embodiment in contemporary religion and spirituality.

Anna Fedele is a senior researcher at the Center for Research in Anthropology of the Instituto Universitário de Lisboa (CRIA, ISCTE-IUL), whose research focuses on the intersections of lived religion, gender and corporeality with a specific interest in ritual and pilgrimage. She obtained her PhD in co-tutelle from the Universidad Autonoma de Barcelona and the EHESS in Paris. She is the author of the award-winning *Looking for Mary Magdalene: Alternative Pilgrimage and Ritual Creativity at Catholic Shrines in France* (Oxford University Press, 2013), and the co-editor of *Gender and Power in Contemporary Spirituality* (Routledge, 2013). She is co-founder of the Network for the Anthropology of Gender and Sexuality of the European Association of Social Anthropologists (EASA) and of the Routledge book series Gendering the Study of Religion in the Social Sciences.

Alexandre Grandjean is a PhD candidate at the University of Lausanne, specializing in the study of the religion/spirituality and sustainability nexus. With socio-anthropological perspectives, he investigates how biodynamic agriculture, an esoterically driven and practitioner-based agronomy, spreads in the Swiss wine-crafting population. He has collaborated on the research projects "Religion and spirituality: The new fuel to energy transition?" (2015–2017) and "Toward a 'spiritualization' ecology?" (2017–2020). In 2019, he received the Best Student Paper Award of the International Society for the Study of Religion, Nature and Culture (ISSRNC) for his contribution "Biodynamic wine-crafting and the 'spiritualization' of agroecology: Case study from Switzerland".

Mar Griera is associate professor of the Department of Sociology of the Autonomous University of Barcelona, and the director of the Centre for the Sociology of Religion (ISOR). She is also the vice-president of the Sociology of Religion Research Committee of the International Sociological

Association. Her research focuses on investigating the intersection between religion, spirituality, identity and politics in contemporary Europe. She has coordinated different competitive projects in these areas, edited several special issues in this area and extensively published the results in academic journals and books.

Cristina Gutiérrez Zúñiga is a full-time professor at Universidad de Guadalajara (Mexico). She has a PhD in social sciences from El Colegio de Jalisco, Mexico (2002). Her work is centred on the pluralizing of religion in Mexico, new religious and spiritual movements, and the transnationalization of religious practices. Her current research projects are on religious diversity and public schools in Guadalajara, and the methodological approach of lived religion in Mexico. Her published works in English include (with De la Torre and Juarez) *New Age in Latin America: Popular Variations and Ethnic Appropriations* (Brill, 2016).

Kim E. Knibbe is Associate Professor Anthropology and Sociology of Religion at Groningen University. She is currently directing the project "Sexuality, Religion and Secularism" (funded by the Netherlands Foundation for Research, NWO). Previous research focused on Catholicism and spirituality in the Netherlands and on Nigerian Pentecostalism in Europe and the Netherlands. Furthermore, she has published a series of theoretical and methodological reflections on studying religion that address how the experience of lived religion, as a mode of experiencing reality that is somehow identified as "different", can be approached in ethnographic research. Publications include the monograph *Faith in the Familiar, Religion, Spirituality and Place in the South of the Netherlands* (Brill, 2013) and the co-edited volume (with Anna Fedele) *Gender and Power in Contemporary Spirituality* (Routledge, 2013).

Martin Lepage has received a PhD in religious studies (Sciences des religions) from Université du Québec à Montréal in 2017. He specializes in the intersection of contemporary religiosities and ritual practices with matters of identity, gender and sexuality. His doctoral thesis explored power relationships around those themes within the Montreal Pagan community, focusing on notions and perceptions of magic, witchcraft and spirituality. He is currently an independent researcher, working mostly on performance, ritual practices, and alternative masculinities among the Radical Faeries.

Chia Longman (PhD in comparative sciences of culture, 2002) is Associate Professor in Gender Studies at the Department of Languages and Cultures at Ghent University, Belgium. She directs the Centre for Research on Culture and Gender (CRCG) and is Programme Director of the Inter University Master Programme in Gender and Diversity. She is a board member of the International Association for the Study of Religion & Gender. Her primary research focus is women's identity and agency within different religious communities and movements in Europe, ranging from

Orthodox Judaism to new spiritualities. Publications include (with T. Bradley) *Interrogating Harmful Cultural Practices: Gender, Culture and Coercion* (Routledge, 2015) and (with G. Coene) *Féminisme et multiculturalisme: Les paradoxes du débat* (Peter Lang, 2010), as well as various book chapters and articles in journals such as *Citizenship Studies, Ethnicities, European Journal of Women's Studies, Gender, Place & Culture, Politics & Gender, Religion & Gender, Religions, Social Anthropology, Social Compass* and *Women's Studies International Forum.*

Stefania Palmisano is Associate Professor in the Sociology of Religion at the University of Turin, where she teaches the sociology of religious organizations and the sociology of religion. She is Visiting Research Fellow at Lancaster University and Wolverhampton University. She is co-ordinator of the research centre CRAFT (Contemporary Religion and Faiths in Transition) based in the Department of Culture, Politics and Society of Turin University. Her research takes the form of ethnographic study of contemporary religious experience in mainstream religions, alternative spiritualities, and possession and exorcism in Catholic Charismatic movements. She is the author of *Exploring New Monastic Communities: The Re-invention of Tradition* (Ashgate, 2015), (with Isabelle Jonveaux) *Monasticism in Modern Times* (Routledge, 2016) and (with Nicola Pannofino) *Invention of Tradition and Syncretism in Contemporary Religions: Sacred Creativity* (Palgrave Macmillan, 2017).

Roberta Pibiri (PhD) is a researcher in the sociology of religions and a member of the research centre CRAFT (Contemporary Religions and Faiths in Transition), Department of Cultures, Politics and Society of University of Turin. Her main research interests are: gender and religion; Goddess Spirituality, Paganism and ancient female sacred paths; alternative spirituality and religious transformations; the sacred and creativity; cultural and religious diversity; religious experience, self-transformation and emotions; and ritual performance. Her recent publications include (with Stefania Palmisano) "'We are all Goddesses': Female Sacred Paths in Italy', in Ruspini, Bonifacio and Corradi (eds), *Women and Religion. Contemporary and Future Challenges in the Global Era* (Policy Press, 2018) and "Re-membering the Goddess: the Avalon Sacred Path in Italy between Tradition and Innovation", in Palmisano and Pannofino (eds), *Invention of Tradition and Syncretism in Contemporary Religion: Sacred Creativity* (New York: Palgrave Macmillan, 2017).

Carine Plancke is a postdoctoral researcher at the Centre for Research on Culture and Gender at the University of Ghent on a research project entitled "Embodying the Feminine Divine: Agency, Subjectivity and Cultural Alterity in Women's Yogic Retreats" and funded by the Flanders Research Foundation (FWO). She holds a PhD in Social and Cultural Anthropology from the School for Advanced Studies in Social Sciences in Paris and the

University of Leuven. From 2011 to 2013 she was a teaching and research fellow at the universities of Nice and Clermont-Ferrand. As a Fernand Braudel and a Marie Curie fellow, she further conducted postdoctoral research at the Centre for Dance Research of the University of Roehampton (2014–2016). Her research interests include gender, embodiment, performance, affect, creativity, ritual and spirituality.

Laurel Zwissler is associate professor of Religion and affiliate faculty member in Women and Gender Studies at Central Michigan University. Her book *Religious, Feminist, Activist: Cosmologies of Interconnection* (University of Nebraska Press, 2018) focuses on global justice activists and investigates intersections between religion, gender and politics, relating these to theoretical debates about religion in the public sphere. As reflected in her contribution in this volume, she is now building on this work with ethnographic research within the North American fair-trade movement to explore emerging definitions of community simultaneously created by economic globalization and its critics. Her fieldwork with contemporary Witchcraft communities also inspired her series of articles about the shadows of women within classical academic theories of religion. These pieces explore challenges to traditional notions of academic knowledge creation, disruptions grounded in imaginaries of female bodies and the moral values ascribed to them.

Introduction

Spirituality, the third category in a gendered triangle

Anna Fedele and Kim E. Knibbe

> You see, regarding these issues I do not agree with the Vatican…,
> I have my own spirituality,
> and I have my own ideas about certain things.
>> (Portuguese pilgrimage guide in Fátima, May 2018)

In 2013, two texts were published that built on qualitative research to argue that current scholarship on the rise of 'spirituality' versus the decline of 'religion' failed to capture the complexity of organized religions as well as that of contemporary forms of spirituality. As often happens in scholarship, scholars who do not know of each other's work on the same topic at the same moment arrived at similar insights. Sociologist Nancy Ammerman published an article titled "Spiritual But Not Religious? Beyond Binary Categories in the Study of Religion" based on research in the United States (Ammerman 2013). The other text was the companion volume to this book, *Gender and Power in Contemporary Spirituality: Ethnographic Approaches*, focusing on anthropological studies in different European countries as well as in Mexico and Israel (Fedele and Knibbe 2013). Both texts acknowledged that the religious/spiritual dichotomy is important for contemporary people and should be taken seriously (see also Klassen 2001, Chapter 4) and proposed to study what people mean when they say that they are spiritual but not religious; in other words, to understand this dichotomy as a cultural phenomenon to study rather than as an analytical tool. Ammerman concluded that "[f]uture research on spirituality should neither presume it to be primarily an extra-institutional phenomenon nor presume that a single umbrella designator can describe the varieties of spiritualities present in U.S. [and European] culture" (Ammerman 2013, 276). She analysed the "moral boundary work" (Lamont 1992) done by those who prefer to identify as spiritual rather than religious and observed that this distinction was made, although in different ways, by members of traditional religions as well as by people with a more secular approach. In both cases, being spiritual implied marking a moral boundary of separation from a religion considered as an immoral enemy. Therefore, she concludes, whenever people refer to themselves as 'spiritual but not religious' "political and not descriptive work is being done" (275).

Similarly, in our 2013 volume we explored what might be included in the category of 'spiritual' and how it sometimes overlaps with religion, sometimes emerges as a distinct category in relation to religion. In our Introduction we advocated for an 'anthropology of the spiritual' as a category that in recent years has emerged as a significant 'other' of the category of religion and that should be studied bearing in mind local and cultural specificities taking into account also its relationship with the secular. Thus, we did not propose our own definition of religion and spirituality, but explored the pairs of opposites that spiritual practitioners associated with these categories. Like Ammerman, we emphasized that spiritual practitioners produce a stereotyped idea of 'religion' that may not always be an accurate reflection of 'lived religion', but does important work in shaping people's idea of what they want to develop under the umbrella term 'spirituality', even when it is in some cases very similar to what people who call themselves religious may be striving for.

Crucially, we argued that gender and power form an important nexus in this religious/spiritual dichotomy. In the previous volume as well as in this one, we propose that reworking valuations of gendered difference is a crucial theme whereby those who claim the label of 'spiritual' simultaneously claim a space to rework oppressive or faulty gender ideologies, distancing themselves from institutionalized religion (see also Aune 2015, reprinted in this volume). This does not mean that we claim that it is impossible to be 'spiritual' and subscribe to oppressive gender ideologies, or to behave in ways that may not further gender equality (see especially Knibbe 2013; Werczberger 2013; Fedele and Knibbe 2016). We simply mean to say that generally, when people claim the label of spirituality, their aim is to do things differently when it comes to gender. They want to do things differently from institutionalized religion but also, as we shall explore in this volume more explicitly, differently from what they identify as secular contexts.

Since these publications in 2013, research on spirituality has become a hot topic in the social sciences and as a result the keyword 'spirituality' is often found alongside religion in the title of call for papers, conferences as well as articles and books. Whereas earlier scholarly debates tended to focus on spirituality as crypto-capitalistic narcissism (e.g. Carrette and King 2005) and spirituality as a revolutionary solution to the crisis of religion (e.g. Heelas and Woodhead 2005), more recently spirituality is increasingly studied from a lived religion perspective. Nevertheless, so far the entanglements of spirituality and religion in relation to the secular have remained underexplored.

In this Introduction we propose to develop the anthropology of spirituality in relation to the anthropology of the secular, bringing it into conversation with the growing body of literature on 'the secular', secularism and secularity. This literature has shifted the conversation on the fate of religion in modern society from a focus on secularization to an analysis of how 'religion' emerges as a category in relation to the secular (Asad 2002, 2003, 2011; Casanova 2009; Agrama 2012; Asad et al. 2009). This analysis developed in tandem with discussions of the merits and limitations of the secularization thesis according to which, in an increasingly secularized world, religion will eventually become irrelevant or disappear (Casanova 2009; see Knibbe in Knoblauch et al. 2011 for a summary of the debate on this topic between Asad and Casanova). In this debate, the consensus that has emerged at least among social scientists studying religion and spirituality in contemporary (Western) societies is that the secularization thesis has only limited validity (Casanova 1994; Davie 2002; Berger 2014). Furthermore, following Asad, one could argue that the whole premise of this thesis is flawed since it misconstrues religion as a universal category, rather than religion and secularity as twin categories that have historically emerged together and derive their meaning in relation to each other.

Interestingly, the relationship of the category of 'spirituality' to the secular is discussed less often (although it is discussed in relation to the secularization thesis; see, e.g., Woodhead 2008). In this book we want to explore how in many countries 'spirituality' has emerged as a category that is relatively 'silent', at least in the public domain. Whereas sociologists and philosophers have celebrated the 'return' or rediscovery of religious actors with an opinion and lots of impact in the public domain, identifying as 'spiritual' seems to guarantee that one can slip away unnoticed. There is a lot of debate on the presence of religious symbols and gatherings in public spaces, but meditating or doing yoga in a public square rarely meets a lot of resistance or raises flags among policy makers.

Based on the research presented in this book and elsewhere we propose that by identifying with this silent category people usually signal two important and entangled strategies for positioning themselves: 1) they are looking for a way to navigate between the religious and the secular; 2) they are working, either explicitly or implicitly, on gendered ways of being and self-constitution that are seen as an alternative to, or at least critically relate to, the secular frames of the society in which practitioners find themselves. It is for this reason that we think it is crucial to examine the relationship between spirituality, religion and the secular through the lens of gender.

Discussions on 'private religion' and 'private spirituality' often seem to depart from the problematic assumption that what happens in the private domain is somehow unimportant (Dobbelaere 1993; Bruce 2003). This 'private equals unimportant' assumption usually goes hand in hand with the expectation that once women enter the labour market, and thus become more socialized into public life, they too will secularize (Brown 2009). But what does it mean when phenomena located in the 'private' sphere are simultaneously dismissed as irrelevant? Why should this private sphere not be a domain for sociological and anthropological enquiry? As many scholars have pointed out, distinctions between public and private spheres historically developed in tandem with new differentiations in gender roles (Scott 2017). At the same time, spiritual practitioners themselves may also take a self-effacing attitude: since this is my own, private preference for how to develop myself and experience the world, it is not of your concern. One could argue that by locating spiritual practices in the private sphere, practitioners can claim some crucial space to develop a way of life away from critical eyes.

In contrast, we propose that as scholars we do not go along with these forms of dismissal and self-effacement of spirituality as 'merely private'. Rather, we propose to understand these minimizing strategies as gendered, and the distinction between public and private as a culturally variable and gendered phenomenon, not as a given. Understanding these strategies as gendered allows us to ask the question how the differentiations between the public and the private map onto the distinctions and overlaps between spirituality, religion and secularity. Thus, this edited volume builds on the previous volume to develop an anthropology of the spiritual that analyses this domain of 'private' practice in relation not just to religion, but also to the secular. In the following, we will first outline what we understand to be the secular and how it can be relevant to understanding spirituality, and reiterate and expand what we mean by the term 'spirituality'. Then, we will link our understanding of the work that is done via the label of spirituality to feminist scholarship on public and private domains, before introducing our proposal to view spirituality as the third category in a gendered triangle. The final part of this Introduction will briefly summarize the chapters.

Secular bodies, secular practices

Religion and spirituality seem to be distinct 'entities'. One can point to a church, and assume that one can find 'religion' there. One can point to a meditation centre, and assume that at least some people there will be calling themselves 'spiritual'. One can point to certain behaviours and practices, and identify those as religious (e.g. prayer, making the sign of the cross, kneeling) or spiritual (e.g. chanting, meditation, inducing altered states of consciousness through ritual). In contrast, the secular is a much more vague and encompassing category, in terms of its practice and material manifestations. How do you observe 'secular behaviour'? What exactly are 'secular practices'? Is there, to speak with Charles Hirschkind, a 'secular body' (Hirschkind 2011; Wiering 2017; Scheer et al. 2019)? So what do we mean when we refer to the secular?

In recent decades, following the call of Asad (2003) to develop an 'anthropology of the secular', literature on this topic has boomed. In adjacent fields (political science, international relations, the sociology of religion, religious studies, history, philosophy) interesting scholarship has emerged as well (e.g. Bracke 2011; Agrama 2012; Burchardt, Wohlrab-Sahr and Middell 2015; Bartelink 2016; Aune et al. 2017; Wilson 2017). For the sake of clarity, we want to distinguish our interest in 'the secular' from 'secularism'. Along with sociologists such as Monika Wohlrab-Sahr and Marian Burchardt, but also anthropologists such as Saba Mahmood, Charles Hirschkind and Webb Keane, we are interested not in the ideologies concerning the differentiation between church and state (secularisms), but rather in the practical arrangements that have been developed historically and culturally, observable in daily life, to delimit what religion is and the ways that religion is separated out from the secular (Bracke and Fadil 2008; Fadil 2011; Hirschkind 2011; Schuh, Burchardt and Wohlrab-Sahr 2012; Wohlrab-Sahr and Burchardt 2012; Mahmood 2015).

Following Agrama, we understand the religious/secular divide as a 'problem space' that is subject to continuous negotiation (Agrama 2012). More recently, a volume by Scheer, Schepelern and Fadil (2019) on the embodied and affective dimensions of the secular has been published that represents an important reference point for thinking about the ways in which we can understand spirituality in relation to the secular and religion. In the Introduction to this last volume, the editors explain that "the secular is nearly always represented in ways that empty it of any such affective and emotional textures, for example by emphasizing neutrality, impartiality, factuality, rationality and reason" (Scheer, Schepelern Johansen and Fadil 2019, 2). These qualifications are also often mobilized in disqualifying the value of spiritual practices. The idea of a secular self relies upon a disconnection of the body and the world (Asad 2011) where the secular self is represented as rational and neutral, and the religious emerges as irrational and emotional. Although the editors do not point to the gendered assumptions associated with this hierarchical ordering, the association of women with the emotional and the irrational and their predisposition towards religion has been widely analysed (for an exploration of how this association emerged, see Scott 2017).

However, as Scheer, Schepelern Johansen and Fadil note, "the secular is not per se 'un-emotional'" and the ideals related to it "are underpinned by a specific mode of emotionality (which might be referred to as subdued or contained), as well as by emotions about secularity" (2019, 2). These emotions become visible in the intense debates over the presence of religious symbols in public spaces or in the moral panic in discussions about religious extremisms. Similarly, the affect-laden reactions against holistic spiritualities as narcissistic and 'dangerous' allies of neoliberalism can well be interpreted as expressions of 'secular affect' (Mahmood 2009). Scheer, Schepelern Johansen and Fadil conclude that "there is no situation in which the secular can be seen to exist in the pure form that some conceptualizations of it postulate; it is always intertwined with and dependent upon the religious" (2019, 3). Or, as Agrama argued, we should see the relationship of the religious and the secular in terms of a 'problem space' of secularism where actors continuously define themselves and are defined by others in relation to these two categories (Agrama 2012).

The question we ask, then, is: what is the role of the behaviours, practices and domains that are indicated with the category of 'spirituality' in this 'problem space'? How and when do these practices and behaviours become visible, when do they remain invisible, how and when do they blend into a religious or secular background? Often, the secular encompasses both the religious and the spiritual in the sense that, to some extent, most of us are socialized not to express certain convictions and do certain things in public, disciplining our bodies to separate religion, spirituality and secularity, or to switch between languages depending on our conversation partners (see Anna Fedele, Mar Griera and Knibbe, Chapters 8, 9 and 10 respectively, but also Utriainen 2011). However, as we shall see, the spiritual can also become a *lingua franca* bridging the secular and the religious (Fedele, Chapter 8).

In the following, we will first outline in more detail how we conceptualize spirituality as a category and as a domain of practice, before going into the theme of gender and how this is linked to the differentiation between public and private domains, secular and religious domains.

Spirituality is not necessarily unchurched

In *Gender and Power in Contemporary Spirituality: Ethnographic Approaches* we used the term 'contemporary spirituality' to refer not only to the different spiritual movements that proposed themselves as alternatives to religion, but also to those that took place within religion. However, considering the growing literature on these topics and the booming of spirituality language everywhere, in this volume we propose to distinguish holistic spirituality from the more general category of spirituality when referring to spiritual movements that claim not to belong to or to be influenced by institutionalized religious traditions. Sointu and Woodhead defined holistic spiritualities as "those forms of practice involving the body, which have become increasingly visible since the 1980s, and that have as their goal the attainment of wholeness and wellbeing of 'body, mind, and spirit'" (Sointu and Woodhead 2008, 259). In contrast, we refer to spirituality as a term that is used both within established religious groups and within groups that can be identified as practising holistic spiritualities.

Since the publication of Fuller's book *Spiritual, But Not Religious* (Fuller 2001), scholars have debated this new category in people's self-identification to get a better understanding of the beliefs of those people who are unchurched, yet not atheist either. The problem is that many of these authors assume that those who identify as spiritual necessarily or almost always belong to holistic spiritualities. However, as the chapters of this volume as well as the companion volume show, many of those who identify as spiritual but not religious also form part of established religions and are not necessarily unchurched. We agree with Huss that spirituality can be seen as an "emergent new cultural category that challenges the binary opposition of the religious and secular realms of life" which "enables the formation of new lifestyles, social practices, and cultural artefacts that cannot be defined as either religious or secular" (2014, 47). However, unlike Huss, we allow for the possibility that identifications as spiritual may emerge within, or overlap with, the religious domain, as explicated in Chapter 8 by Fedele, for example.

So when did 'spirituality' emerge as something that can be distinguished from religion and the secular? According to van der Veer, the category of spirituality emerged during the nineteenth-century Great Transformation, when the world became integrated in terms of economics, politics and culture. He argues that the spiritual is produced in interaction with the secular, and has become universalized along with the notion of religion (Van der Veer 2009). Spirituality, in this nineteenth-century history, came to position itself as an alternative to institutionalized religion, often aligning with scientific interests and progressive ideals regarding gender relations and anti-colonialism (exemplified by Annie Besant, for example). According to van der Veer, spirituality should not be seen as a fringe phenomenon in relation to modernity, but as something lying at the heart of Western modernity. As other scholars have argued, spirituality and New Age have their roots in the romanticist reaction to the Enlightenment and the rise of science, but at the same time, especially through the development of spiritualism, they often aim to supersede and/or integrate science (Hanegraaff 1996; Campbell 2005). Furthermore, through its position as an intermediate category, spirituality often aligns well with projects of secularism (for example through Gandhi's association of spirituality with the secularity of the Indian nation).

This analysis of the historical rise of the category of spirituality links up with our own analysis of the ways identifications with the term spirituality are dynamic and fluid, but usually informed by pairs of opposites, as we outlined previously (Fedele and Knibbe 2013). There, we found that, across the various contexts that were represented in the chapters of that edited volume, the following pairs of opposites continuously recurred (Fedele and Knibbe 2013, 6):

Religion–spirituality
Fixed–flexible
Authority–absence of authority
Gender inequality–gender equality
Hierarchy–non-hierarchical structure
Status oriented–inner development oriented
Mediated access to divinity–unmediated access to divinity
Body/sexuality hostile–body/sexuality friendly

What makes it particularly interesting to develop an anthropology of spirituality in relation to religion and secularity is the fact that, very often, spirituality positions itself as an alternative to both religion and the secular, without completely rejecting either. Thus, for example, if spirituality presents itself as recognizing the value of femininity, the default, which can be either secular or religious, is assumed to devalue the feminine. Simultaneously, spiritual practitioners affirm the emancipatory and democratic claims of the secular, while also recognizing the rich stores of wisdom hidden away in religious traditions. Thus, they are able to reclaim this wisdom while doing away with the hierarchies and stodgy traditions associated with 'religion'. Furthermore, spirituality introduces enchantment through its emphasis of what Fedele has termed an 'energy grammar' (2013, 2018), while simultaneously affirming that spiritual practice is a personal choice; thus depoliticizing any appearance of spiritual practices in the public spaces. At the same time, it is seen by its practitioners as well as by scholars such as Ammerman and ourselves, as a form of 'practical politics', creating alternatives to the destructive workings of modern society through exploring new ways of living, working, and forming communities (Ammerman 2013; Longman 2018). The 'work on the self' is both adaptive and privatized, as Carette and King argue, and subversive, as Sointu and Woodhead demonstrate (Carrette and King 2005; Sointu and Woodhead 2008).

Whereas previous activisms often rejected spiritual practices, current activists sometimes turn to spiritual practices while referring to Audre Lorde's injunction that self-care, in a society that is bent on destroying you, is a political act (Michaeli 2017). As we will explain in more detail below, when studying spirituality it is therefore essential to problematize the private–public divide, taking into account the political work that can be entailed in practices of self-care as well as in practices of emotional labour that seem private, yet are strongly informed by societal structures and gendered expectations (Hochschild 2003).

The scholarship on spirituality collected in this volume introduces a third dimension to the scholarship on the secular–religious divide that has become such a fruitful area of enquiry in recent years. As Chia Longman observes in Chapter 3, some courses, lectures and books related to personal growth and self-development have been described by scholars as 'secular spiritualities'. This expression, which may initially appear as an oxymoron, turns out to describe very well the kind of mediatory role played by the spirituality explored in this volume. The blurred boundaries between the spiritual and the secular are also evident in so-called 'invented religions'. The blurry outlines of spirituality may be one of the reasons that it has so far been little discussed in scholarship on the religious–secular tensions.

Linked to this mediatory role is the apolitical appearance of spirituality. Despite the fact that spiritual practitioners and activists might conceive of spiritual practice as political, the ambiguous and fluid nature of the category of spirituality in Western modernity has contributed to its appearance as a depoliticized option, as van der Veer argues (2009). Indeed, as we explained above, spiritual practice taking place in public space is often silent, unprovoking, maybe faintly embarrassing. While religion in public institutions is subject to careful governance, the practice of yoga and the holistic spirituality that accompanies it remains below the radar (Griera and Clot-Garrell 2015). Yoga clothes do not attract the intense debates that the hijab, niqab or burqa do. At most, clothes and events associated with yoga and meditation may be perceived as faintly ridiculous and/or a bit embarrassing, as if doing something very private while visible to the whole world. This depoliticized appearance, then, also has to do with the fact that it is often seen as a personal choice, a privatized form of religion and therefore of no consequence for society. However, as we know from feminist scholarship, the public–private divide and the valuations that arise from this divide are deeply gendered, as well as historically linked to the separation of religious and secular domains of society. Building on this recognition, we can gain more insight into exactly what is problematized both by spiritual practitioners and by feminist scholarship.

Public religion, private spirituality?

Following the publication of Casanova's influential book *Public Religions in the Modern World* in 1994, attention in the sociology of religion turned towards the role of religion in the public sphere (Casanova 1994). Often, as already noted in Casanova's book, the public role of religion focuses on issues to do with gender roles and sexuality, whereby religious positions become conflated with conservative stances. At the same time, religious contexts are generally at least numerically (but not in terms of leadership) dominated by women. Influenced by the post-secular turn in feminism (e.g. Braidotti 2008), religious studies scholars focusing on gender have increasingly recognized that although second-wave feminism is generally considered to be and presented itself as anti-religious and shaking off the chains of religion and tradition (Aune 2011; Reilly and Scriver 2014; Aune, Toldy et al. 2017; Longman this volume), the automatic identification of religion with patriarchal arrangements must be critiqued. Certainly, as Scott has shown in her various works, an identification with secularism must not be confused with an automatic support for women's rights and gender equality (Scott 2017). Several authors have observed that a focus on emancipation and gender equity can certainly be combined with a religious identification (e.g. Zwissler 2018). Furthermore, within religious traditions that are overwhelmingly patriarchal, women have nevertheless been able to create significant alternative spaces for developing their own religious practices (Mahmood 2011). In other cases, women have deliberately constructed their theories and practices in open criticism and opposition to Judeo-Christian religions, aiming to create a form of religiosity that is gender equal, non-hierarchical and post-patriarchal.

The numerical dominance of women in both religious and spiritual domains of practice has often been an object of analysis and comment (Heelas and Woodhead 2005; Aune, Sharma, and Vincett 2008; van Osselaer and Buerman 2008; Pasture, Art, and Buerman 2012). The predominance of women in religious contexts has led some authors to speak of the feminization of the religious domain, usually abbreviated as the 'feminization thesis'. As others have shown, this thesis in fact has four different meanings: 1) the numerical increase of women in religious domains since the early nineteenth century; 2) the increase of the number of female congregations in the Catholic world; 3) a change in the character of piety towards more sentimental and emotional forms of religious life and material culture; and 4) a shift in Christian culture through the increased significance of the Virgin Mary, which was sometimes expressed through a strong association between domestic life, religiosity, femininity and anti-intellectualism, as well as the sacralization of feminine virtues through which, in contrast, men came to be seen as inherently more prone to gamble, have extra-marital relations, and so on (Pasture, Art, and Buerman 2012).

The feminization thesis has been helpful in rethinking the history of religion in Europe in two ways: through centralizing women, the secularization thesis was destabilized. By trivializing the role of women and the private domain, this thesis could maintain that religion was becoming less important. Although some scholars did note that to women and the private domain, religion remained important (Dobbelaere 1993), this was not embedded within wider (feminist) theorizing that problematized the distinction between public and private (Casanova 1994; Canaday 2003; Fraser 2009). There are several reasons to problematize this distinction in relation to the structural location of religion and spirituality. For example, one could read the distinction between public and private as a structure of power, by which certain kinds of knowledge, opinions and arguments are seen as fit for public debate, and others are kept out of this debate since they are deemed to be 'merely private'. Thus, the privatization and simultaneous feminization of religion could be read as indeed a disempowering of religion. Simultaneously, the feminization thesis has been helpful in directing attention towards the religious domain as an important area in which female agency has developed.

As many scholars have pointed out, with the rise of modern liberal political arrangements, historically religion came to be identified with the private domain (e. g. most recently Mahmood 2015; Scott 2017), while at the same time women came to be seen as the guardians of the values of an orderly and warm society embodied in this private domain, necessary for creating the nation (see, e.g., the discussion of the influence of French philosopher Rousseau on this idea in Kukla 2005). In the meantime, the public domain came to be thought of as secular, governed by arguments based on reason and science. For men, the private domain was a space where they could rest and recuperate from their duties and activities in the public domain. Like Trzebiatowska and Bruce (2013) we would resist any conclusions that women have a 'natural' tendency to feel attracted to religion, or for that matter spirituality. Rather, we think this needs to be understood in relation to the historical developments of society, through which women came to be regarded as more religious or open to the transcendent, and religious contexts came to be an important domain of female agency. Gendered pairs of opposites are at work here:

secular–religious
public–private
rational–emotional
strong–vulnerable
male–female

Thus, while in current debates secularism is often equated with the emancipation of women as a matter of course, historian Scott has shown that, in fact, the rise of secular discourses was premised on gendered difference that accompanied the differentiation of public and private domains (Scott 2017). The anti-clerical French Revolution, while emphasizing liberty, equality and fraternity, did not extend these values to women. Ideas about what it means to be secular or religious, and the very notion of secularism as a higher, more evolved form of organizing society with its roots in the historical development referred to as the Enlightenment, is inevitably connected with the secular–religious binary. As Longman argues in Chapter 3, the secularization process as a fundamentally sexed and gendered process continues to allocate women and femininity to the sphere of the religious *and* the realm of spirituality, opposed to men, masculinity and the secular, modern, rational public sphere; women, to date, are on the whole 'more' religious and spiritual than men (Houtman and Aupers 2006; Aune, Sharma, and Vincett; 2008).

This association of religiosity and spirituality with femininity and the numerical dominance of women in religious domains has also led to quite a bit of anxiety among religious actors. For example, within Christianity, there has long been an anxiety around the 'feminization of religion'. This has led to developments such as a 'muscular Christianity' (Higgs 1983; Hall 2006; Putney 2009; McCleod 2012). Fast-growing forms of Christianity such as evangelicalism and Pentecostalism have a strong focus on 'reforming men' and introducing new models of relating particularly to men, which, ironically, makes them very attractive to women (Brusco 1995; Martin 2001; Bochow and van Dijk 2012; Klinken 2013; Kamp 2016). Interestingly, this volume contains some chapters that are focused on men in spiritual contexts, showing how men use yoga to think differently about what it means to be masculine and strong (Griera, Chapter 10). This important chapter shows that the gendered differentiations associated with religion, spirituality and the secular also affect the possibilities men have in their subjective self-formation. We suspect that there may be many more 'male' practices that remain even more invisible than those practised by women because of the taboo on appearing vulnerable and emotional, and therefore feminine (Fedele 2018).

Similar to religious contexts, domains that identify with the term spiritual are at least numerically dominated by women (Houtman and Aupers 2006; Woodhead 2007). Often, there is an emphasis on equality and a developed critique of traditional gender roles. New ways of valuing the body and sexuality are offered that are felt to be empowering for women and the female body is celebrated in more positive ways, it is felt, than in traditional male-dominated religion. Spiritual practitioners celebrate the massive participation of women as evidence of the empowering effects of spirituality on women, but they also wish that more men would get involved. Furthermore, Sointu and Woodhead have argued that spirituality, in the form of new-age practices, for example, allows women to negotiate the contradictory demands of modern society, by validating practices and values associated with women, such as caring work, but at the same time encouraging them to develop what they call an 'expressive selfhood' (Woodhead 2007; Sointu and Woodhead 2008). Whereas religious traditions value care work within narrowly confined gender roles, spirituality values care work and work on the self, as well as on redefining oneself in relation to others (Woodhead 2007; Fedele and Knibbe 2016).

So how does spirituality relate to the pairs of opposites outlined above? At the level of public debate in societies across the globe, 'religion' is usually associated with conservative gender politics, whereas feminist positions are usually associated with a secularist, liberal position. Religion, when it goes public, often does so with an agenda that concerns the 'pelvic issues' (i.e. a concern with sexual morality) and an 'anti-gender' agenda. Resistance against gay marriage, against the legalization of abortion and so on is often led by religious actors. At the level of these polarized debates, there is little room for recognizing the variations within religious traditions, as well as the emergence of strong feminist positions within the domain of spirituality and paganism (Zwissler 2018). Often, as we showed above, spiritual practitioners reproduce this image of religion as inherently conservative. Even when not explicitly feminist, spiritual practitioners often relate in specific ways to both the 'patriarchal' tendencies of religion, as we showed in the previous edited volume, but also the disenchanting forces of secularity, as has been noted from the beginning of the emergence of the field of 'New Age' and contemporary spirituality studies (e.g. Hanegraaff 1996; Heelas 1996). A new area within the study of spirituality is the link with LGBTI issues. In recent years, queer and LGBTI communities have taken up paganism and spiritual practices, transforming the often quite essentializing discourses around masculinity and femininity in spiritual settings (see for example the podcast 'Tarot for the Wild Soul'[1] from NYC as well as Chapter 11 by Lepage in this volume on pagans in Montreal).

Yet, within the sociology of religion attention to spirituality in the past has sometimes tended to be either dismissive (spirituality is just a private activity, not relevant) or derogatory (critiques of spirituality as simply a way to make employees more productive, for example). And it is true that, for the most part, barring some pagan rituals that are performed publicly (and seem to have gained a certain notoriety after Trump was elected), spiritual practitioners do their thing in the private domain, or form parallel communities (as described by Becci, Farahmand and Grandjean in this volume). However, from a feminist perspective, equating the private sphere with irrelevance does not make sense, since it is in the private sphere that most of the reproduction of society goes on in the form of mostly unpaid labour done predominantly by women. As Fraser, Benhabib and others have argued, the notion of the public domain, as well as the communicative practices taking place in this domain, are strongly gendered and biased towards white, heterosexual masculinity (Fraser 1990; Benhabib 1998; for a summary of these critiques see Canaday 2003). Keeping 'women's concerns' out of the public domain and confining them to the private sphere is a way of depoliticizing these concerns, which second-wave feminism successfully resisted through the slogan that the 'personal is political'. In light of this, we can ask: what does it mean when spirituality is posited as privatized religion? Conversely, what does it mean when 'real religion' is seen as public?

As stated in the introduction of this chapter, we argue for developing a different, less dismissive view of spirituality based on the recognition that the distinction between public and private is gendered, and thus political. In some ways, the spiritual could be argued to be a label that properly confines what could be called 'religious' to the private sphere, submitting to an order by which secularity encompasses religion as something that needs to be managed and circumscribed (Wohlrab-Sahr and Burchardt 2012). As such, religion should know its place and is allowed to be part of modern society only in a privatized form, because it is emotional and irrational and cannot be allowed into the public sphere that should be secular, neutral and rational. However, if we dismiss spirituality as irrelevant this implies that we also assume that the work that goes on in the private sphere and the values this work is guided by are irrelevant. Taking seriously what goes on in the private domain also means recognizing that the personal and the private are intricately linked with the political arrangements of our societies (see, for example, the discussion of mothering as citizenship practice and cultural work in Longman, De Graeve and Brouckaert 2013). Self-care, as well as emotional labour, is relevant political work for those who only fit into existing structures awkwardly. Furthermore, spiritual practice, as we will see, is often quite critical towards current societal arrangements and can provide the basis for both environmental and feminist activisms, as well as the fostering of new forms of community.

Recognition that the work that goes on under the label of spirituality can be important does not mean that we promote an uncritical acceptance of spirituality as the solution to present-day evils related to gendered hierarchies or the ecological crisis. As individualized practices and with an individualist epistemology that takes its own body and experience as sites for fact-finding, a focus on self-improvement also fits with the neoliberal ideologies that current practices of work and ideas of citizenship encourage, as De La Torre and Gutiérrez Zúñiga show in Chapter 4. However, we do not want to go along with the dismissive ridiculing or belittling of spirituality as somehow 'not real' religion, not properly a social actor. Perhaps spiritual practice is considered subversive because it is, after all, political. Certainly, in the ethnographies presented here but also elsewhere in the literature, we can see how spiritual practices can be used to rework the 'microphysics of power' in one's own life and embodiment. The injunction to 'listen to yourself, pay attention to how you feel' may sound narcissist, but it is subversive when this is addressed to a self whose perspectives and experiences are usually dismissed.

Moving beyond the binary: spirituality as the third term of a gendered triangle

After all these explorations, what can we say about the work that the category of the spiritual does, or, to put it differently, what is the work that is being done in the domain of spiritual practice?

The chapters of this edited volume explore the intersections between spirituality, religion and secularism in different geographical areas ranging from European countries such as the Netherlands, Portugal and Italy over to Canada, the United States and Mexico. They address the meaning of spirituality in the context of a variety of spiritual movements as well as in the context of social movements that are often considered to be secular rather than religious, such as the ecologist movement (Becci, Fahramand and Grandjean, Chapter 5). They explore the spiritual experiences of women and their struggle for a more gender equal way of approaching the divine, without neglecting the experience of men and of those who challenge binary sexual identities advocating for a queer spirituality.

What emerges from these ethnographically grounded chapters is a kind of spirituality that challenges as well as reproduces secular theories and practices. If certain spiritual actors present their spirituality as a sort of remedy against the progressive secularization of Western society (Lepage, Chapter 11), others use spirituality to find a middle way between religion and secularism (Zwissler, Fedele, and Knibbe, Chapters 7, 8 and 9 respectively). Rather than forming distinctly different domains, the secular, religious and spiritual appear to be overlapping but also stand in creative tension to each other. These domains include diverse practices, discourses and strategies that have to be understood in relation to each other. The contributors' chapters not only provide different examples and analyses of this interplay, they also emphasize the importance of using a gender lens to improve an understanding of how and why the religious, the secular and the spiritual mutually create each other and the gendered power relations involved in their interplay.

Whereas in the previous volume we explored the dichotomy of religion and spirituality, including the secular has led us to view the 'boundary work' (Ammerman 2013) and political work that spirituality does in a new light. While often spiritual practitioners do not explicitly reference the secular, it is present as a third element, as the chapters in this volume will demonstrate. Sometimes, this is very visible, as in the cases described by Longman and Plancke (Chapters 6 and 3 respectively), where female spiritual practitioners explicitly set out to rediscover their femininity against the background of a secular mainstream society that in their eyes ultimately disempowers female sexuality and feminine values. Sometimes it is implicit, as in the case of Griera's men, who develop a different view of what it means to be a man. In most cases, holistic practices present themselves as forms of enchantment, a way of getting in touch with energies, authenticity and realness in a world where meaning has leaked away through monetization and exploitation that are the consequences of instrumentalist ideologies and the accompanying exploitation of the earth that dominate economic life. At the same time holistic spirituality recuperates core ideas of secularism such as the idea of empowerment of the self, and the overcoming of moralistic and constraining ways of life associated with religion and tradition.

Thus, we argue that spirituality should be seen as the third term in relation to the religious–secular divide. The model along which to guide the enquiry and analysis that we propose is not a binary but a triangle. While writing this chapter, we came to refer to this triangle as the 'vagina triangle'. This is a bit tongue in cheek, and we are aware that many scholars will not want to refer to it in this way. However, the subversiveness of this designation is helpful to highlight the importance of gender when analysing religion, spirituality and the secular, as well as to point out the ongoing gendered hierarchies that inevitably associate what is feminine with elements perceived as weaker and less valuable. As we showed previously (Fedele and Knibbe 2013), these hierarchies also continue to be present within holistic spiritualities.

We propose this triangle as an exploratory model to open new pathways, rather than a rigid categorization, a tool that makes it possible to develop an anthropology of spirituality in relation to religion and to the secular, and to explore the gendered boundary work that is going on between the different points of the triangle. Deliberately, and in a play on the associations with the feminine, we place the term spirituality at the lowest point of the triangle, indicating its association with the private domain, as something that is often hidden away and taboo. Eve Ensler's *Vagina Monologues* (2003) helped to give visibility to the taboo around female genitals that still persists also in Western societies, as well as its links with gendered violence. Similarly, by introducing the third category of spirituality in relation to the secular–religious binary we aim to counter the gender bias that affects not only social actors but also the scholars who study them.

Thus, we get trios of linked descriptors rather than pairs, as we summarize in Figure 0.1. Note that here these descriptors are developed from the perspective of spiritual practitioners; they would look very different from a religious perspective, and again different from a secularist perspective.

This model makes visible the negotiations between the religious and the secular informed by the two strategies that we proposed as linked to the identification with spirituality. In each context, the exact descriptors linked to each of the three categories may vary, as well as their prominence. However, we do think that the ease with which those who identify as spiritual are able to move between different particular contexts is informed by the sharing of the notions of energy, the revaluing of the feminine and a willingness or commitment to see the earth as Mother. Furthermore, we maintain that these notions are developed in explicit or implicit contradistinction to the notions and strategies associated with the domains of the secular and of the religious.

Interestingly, describing the religious and secular domains from the point of view of the spiritual domain, the distinction between public and private disappears. Yet,

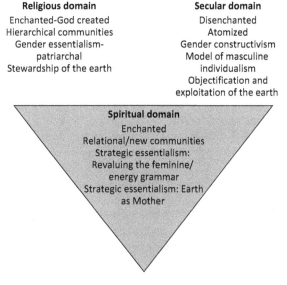

Figure 0.1 The gendered triangle of religion, secularity and spirituality

we would argue that it is still there, in the code switching that is often part and parcel of being spiritual in a secular world, for example. This becomes visible especially in those moments when people are not able to switch codes, present themselves as secular subjects, and become faintly ridiculous, as Knibbe explores in Chapter 9 on spiritual practitioners with a lower-class background.

Exploring spiritual selves: the contributions to this volume

Continuing with the practice-oriented approach of the companion volume, we wanted to understand what people mean when they say that they are spiritual but not religious. Rather than offering a definition of spirituality, religion and secularism we wanted to understand what spirituality does and how this relates to the secular and the religious. We proposed an approach that challenges the private/public divide as well as the mind/body binary (Rosaldo 1989; Csordas 2002; Fedele and Llera Blanes 2011), conceptualizing the spiritual, the religious and the secular as lived phenomena that are experienced through the mind as well as the body. The study of the spiritual is therefore necessarily an ongoing process that aims to analyse what the spiritual does and how it unfolds in relation to the religious and the secular.

When inviting the contributions to this volume we also aimed to blend anthropological and sociological approaches in the hope of fostering a more fruitful dialogue between these two disciplines in the context of the study of religion. We chose to foreground an ethnographic approach that in our eyes is essential to grasp the complexities of holistic spiritualities and chose mostly colleagues who had a wide experience investigating these topics. Also the voices of young scholars emerge. To overcome the Anglo-centrism that often characterizes the social sciences, we solicited contributions from a wide range of settings; most authors are not native English speakers. The result is a rich mixture of ethnographic insights that portray the local diversities of holistic spiritualities but point also towards common themes.

In the companion volume we had identified 'vernacular religion' as a useful term and scholarly approach to overcome the religion–spirituality dichotomy and used an empirical approach to understand the growing phenomenon of contemporary forms of spirituality (Sutcliffe and Bowman 2000; Claverie and Fedele 2014; Fedele 2014b). In recent years there has been a spread of research using a similar, but more appropriate term, namely 'lived religion' (Ammerman 2013; Knibbe and Kupari forthcoming) as well as on contemporary forms of spirituality (Aune 2015, reprinted in this volume in Chapter 1). Whereas vernacular religion still (implicitly) maintains the distinction between official doctrine and unofficial practice, the lived religion approach has developed the position that even 'official' religion and doctrine must be studied as products of human action. This move to a lived religion approach, connecting the sociology of religion more closely to anthropological approaches to religion, is reflected in the essay by Kristin Aune, analysing how feminists in the UK see spirituality and religion, first published in 2015 in the journal *Gender and Society*.

Analysing findings from an interview-based sociological study in England, Scotland and Wales, Aune refuses to equate feminism with secularism or with spirituality and analyses the complex interweaving of religion, spirituality and secularism through a gender lens. The 30 feminists Aune interviewed from different parts of the UK are de-churched, relational and emphasize practice. From Aune's analysis we can see that reducing feminist spirituality only to holistic spiritualities does not do justice to the complexity and creativity of these women's encounters with the divine. Drawing on scholars investigating lived religion (Hall 1997; McGuire 2008) the author concludes that it is more fruitful to see feminist spirituality as yet another form of lived religion. This approach makes it possible to overcome both the religion/spirituality divide and the idea that embracing feminist ideas necessarily leads to secularization. Even if some feminists abandoned the established religions they grew up with, because they felt the church did not respect women's experiences, this should not be misinterpreted as a form of religious decline or as a rejection of Christian beliefs and practices as a whole. Religion and spirituality were "embedded in their childhoods and relational networks", or for the atheists especially, "functioned as something to define themselves against" (2015, 142).

It would be interesting to know whether the feminists Aune interviewed would be comfortable being described as embracing religion, even if it is a lived and lively one. As we observed in the companion volume, spiritual practitioners tend to have a stereotyped idea of what religion and especially Christian religions are like, often dismissing the creative and very diverse ways in which Christians live their faith. We hope that this volume can contribute to further dismantling this idea as well as to conveying that, like any other form of religion or spirituality for that matter, holistic spiritualities are made up by human beings in the context of local cultures and societies. As such, spiritual practitioners are "neither passive victims of the neoliberal society nor religious heroes bringing about a spiritual revolution" (Fedele and Knibbe 2013, 19). An ethnographic approach "gives us privileged access to people's religious lives and their complexity" and "precludes simplifications or reductionist dichotomies" (*ibidem*).

Like Aune's UK feminists, Italian Goddess spiritualists described by Stefania Palmisano and Roberta Pibiri are de-churched, relational and emphasize practice. The two Italian sociologists analyse the Goddess Spirituality movement in Italy, focusing on the ways in which its practitioners are influenced by the global Goddess Spirituality movement, through internationally recognized leaders and authors such as Riane Eisler, Kathy Jones and Starhawk, but also adapt their theories and practices to the traditionally Catholic context of their country. Adopting social and cultural models based on partnership in their everyday life, they are convinced that the personal can be political and that not only collective but also individual spiritual practices can lead to personal as well as to collective empowerment as well as to social change. This contribution emphasizes Goddess Spirituality's ability to create an interweaving of secular and spiritual spheres through social, cultural and spiritual models based on partnership (see also

Palmisano and Pannofino 2020). The challenges that this kind of approach entails are further analysed in the following two chapters that explore different ways in which spirituality is intertwined with neoliberalism. They emphasize, however, that this relationship cannot simply be reduced to considering spiritual practitioners as empty vessels passively receiving neoliberal and postfeminist theories (Fedele 2013, 2014b).

Exploring women spirituality movements in Germany, Belgium and the Netherlands, Chia Longman analyses the life-story interviews she conducted with the leaders of groups and workshops fostering female empowerment. Building upon the work of scholars exploring the intersections between gender and secularism (Scott 2017) as well as the predominance of women in contemporary spiritualities (Trzebiatowska and Bruce 2013), she explores the empowering and agentic potentialities of religion/spirituality for women from a post-secular perspective on gender and religion. She convincingly shows that the complex and intersectional identities and experiences of these female empowerment groups cannot easily be reduced into categories of secular/religious/spiritual and that the "often assumed class, age and ethnic homogeneity within the women's wellbeing milieu" (Longman, Chapter 3) needs to be challenged. Longman argues that this stereotype does not do justice to the legacy of black, coloured, minority and non-Euro-American women's spiritualities nor does it take into account the current globalization of women's wellbeing-culture beyond the Global North. Moreover, Longman, as well as other researchers doing research in Europe (e.g. Fedele 2013, 2016; Fedele and Knibbe 2013; Knibbe 2013), found that her ethnographic data did not confirm this thesis. Without neglecting recent criticism of the therapy culture (e.g. Furedi 2004) as well as scholars analysing 'technologies of the self' as the product of a neoliberal (and secular) project that forecloses political critique and social change. Longman shows that the scenario is more complex and that women's empowerment groups cannot simply be labelled as disempowering movements for women who are passive recipients of these kinds of discourses. Longman agrees that the cultivation of the feminine is related to an inbuilt gender inequality. However, she also finds that her informants cannot be dismissed as "postfeminist dupes" and that they emerge "in a very somatic, practical and communal activist sense as critics and agents of the system in which they are subjects" (Chapter 3).

Focusing on the growing phenomenon of Neomexican ceremonies and their connection with women circles in Mexico, Renée de la Torre and Cristina Gutiérrez Zúñiga show how some of the topics addressed by Chia Longman play out in Latin America where neo-indigenous movements (also called Neo-Indian movements; Galinier and Molinié 2006) blend with holistic spiritualities. Analysing the Regina spiritual movement, the authors show how these women's circles use terms and symbols related to Mexican identity, reinterpreting them in terms of female empowerment. The ceremonies, workshops and courses related to this phenomenon result in career opportunities for women and allow them to voice their criticism of patriarchy, capitalism and (mainly Catholic) religion. However, like other spiritual practitioners analysed in the previous contributions, these women also reproduce gendered stereotypes, tend to romanticize indigenous cultures and often end up embracing the very capitalistic logics they criticize. There is an evident tension between what the authors describe as a "postcolonial" and one might add, post-patriarchal, criticism and the reproduction of the very colonial and patriarchal mechanisms that have led to the exoticization of indigenous cultures, the undervaluation of women and capitalistic exploitation.

The complex scenario of Mexican feminine spirituality also provides the ethnographic flesh for part of the following chapter by Irene Becci, Manéli Farahmand and Alexandre Grandjean. The authors explore the intersections of spirituality and ecology in three different national contexts, namely Switzerland, Italy and Mexico. The authors found that even if there are important differences among the Maya revival networks in Yucatán, Swiss eco-spiritual movements and the eco-esoteric community of Damanhur in Northern Italy they studied, all three share "a global framing of 'spirituality' understood as part of a global ecological commitment" (Chapter 5) that is also related to a questioning and challenging of dominant gender norms in the specific local contexts. Ecology emerges in these contexts not as a merely secular and technical subject but as being interwoven with religious theories, practices and symbols. These authors also observe the increasing influence of a language related to contemporary forms of spirituality that tends to see nature as the physical manifestation of a being, usually identified as 'Mother Earth' that has also religious features and is related to a 'sacred feminine' that needs to be protected and honoured (Harvey 1997; Pike 2017). Like other authors before them (Pike 2001; Fedele 2013, 2016), Becci, Fahramand and Grandjean point out the problems related to this essentialization of gender differences that perpetuates the idea of nature as feminine, nurturing and good. This approach also neutralizes more aggressive and destructive images of Mother Earth that were present in the Mayan tradition and are still to be found in indigenous groups in Yucatán. What emerges from the analyses of these different ecological activisms is a form of social action that is gendered and spiritual but seems to be disconnected from feminist agendas.

So far we have seen how contemporary spiritualities often tend to navigate between gendered empowerment and the replication of gendered hierarchical ideologies. Through the feminine–masculine polarization spiritualities tend to replicate a classical dichotomy that has been deconstructed by feminists according to which the feminine is closer to nature, passive intuitive, and so on, and the masculine is active, rational, closer to technology. In the companion volume we had shown that although contemporary spiritualities present themselves as non-hierarchical and gender equal, the scenario is more complex and should always be analysed keeping in mind local contexts as well as the relationship with the secular sphere. Although highlighting the ways in which spiritualities sometimes tend to reproduce the very ideological constructs they criticize (neoliberalism, patriarchy, colonialism), we need to be careful not to overlook the important contributions they make in terms of female empowerment and rendering certain problems visible. This becomes particularly evident in the following contribution.

Carine Plancke shows that, just like religion and spirituality have never disappeared and are intimately intertwined with secularism, the disenchantment of the world advocated by secularists has also never totally arrived. She argues that the alternating phases of enchantment and disenchantment should be studied as well as the different forms of conceiving enchantment. This study of (dis)enchantment needs to be gendered in a similar way as the study of secularism (Woodhead 2008) should be. Analysing women only workshops centring on the re-connection with the "inner wild woman", which was supposedly lost due to a modern lifestyle, Plancke describes how participants learn "to be for oneself and to be for others". Following Woodhead (2008) she argues that holistic spiritualities allow women to deal with these two contradictory demands. For contemporary women, for whom the discovery of their self is already an important step, the process of creating a self implies a double movement: going beyond the closed-off self but also preventing a complete sacrifice of the self. "This experience of a balanced, relational self results in the development of a new understanding of femininity." Comparing this kind of contemporary form of enchantment with earlier forms promoted by Romanticism or Theosophy, Plancke convincingly shows that in "present day spiritualities there seems to be little or no desire to merge the self into some greater whole, or to dissolve individuality into oneness" (Chapter 6). She concludes that although most women she met tend to criticize feminism as inviting women to imitate men, these forms of spirituality "are not necessarily incompatible with a sense of empowerment for women – whether framed in feminist terms or not".

Laurel Zwissler explores the gendering of spiritual consumption based on fieldwork in charity shops of a fair-trade organization with an originally Mennonite background, ten thousand villages. Since the stores implicitly present themselves as secular, certain participants have to negotiate between their loyalty to the Mennonites who founded the project and their desire to compete in a secularized retail market. Focusing on the "cosmology of interconnection" widely used by fair-trade organizations, Zwissler observes how this cosmology not only implicitly invokes religious values, but is also deeply gendered. Through processes echoing Victorian moralized gender complementarity, women are "burdened with informally mitigating damages caused by the systemic inequalities of formal economic, religious and political systems" (Chapter 7). Zwissler analyses what she calls the "language of spirituality" as "a means to get around conflicts over religion and, instead, to emphasize a universally accessible experience of peace and contentment". This language, which has many elements in common with what Fedele called "energy grammar" (2013, 2018), allows Zwissler's informants to promote gendered ethical values that are originally grounded in a particular religious community, as universal. This relational approach and cosmology of interconnection also has elements in common with the models of partnership used by Goddess Spirituality practitioners in Italy described in by Palmisano and Pibiri in Chapter 2 to contrast the individualization and atomization of capitalistic societies.

Zwissler's findings provide a good introduction to the following contribution by Fedele, showing how spirituality provides a middle ground between religion and secularism, in a context in which religion is increasingly perceived as the bad, disempowering guy, following secular discourses related to the Enlightenment. Fedele's analysis of pilgrims visiting the Marian shrine of Fátima in Portugal builds on Ammerman's findings about the religious/spirituality binary in the United States as "moral boundary work" (2013) to explore what Catholic pilgrims mean when they say that they are spiritual but not religious, and how this relates to gender. Calling themselves spiritual, the pilgrims draw a moral boundary towards institutionalized Catholicism, represented by the Vatican and in Fátima more specifically by local Catholic authorities in charge of the sanctuary. These ecclesiastical authorities often emerge as a sort of religious, immoral enemy misinterpreting the true, spiritual message of Jesus. The pilgrims strategically use a spiritual *lingua franca* they feel can be acceptable for both those representing Catholic local institutions and secular institutions or viewpoints. Using this distinction, pilgrims engage in political work: challenging certain positions adopted by the Vatican, in general, and the local Church, in particular, and embracing what they perceive as more secular values, especially those related to feminism, such as gender equality and the freedom of sexual orientation. Fedele shows how the distinction between spirituality and religion should, therefore, not be underestimated as a temporary trend but understood as an expression of discontent towards religious institutions as well as an effort of dialogue with the secular sphere.

Knibbe's findings in the following chapter further complicate the scenario, showing how in the southern part of the Netherlands the term spirituality and its accompanying practices allow women to position themselves critically vis-à-vis both religious and secular forms of authority that are disempowering to them in terms of the modes of selfhood that they promote. Many of these women found their self-worth primarily in their role as housewife and carer, a choice validated by the Catholic world they grew up in but later invalidated by the disappearance of this world, and the emergence of professional identity as the primary locus of self-worth. While they are themselves critical of the commercial character of services provided in the spiritual marketplace, it is exactly this commercial character that allows them to form a relationship of choice with a source of authority, based on the criterion of what works for them. In this way, and by framing their engagement with spiritual practices as a personal choice, women are able to recast their relationship to authority, tapping directly into the supernatural rather than via the mediation of priests, as they were used to in their youth, or later, in adulthood, via professional secular authorities.

Mar Griera explores, from a sociological perspective, how holistic practices such as yoga find their place among male prisoners in Barcelona. If we consider that holistic spiritualities have so far been analysed as being predominantly attractive for middle-class, educated women, prisoners, especially male inmates, appear an unlikely target. Analysing how yoga helps to refashion conceptions of masculinity in a working-class male-dominated environment, Griera shows, how yoga gets legitimated and easily enters prison because it is presented as a secular activity that helps to improve physical well-being. As a result, yoga is not inserted into the problematic and restrictive legal-bureaucratic apparatus regulating religion in public institutions and is also more easily accepted by inmates. Drawing from her fieldwork data, Griera convincingly demonstrates that the impact of yoga goes well beyond its physical effects and implies the acquisition of "new languages related to the care of oneself and the others and attention to emotions that blur traditional working-class conceptions of masculinity" (Chapter 10). Although penitentiary institutions are not favourable contexts for the reshaping of traditional forms of masculinity but on the contrary promote often violent behaviours related to hypermasculinity, yoga classes provide a safe space where emotions and vulnerability can be shown. Through yoga and the holistic language associated to it, these inmates learn new narratives and practices of masculinity that "play a strategic role in prison since they hold an affinity with the spiritual therapeutic culture that is gaining credibility among penitentiary authorities and staff". Through yoga, inmates learn to focus on their inner rather than their physical strength. They gradually come to reinterpret their lives through what Griera, referring to Schütz, calls a spiritual stock of knowledge, and to see their time in prison as an opportunity for a change towards a more spiritual life. Through the acquisition of this kind of "middle-class therapeutic/spiritual language", male prisoners more easily adapt to a penitentiary context that is increasingly focused on therapy and expects them to actively participate in their own rehabilitation process. Like other contributors analysing spiritual practices, Griera observes that yoga appears not to contradict the secular ethos and tends to be assimilated with therapy and physical and mental well-being rather than with religion.

Martin Lepage's contribution explores how queer Montreal Pagans perceive their own spirituality. He focuses in particular on this spirituality's position in regard to Quebec's alleged secularization, analysing how queer Montreal Pagans understand and integrate negative perceptions of religion that are typical of Quebec 'secular' society. He describes how contemporary spiritualities facilitate the construction of queer identities and are in constant dialogue and exchange with the established religions and gender norms they challenge. Lepage shows how different Pagan groups perceive masculinity and femininity in more or less rigid ways depending not only on the Pagan tradition they follow but also on the personal positioning of their leaders. Particularly interesting is the figure of Santa Muerte, a popular Mexican saint that emerges as a multicultural figure protecting, in the words of an informant: "queers, the sex workers, people who ride motorcycles, drug dealers, people who cross the border, the things that institutions are against" (Chapter 11). Lepage's chapter points to new directions for research into holistic spiritualities; namely the exploration of the ways in which marginal social groups live their spirituality, challenging the assumption that spiritual practitioners are white, middle class, cisgender and usually women (see also Longman, Chapter 3).

The chapters of this book cover a wide range of geographical areas although this volume by no means pretends to cover all. It does not include chapters based on ethnographic research in Africa or Asia. Some scholars investigating spirituality in China and India (e.g. Van der Veer 2013; Kwan 2018) as well as in Japan (e.g. Shimazono 1999, 2004) have problematized the Eurocentrism of definitions and analyses of spirituality. We think that proposing to study 'spirituality' as a globalized and globalizing category in relation to religion and the secular can make visible the specific historical trajectories and layered histories of spirituality in various contexts. Research in Africa (e.g. Steyn 2003; Spiegel and Sponheuer 2011; Salomonsen 2014) has pointed towards the increasing influence of holistic spiritualities and their blending with local, traditional forms of magic and witchcraft. Given the demonic representation of local cosmologies forged by the rise of Pentecostalism in many countries, linking these cosmologies with transnational spiritual networks creates interesting new possibilities. The continuous links between South America and (mostly West) Africa exemplified by religious practices such as Candomblé and Vodoun create a transnational social field that often overlaps with that of spiritual practitioners (Adogame 2016; Schmidt 2016).

Research especially about Neopaganism in Australia and New Zealand is growing but not represented here (Possamai 2003; Rountree 2004). Also in Latin America there has been recent research on the important expansion of new spiritualities that is taking place especially in Mexico, maybe also because of proximity to United States, as shown in chapters by De la Torre and Zúñiga (Chapter 4) as well as by Manéli Farahmand's research (Chapter 5). However, the spreading of holistic spirituality and its entanglements with native religions has been analysed also in the contexts of Brazil (Dawson 2007), Colombia (Losonczy and Mesturini Cappo 2010, 2011) and Peru (Galinier and Molinié 2006; Hill 2008; Fedele 2013), among others. There have been important debates about the appropriation of indigenous traditions and here again overlap with secular political spheres (e.g. Pike 2001; Galinier and Molinié 2006) becomes evident.

We regret that this volume does not include contributions focusing on Eastern Europe where researchers have analysed the problematic entanglements of Neopagan movements with right-wing nationalism as well as the entanglements of spirituality with local, traditional forms of religiosity (Aitamurto and Simpson 2013). More research needs to be done in all these geographical areas also to contrast the Eurocentric bias of studies on spirituality. Another gap regards research on men's experiences as well as those of LGBTQI spiritual practitioners, although some chapters here do address this topic (see also Woodhead 2007; Fedele and Knibbe 2013).

We hope that this volume can open the way for a larger discussion about spirituality that goes beyond the religious–secular divide as well as the religious–spiritual divide, adopting a practice-oriented, 'lived religion' approach. As Linda Woodhead states in her Afterword to this volume, such an approach may well be the best way to construct new 'mid-level' theories to replace the dominance of the secularization theory that has so long dominated the field. This implies analysing the ways in which these three domains mutually construct each other, paying close attention to gender and deconstructing the ways in which binaries such as mind/body, public/private and secular/religious are interlinked with the male/female binary, and used once again to perpetuate the superiority of the rational, public, secular (and, one might add, white, Western) male. Furthermore, it implies a recognition of our own positioning and embodiments as researchers, a theme that, while not addressed here, is often implied in the methodologies employed.

Note

1 https://wildsoulpodcast.com/

Acknowledgements

Anna Fedele's contribution for this text (pages 13-29) was mainly funded by FCT/MCTES as part of the strategic research plan of CRIA (UID/ANT/04038/2013) and as part of her activities as an FCT investigator (IF/01063/2014). This project has also received funding from EU's Horizon 2020 under grant agreement No. 649307.

References

Adogame, Afe, ed. 2016. *The Public Face of African New Religious Movements in Diaspora: Imagining the Religious 'Other'*. London: Routledge.

Agrama, Hussein Ali. 2012. "Reflections on Secularism, Democracy, and Politics in Egypt." *American Ethnologist* 39(1): 26–31. https://doi.org/10.1111/j.1548-1425.2011.01342.x.

Aitamurto, Kaarina, and Scott Simpson, eds. 2013. *Modern Pagan and Native Faith Movements in Central and Eastern Europe*. London: Acumen Publishing.

Ammerman, Nancy T. 2013. "Spiritual But Not Religious? Beyond Binary Choices in the Study of Religion." *Journal for the Scientific Study of Religion* 52(2): 258–278. https://doi.org/10.1111/jssr.12024.

Asad, Talal. 2002. "The Construction of Religion as an Anthropological Category." In *A Reader in the Anthropology of Religion*, edited by Michael Lambek, 114–132. Blackwell Anthologies in Social and Cultural Anthropology. Malden: Blackwell.

Asad, Talal. 2003. *Formations of the Secular: Christianity, Islam, Modernity*. Stanford: Stanford University Press.

Asad, Talal. 2011. "Thinking About the Secular Body, Pain, and Liberal Politics." *Cultural Anthropology* 26(4): 657–675. https://doi.org/10.1111/j.1548-1360.2011.01118.x.

Asad, Talal, Wendy Brown, Judith Butler, and Saba Mahmood. 2009. *Is Critique Secular? Blasphemy, Injury, and Free Speech*. http://escholarship.org/uc/item/84q9c6ft.

Aune, Kristin, Sonya Sharma, and Giselle Vincett. 2008. *Women and Religion in the West: Challenging Secularization*. Aldershot: Ashgate.

Aune, Kristin. 2011. "Much Less Religious, a Little More Spiritual: The Religious and Spiritual Views of Third-Wave Feminists in the UK." *Feminist Review* 97(1): 32–55. doi:10.1057/fr.2010.33.

Aune, Kristin. 2015. "Feminist Spirituality as Lived Religion: How UK Feminists Forge Religio-Spiritual Lives." *Gender & Society* 29(1): 122–145. https://doi.org/10.1177/0891243214545681.

Aune, Kristin, Mia Lövheim, Alberta Giorgi, Teresa Toldy, and Terhi Utriainen. 2017. "Introduction: Is Secularism Bad for Women? La Laïcité Nuit-Elle Aux Femmes?" *Social Compass* 64(4): 449–480. https://doi.org/10.1177/0037768617727464.

Aune, Kristin, Sonya Sharma, and Giselle Vincett. 2008. *Women and Religion in the West: Challenging Secularization.* Aldershot: Ashgate.

Bartelink, Brenda. 2016. "Cultural Encounters of the Secular Kind: Religious and Secular Dynamics in the Development Response to HIV/AIDS." Groningen: University of Groningen.

Benhabib, Seyla. 1998. "Models of Public Space: Hannah Arendt, the Liberal Tradition, and Jürgen Habermas." In *Feminism, the Public and the Private*, edited by Joan B. Landes, 65–99. Oxford: Oxford University Press.

Berger, Peter L. 2014. *The Many Altars of Modernity: Toward a Paradigm for Religion in a Pluralist Age.* Berlin: De Gruyter.

Bochow, Astrid, and Rijk van Dijk. 2012. "Christian Creations of New Spaces of Sexuality, Reproduction, and Relationships in Africa: Exploring Faith and Religious Heterotopia." *Journal of Religion in Africa* 42(4): 325–344. https://doi.org/10.1163/15700666-12341235.

Bowman, Marion, and Ülo Valk. 2012. *Vernacular Religion in Everyday Life: Expressions of Belief.* London: Equinox.

Bracke, Sarah. 2011. "Subjects of Debate: Secular and Sexual Exceptionalism, and Muslim Women in the Netherlands." *Feminist Review* 98(1): 28–46.

Bracke, Sarah, and Nadia Fadil. 2008. "Islam and Secular Modernity under Western Eyes: A Genealogy of a Constitutive Relationship." Mediterranean Programme Series, EUI Research Repository. http://cadmus.eui.eu/handle/1814/8102.

Braidotti, Rosi. 2008. "In Spite of the Times: The Postsecular Turn in Feminism". *Theory, Culture & Society* 25(6): 1–24. https://doi.org/10.1177/0263276408095542.

Brown, Callum G. 2009. *The Death of Christian Britain: Understanding Secularisation, 1800–2000.* Taylor & Francis.

Bruce, Steve. 2003. "The Social Process of Secularization." In *The Blackwell Companion to Sociology of Religion*, edited by Richard K. Fenn, 249–263. Oxford: Wiley-Blackwell.

Brusco, Elizabeth E. 1995. *The Reformation of Machismo: Evangelical Conversion and Gender in Colombia.* Austin: University of Texas Press.

Burchardt, Marian, Mar Griera, and Gloria García-Romeral. 2015. "Narrating Liberal Rights and Culture: Muslim Face Veiling, Urban Coexistence and Contention in Spain." *Journal of Ethnic and Migration Studies* 41(7): 1068–1087. https://doi.org/10.1080/1369183X.2014.957170.

Burchardt, Marian, Monika Wohlrab-Sahr, and Matthias Middell. 2015. *Multiple Secularities Beyond the West: Religion and Modernity in the Global Age.* Berlin: De Gruyter.

Burchardt, Marian, Monika Wohlrab-Sahr, and Matthias Middell. 2015. *Multiple Secularities Beyond the West: Religion and Modernity in the Global Age.* Boston: Walter de Gruyter GmbH & Co KG.

Campbell, Colin. 2005. *The Romantic Ethic and the Spirit of Modern Consumerism.* Alcuin Academics/Writers Print Shop.

Canaday, Margot. 2003. "Promising Alliances: The Critical Feminist Theory of Nancy Fraser and Seyla Benhabib." *Feminist Review* 74(1): 50–69.

Carrette, Jeremy R., and Richard King. 2005. *Selling Spirituality: The Silent Takeover of Religion.* Abingdon: Routledge.

Casanova, José. 1994. *Public Religions in the Modern World.* Chicago: University of Chicago Press.

Casanova, José. 2009. "The Secular and Secularisms." *Social Research* 76(4): 1049–1066.

Claverie, Élisabeth, and Anna Fedele. 2014. "Incertitudes et Religions Vernaculaires/ Uncertainty in Vernacular Religions." *Social Compass* 61(4): 487–496. doi:10.1177/ 0037768614546996.

Csordas, Thomas J. 2002. *Body/Meaning/Healing.* 1st edn. Contemporary Anthropology of Religion. New York: Palgrave Macmillan.

Davie, Grace. 2002. *Europe – the Exceptional Case: Parameters of Faith in the Modern World.* London: Darton, Longman & Todd.

Dawson, Andrew. 2007. *New Era, New Religions: Religious Transformation in Contemporary Brazil.* 1st edn. Aldershot: Ashgate.

Dobbelaere, Karel. 1993. "Church Involvement and Secularization." In *Secularization, Rationalization and Sectarianism*, edited by Eileen Barker, Karel Dobbelaere, and James A. Beckford, 19–36. Oxford: Clarendon Press.

Fadil, Nadia. 2011. "Not-/Unveiling as an Ethical Practice." *Feminist Review* 98(1): 83–109. https://doi.org/10.1057/fr.2011.12.

Fedele, Anna. 2013. *Looking for Mary Magdalene: Alternative Pilgrimage and Ritual Creativity at Catholic Shrines in France.* Oxford Ritual Studies. New York: Oxford University Press.

Fedele, Anna. 2014a. "Reversing Eve's Curse. Mary Magdalene Pilgrims and the Creative Ritualization of Menstruation", *Journal of Ritual Studies,* 28(2), 497–510.

Fedele, Anna. 2014b. "Creativité et incertitude dans les nouveaux rituels contemporains", *Social Compass,* 61(4), 497–510.

Fedele, Anna. 2016. "'Holistic Mothers' or 'Bad Mothers'? Challenging Biomedical Models of the Body in Portugal", *Gender and Religion*, 6(1), 95–111.

Fedele, Anna. 2018. "'The Craziness Reached My Head, I Will Go to Fátima by Foot': Gendered Reflections about Male Pilgrims' Experiences", paper presented at the 15th Biennial Conference of the European Association of Social Anthropologists, Stockholm, August.

Fedele, Anna. 2019. "Spirituality and Gender." In *The Routledge International Handbook of Spirituality in Society and the Professions*, edited by Bernadette Flanagan and Laszlo Zsnolnai. London: Routledge, 135–141.

Fedele, Anna, and Kim Esther Knibbe, eds. 2013. *Gender and Power in Contemporary Spirituality: Ethnographic Approaches.* London: Routledge.

Fedele, Anna, and Kim Esther Knibbe, eds. 2016. "From Angel in the Home to Sacred Prostitute: Unconditional Love and Gendered Hierarchies in Contemporary Spirituality." In *Contemporary Encounters in Gender and Religion*, 195–216. Cham: Springer International Publishing.

Fedele, Anna, and Ruy Llera Blanes, eds. 2011. *Encounters of Body and Soul in Contemporary Religious Practices: Anthropological Reflections.* EASA Series 16. New York: Berghahn Books.

Fraser, Nancy. 1990. "Rethinking the Public Sphere: A Contribution to the Critique of Actually Existing Democracy." *Social Text*, 25/26, 56–80.

Fraser, Nancy. 2009. "Feminism, Capitalism, and the Cunning of History." *New Left Review* 56, 97–117.

Fuller, Robert C. 2001. *Spiritual, But Not Religious: Understanding Unchurched America.* Oxford: Oxford University Press.

Furedi, Frank. 2004. *Therapy Culture: Cultivating Vulnerability in an Uncertain Age.* London: Routledge.

Galinier, Jacques, and Antoinette Molinié. 2006. *Les néo-Indiens: Une religion du IIIe millénaire.* Paris: Odile Jacob.

Griera, Mar, and Anna Clot-Garrell. 2015. "Doing Yoga Behind Bars: A Sociological Study of the Growth of Holistic Spirituality in Penitentiary Institutions." In *Religious Diversity in European Prisons: Challenges and Implications for Rehabilitation*, edited by Irene Becci and Olivier Roy, 141–157. Cham: Springer International Publishing. https://doi.org/10.1007/978-3-319-16778-7_9.

Hall, David D., ed. 1997. *Lived Religion in America: Toward A History of Practice*. Princeton: Princeton University Press.

Hall, Donald E. 2006. *Muscular Christianity: Embodying the Victorian Age*. Cambridge: Cambridge University Press.

Hanegraaff, Wouter J. 1996. *New Age Religion and Western Culture: Esotericism in the Mirror of Secular Thought*. Leiden: Brill.

Harvey, Graham. 1997. *Contemporary Paganism: Listening People, Speaking Earth*. New York: New York University Press.

Heelas, Paul. 1996. *The New Age Movement: the Celebration of the Self and the Sacralization of Modernity*. Oxford: Blackwell.

Heelas, Paul, and Linda Woodhead. 2005. *The Spiritual Revolution: Why Religion Is Giving Way to Spirituality*. Oxford: Wiley-Blackwell.

Higgs, Robert J. 1983. "Muscular Christianity, Holy Play, and Spiritual Exercises: Confusion about Christ in Sports and Religion." *Arete* 1(1): 59–85.

Hill, Michael. 2008. "Inca of the Blood, Inca of the Soul: Embodiment, Emotion, and Racialization in the Peruvian Mystical Tourist Industry." *Journal of the American Academy of Religion* 76(2): 251–279. doi:10.1093/jaarel/lfn007.

Hirschkind, Charles. 2011. "Is There a Secular Body?" *Cultural Anthropology* 26(4): 633–647.

Hochschild, Arlie Russell. 2003. *The Managed Heart: Commercialization of Human Feeling, with a New Afterword*. Berkeley: University of California Press.

Houtman, Dick, and Stef Aupers. 2006. "The Spiritual Revolution and the New Age Gender Puzzle: The Sacralisation of the Self in Late Modernity (1980–2000)." http://hdl.handle.net/1765/7576.

Kamp, Linda van de. 2016. *Violent Conversion: Brazilian Pentecostalism and Urban Women in Mozambique*. Woodbridge: Boydell & Brewer.

Kaplan, Dana, and Rachel Werczberger. 2017. "Jewish New Age and the Middle Class: Jewish Identity Politics in Israel under Neoliberalism." *Sociology* 51(3): 575–591.

Klassen, Pamela E. 2001. *Blessed Events: Religion and Home Birth in America*. Princeton Studies in Cultural Sociology. Princeton: Princeton University Press.

Klinken, Adriaan van. 2013. *Transforming Masculinities in African Christianity: Gender Controversies in Times of AIDS*. Farnham: Ashgate.

Knibbe, Kim. 2013. "Obscuring the Role of Power and Gender in Contemporary Spiritualities." In *Gender and Power in Contemporary Spirituality: Ethnographic Approaches*, edited by Anna Fedele and Kim Knibbe, 104–119. New York: Routledge.

Knibbe, Kim Esther, and Helena Kupari. Forthcoming. "Theorizing Lived Religion." *Journal of Contemporary Religion*.

Knoblauch, Hubert, Grace Davie, Kim Knibbe, Manuel A.Vasquez, and José Casanova. 2011. "I. Portrait: Jose Casanova." *Religion and Society: Advances in Research* 2(1): 5–36. https://doi.org/DOI:10.3167/arrs.2011.020102.

Kukla, Rebecca. 2005. *Mass Hysteria: Medicine, Culture, and Mothers' Bodies*. Lanham: Rowman & Littlefield.

Lamont, Michèle. 1992. *Money, Morals, and Manners*. Chicago: University of Chicago Press.

Longman, Chia. 2018. "Women's Circles and the Rise of the New Feminine: Reclaiming Sisterhood, Spirituality, and Wellbeing." *Religions* 9(1): 1–17.

Longman, Chia, Katrien De Graeve, and Tine Brouckaert. 2013. "Mothering as a Citizenship Practice: An Intersectional Analysis of 'Carework' and 'Culturework' in Non-Normative Mother–Child Identities." *Citizenship Studies* 17(3–4): 385–399. https://doi.org/10.1080/13621025.2013.791540.

Losonczy, Anne-Marie, and Silvia Mesturini Cappo. 2010. "Entre l''Occidental' et l''Indien': Ethnographie des routes du chamanisme ayahuasquero entre Europe et Amériques." *Autrepart* 56(4): 93–110. https://doi.org/10.3917/autr.056.0093.

Losonczy, Anne-Marie, and Silvia Mesturini Cappo. 2011. "Pourquoi l'ayahuasca? De l'internationalisation d'une Pratique Rituelle Amérindienne." *Archives de Sciences Sociales Des Religions* 56(153): 207–228.

Mahmood, Saba. 2009. "Religious Reason and Secular Affect: An Incommensurable Divide?" *Critical Inquiry* 35(4): 836–862. https://doi.org/10.1086/599592.

Mahmood, Saba. 2011. *Politics of Piety: The Islamic Revival and the Feminist Subject.* Princeton: Princeton University Press.

Mahmood, Saba. 2015. *Religious Difference in a Secular Age: A Minority Report.* Princeton: Princeton University Press.

Martin, Bernice. 2001. "The Pentecostal Gender Paradox: A Cautionary Tale for the Sociology of Religion." In *The Blackwell Companion to Sociology of Religion*, edited by Richard K. Fenn, 52–66. Oxford: Wiley-Blackwell.

McLeod, Hugh. 2012. "The 'Sportsman' and the 'Muscular Christian': Rival Ideals in Ninteenth-Century England." In *Gender and Christianity in Modern Europe: Beyond the Feminization Thesis*, edited by Patrick Pasture, Jan Art, and Thomas Buerman, 85–107. Leuven: Leuven University Press.

Michaeli, Inna. 2017. "Self-Care: An Act of Political Warfare or a Neoliberal Trap?" *Development* 60(1): 50–56. https://doi.org/10.1057/s41301-017-0131-8.

Osselaer, Tine van, and Thomas Buerman. 2008. "Feminization Thesis: A Survey of International Historiography and a Probing of Belgian Grounds." *Revue d'Histoire Ecclésiastique* 103(2): 497–544. https://doi.org/10.1484/J.RHE.3.180.

Palmisano, Stefania, and Nicola Pannofino. 2020. *Contemporary Spiritualities: Enchanted Worlds of Nature, Wellbeing and Mystery in Italy.* London: Routledge.

Pasture, Patrick, Jan Art, and Thomas Buerman. 2012. *Beyond the Feminization Thesis: Gender and Christianity in Modern Europe.* Leuven: Leuven University Press.

Pike, Sarah M. 2001. *Earthly Bodies, Magical Selves: Contemporary Pagans and the Search for Community.* Berkeley: University of California Press.

Pike, Sarah M. 2017. *For the Wild: Ritual and Commitment in Radical Eco-Activism.* 1st edn. Berkeley: University of California Press.

Possamai, Adam. 2003. "Alternative Spiritualities, New Religious Movements, and Jediism in Australia." *Australian Religion Studies Review* 16(2). https://openjournals.library.sydney.edu.au/index.php/ARSR/article/view/8998.

Putney, Clifford. 2009. *Muscular Christianity: Manhood and Sports in Protestant America, 1880–1920.* Cambridge, MA: Harvard University Press.

Rosaldo, Renato. 1989. "Introduction: Grief and a Headhunter's Rage." In *Culture and Truth: The Remaking of Social Analysis.* Boston: Beacon Press.

Rountree, Kathryn. 2004. *Embracing the Witch and the Goddess: Feminist Ritual-Makers in New Zealand.* London: Routledge.

Salomonsen, Jone. 2014. "The Affective Work of (Non)Ritual for HIV Positive Women, South Africa." *Journal of Ritual Studies* 28(2): 9–22.

Scheer, Monique, Birgitte Schepelern Johansen, and Nadia Fadil. 2019. "Secular Embodiments: Mapping an Emergent Field." In *Secular Bodies, Affects and Emotions: European Configurations*, 1–14. London: Bloomsbury.

Schmidt, Bettina E. 2016. "Contemporary Religions in Brazil." Oxford Handbooks Online. https://doi.org/10.1093/oxfordhb/9780199935420.013.50.

Schuh, Cora, Marian Burchardt, and Monika Wohlrab-Sahr. 2012. "Contested Secularities: Religious Minorities and Secular Progressivism in the Netherlands." *Journal of Religion in Europe* 5(3): 349–383.

Scott, Joan Wallach. 2017. *Sex and Secularism*. Princeton: Princeton University Press.

Shimazono, Susumu. 1999. "'New Age Movement' or 'New Spirituality Movements and Culture'?" *Social Compass* 46(2): 121–133. doi:10.1177/003776899046002002.

Shimazono, Susumu. 2004. *From Salvation to Spirituality: Popular Religious Movements in Modern Japan*. Trans Pacific Press.

Sointu, Eeva, and Linda Woodhead. 2008. "Spirituality, Gender, and Expressive Selfhood." *Journal for the Scientific Study of Religion* 47(2): 259–276.

Spiegel, Andrew, and Silke Sponheuer. 2011. "Transforming musical soul into bodily practice: Tone eurythmy, anthroposophy and underlying structures." In *Encounters of Body and Soul in Contemporary Religious Practices: Anthropological Reflections*, edited by Anna Fedele and Ruy Llera Blanes. 2011 EASA Series 16. New York: Berghahn.

Steyn, Christina W. 2003. "Where New Age and African Religion Meet in South Africa: the case of Credo Mutwa." *Culture and Religion* 4(1): 67–158.

Sutcliffe, Steven, and Marion Bowman, eds. 2000. *Beyond New Age: Exploring Alternative Spirituality*. Edinburgh: Edinburgh University Press.

Trzebiatowska, Marta, and Steve Bruce. 2013. "'It's All for Girls': Re-Visiting the Gender Gap in New Age Spiritualities." *Studia Religiologica* 46(1): 17–33. doi:10.4467/20844077SR.13.002.1223.

Utriainen, Terhi. 2011. "The Post-Secular Position and Enchanted Bodies." *Scripta Instituti Donneriani Aboensis* 23 (January): 417–432. https://doi.org/10.30674/scripta.67399.

van der Veer, Peter. 2009. "Spirituality in Modern Society." *Social Research: An International Quarterly* 76(4): 1097–1120.

Werczberger, Rachel. 2013. "Spirituality, Charisma and Gender in a Jewish Spiritual Renewal Community in Israel." In *Gender and Power in Contemporary Spirituality: Ethnographic Approaches*, 126–141. London: Routledge.

Wiering, Jelle. 2017. "There Is a Sexular Body: Introducing a Material Approach to the Secular." *Secularism and Nonreligion* 6(8): 1–11.

Wilson, Erin. 2017. "'Power Differences and the 'Power of Difference': The Dominance of Secularism as Ontological Injustice." *Globalizations* 14(7): 1076–1093. http://dx.doi.org/10.1080/14747731.2017.1308062.

Wohlrab-Sahr, Monika, and Marian Burchardt. 2012. "Multiple Secularities: Toward a Cultural Sociology of Secular Modernities." *Comparative Sociology* 11(6): 875–909. https://doi.org/10.1163/15691330-12341249.

Woodhead, Linda. 2007. "Gender Differences in Religious Practice and Significance". In *The Sage Handbook of the Sociology of Religion*, edited by James A. Beckford and N.J. Demerath III, 550–570. London: Sage.

Woodhead, Linda. 2008. "Gendering Secularization Theory." *Social Compass* 55(2): 187–193.

Zwissler, Laurel. 2018. *Religious, Feminist, Activist: Cosmologies of Interconnection*. Lincoln: University of Nebraska Press.

1 Feminist spirituality as lived religion

How UK feminists forge religio-spiritual lives

Kristin Aune[1]

How do feminists in the United Kingdom view spirituality and religion? What are their religious or spiritual attitudes, beliefs, and practices? What role do spirituality and religion play in feminists' lives? This essay presents findings from an interview-based study of 30 feminists. It identifies three characteristics of feminists' religio-spiritual approaches: they are de-churched, are relational, and emphasize practice. These features, I argue, call for a new approach to feminists' relationship to religion and spirituality, so I propose conceptualizing feminist spirituality as lived religion.

Just as feminisms are diverse and the term "feminism" is continually interrogated, defining "religion" and "spirituality" has preoccupied scholars for over a century. Sociologists of religion have taken two broad approaches. *Substantive definitions* seek to interrogate what religion *is*: its essence or substance. Belief in something otherworldly is emphasized, often one or more deities who govern or intervene in the world. Tylor (1873), for instance, held that religion was "belief in Spiritual Beings." *Functional definitions* explain what religion *does*: its function in society, for instance, providing a worldview that helps people cope with questions of meaning, or bringing people together in worship. Luckmann's (1967, 49) notion of religion as "the transcendence of biological nature by the human organism" is a well-known functional definition.

For most scholars, "spirituality" is an aspect of religion. But in post-industrial contexts, some argue that non-institutional spiritualities deserve attention apart from "religion." Observing that many people refer to themselves as "spiritual but not religious," some have taken this "emic" (insider) notion of spirituality and made it an "etic" (outsider) one too (Vincett and Woodhead 2009; Wuthnow 2001).

However, a group of scholars have begun employing the term "lived religion" to encompass religion *and* spirituality. Like them, I use "spirituality," "religion," and "religio-spiritual" interchangeably when discussing feminists' approaches (see McGuire 2008, 6). I believe distinguishing religion from spirituality is unhelpful analytically and does not reflect the narratives of the feminists interviewed for this study. While some of them viewed spirituality as more open and indeterminate than religion (religion connoting a misogynistic institution), others thought differently, experiencing spirituality within religion, seeing no need for either, or possessing a spiritual worldview interpretable (cf. Luckmann 1967) as religious in itself. Their experiences cannot be differentiated as *either* religious *or* spiritual. But treating the terms as synonymous does not obfuscate the need for discussion of the light my findings shed on how to define religion and spirituality. So after outlining characteristics of feminists' religio-spiritual approaches, I will suggest that the concept of lived religion captures their approaches well, and will prove influential in taking forward analysis of religion in late modern societies.

Feminist sociological literature on religion

This research speaks to three themes in feminist sociological literature on religion. The first equates feminism with secularism and secularization. The second links feminism to women's turn to alternative forms of spirituality. The third concerns religious feminisms. These trajectories are partly chronological—they move historically from a "feminism vs. religion" position to the feminist turn to spirituality and then to religious feminisms—but they are also overlapping discourses about religion that continue to be articulated in academic literature.

Feminism vs. religion: secularism and secularization

As women's and gender studies developed from the 1970s, its scholars often portrayed religion negatively, as an obstacle to feminism. In women's movement histories and feminist texts, religion is either absent or treated negatively, as a patriarchal impediment to liberation (Braude 2004; Llewellyn and Trzebiatowska 2013). Consequently, the study of religion is at best a marginal field within gender studies; the study of gender in the sociology of religion is also relatively new (Woodhead 2001). This neglect of religion betrays secularist assumptions (that gender equality is antithetical to religion, and that religions should not be given power in the public sphere to control women's lives), Reilly (2011) and Mahmood (2005) argue, secularist assumptions that derive partly from liberal feminism's genesis in the Enlightenment rejection of non-scientific meta-narratives. Liberal feminist views of agency as autonomy and resistance to patriarchal norms often contradict religious understandings of agency (Mahmood 2005). Feminism's secularist assumptions derive also from feminism's socialist or Marxist inheritance, wherein religion is rejected as a form of false consciousness blinding women to their oppression or teaching that freedom is for a utopian afterlife (Braidotti 2008).

Many social theorists, like feminists, consider modernity the antithesis of religion. Secularization theorists argue that modernization brought about democracy, egalitarianism, and religion's demise (Wilson 1966). As the revitalized nature of religion in today's world calls secularization theories into question (P. Berger 1999), secularism too is being interrogated. Not only is secularism a historical product of modernity, the eventual outcome of Protestant Christianity prioritizing personal choice in religious matters (Jakobsen and Pellegrini 2008), but the assumption that secularism is *the* superior feminist position is being called into question as women exercise agency through religion, and because it marginalizes religious women, labeling them victims of religious oppression (Reilly 2011).

Feminism played a role in the process of secularization in Western Europe and North America, historians and social scientists argue. Secularization is "the process whereby religious thinking, practices and institutions lose social significance" (Wilson 1966, xiv). Religion remains, but only in the private sphere. Insofar as secularization occurred, gender scholars argue that men and women encountered it differently because of their different public/private positioning (Aune, Sharma and Vincett 2008; Brown 2001, 2007; Woodhead 2005). During the nineteenth and early twentieth centuries, more women than men stayed religious because they were occupied by domestic work in the private sphere. But women's lives diversified in the late twentieth century, giving women freedom beyond the private (religious) sphere. Second-wave feminism raised women's aspirations beyond *a* female role to diverse options—motherhood, marriage, sexual relationships outside heterosexual marriage, employment, travel, education, and so on. In the 1960s, Brown (2001, 192) argues, "British women secularized the construction of their identity, and the churches started to lose them." Brown believes that feminist narratives of female freedom partly explain the steep decline in institutional Christianity (e.g., churchgoing, baptisms, and confirmations). For Brown (2001, 192), "the keys to understanding secularization in Britain are the simultaneous de-pietization of femininity and the de-feminization of piety."

Oral history interviews endorse Brown's thesis that feminism supported British women's religious disaffiliation (Browne 2013). Quantitative evidence from the UK and US illustrates that women whose lives diversify from wifehood and motherhood are less likely to stay at church or report feeling close to God (Marler 2008; Woodhead 2005). Secularization is "almost entirely de-Christianization" (Brown 2007, 394) in this body of work, which connects the diversification of women's lives with church decline.

The feminist turn to spirituality

While feminism encouraged de-Christianization, it precipitated alternative spirituality. Previously called "New Age," Sointu and Woodhead (2008, 259) define holistic spiritualities as "those forms of practice involving the body, which have become increasingly visible since the 1980s, and that have as their goal the attainment of wholeness and well-being of 'body, mind, and spirit'." Complementary medicine, shiatsu, and Wicca are examples. Proportions of European and North American populations actively committed to holistic spiritualities stand at around 2–5 percent, while a larger 10–20 percent see themselves as "spiritual not religious" (Sointu and Woodhead 2008). There is a large literature on the growth of alternative spiritualities in the US (Roof

1999), Europe (Houtman and Aupers 2007), and the UK (Heelas and Woodhead 2005). These spiritualities are often described as creating a "spiritual marketplace" (Roof 1999) reflecting the consumerism of late modernity, or as individualistic and narcissistic (Bellah et al. 1985). Sointu and Woodhead consider the individualistic charge unfair, since their focus on the self is a corrective to traditional notions of femininity as self-sacrifice. They are popular with women because

> holistic spiritualities align with traditional spheres and representations of femininity, while simultaneously supporting and encouraging a move away from selfless to expressive selfhood. By endorsing and sanctioning "living life for others" and "living life for oneself," holistic spiritualities offer a way of negotiating dilemmas of selfhood that face many women—and some men—in late modern contexts.
>
> (Sointu and Woodhead 2008, 259)

Moreover, alternative spiritualities are relational, directed toward others as well as enriching women's neglected selves.

Since the 1970s, feminism has been associated with alternative spiritualities; this is the form of religion/spirituality that feminist scholars have shown most interest in. Practitioners argued that rather than getting rid of the concept of the divine, women needed a female divine figure to reaffirm women's bodies, which were traditionally denigrated as impure or purely sexual. From Carol Christ's 1978 conference address "Why women need the Goddess," feminist spirituality spread through a range of pagan, Wiccan, and goddess-focused spiritualities, as Eller's (1993) American study demonstrates. In Heelas and Woodhead's (2005) study of Kendal, a northern English town where 2–3 percent of the population were involved in alternative spiritual activities (against a weekly churchgoing rate of 7.9 percent), 80 percent of participants in New Age spirituality were women. Brown suggests (2007, 414), perhaps prematurely, that today "the New Age ... is the site for the new femininity of British religion." These British examples fit within a large North American feminist literature that sees holistic spirituality as a way in which feminist and religio-spiritual identities can be aligned (e.g., H. Berger 1999; Eller 1993; Salomonsen 2002).

Religious feminisms

Less visible in feminist literature is the third theme, religiously based feminisms. These have begun to be investigated in the twenty-first century and include Ingersoll's (2003) research with the American evangelical Christian feminist movement, McGinty's (2007) with Swedish feminist converts to Islam, Zwissler's (2007) with Canadian feminist social justice activists, and Klassen's (2009) essay collection on third-wave feminists and spirituality. The few European studies include Daggers' (2002) on the 1970s and 1980s British Christian feminist movement. Fedele's (2013) anthropological journeys with pilgrims visiting French Catholic shrines to Mary Magdalene reveal the complex ways women fuse Catholic spirituality with feminist notions of the "sacred feminine" and neo-pagan and indigenous traditions. Vincett's (2008) UK study of Christian and goddess feminists reveals a similar fusion of neo-pagan and Christian feminist spiritualities. These new studies show feminists using religious resources to negotiate and challenge gender inequalities within their religious traditions, personal lives, and societies.

The literature, then, posits three trajectories in feminists' engagement with religion: feminist secularism and secularization, the feminist turn to spirituality, and religio-spiritual feminist groups. My study builds on, yet challenges, this literature. It also builds on an article in which I analyzed survey data (n = 1,265) on UK feminists' religious and spiritual views (Aune 2011). Survey participants were asked, "Describe your religious and spiritual views (including none/atheist/agnostic)." Comparison with surveys of religious adherence revealed that these feminists are significantly less traditionally religious and somewhat more "spiritual" than the UK female population. Over half of the sample were atheist (39 percent) or had no religion (15 percent). Agnostics made up 15 percent. 11 percent supported a major world religion. Eight percent were spiritual (in a general sense or identifying with alternative spiritualities). The final 12 percent displayed three tendencies: merging or blurring positions ("spiritual atheist" or "Jewish agnostic"), difficulties in defining their religious views, or describing previous religious positions ("lapsed Catholic"). Asking why it might be that they were much less religious yet slightly more spiritual, I posited three explanations: feminism's alignment with secularism, secularization and feminism's role within it, and feminism's association with alternative spiritualities. This essay develops that work through an analysis of interview data. While this study does not claim to produce generalizable findings, the data are rich and indicative of trends and patterns that should be explored further.

In this interview study of UK feminists, I argue that feminists' religio-spiritual approaches should not simply be equated with secularism, secularization, or alternative spiritualities. Instead, feminists forge religio-spiritual lives in complex ways. The spiritual approaches of those I interviewed had three main characteristics: they are *de-churched*, are *relational*, and emphasize *practice*. Moreover, contrary to some scholarly approaches that see "spirituality" and "religion" as analytically distinct, I argue that feminist spirituality should be conceptualized as "lived religion".

Methods

Semi-structured interviews were conducted with a quota sample of 30 participants drawn from the survey of feminists. The survey targeted those involved in new forms of feminism that had emerged in the UK since 2000; this emphasis on new groups accounts for the high proportion (three-quarters) in their 20s and 30s. Interview participants were selected to ensure a geographical spread across

England, Scotland, and Wales.[2] Sampling reflected the survey patterns in relation to age, sexuality (40 percent of survey participants identified as lesbian, gay, bisexual, queer, or otherwise non-heterosexual), gender (91 percent identified as female, 7 percent as male, and the rest as "other" or withheld a response), ethnicity (91 percent were white), and religio-spiritual views. Interviewees were between 18 and 80 years of age when surveyed (2008–2009); interviews took place nearly two years later (2010). Twenty-seven identified as female, two as male, and one as "other." Fourteen were heterosexual, nine bisexual, three lesbian or gay, and three "other" ("pansexual," "politically celibate," and "unsure"); one participant selected "prefer not to say." Interviews were digitally recorded, transcribed, and thematically coded.

Participants were asked about: a) religious background and upbringing (including family and schooling); b) spiritual and religious attitudes and beliefs (whether they held religious or spiritual beliefs, how these had developed, and what might have influenced any changes); and c) spiritual and religious practices (attendance at places of worship, individual practices such as meditation, prayer, or clothing, or engagement with spiritual literature, art, or music).

My survey research categorized feminists' approaches to religion on two levels: in broad categories ("atheist," "no religion," "agnostic," "major world religion," "spiritual," and "other"), and detailed categories of specific world religions and manifestations of spirituality (e.g., "spiritual but not religious" or "alternative spirituality"). Such simplifications, while useful in quantitative work, ignore commonalities in feminists' responses across these constructed categories, complexities that become visible through qualitative research, as this article will show. Data analysis took place in two stages: first, to get an overview of participants' responses to the main interview topics (religious background and upbringing, spiritual and religious attitudes and beliefs, and spiritual and religious practices), key themes were identified (for example, each participant's upbringing was categorized as "Muslim", "Christian", "non-religious" or "background Christianity" and placed alongside written summaries of the participants' narratives about their upbringing). Second, transcripts were examined and coded to identify broader themes and characteristics of feminists' spiritual approaches that recurred across the interviews. Three emerged: feminist spiritualities are *de-churched*, are *relational*, and emphasize *practice*.

Findings

Feminist spiritualities are de-churched

The first characteristic of feminist spirituality is that it is *de-churched*. This term rarely appears in the sociology of religion (for an exception, see Wood 2010), but it is more accurate than *de-institutionalized* (which obscures the fact that it is the Christian church and not another religious institution that these feminists have become distanced from) or *de-Christianized* (which falsely conflates distance from the church with no longer being Christian). Almost all participants were no longer involved with the institutional church. During childhood and youth, two-thirds of participants were engaged, to varying degrees, with the church. For some, especially the five with Christian parents, the church was in the foreground. Gabriella's[3] (age 28) family were Italian Catholics:

GABRIELLA: I've never been religious as such although I followed the Catholic faith up to when I was 12, I mean, there are different steps in the Catholic religion.
INTERVIEWER: Like the Holy Communion.
GABRIELLA: Yes, Holy Communion, all that. So until the age of reason basically, I was sent to Sunday school and all the rest of it and then when I was about 12 I decided to stop. I was part of the Scouts, which here is called Girl Guides,[4] so I had to go to church and then I had, like, the break-off when I was 17 and decided, "OK, that's not for me," because I never believed.

Similarly, Jennifer's (age 59) father was a Presbyterian church elder. She grew up reading the Bible regularly and attending church. Theology was one of her majors at university, she explained, laughing, "at which point of course I totally stopped believing in God."

For half of the participants—who had attended Church of England or Roman Catholic schools, or had a churchgoing friend or family member—church formed more of a childhood backdrop. Karen's (age 25) mother worked at a Catholic secondary school:

I went there because Mum worked there, and our family wasn't religious but a lot of the people at the school were... We went to Mass every week and a lot of the people took Holy Communion, and we had a lot of religious education... I know quite a lot about Christian religion and I studied aspects of Judaism as well, but apart from that I don't really... the things that I learnt about Christian religion I never believed and I never really took it at face value.

For Karen, Christianity was something she learnt about at school and participated in there when required, but it never became a personal faith or a feature of her adult life.

By adulthood, all participants were dissociated from the institutional church, and none attended regularly. Christianity remained in the self-descriptions of only three (Harriet, a liberal Christian, Beth, a Roman Catholic, and Melanie, a Buddhist Anglican). As will be discussed, spiritual practices remained important to many of them, but did not require close ties with the church.

Some, like Karen and Gabriella, ceased contact with the church because they did not "believe." Some associated church with school life, and, on leaving school, they did not seek out a church. This reflects what happens to most British people as they reach adulthood. The Anglican and Roman Catholic churches run a third of UK schools, but weekly church attendance currently stands at only 6 percent. By adulthood, most British people take what Davie (2007) terms a "vicarious" approach to religion: it is as if a small number of people (religious professionals, Sunday school teachers, religious broadcasters) perform religion on behalf of a much larger population, who participate vicariously. The movement of these feminists toward perceiving Christianity vicariously or as a cultural backdrop reflects its status for most British people.

Not all perceived their childhood Christianity negatively. Deborah's (age 29) Church of England school had inculcated morality and "Golden Rule Christianity." While she later disconnected from church, she had found these experiences positive:

> I went to a C of E primary school so we had a lot of... religious-y things going on there although there were some students who were not Christian, probably Hindu I think, or Sikh. There was a vicar who was tied quite closely to the school and came in a lot to do assemblies and things. I went to Brownies and Guides and I suppose they were fairly religious, it's more just like church attendance and knowing about stories from the Bible... I think the primary schools are quite good. It made us see the more good things about Christianity and the sort of the moral of the story is like, be nice to people, take care of everyone, and be respectful... I never got any of the sort of God-fearing, strike-you-down-with-lightning and things like what not to do.

Others dissociated because of a negative experience with the church. Raised by humanist "ex-Christian" parents, Tamara, 39, turned to the church at age 10 or 11 to explore her spiritual feelings. Her parents opposed her churchgoing, but she persevered until she felt that her feminist and pagan views were incompatible with Christianity:

> My parents gave me such a hard time... I carried on, but in the meantime I was reading books about witchcraft and paganism... Eventually I stopped going to church... Having read these books I thought, "Oh, I'm clearly not a Christian," and having been to church I realized I wasn't a Christian because I wasn't that excited by that whole thing of the patriarchal father, son, and holy ghost thing and the whole guilt stuff and about Jesus rising from the dead and our sin and... it just wasn't really a life-giving religion... It didn't feel like a religion that had any place for my feminist view of the world... It felt like a religion that had no sympathy for women... By the time I was 16 I was calling myself a pagan.

Now I don't think I have a religion because I don't follow any religious practices... but I do have very strong spiritual feelings.

Harriet, 24, one of the few who became more engaged with organized religion during adolescence, was taken to church by her parents who believed it would win her a place at a respected church-run school. She developed a Christian spirituality, helped by her friends, but was critical of the institutional church:

My parents aren't religious at all, really. I had to go to church until I was 11 but that was mainly to get me into secondary school. Then a couple of my friends made me see that Christianity wasn't necessarily as constraining as it had been put about that it was so I sort of found it my own way... I went to church for a little bit without my parents but I realized I didn't really like what the church was saying either and I thought it should be about your personal relationship with God and the things that you do rather than some sort of regimented "stand up now, sit down now, say a prayer now." I think it should get into everyday life by being nice to people and always just trying to be the best person that you can be.

Of the two women who identified as Muslim, one had distanced herself from some Islamic practices. However, religious observance for Muslims—especially for women, who are not expected to attend mosque if they have family responsibilities—is less focused around the mosque and more around practicing the five pillars (declaration of faith, five daily prayers, fasting during Ramadan, pilgrimage to Mecca, and charity) (Hussain 2008). Ceasing mosque attendance does not take on the same significance as ceasing attending church. Aisha, 45, said that, now in her second marriage to a non-practicing Catholic, she prays and fasts less than she did when married to her first husband, who was Muslim. Laila, 65, was brought up in the Swedenborg New Church but converted to Islam upon marriage. One of the things that attracted her to Islam was its lack of traditions and formalities:

What attracted me to Islam was it didn't have all the trappings of the Christian religion that I was brought up in, that we don't have idols and we don't have statues and we don't have all those sorts of things, there's no intermediaries.

Those raised without a religion remained distant from religion as adults. A few became more or less strongly atheist: Ruth, 31, became more "actively atheist." Paul, 20, was "against religion" but less of a "militant atheist" than he had been a few years before. Margaret, 82, Jackie, 44, and Nerys, 29, embraced humanism. Margaret joined a humanist organization in her 70s, and gave her husband and mother humanist funerals. All three saw humanism as an ethical stance asserting the importance of being good to others; as Nerys put it, "I became more positive about humanism rather than negative about the rest of the moralists." With all participants disconnected from the institutional church by adulthood, de-churching is a hallmark of feminists' spiritual approaches.

Feminist spiritualities are relational

Feminists' spiritual approaches are, secondly, *relational*. As the excerpts above indicate, feminists describe their movement away from the church as a decision shaped by and embedded in relationship networks. During childhood, many experienced socialization into Christianity by parents, schools, and churches. Others experienced socialization into non-religion, and this sense of spiritual deficit led a few to explore spirituality, either by attending church or reading about paganism. Circumstances relating to their relationships also contributed to feminists changing their views about spirituality—for instance, parents' deaths or intimate relationships with partners who were more or less religious. When discussing their movement toward or out of religion, participants mentioned the influence of parents, grandparents, siblings, friends, and partners.

The impact of relational networks on feminists' spiritual formation reflects a body of work demonstrating that families are central to the transmission of faith; people's spiritual approaches are often similar to those of their families (Arweck and Nesbitt 2010; Voas and Crockett 2005). Voas and Crockett (2005) also reveal an erosion of churchgoing religiosity between generations in Britain: In their study, even with two churchgoing parents, only 50 percent of young adults remained church attendees. A landmark longitudinal study of 200 Americans' religious lives, consisting of interviews at five points from the 1930s to the 1990s, found "the specific sociobiographical, cultural, and historical contexts in which lives unfold" (Dillon and Wink 2007, 11–12) to be key to understanding "the nature, place, and meaning of religion."

Stephanie, 24, presents a poignant example of the interaction of family, friends, and religious attitudes. Stephanie was not brought up in a religion. At age 12, she started to go to a large evangelical church with other local children. The church had a lively children's program, which she enjoyed. However, her stepfather ridiculed her, so a year later she stopped going. At the time of interview, she described herself as "not really religious." But her mother's death when she was in her late teens had an impact on her views of religion/spirituality. "It was comforting to believe in angels," she said. "It was nice to think that maybe she was one or that she was looking down on me." But the experience alienated her from conventional religious belief, as she wondered why God would allow her mother's early death.

Many of those who were not brought up religious were the children of parents who disengaged from church before having children. Marie, 24, explained:

> I didn't really have a religious upbringing. My parents chose not to baptize me. They come from... obviously my dad, because he's English he's Protestant, he doesn't practice at all. My mum would be Catholic, I guess, but she

didn't practice either. So they just—I thought it was pretty nice of them actually—they chose not to baptize me. They told me, "We want you to choose whichever religion, you know, when you grow up. If you're religious you can get baptized and join the church or be a Muslim, or whatever you want to be."

While Marie's parents were deinstitutionalized, Marie herself was simply brought up without a religion. Like Marie's parents, Nerys and Melanie's presented religion as a choice they could make in later life. But given the extent to which choosing a spiritual practice is embedded in relational contexts, the absence of religion in their key relational networks makes it unlikely that they will adopt a spiritual practice.

Deborah's childhood Anglicanism was challenged at university by friends:

> I was at my first year in uni and I used to wear a crucifix on a chain, just because it was a bit of jewelry, and a friend of mine went off on this big rant about organized religion and how it was really bad. I'd never really come across views like that before so it was just, like, "Well, it's just a cross on a chain, I just wear it because it's pretty," and he was a bit like, "Hmm, not sure about that," and I suppose that was the first time I started thinking, "Hmm, okay...," started being a bit more open to other ways of thinking.

While she had not stopped thinking or reading about religion, her skeptical attitude made her feel at odds with her family who were "still a little bit religious".

A similar experience was recalled by Iona, 41, whose Catholic parents had brought her up attending Mass weekly and sent her sister to a convent school. Her sister is still a practicing Catholic, but Iona and her brother are atheists. To avoid conflict, Iona and her family avoid talking about religion:

> I tend not to discuss religion with my family, my parents luckily completely respect my views, we don't really go there, other than when something the Pope says really upsets me and I just have to let it out... I wouldn't take Communion now, so I didn't take Communion at my grandmother's funeral a couple of years ago, which was a bit sticky, but you know, I couldn't do that.

Occasionally, as Iona experienced when she refused Communion at her grandmother's funeral, it is necessary to risk family disapproval in order to stay true to one's conscience.

Along with friends and family, sexual partners were important conversation partners. For some, religious differences raised conflict: Emily's (21) female partner was a Christian, which atheist Emily found difficult, and lesbian Frances, 46, was distressed when her sister became an evangelical Christian.

Others shared their partners' views. Melanie, 54, was encouraged to explore Buddhism by her female partner, and prompted to return to the church she had left by Jewish friends.

Some of the queer feminists came up against negative attitudes from the church as they developed their sexual identities and relationships. Naomi, 21, who identified as "pansexual," explained: "A lot of the religions just, well, for a start, they would probably discriminate against me a little bit... So I can't identify with something which doesn't seem to like me very much." Given that half of the feminist participants identified as lesbian, bisexual, queer, or otherwise non-heterosexual (reflecting the survey findings), LGBT sexuality emerges in this study as a significant relational context for the formation of spiritual attitudes. These findings challenge recent work presenting LGBT or queer spiritualities as individualistic rather than relational (Wilcox 2009; Yip 2005).

Feminist spiritualities emphasize practice

Feminists' religio-spiritual approaches are, thirdly, oriented toward *practice*. The Muslim and Christian participants followed a range of religious practices. The daughter of Pakistani parents (a Muslim mother and a communist father), Aisha describes herself as having a strong faith in God but engages in Islamic practices less since remarrying. She describes her adult children as more religiously observant than she (for instance, she no longer always fasts during Ramadan). However, her daily life accords with Islamic behavioral codes: she neither drinks alcohol nor eats non-halal food, and dresses "conservatively," wearing a locket inscribed with an Arabic prayer most days. She celebrates Ramadan with her extended family, friends, and neighbors. Asked if she attends mosque, she replied:

> I wouldn't go on a regular basis. If I was going there for a particular event and I was going with my mum, I would go. And I don't get my prayer mat out and do my five prayers, but what I do, I don't know if it's habit, but there are certain prayers that you say quietly, which I do all the time. I say my prayers every night before I go to sleep. That's just something I've always done, I've never not done it and I say, because it's part of the language, things like, "Shukar Alhamdulillah, thanks be to God", and they're just part of my vocabulary.

The extent to which religion remains a habit or, as Bourdieu (1977) puts it, part of someone's "habitus" (deep-rooted dispositions governing actions) is a question Aisha's response raises; as Mahmood (2005) argues, the role of the habitus should be examined when investigating women's religiosity.

Raised Roman Catholic, Beth, 25, maintained a strong faith throughout childhood, aspiring to be a nun. She developed socialist political views as a teenager and rejected the church's stance on abortion. Attending a Christian group at university, she became critical of the way the Bible was used against women. These attitudes distanced her from the church, yet she still identifies as Roman Catholic, attends confession occasionally, and does the rosary. Christian art (especially pietas) and music move her, and she sings hymns while doing domestic chores. She likes a poem she has on her wall, Kaylin Haught's "God Says Yes to Me," which speaks about God as female. Like other participants, she values ritual:

> I like the rituals of it, and I like the aesthetics, which is part of why I like Ash Wednesday and Palm Sunday, 'cause you've got the symbols and the crosses and I like sort of thinking about the way that we develop these traditions and how old they are and how they must have come... it all developed slowly and I really like sort of feeling part of that history.

Buddhist Anglican Melanie fuses an agnostic approach with Buddhism and Anglican Christianity. "Fusers," a term coined in Vincett's (2008, 133) study of Christian and neo-pagan feminists, "represent a new form of 'spiritualized Christianity'." Fusers comprise a spectrum, incorporating elements of the holistic "subjective turn" (Heelas and Woodhead 2005) into their Christianity, or, for those more committed to paganism, retaining only small elements from their Christian past. In Vincett's (2008, 137) study, the trend toward fusing was "unidirectional"; all fusers were previously Christian or raised as such, but none moved from paganism toward Christianity. Like Vincett's participants, Melanie's childhood connection to Christianity had been strong: She chose to be christened at the age of ten and attended different denominational services during her teens with her father. Beginning university and coming out as a lesbian, she abandoned Christianity as patriarchal. Later she became interested in Judaism and Buddhism, and, as described previously, was encouraged by Jewish acquaintances to return to church. Having attended a Buddhist retreat two years before the interview with her female partner (whose father is Buddhist), she took up Zen Buddhist meditation and attended church regularly. She got on well with the vicar and joined the Bible-reading rota, but was disappointed by the lack of religious practice she observed. Quakers, she felt, were better at integrating faith into their lives:

> My vicar's very clear that it doesn't matter a jot whether you go to church or not, what matters is what you do, but... as an Anglican I don't think it's really in our consciousness, the real everydayness about it. But it's, for me, about every day, the details of how we treat every moment of every day and how we treat each other, it's just really, really important, so I like that word "practice" because that's all you do, you're practicing—practice practice [laughs]. I'm not a Buddhist or a Christian, I'm practicing!

For her, ritual is important. Recalling Aisha's question about the extent to which Islamic prayer is a "habit," "just part of my vocabulary," Melanie described how repeating the words of confession of sin during the Anglican service recalls for her how Christianity has negatively shaped UK society. While this might appear an off-putting experience, it is as if the words of confession provide a perverse comfort, recalling the familiar structures of her childhood and society:

> There's something about the ritual of communion that I like... the con-gregational saying confession at the same time just makes me laugh inside. I just think, well, that's a good reminder of why we're such dowdy whatsits... Most of my childhood I wasn't at church, but going back and then hearing the words again I just think, yeah, that just sums up the oppression in the society. So I find that very useful.

The three pagan or alternative spirituality practitioners also emphasized ritual and daily practice. These practices included making a sacred space at home (an altar for Anya, 23, a garden for Sandy, 36), wearing special jewelry (Anya's owl necklace represented the goddess Athena, and Sandy wears a goddess ring), and celebrating pagan festivals; Sandy also had a pagan wed-ding. Sonia, 37, who rejected Christianity for Wicca and paganism in her teens, saw paganism as an "earth-based spirituality with magic and witchcraft involved." Paganism sees everything and everyone as "made of the same stuff," she explained, and all actions have effects. She practices spellwork, likening it to prayer:

> I don't like to say that spellwork and magic is like prayer but there are similarities; whereas a Christian or Muslim would pray to their God, my spell is more of a kind of interactive version of that... I talk to what I presume to be sort of a deity in my head, not as a sort of kneel down, put my hands together, but if I want something to happen I might do a ritual that essentially is asking for that to happen. I send emotion, my energy to get it to happen, but I also would then add into it normal things... The classic one is hunting for a job or finding a partner, you do all the rituals in the world but if you sit in your living room or your garden and don't actually do anything about it, it's not going to turn up on your doorstep.

Participants' focus on action, not just belief, is important, and is a feature of work on lived religion, as I will discuss. Practice is both a noun and a verb; as Bender (2012) points out, religion is not simply a series of practices, but something that people are constantly doing. This is not to say that all spiri-tual practices are understood as such by those doing them. Karen, an agnos-tic, practiced yoga for exercise, not spiritual reasons.

Moreover, practices some scholars class as "spiritual" were also found among atheists and humanists, who saw atheism or humanism as a positive engagement with the world, as Ruth put it, as the practice of doing good to others. Jackie explained:

It's the acts that people do, the help that you get from people. I don't think there's a higher being, a greater force. I think we're here and we're on our own, and it's down to us to get on with it... I try to be tolerant ... I try to act in the way that I would like people to treat me. Sometimes if I see a stranger on the bus—I just see a girl and she's wearing a really nice dress—I will say to her, "I really like your dress, it really suits you," because I know that if somebody pays me a compliment it makes me feel good... So those are the ways I try and be a humanist. I give to charities.

Lynne, 24, said she had no religion, but her values shape her actions. Raised by atheist parents but with a Christian grandmother, she believes in energy and balance but would not refer to them as "God." Balance is important to her, and she believes that good actions will reap rewards, using the illustration of "driving karma":

One of my main ideas is about balance and how if you do something good, that makes you a good person and good things will happen to you and if you look out for someone else they'll look after you... if you've got good driving karma you'll get a space at the car park, if you've got bad driving karma you don't get a space. So I often think... how can I go about something the right way? I don't know if I'd call that meditating or not, because I still haven't decided if this is a religion or if this is what most people do. But I try and take time out every day and think, "Am I doing it right?," "Am I a good person?," "Have my actions today made the world a better place?," or, y'know, "Do I need to do some recycling?!"

Lynne is not conventionally religious, but is open to the idea that practicing doing good might constitute a religio-spiritual act.

Conclusions

How do these findings inform existing debates? First, the feminism vs. religion approach common in earlier feminist scholarship was evident for some participants, but a minor theme. Although they rarely used the term "secularism," most of them felt that institutional religion was implicated in, and even caused, women's subordination.

In relation to secularization, feminism appears to have led some participants away from the church, and many felt that religious institutions fail to respect women's experiences. Other factors—relationships with family, friends and partners, sexuality, and education—also influenced my interviewees. Feminism is associated with disaffiliation from church but only slightly with rejection of Christian practices or beliefs. This is important, suggesting to scholars of secularization that disaffiliation from church should not be assumed to constitute religious decline; church attendance is just one measure of religiosity.

The second feminist trajectory, emphasizing holistic feminist spirituality, was evident; I also observed a movement toward alternative religio-spiritual manifestations that were embodied and practiced in daily life. But distinctions between institutional Christianity ("religion") and alternative spiritualities ("spirituality")—epitomized in Heelas and Woodhead's (2005) contrast between "life-as" religion and "subjective-life" spiritualities—fail to reflect feminists' experiences. Third, in showing how feminist activists utilize spiritual resources, this study mirrors the new studies of religiously based feminisms. Moreover, I observed three characteristics present in feminists' spiritual approaches: they are de-churched, are relational, and emphasize practice. These characteristics make it appropriate, I propose, to conceptualize feminist spirituality as lived religion.

Coined by Hall (1997), the term "lived religion" involves a focus on people's everyday religious experiences. Hall preferred "lived religion" to "popular religion" (which had developed to signify the difference between official forms of religion propagated by religious leaders and institutions, and how religion was lived out in daily life) because it lacks "the distinction between high and low that seems inevitably to recur in studies of popular religion" (Hall 1997, ix). The term, explains McGuire (2008, 12), "is useful for distinguishing the actual experience of religious persons from the prescribed religion of institutionally defined beliefs and practices." Everyday bodily experiences—like gardening, walking, or domestic work—are often the means by which people experience the sacred. Emotion is integral. Lived religion incorporates how the material body experiences the spiritual with everyday material culture—clothing, household consumption, or religious objects—and with locality—place, geography, the global, and the local (Neitz 2011).

Lived religion scholars emphasize the *practice* of religion, but the spiritual practices of which they write are far broader than sociologists have conventionally examined, and take place across multiple contexts. Ammerman (2007, 12), using the related term "everyday religion," explains that in the contemporary "dynamic religious culture" "official and unofficial religious ideas and practices are shaped into everyday strategies of action" that "take place not only across cultural and religious traditions but also across the multiple settings in which modern people create life."

In emphasizing *practice*, lived religion differs from substantive understandings of religion as belief, dispensing with the view that one is not religious unless one adheres to officially recognized doctrines. It offers scholars "a fundamental rethinking of what religion is and of what it means to be 'religious'" (Orsi 1997, 7). Importantly, the lived religion concept gets over the spirituality versus religion dichotomy. Religious and spiritual phenomena overlap; they are interconnected and complex, not distinct and distinguishable.

This study of UK feminists illustrates these points. For them, religion and spirituality are complex phenomena. Some of them saw institutionalized spiritualities, especially Christianity, as restrictive or oppressive. Some considered holistic or pagan spirituality a better alternative. But they did not tell a simple story of movement from institutional religion to individualized, or holistic, spirituality. They experienced spirituality and religion in more complex ways than the religion vs. spirituality distinction allows for: religion and spirituality were embedded in their childhoods and relational networks, even while, for the atheists especially, they functioned as something to define themselves against or sources of family conflict. Practice was important to their spirituality. Religion and spirituality were *lived*. The study's key finding is that feminist spirituality *is* lived religion.

In arguing this, my study supports not only the work of lived religion scholars, but also Fedele and Knibbe's (2012) new ethnographic work on gender and spirituality. They also reject the spirituality/religion distinction, since there is no clear difference between people who describe themselves as spiritual and those calling themselves religious, and many people see themselves as both; Roussou's (2012, 57) ethnography in Fedele and Knibbe's volume of Greek women who "perceive religion and spirituality as complementary and amalgamate the two" illustrates this. Writing favorably of the lived religion approach, Fedele and Knibbe (2012, 3) also critique "the claims of contemporary 'spirituality' to offer (gendered) empowerment and to be free from the 'traditional' gendered hierarchies (in contrast to 'religion')." "Institutional religions can empower women, just as alternative spiritualities can end up reproducing gender stereotypes or gendered domination" (2012, 5).

Building on recent empirical studies of religious feminism, I argue for a new conceptualization of feminist religio-spiritual approaches as lived religion. While feminist scholars' journey from critiquing religion to exploring feminist spirituality has contributed important insights about how individuals blend feminist and feminist identities, neither approach takes into account the full feminist experience. The full femin

ist experience includes, as this study shows, a blend of elements often categorized as *either* "spiritual" *or* "religious"; it includes recourse to religious traditions (Islamic, Jewish, Christian, Buddhist), such as the singing of Christian hymns or recitation of Islamic prayers, alongside detachment from religious institutions (in this British example, the Christian church). The feminist experience prioritizes relationships as the context for religio-spiritual formation, while foregrounding, as alternative spiritualities do, the need to nourish the self. The full feminist experience emphasizes religio-spiritual practices, not doctrines, but this does not mean beliefs play no part.

The feminist religio-spiritual experience also offers sociologists of religion an empirical basis for the critique of the conceptual distinction between religion and spirituality. As Wood (2010, 281) argues:

> Ethnographic evidence shows that people's discourses, practices and interactions in contexts considered (by themselves or sociologists) as "spirituality" in fact relate explicitly to contexts labeled as "religion" ....
> whilst "religion" and "spirituality" may sometimes and in some contexts

relate to distinct discourses and practices, the clear linkage between these necessitates a *single* analytical category.

Wood contends that the posited religion/spirituality distinction is not sufficiently sociological, because it ignores the social context of people's lives:

> Through its conceptual distinction between "religion" and "spirituality," this sociology lifts people out of their social contexts, with the result that it fails adequately to address social practice, social interaction, and the wider contexts of people's lives and biographies.
>
> (2010, 267)

There is a need for more thoroughly sociological explorations of religio-spirituality or, to use my preferred term, "lived religion." As this study shows, feminists' religio-spiritual approaches are socially located and tied to social practice, social interaction, and the wider context of their biographies and lives; "'spirituality' or 'religion' can be understood only within the social and cultural configurations and historical trajectories in which such self-identifications occur" (Fedele and Knibbe 2013, 6).

This study contributes to the growing field of research on gender, feminism, and religion. To scholars of gender, it demonstrates the importance of taking seriously the role spirituality and religion play in feminists' lives. To scholars of religion it challenges the conceptual dichotomy between religion and spirituality and provides an empirical basis for doing so. That these feminists forge religio-spiritual lives in ways that are de-churched, relational, and oriented toward practice provides further endorsement for the concept of lived religion. Moreover, this study has ramifications beyond the field of feminism and religion. If feminists, as the evidence suggests, represent the vanguard of new forms of femininity that later spread to the wider culture (Brown 2007, 414), this study is of wider significance: the forms of spirituality and religion expressed, rejected, and wrestled with by these UK feminists may become increasingly present, in European and other post-industrial societies. To understand the future of religion we must not only, as Marler (2008) argues, "watch the women"; we must also watch the feminists.

Notes

1 This essay was first published in *Gender & Society* 29(1): 122–145, copyright © 2015 by Sage Publications. Reprinted by Permission of SAGE Publications, Inc. This research received no specific grant from any funding agency in the public, commercial, or not-for-profit sectors.
2 Because few respondents resided in Northern Ireland, and to reduce travel costs, no interviews were conducted there.
3 Participants' names are pseudonyms.
4 Girls' clubs with loosely Christian roots; these are part of the international Scouts and Guides movement, first established in the early twentieth century.

References

Ammerman, Nancy T., ed. 2007. *Everyday religion: Observing modern religious lives.* New York: Oxford University Press.

Arweck, Elisabeth and Eleanor Nesbitt. 2010. "Young people's identity formation in mixed-faith families: Continuity or discontinuity of religious traditions?" *Journal of Contemporary Religion* 25(1): 67–87.

Aune, Kristin. 2011. "Much less religious, a little more spiritual: The religious and spiritual views of third-wave feminists in the UK." *Feminist Review* 97: 32–55.

Aune, Kristin, Sonya Sharma, and Giselle Vincett, eds. 2008. *Women and religion in the west: Challenging secularization.* Aldershot: Ashgate.

Bellah, Robert, Richard Madsen, William Sullivan, Ann Swindler, and Steven Tipton. 1985. *Habits of the heart: Individualism and commitment in American life.* Berkeley, CA: University of California Press.

Bender, Courtney. 2012. "Practicing religions." In *The Cambridge companion to religious studies,* edited by Robert A. Orsi. Cambridge: Cambridge University Press.

Berger, Helen A. 1999. *A community of witches: Contemporary neo-paganism and witchcraft in the United States.* Columbia, SC: University of South Carolina Press.

Berger, Peter, ed. 1999. *The desecularization of the world: Essays on the resurgence of religion in world politics.* Grand Rapids, MI: William B. Eerdmans.

Bourdieu, Pierre. 1977. *Outline of a theory of practice.* (Richard Nice, trans.) Cambridge: Cambridge University Press.

Braidotti, Rosi. 2008. "In spite of the times: The postsecular turn in feminism." *Theory, Culture & Society* 25(6): 1–24.

Braude, Ann. 2004. "A religious feminist—who can find her? Historiographical challenges from the National Organization for Women." *The Journal of Religion* 84(4): 555–572.

Brown, Callum. 2001. *The death of Christian Britain: Understanding secularisation, 1800–2000.* London: Routledge.

Brown, Callum. 2007. "Secularization, the growth of militancy and the spiritual revolution: Religious chance and gender power in Britain, 1901–2001." *Historical Research* 80(209): 393–418.

Browne, Sarah F. 2013. "Women, religion, and the turn to feminism: Experiences of women's liberation activists in Britain in the seventies." In *The sixties and beyond: Dechristianisation in North America and Western Europe, 1945–2000,* edited by Nancy Christie and Michael Gauvreau. Toronto: University of Toronto Press.

Daggers, Jenny. 2002. *The British Christian women's movement.* Aldershot: Ashgate.

Davie, Grace. 2007. *The sociology of religion.* London: Sage.

Dillon, Michele and Paul Wink. 2007. *In the course of a lifetime: Tracing religious belief, practice, and change.* Berkeley, CA: University of California Press.

Eller, Cynthia. 1993. *Living in the lap of the goddess: The feminist spirituality movement in America.* New York: Crossroad.

Fedele, Anna. 2013. *Looking for Mary Magdalene: Alternative pilgrimage and ritual creativity at Catholic shrines in France.* Oxford: Oxford University Press.

Fedele, Anna and Kim Knibbe, eds. 2013. *Gender and power in contemporary spirituality.* New York: Routledge.

Hall, David D. 1997. "Introduction". In *Lived religion: Toward a history of practice,* edited by David D. Hall. Princeton, NJ: Princeton University Press.

Heelas, Paul and Linda Woodhead. 2005. *The spiritual revolution: Why religion is giving way to spirituality*. Oxford: Blackwell.

Houtman, Dick and Stef Aupers. 2007. "The spiritual turn and the decline of tradition: The spread of post-Christian spirituality in 14 western countries, 1981–2000." *Journal for the Scientific Study of Religion* 46(3): 305–320.

Hussain, Serena. 2008. "Counting women with faith: What quantitative data can reveal about Muslim women in 'secular' Britain." In *Women and religion in the west: Challenging secularization*, edited by Kristin Aune, Sonya Sharma, and Giselle Vincett. Aldershot: Ashgate.

Ingersoll, Julie. 2003. *Evangelical Christian women: War stories in the gender battles*. New York: New York University Press.

Jakobsen, Janet R. and Ann Pellegrini, eds. 2008. *Secularisms*. Durham, NC: Duke University Press.

Klassen, Chris, ed. 2009. *Feminist spirituality: The next generation*. Lanham, MD: Lexington Books.

Llewellyn, Dawn and Marta Trzebiatowska. 2013. "Secular and religious feminisms: A future of disconnection?" *Feminist Theology* 21(3): 244–258.

Luckmann, Thomas. 1967. *The invisible religion*. New York: Macmillan.

Mahmood, Saba. 2005. *Politics of piety: The Islamic revival and the feminist subject*. Princeton, NJ: Princeton University Press.

Marler, Penny Long. 2008. "Religious change in the West: Watch the women." In *Women and religion in the West: Challenging secularization*, edited by Kristin Aune, Sonya Sharma, and Giselle Vincett. Aldershot: Ashgate.

McGinty, Anna. 2007. "Formation of alternative femininities through Islam: Feminist approaches among Muslim converts in Sweden." *Women's Studies International Forum* 30(6): 474–485.

McGuire, Meredith. 2008. *Lived religion: Faith and practice in everyday life*. New York: Oxford University Press.

Neitz, Mary Jo. 2011. "Lived religion: Signposts of where we have been and where we can go from here." In *Religion, spirituality and everyday practice*, edited by Giuseppe Gordon and William H. Swatos, Jr. London: Springer.

Orsi, Robert. 1997. "Everyday miracles: The study of lived religion." In *Lived religion: Toward a history of practice*, edited by David D. Hall. Princeton, NJ: Princeton University Press.

Reilly, Niamh. 2011. "Rethinking the interplay of feminism and secularism in a neo-secular age." *Feminist Review* 97(1): 5–31.

Roof, Wade Clark. 1999. *Spiritual marketplace: Baby boomers and the remaking of American religion*. Princeton, NJ: Princeton University Press.

Roussou, Eugenia. 2012. "Spirituality within religion: Gendered responses to a Greek 'spiritual revolution.'" In *Gender and power in contemporary spiritualities*, edited by Anna Fedele and Kim Knibbe. London: Routledge.

Salomonsen, Jone. 2002. *Enchanted feminism: The Reclaiming Witches of San Francisco*. London: Routledge.

Sointu, Eeva and Linda Woodhead. 2008. "Spirituality, gender and expressive selfhood." *Journal for the Scientific Study of Religion* 47(2): 259–276.

Tylor, Edward. 1873. *Primitive culture, vol. II*. London: John Murray.

Vincett, Giselle. 2008. "The fusers: New forms of spiritualized Christianity." In *Women and religion in the west: Challenging secularization*, edited by Kristin Aune, Sonya Sharma, and Giselle Vincett. Aldershot: Ashgate.

Vincett, Giselle and Linda Woodhead. 2009. "Spirituality." In *Religions in the modern world: Traditions and transformations, 2nd edition*, edited by Linda Woodhead, Hiroko Kawanami, and Christopher Partridge. London: Routledge.

Voas, David and Alasdair Crockett. 2005. "Religion in Britain: Neither believing nor belonging." *Sociology* 39(1): 11–28.

Wilcox, Melissa M. 2009. *Queer women and religious individualism*. Bloomington, IN: Indiana University Press.

Wilson, Bryan. 1966. *Religion in secular society*. Harmondsworth: Penguin.

Wood, Matthew. 2010. "The sociology of spirituality: Reflections on a problematic endeavour." In *The New Blackwell Companion to the Sociology of Religion*, edited by Bryan S. Turner. Malden, MA: Wiley-Blackwell.

Woodhead, Linda. 2001. "Feminism and the sociology of religion: From gender-blindness to gendered difference." In *The Blackwell Companion to Sociology of Religion*, edited by Richard K. Fenn. Malden, MA: Blackwell.

Woodhead, Linda. 2005. "Gendering secularisation theory." *Kvinder, Køn og Forskning* 1–2: 24–35.

Wuthnow, Robert. 2001. "Spirituality and spiritual practice." In *The Blackwell companion to sociology of religion*, edited by Richard K. Fenn. Oxford: Blackwell.

Yip, Andrew. 2005. "Queering religious texts: An exploration of British non-heterosexual Christians' and Muslims' strategy of constructing sexuality-affirming hermeneutics." *Sociology* 39(1): 47–65.

Zwissler, Laurel. 2007. "Spiritual, but religious: 'Spirituality' among religiously motivated feminist activists." *Culture and Religion* 8(1): 51–69.

2 Goddess Spirituality in Italy

Secular and spiritual – two sides of the same coin?

Stefania Palmisano and Roberta Pibiri

Introduction

Based on an analysis of the Italian Goddess Spirituality movement, this chapter aims to investigate – through the lens of gender – relations among secularism, religion and nascent forms of spirituality. We argue that the Goddess Spirituality movement – also called feminist spirituality – appears as an emblematic example of secular–spiritual integration. Goddess Spirituality is a quintessentially female religiosity, based on a regulative divine, symbolic principle of female qualities – represented by the Goddess – which originates from feminist movements, in particular the academic work of feminist studies (see Eisler 1987; Gimbutas 1989) in different disciplines which have attested to the existence, in the Neolithic Age,[1] of ancient matrifocal societies and pre-Christian cults honouring the female divine symbolized by the Goddess.[2] The gender question to which the feminist movement has drawn attention, focussing on social and political needs, has encouraged the development of this new countercultural form of spirituality (Woodhead 2008) where the female is endowed with spiritual significance and appreciated as a sacred, divine principle.

As a consequence, in Italy too Goddess Spirituality is slowly becoming an advocate of spiritual and social demands, integrating them into a coherent framework in which the transformation of the self (understood as healing one's emotional wounds generated by the patriarchy), personal empowerment, individual and social responsibility and effectiveness of ritual practice are central.

In this chapter we shall outline how this kind of spirituality is able to combine and transmit spiritual as well as secular concepts and values by means of alternative political, economic (gift and exchange economy), educational and social development models. We shall also show how this spirituality is integrated into its members' daily lives through collective and individual practices and/or forms of activism combining the material and spiritual dimensions of life.

Due to its peculiar worldview and practices depending on specific attitudes towards the sacred, Goddess Spirituality in Italy reveals the distance between what in this essay we identify as "religion" and what we identify as "contemporary spirituality". We suggest that in the Italian case it is useful to distinguish between these two concepts not only on an emic but also on an analytical level considering them as opposite poles of a continuum. At one extreme we define religion as an experience of the sacred mediated by institutions which, by virtue of a tradition, regulate its beliefs and practices (orthodoxy and orthopraxis). "Contemporary spirituality", on the other hand, is understood as an experience of the divine regulated by the subject without a strict regulation of the dominant Western religious institutions and traditions. Such experience is often described as personal seeking after meaning, satisfying mind, body and spirit (see also Heelas and Woodhead 2005).

This distinction between religion and spirituality, mirroring the distinction that the exponents of Goddess Spirituality themselves make, is useful to understanding the place that contemporary forms of spirituality (such as Goddess Spirituality) have in Italy. While these spiritualities are slowly becoming institutionalised over time, their peculiarities also derive from the relationship of distance and almost of opposition (see also Fedele 2013a; Fedele and Knibbe 2013) that exists between them and the religion that is predominant in Italy: Catholicism. In other words, the distinction between religion and spirituality permits greater understanding of the various modalities of relating to the sacred and to practitioners' "emic" discourses.

Although religion and spirituality should be distinguished analytically, we believe that they are not autonomous in practice and have a dialectical relationship, as also happens in other traditionally Catholic countries of Southern Europe (Fedele and Knibbe 2013; Fedele 2013b). Both historical analysis and contemporary reality reveal that the two phenomena enjoy continuous exchange and exercise reciprocal influence (see also von Stuckrad 2005; Hanegraaff 1996). A good example of the influence of spirituality on religion is a recurrent theme in many international surveys: most people conjoin "religious seeking" and "spiritual seeking" (see also Ammerman 2013). Institutionalized religious traditions remain a model of reference even for alternative spiritualities, where discursive registers, theological conceptions and values derive prevalently from Christianity and from Buddhism.

Defending the use of spirituality as a useful category to study contemporary forms of religiosity, however, does not imply that we agree with current sociological approaches that interpret spirituality as *designer religion* (Rountree 2004), *bricolage* or *religion à la carte* (Hamilton 2000). The idea that within contemporary forms of spirituality the authority of the subject substitutes the authority of religious institutions is central to this view of *bricolage*.[3] In other words, religion subordinates the self to external authorities while spirituality exercises the authority of the self.

When we refer to contemporary spirituality, however, we take our distance from the previous approaches: it cannot be taken for granted that in the alternative-spirituality field (the holistic milieu) the inner self really does exercise its authority because here too there are multiple authorities (shamans, priestesses, spiritual guides, educators, coaches) and traditions of reference which subjects give credit and obey. As Wood (2009) has noted, authorities in the spiritual field usually become potential – no longer binding – references and their multiple presence, through the prism of eclecticism, ends up relativizing them so that none is any longer exclusive. In addition, authority and traditions survive in the holistic milieu partly because the subject does not personally substitute them, in the sense that s/he does not create new beliefs and practices. In a more restricted way s/he chooses to what extent to adopt them and whether/how to combine them: to use a metaphor, the subject is not an author but a director.

In the next section we sketch three ethnographic reports which help us to reflect upon relations in Goddess Spirituality among religion, spirituality and secularism through the gender category prism. Specifically, the argumentations illustrated in this chapter are derived from the results of ethnographic research carried out within two of the most prominent and active groups of practice belonging to Goddess Spirituality in Italy, its headquarters in Turin, a northwestern city: Il Tempio della Dea[4] and the Laima Cultural Association.[5] On a methodological level, fieldwork – which lasted two years (2013–2014) – consisted of ethnographic research within the groups being examined, mainly based on participant observation. In addition, biographical interviews were conducted with group members (both women and men)[6] and an analysis of documents was produced by the groups themselves during fieldwork. The third section discusses theoretically the interpenetration of religion, spirituality and secularism. The fourth section describes Goddess Spirituality's beliefs and practices as a function of its capacity in this context to give rise to alternative economic, social and political models. In the fifth section we discuss how the partnership model, as theorized by sociologist Riane Eisler (1987), is the key to the fusion of spiritual and secular elements within Goddess Spirituality. In particular, partnership is the founding principle of the social system which Eisler calls "mutual", inspiring Goddess Spirituality's spiritual path, worldview and practices. In Eisler's definition, a "mutual" social system is based on "alternative" ways of (re)thinking the female and a balanced union between the female and male halves of humanity, whose relationship aims at gender equality focused on reciprocal valorization of their differences.

Fieldwork voices

The following passages are contained in field notes from ethnographic research carried out by one of the two authors into different groups belonging to Goddess Spirituality in Italy.[7] The notes refer in particular to the international conference "Indigenous Peace Cultures: Re-educating Oneself to Partnership" held in Turin in April 2013. The conference was organized by the Laima Cultural Association, an Italian group actively interested in practising and spreading female spirituality, inspired by shamanism and the teachings of Vicki Noble. It involved the main national and international spiritual practitioners and exponents of Goddess Spirituality and its variegated streams (the Avalonian tradition, Reclaiming, Female Shamanism), scholars and intellectuals, representatives of matrifocal indigenous societies. This was an important occasion of debate, reflection and comparison for the movement both at national (Italy) and international (UK and US)[8] levels. It was further possible to observe that the particular spiritual–secular interweaving became visible and legitimate through the production of shared discourses and narratives. These are transmitted by the main spiritual mentors of Goddess Spirituality's different traditions, which characterize the alternative interpretative framework transmitting the movement's vision of the world, values and spiritual practice. The concept of partnership is the main guiding principle of most of the female spirituality groups, fuelling the creation of alternative social, cultural, spiritual and existential models.

The following field notes were taken during the address of Riane Eisler, one of the most important scholars contributing to the development of this new form of spirituality and the creation of its historical, interpretative framework, explaining what she calls "the partnership way".

Sunday 28 April 2013, 9.00

The hall is packed and a slight buzz accompanies the appearance of one of the conference's most important speakers (via Skype), the sociologist Riane Eisler. Her theories about the evolution of humanity – presented in her greatly admired book *The Chalice and the Blade* – were a milestone in the diffusion of Goddess Spirituality, contributing to the body of knowledge and the innovative, alternative framework upon which this spirituality is based. When Riane Eisler starts to speak about the Goddess Spirituality path and the "partnership way" (her words), the buzz gives way to a profound silence. According to Eisler, "it is the only possible way to bring about a better world based on relations among human beings (men/women; parents/children) oriented towards more egalitarian reciprocity and on valuing male-female differences" … "The real challenge of our times", she says, "is the passage from the dominant (i.e. patriarchal) to the non-hierarchical model in which the condition of women is not only a female matter but a pillar upon which social development and a caring economy rest." She continues: "Our societies are characterized by a devaluation of everything female, an attitude resulting from stereotypical models belonging to the past – especially the dominator models – which have created a high level of gender inequality." For this reason, "it is necessary to change the structure of society, appreciating the female and women's role in the family, because high-quality human capital greatly depends on the quality of lifelong care received". She concludes by pointing out how important it is to work on new gender relations informed by the partnership principle, entitling her talk with the formula "What is good for women is good for the world".

Among the international exponents of Goddess Spirituality at this conference were Kathy Jones, a Goddess priestess, founder of the Glastonbury Goddess Temple (UK)[9] and the main representative of the Avalonian tradition.[10] Her contribution focusses on her elaboration of the MotherWorld project, aimed at a social model and liveable sacred paths for the contemporary world, based mainly on reclaiming the female sacred dimension, the sacralization of the body and the deconstruction of patriarchal cultural patterns of thought. The specific spiritual proposal of Goddess Spirituality, also shared by the Italian groups we are considering, is to promote social change by transmitting innovation through developmental social models that are alternatives to the patriarchal, dominating model of Western societies. As we shall see through the analysis below, in these new, alternative models spiritual and secular values are closely related. The following ethnographic account gives an idea of the social changes implied.

Saturday 27 April 2013, 14.30

"The vision of the MotherWorld project is a matrifocal society inspired by the Goddess and by female, maternal values where Mother Earth is the basis of all that we are and have ... inclusive and focused on retrieving female values in our society." Kathy Jones continues by explaining the basic values of MotherWorld including:

> to venerate Mother Earth as a living being; to stimulate reciprocal love, care and kindness; to honour all forms of maternal caregiving and to protect children; to encourage emotional expression and non-violent methods for resolving conflicts; and to appreciate the wisdom of the elderly and ancestors.... Healing practices – particularly of emotional wounds caused by patriarchy – are encouraged and made available to everybody in order to boost skills and techniques developing emotional expression and reciprocal love and support, thereby assuming the responsibility of one's repressed, dysfunctional emotions.

However, change is not possible without social action, which is usually expressed through multiform activism, as claimed by Starhawk, one of the most important representatives worldwide of female earth-based spirituality and ecofeminism. Founder of the San Francisco Reclaiming movement,[11] writer and activist, her talk illustrates another element demonstrating the intimate interweaving between sacred and secular. She attributes great importance to social activism and political action as an integral part of Goddess Spirituality's basic message. The meaning and modalities of interaction between the spiritual and material dimensions of Goddess Spirituality have become blindingly clear, as have the close link between activism and spiritual life and this form of religiosity's ability to contribute actively to social, cultural and spiritual innovation – a new symbolic resource capable of defining new languages.

The following passage is an example of Goddess Spirituality's tendency to promote social, cultural and spiritual innovation through the creation of new languages capable of integrating the spiritual (female earth-based) and secular (ecofeminism) dimensions:

Sunday 28 April 2013, 14.30

"Women Take Action" is the title of Starhawk's talk. Sharing her spiritual and activist experience in various (social, educational, ecological) environments, she reflects upon how feminine intuition can be used to bring about significant change in the world. Against a background of photographs testifying to her protest activities and women in action, Starhawk focusses on the theme of responsibility and the real meaning of being indigenous. "Each of us has a duty to be a native of somewhere, accepting our responsibility to be guardians of the Earth and look after the place where we live and our community." Particularly when – as now – the Earth is undergoing a period of transition and crisis – not only economic –

> it is useful to make use of female intuition to bring about social, economic and cultural change .... If one wants to change an oppressive system, one should not be afraid of creating a disturbance in that system ... [for example], obtaining the vote was just a first step for women, which did not change the dominant patriarchal culture. What can one believe in, when everything that one has believed in hitherto turns out to be false? That which allowed the transformation of a personal – rather than gender or female – problem into a political, social question was the formation of self-awareness groups with whom one could share one's experiences. The platform of the feminist movement and its accompanying revolution derives from the existence of these groups .... Feminist movement intuitions are necessary to identify actions which can be put into practice today to bring about important social change by finding the most suitable tools to collaborate effectively with one another .... The next step is to reflect on how religion contributes to our perception of reality. Up to now, religion has been shaped by men for men. But we have to ask: has there ever been, or can there ever be, another way?

For Starhawk there is the necessity of "new creations, new ways of being together, growing and sharing our spirituality, challenging the patriarchate by developing and activating new forms of spirituality rooted in new ways of living". She then asks herself and the public: "What can we do to change the world?" and her answer is to act in favour of peace by

> listening to women (especially native women), paying attention to the subject of food, a key point of intersection between the present economic-ecological crisis ... indeed, one of the forms of action is to work with food, which is to say, feed people and teach them to feed themselves. For example, for years I have been actively engaged in the permaculture movement. Another traditional activity is for us women to become involved on behalf of peace.

Her activism implies the integration of rituals into political protest, particularly the spiral dance: a ritual performance, which she created in 1969 in San Francisco where all participants actively contribute. Finally, alluding to her original title "Women Take Action", Starhawk asserts that "as women we can make use of our proudest and most warrior-like values, not only those of giving and care".

These ethnographic excerpts that present the international authors that influence Goddess Spirituality in Italy aim to stimulate reflection on the relations among spirituality, religion and the secular in the light of the gender category, representing/acting as an exemplary case study where secular–spiritual integration can conciliate different impulses and tendencies through its symbolic-axiological spiritual universe. Such integration is defined on the basis of Goddess Spirituality's vision of the world, values, images of the divine and the sacred and spiritual experience, making it a particularly relevant example of the topic under discussion. We shall further analyse this integration below, referring to interviews and ethnographic excerpts from Italian practitioners of Goddess Spirituality.

Religion, spirituality and secularity: an Italian insight

In recent years, a large body of literature on "the secular", secularism and secularity has shown that religion and secularity should be considered as intertwined categories that have historically emerged together and derive their meaning in relation to each other (Asad 2003; Knoblauch et al., 2011). In this section, our aim is to take a further step and to engage with the relationship between the category of spirituality and that of secularity, passing through that of religion. We claim that contemporary spirituality, historically rooted both in the Enlightenment and Romanticism, has also realized these movements' common project of a secular ideology (Palmisano and Pannofino 2017).

The sociology of religion recognizes pragmatism as a constituent trait of contemporary spirituality. More than faith and cognitive adherence to a doctrine, and more than respect for ethical norms, it is the experiential, corporeal and emotional dimension which counts (Heelas 2006; Hamberg 2009; Riis and Woodhead 2010). Spiritual seekers feel an urgent need to orient their relationship with the sacred towards the worldly sphere of daily life in order to satisfy concrete exigencies such as healing, psychological and material wellbeing, and personal growth (Barker 2008). This pragmatism is what endows modernity with the spirituality begun in the 1960s and 1970s, which may be summed up in the "It's true if it works" formula, where the centrality of the self and a direct, personal relationship with religious truth can be seen, measured by its effectiveness (Lenoir 2003; Fedele and Knibbe 2013).

This pragmatic, experiential approach has a double historical root – the Enlightenment and Romanticism – traceable to Western movements which gave its cultural impulse to the very birth of modernity. "Experience" is one of the distinctive categories of the modern age and philosophy, the counterpart of dogma in medieval thought (Thomassen 2014). Both the Enlightenment and Romanticism constructed their concepts of the world on the idea of experience – the former considering it as experimental and the latter as experiential – albeit reaching different, antithetical conclusions. The main attribute of contemporary spirituality is that it has inherited both these contradictory conceptions, joining them together in an original way. By now, several scholars have recognized the Enlightenment-Romantic heritage of some of the new spirituality's themes and ideology (Heelas 2008). In Italy, as elsewhere, contemporary spirituality has united those two conceptions of experience, producing a historically innovative vision of its value in the religious field (Hanegraaff 1996; von Stuckrad 2005).

This vision of experience fuelled in the spiritual seekers a critical-rational-type cognitive orientation according to which the plausibility of religious beliefs and truths can be measured not only in relation to subjective legitimation but also by their compatibility with a shared repository of knowledge deriving from other cultural fields which are not subordinate to religious knowledge but construct a framework of explanation of the real on an equal footing. A good example of this within contemporary spiritual movements is that of Goddess Spirituality which, according to scholars (historians, archaeologists, anthropologists, mythologists, philosophers and theologians), makes up the interpretative framework of the tradition. While the structural differentiation of complex societies has made these cultural fields autonomous and specialized, the borders between them are no less porous and overlapping. The result is *bricolage*, the eclecticism of knowledge deriving from different conceptual realms, a main element of recent forms of spirituality (Hamilton 2000; Lyon 2000; Possamai 2003).

Therefore, since contemporary spirituality has inherited the primacy of experience equally from the Enlightenment and Romanticism, it has also realized their joint historical project of secular ideology. Rather than being antagonistic, spirituality and secularity have a common genealogy, a common lay inspiration and a common aversion against both dogmatism and the power of hierarchical institutions (Van der Veer 2009). This antipathy is expressed in both cases in the concept of truth as pragmatic seeking to be tested by critical reason and by subjective meaning. This ideology derives from liberal Western societies and, albeit developed outside – and in opposition to – churches and traditional religions, it has not produced its own fully anti-traditional spirituality.

The idea that spirituality and secularity interpenetrate – that is to say they are related rather than opposite categories – is not only fuelled by ethnographic research about spirituality, as we see in this chapter's case study on Goddess Spirituality. Sociological quantitative studies devoted to measuring the growth of spiritual identity in different countries point in the same direction. Some findings from a sample survey[12] of the Italian population and interviews carried out with young people in various cities reveal that religion, spirituality and secularity are not separated and it is useful to problematize the borders among them (Palmisano and Pannofino 2016). In that study a typology of religious, spiritual and secular attitudes expressed ideally in the space between two opposite poles is traced: the hot pole of "re-sacralization" in terms of "spiritual revolution" (Heelas and Woodhead 2005) and the cold pole of radical secularization as effective indifference towards the religious question and the problem of God (Bruce 2002).

We labelled three profiles: 1) the spiritual religious (yearning for the Christian God); 2) the spiritual alternatives (open to the supra-natural, seeking an impersonal, immanent, pantheistic deity and expecting the divine to manifest itself in incomprehensible, mysterious forms); and 3) the spiritual atheists (who use the language of spirituality to describe not a transcendental, supra-natural "Other" but an immanent, ordinary "other" understood, for example, as humanity, society, community and nature). Hierophany, the manifestation of the sacred, is here situated in the worldly sphere, which is, however, sacralized. In this way, according to a small number of interviewees, beauty too – in the forms of art, in ecology, music, literature and philosophy – becomes a kind of "rumour of angels": books, songs, landscapes, paintings and poetry trigger spiritual experiences by revealing hidden connections, evoking wonder, encouraging reflection, offering a break in one's daily routine and motivating self-awareness. The differences among the three profiles clarify the necessity of problematizing the confines between what is, and what is not, religious. In other words, a spiritual profile fuels styles of life, social practices and cultural objects which may not be exclusively assigned either to the "religious" or the "secular" realm. From the sociological perspective these findings demonstrate that religion and secularism are not fixed, monolithic categories (Asad 2003). The modern opposition between them needs to be reconsidered because, as the profiles above show, the spiritual may contain characteristics of both religion and secularism.

Goddess Spirituality as a case of spiritual and secular integration

Goddess Spirituality is ontologically female, which is to say based on a conception of the divine with female qualities. More precisely, the divine force is conceived as energy revealing itself both in nature (through the cycle of the seasons) and in human beings (of both genders) whose individual self is considered at the same time as a reflection of – and a means of contacting – the divine. According to this pantheistic and immanent view, everything is sacred since it is an expression of female divine energy, which explains the overlapping – or convergence – of the spiritual and material dimensions of existence. Gender becomes informed with a spiritual component and integrated into a symbolic, axiological universe capable of bringing about a consistent secular–spiritual synthesis. Symbolically, this divine energy is represented by the Mother Goddess whose specific qualities are incorporated by different goddesses;[13] its cyclic nature can be seen in the Wheel of the Year, the symbolic, seasonal ritual calendar. It comes as no surprise in the light of these characteristics that Goddess Spirituality occupies a marginal position in the current religious and socio-cultural environment. More specifically, it is opposed to prevailing theologies and values because of its alternative conception of the sacred and the divine (the*a*logy, Goldenberg 1979) and its criticism of conventional gender concepts (Woodhead 2008) and of religion.

The Goddess Spirituality path is characterized by teachings and practices aimed at encouraging change through more-or-less explicit forms of activism implying alternative ways of experiencing the secular sphere, as demonstrated in the field notes presented in the second section. It demonstrates its ability to contribute actively to social, cultural and spiritual innovation by becoming a symbolic resource laden with new practices and discourses. This happens through the rejection of traditional forms of religion, which are considered patriarchal, authoritarian and dogmatic, and of a male-type conception of the divine embodying norms and dogmas rather than direct, intimate relationship with the sacred. The process of reclamation and re-actualization of Goddess Spirituality in Italy, as in other European countries (especially the UK), coincide with a process of rediscovery of the ancient, pre-Christian spiritual traditions of so-called "Ancient Europe" (Gimbutas, 1989). Through countercultural narrations based on the mechanism of "re-membering" (Pibiri 2017), adherents aim to reclaim and actualize ancient spiritual traditions of the female sacred and to establish continuity and a connection with the Goddess spiritual traditions which are considered the authentic spiritual heritage of Europe, in opposition to traditional – especially monotheistic – religions (*ibidem*). By valorizing a divine principle with female qualities, Goddess Spirituality brings to light the urgency of developing a *modus vivendi* in tune with a "shared" social model based on the partnership principle (Eisler 1987).

To this end Goddess Spirituality considers direct, intimate experience of divine female energy – which is mainly felt through ritual seasonal practices celebrating the Wheel of the Year – as the core of its itinerary. Direct spiritual experience in function of the central position accorded to the authority of the self becomes the yardstick of religious "truth", as a Priestess of the Glastonbury Goddess Temple (UK) states: "One is encouraged to find one's own truth, to accept one's own feelings, one's truth based on experience."[14]

This truth coincides with the effectiveness of the spiritual practice. Direct experience of this effectiveness gives rise to a process of personal empowerment (deriving from valorization of female qualities) accompanied by an increased sense of individual and social responsibility on the part of both men and women members of Goddess Spirituality groups, revealed by the interviews as premises for transformation of the self and, as a consequence, of the world. In other words, empowerment results in increased awareness of one's own effectiveness, which is to say personal ability and power to become co-creators of reality by exercising one's willingness and active participation, from which the above-mentioned sense of individual and social responsibility derives. Based on this observation it is possible to understand secular–spiritual integration at the heart of Goddess Spirituality and the necessity – expressed by most of the members of the studied groups – to unite daily and spiritual life, to live every moment of one's existence with sacrality. In the words of one interviewee:

It is necessary to work deeply on oneself, to transform oneself... implying first of all recognition of the sacred in oneself and in others... the Goddess in them. To do this one must immerse oneself in the real, to experience the sacred dimension of existence and translate it into concrete attitudes and actions. The sacred imbues every area of our lives and being attentive towards it is the first – basic – step.

(Viviane the Lady of the Lake)

In this process ritual performance plays a major part. It defines a space where women and men may connect with the various qualities of divine energy demonstrated by the cyclical nature of the seasons (represented symbolically by different Goddesses). According to the interviewees, ritual practice facilitates awareness of one's own sacred part (which is to say, the authentic, archetypal self) considered an emanation and reflexion of the female divine. This process of recognition and valorization of the female divine within oneself and the consequent transformation implies working on one's emotions – considered, along with sexuality – as a fast track to the female divine.

Again, according to the interviewees, increased awareness of one's sacred part – acquired through practices such as visualization, meditation and symbolic acts – derives from contact, acceptance and integration of one's shadowy, emotional (mostly negative) parts. This triggers a self-transformation process coinciding with the healing of one's emotional wounds caused by patriarchal religious, social and cultural models relative to ways of conceiving gender, male–female relations and religiosity itself. In this sense, therefore, self-transformation aims at integrating one's shaded areas and wounds with the purpose of synthesizing the archetypal polarities of the human being, female and male. As one interviewee says:

Working on the emotions and emotional healing are at the heart of the Goddess Spirituality vision because the creation of dependable, repeatable models, the integration of the male and female in the human being, can only come about if our wounds (generally of an emotional type) heal.

(Elen of the Ways)

Individual internal work is a precondition for activating collectively the desired change, supported by the creation of social, cultural and spiritual models tending towards partnership, which is to say inspired by a principle of gender equality based on valorization of differences.

Goddess Spirituality's ideological horizon becomes concrete in various secular spheres of existence which in turn are informed by a spiritual dimension, as can be seen from the fieldwork. In practical terms, this variety develops through the adoption of lifestyles which are respectful of nature and its cycles; the creation of groups and communities inspired by matrifocal, caring values; use of language attentive to gender differences; being careful about using cultural products with implicit patriarchal messages. Furthermore, this secular–spiritual interweaving can be found in the health field in the adoption of holistic cures respecting the female body and its cyclic nature; in the choice of professions in tune with matrifocal, healing values; in intransigent insistence on natural (non-medicalized) methods of conception and delivery (e.g. home birth, lotus birth),[15] childcare (e.g. opposition to vaccination). The interweaving of the spiritual and the secular can also be seen in the economic and educational areas (e.g. parental teaching) where they experiment with alternative economics (e.g. gift economy, green economy, cooperation) and professions (e.g. holistic workers, psychologists, researchers, teachers, educators and pedagogues) contributing to the wellbeing of the community.

The close link among self-transformation, personal responsibility and desire for social change of the Goddess Spirituality's itinerary is described by an interviewee:

> Since it is based on a personal reconnection with both natural rhythms and the divine, infusing every aspect of daily life, the acquisition of a sense of responsibility is favoured in order to remind us that every action we carry out honours the divine within us and in nature. If I act with awareness and responsibility I consciously co-create with the energy of the Goddess, which is consequently reflected in the fact that my behaviour will change, respecting nature, people and natural rhythms, no longer contributing to dysfunctional systems such as that of the patriarchal dominator. This is the main emotional change which can be seen: only through individual change can one hope to bring about collective change.
>
> (The Lady of Avalon)

The next section will illustrate that Goddess Spirituality is characterized by a double (secular and spiritual) value which is useful for illuminating the relationship among secular, spiritual and religious.

The partnership way: where secular and spiritual meet each other

As we have seen up to now, Goddess Spirituality is emblematic of the secular–religious–spiritual relationship because of its tendency to integrate spiritual and material life on both the individual and collective levels, both through ritual practices and alternative "mutual"-type (Eisler 1987) social, cultural and spiritual models leading to the adoption of modalities of existence and action inspired by Goddess Spirituality principles.

This interweaving between the spiritual and secular dimensions of existence can be more easily understood in the light of Goddess Spirituality's concepts of the divine and of gender characterizing our sample groups.

To clarify further how this integration works, it is worthwhile to recall the genesis of Goddess Spirituality and the influences contributing to its development. As hinted in the first section, two main elements related to secular spheres and dynamics contributed to recovering and re-actualizing the ancient paths of the female sacred upon which Goddess Spirituality is based. First, the principally academic research of feminist scholars belonging to different disciplines (history, archaeology, sociology, anthropology, classical and mythological studies, e.g. Daly 1973; Stone 1976; Eisler 1987; Gimbutas 1989, 1991) who rediscovered ancient, pre-Christian religiosity devoted to worship of the Goddess – in particular, their critical theories focussed upon matrifocal societies – form the framework legitimating tradition. Second, the political and social demands of feminist movements have helped this re-birth of forms of religiosity centred on the female divine. The valorization of the female in a spiritual key would not have been possible without the contribution of feminism, whose struggles for political and social rights and women's emancipation opened the door to the development, some decades later, of these "counter-cultural" forms of spirituality/religiosity (Woodhead 2008).

The roots of Goddess Spirituality demonstrate the influence of secular dynamics which are reflected in its capacity to contribute actively to social, cultural and spiritual innovation by becoming an alternative symbolic resource in order to define and disseminate new – and not only religious – languages and discourses. For example, self-transformation implicit in spiritual practice and translated into healing one's emotional wounds, personal empowerment, greater awareness of one's self, one's place in the world and sense of responsibility stimulate adherents to action suggesting alternative modalities of experiencing secular spheres. Thus, Goddess Spirituality demands a more prominent role for women in society and is an important symbolic resource for men who do not identify with traditional models of masculinity. More particularly, it stimulates radical social, cultural and spiritual change hinging on the mutual social system inspired by the partnership principle (Eisler 1987).[16] The partnership concept, integrating individual and collective needs, is the key to understanding Goddess Spirituality's orientation towards spiritual–secular integration, an orientation emphasizing union between equals rather than patriarchal domination.

Finally, it is worth underlining that the kind of rebirth proposed by the Goddess Spirituality movement leads to a re-emergence of awareness of the female principle – as an archetypal quality – among both women and men. Although most followers are women, its spiritual proposal is also relevant to men because gender is not understood as merely physical or biological. The female and the male, being complementary, are considered as two aspects of the human being: a being characterized by equality of status, which is a precondition of cultural evolution embracing the totality of human society (Mercanti 2011) and not just the male half.

Conclusion

Hitherto we have seen that Goddess Spirituality in a traditionally Catholic country such as Italy represents an interesting case for analysing the relationship among religion, spirituality and secularism by virtue of its ability to fuse religious, spiritual and secular elements into a consistent framework. This capacity manifests itself in its tendency to integrate spiritual and material life, an interweaving generating – at collective levels – social, cultural and spiritual models based on partnership, which is inspiring changes in the wider society. This universe is characterized by a specific conception of the divine, which is ontologically female, immanent and pantheistic and is experienced by means of a ritual practice. The transformative effects of the ritual practice on the self correspond to an augmented empowerment, responsibility and personal efficacy, preconditions of the social change envisioned by the Goddess Spirituality. Hence it can be seen how such spirituality has succeeded in combining the spiritual and pragmatic dimensions and combines spiritual and secular values. The examples we have given stimulate reflection on the secular–religious–spiritual debate, opening the door to various ways of thinking about their relationships and suggesting the importance of giving due consideration to the different – the etic and the emic – levels of analysis without making the reductionist mistake of emphasizing one at the expense of the other.

Notes

1 For a critical reading and interpretation of Gimbutas's theories, see Goodison and Morris (1999); Eller (2000). See also Fedele (2013, 10–11).
2 Different feminist movements are critical of Goddess Spirituality; see, for instance, the debate between Carol Christ and Miriam Peskowitz in *Women, Gender, Religion: A Reader* (2001), edited by Castelli and Rodman.
3 Heelas and Woodhead (2005) exemplify this position in their well-known distinction between religion and spirituality: the former sacralizes conformity with a transcendent authority and with tradition which mediates its will; the latter sacralizes the authentic personal experience of meeting one's inner self.
4 Il Tempio della Dea di Torino was founded in 2015 by Sarah Perini, Priestess and chairwoman of the Temple and also founder in 2012 of the Circle of the Wheel of Avalon and Diana.
5 Laima Cultural Association was founded in 2010 by Morena Luciani.
6 In biographical interviews and ethnographic accounts, members' names have been replaced with specific Goddesses or the names of archetypal figures or characters (e.g. Viviane the Lady of the Lake) related to the Goddess Spirituality tradition.
7 One of the Turin groups is inspired by Vicki Noble's teachings and female shamanism; the other by the Avalonian tradition based on the spiritual itinerary and teachings of Glastonbury's Goddess Temple. The groups consist of 20 to 50 participants of varying ages (women between 25 and 65, men between 25 and 50), and of a second-to-third educational level. The majority work in caring professions (e. g. psychologists, holistic operators, midwives), as educators, academics and artists. Although these groups are predominantly female, they are also open to men.
8 In this regard, it is worth noting that most Italian Goddess Spirituality groups belong to international and European networks and that there are strong bonds and exchanges between the exponents of Goddess Spirituality streams. Therefore, the Italian groups we are examining, established as means of spreading in Italy and affirming spiritual itineraries basic to the main currents of Goddess Spirituality, may be considered as fully representative of Goddess Spirituality in Italy.
9 The first European temple dedicated to the worship of the Goddess officially recognized as a sacred place in 2001.

10 One of the main Goddess Spirituality groups active in Italy – the Circle of the Wheel of Avalon and Diana that is based at Il Tempio della Dea in Turin – in addition to adhering to the MotherWorld project, offers structured paths based on the Glastonbury Goddess Temple model and giving rise to the Avalon and Diana Wheel. Although the group derives its inspiration from Avalonian tradition, it nevertheless pursues the goal of rediscovering and reclaiming an Italian specificity of pre-Christian sacred feminine paths and creating a Wheel of the Year dedicated to Diana, regarded as the Italic deity of pre-Christian times and symbol of the Goddess manifestation in Italy. The Turin group is one of the first Italian-founded circle to practise and transmit the Avalonian tradition based on the teachings of the Glastonbury Goddess Temple and has been approved by Kathy Jones. For a detailed study of the Goddess Spirituality movement and the Avalonian Tradition in Italy, see Pibiri (2016, 2017).

11 For a detailed study of Starhawk's movement, see Salomonsen (2002).

12 The survey was carried out in Italian among a random sample of 1,450 young people between 18 and 29 years old (divided into two groups: 18–24 and 25–29) living in Italy, representative of geographical areas, the size of their commune of residence and gender. The questionnaire consisted of 50 questions about the main religious dimensions (belief, practice, belonging, experiences), focussing particularly on the themes of atheism, the plausibility of believing and of religious and spiritual socialization. In tandem, during 2014 and 2015, 144 interviews were carried out among university students from various faculties in two Italian cities (Turin and Rome) that have very different socio-cultural variables. For more information about this survey see Garelli 2016.

13 The variety in the symbolic representation of the Mother Goddess is linked to existing differences between geographical and cultural context characterized by a pantheon of specific goddesses (e.g. Greek, Roman, Egyptian, Hindu, Celtic), generally dating back to ancient times.

14 Taken from fieldwork notes during the workshop on the Cerimonial Labyrinth, Turin, 1–2 March 2014, held by Kathy Jones, founder of the Goddess Temple of Glastonbury. Interviews (20 with members and 6 with priestesses and group founders) were carried out as part of ethnographic research conducted by one of the two authors, Roberta Pibiri, among the two main female spirituality groups practising in Italy with their headquarters in Turin. Interviewees' names have been substituted with the names of Goddess Spirituality divinities or female figures belonging to Arthurian Cycle symbolic imagination, considered to be the expression of female divine energy in Avalon tradition.

15 For more information, see Fedele and Knibbe (2013) and Fedele (2016).

16 Eisler defines "mutual" as the union between the two halves of humanity whose relations are centred on care and empathy, and whose diversity enriches and is the very foundation of evolution.

Acknowledgements

Whereas this chapter is the result of collaboration, the second and fourth sections can be attributed to Roberta Pibiri and the third section to Stefania Palmisano. The introduction, the fifth section and the conclusion are a joint effort

References

Ammerman, Nancy T. 2013. "Spiritual but Not Religious? Beyond Binary Choices in the Study of Religion." *Journal for the Scientific Study of Religion* 52(2):258–278.

Asad, Talal. 2003. *Formation of the Secular: Christianity, Islam, Modernity.* Stanford, CA: Stanford University Press.

Aune, Kristin. 2015. "Feminist Spirituality as Lived Religion: How UK Feminists Forge Religio-Spiritual Lives." *Gender & Society* 29(1): 122–145.

Bainbridge, William. 2009. "Science and Religion." In *Oxford Handbook of the Sociology of Religion*, edited by Peter Clarke, 303–318. Oxford: Oxford University Press.

Barker, Eileen. 2008. "The Church Without and the God Within: Religiosity and/or Spirituality?" In *The Centrality of Religion in Social Life*, edited by Eileen Barker, 187–202. Aldershot: Ashgate.

Bruce, Steve. 2002. *God Is Dead: Secularization in the West*. Oxford: Blackwell.

Castelli, Elizabeth, and Rosamond, Rodman (eds). 2001. *Women, Gender, Religion: A Reader*. Berlin: Springer.

Daly, Mary. 1973. *Beyond God the Father: Toward a Philosophy of Women's Liberation*. Boston, MA: Beacon Press.

Eisler, Riane. 1987. *The Chalice and the Blade: Our History, Our Future* (1st edn). San Francisco, CA: HarperCollins.

Eller, Cynthia. 2000. *The Myth of Matriarchal Prehistory: Why an Invented Past Won't Give Women a Future*. Boston: Beacon Press.

Fedele, Anna. 2013a. "The Metamorphoses of Neopaganism in Traditionally Catholic Countries in Southern Europe." In *Sites and politics of religious diversity in Southern Europe*, edited by Ruy Blanes and José Mapril, 51–72. Leiden: Brill.

Fedele, Anna. 2013b. "'Black' Madonna Versus 'White' Madonna: Gendered Power Strategies in Alternative Pilgrimages to Marian Shrines." In *Gender and Power in Contemporary Spirituality: Ethnographic Approaches*, edited by Anna Fedele and Kim Knibbe, 96–114. New York: Routledge.

Fedele, Anna. 2016. "'Holistic Mothers' or 'Bad Mothers'? Challenging Biomedical Models of the Body in Portugal." *Religion and Gender 6* (1): 95–111

Fedele, Anna and Kim Knibbe (eds). 2013. *Gender and Power in Contemporary Spirituality. Ethnographic Approach*. New York: Routledge.

Garelli, Franco. 2016. *Piccoli atei crescono: Davvero una generazione senza Dio?* Bologna: Il Mulino.

Gimbutas, Marjia. 1989. *The Language of the Goddess*. San Francisco, CA: Harper & Row.

Gimbutas, Marjia. 1991. *The Civilisation of the Goddess*. San Francisco, CA: Harper San Francisco.

Goldenberg, Naomi. 1979. *Changing of the Gods: Feminism and the End of Traditional Religions*. Boston, MA: Beacon Press.

Goodison, Lucy and Christine Morris. 1999. *Ancient Goddesses: The Myths and the Evidence*. Madison, WI: University of Wisconsin Press and British Museum Press.

Hall, David D. 1997. *Lived Religion in America: Toward a History of Practice*. Princeton, NJ: Princeton University Press.

Hamberg, Eva. 2009. "Unchurched Spirituality." In *The Oxford Handbook of the Sociology of Religion*, edited by Peter Clarke, 742–757. Oxford: Oxford University Press.

Hamilton, Malcom. 2000. "An Analysis of the Festival for Mind-Body-Spirit, London." In *Beyond New Age: Exploring Alternative Spirituality*, edited by Steven Sutcliffe and Marion Bowman, 188–200. Edinburgh: Edinburgh University Press.

Hanegraaff, Wouter J. 1996. *New Age Religion and Western Culture: Esotericism in the Mirror of Secular Thought*. Leiden: Brill.

Heelas, Paul. 2006. *The New Age Movement: The Celebration of the Self and the Sacralization of Modernity*. Oxford: Blackwell.

Heelas, Paul. 2008. *Spiritualities of Life: New Age Romanticism and Consumptive Capitalism*. Malden, MA: Blackwell.

Heelas, Paul, and Linda Woodhead. 2005. *The Spiritual Revolution: Why Religion is Giving Way to Spirituality.* Oxford: Blackwell.

Knoblauch, Hubert et al. 2011. "Portrait: José Casanova." *Religion and Society* 2(1): 5–36.

Lenoir, Frédéric. 2003. *Les métamorphoses de Dieu: La nouvelle spiritualité occidentale.* Paris: Editions Plon.

Lewis, James. 2007. "Science and the New Age." In *Handbook of the New Age*, edited by Daren Kemp and James Lewis, 207–230. Leiden: Brill.

Lyon, David. 2000. *Jesus in Disneyland: Religion in Postmodern Times.* Cambridge: Polity Press.

McGuire, Meredith B. 2008. *Lived Religion: Faith and Practice in Everyday Life.* Oxford: Oxford University Press.

Mercanti, Stefano. 2011. "Glossario mutuale." In R. Eisler, *Il calice e la spada: La civiltà della Grande Dea dal Neolitico a oggi.* Udine: Forum.

Palmisano, Stefania, and Nicola Pannofino. 2017a. "So Far and Yet So Close: Emergent Spirituality and the Cultural Influence of Traditional Religion among Italian Youth." *Social Compass* 64(1): 130–146.

Palmisano, Stefania, and Nicola Pannofino. 2017b. *The Emergent Tradition of the New Spirituality*, in Stephen D. Mills, *Religion: Past, Present and Future Perspectives.* New York: Nova.

Pibiri, Roberta. 2016. "Genere e religione: la costruzione del femminile nella Spiritualità della Dea in Italia." In *D come Donne, D come Dio*, edited by Alberta Giorgi and Stefania Palmisano, 79–97. Milano-Udine: Mimesis.

Pibiri, Roberta. 2017. *Re-Membering the Goddess: The Avalon Sacred Path in Italy between Tradition and Innovation.* In *Invention of Tradition and Syncretism in Contemporary Religions. Sacred Creativity*, edited by Palmisano Stefania and Pannofino Nicola, 91–119. Cham: Palgrave Macmillan.

Possamai, Adam. 2003. "Alternative Spiritualities and the Cultural Logic of Late Capitalism." *Culture and Religion* 4(1): 31–45.

Riis, Ole, and Linda Woodhead. 2010. *A Sociology of Religious Emotions.* New York: Oxford University Press.

Rountree, Kathryn. 2004. *Embracing the Witch and the Goddess. Feminist Ritual-Makers in New Zealand.* New York: Routledge.

Salomonsen, Jone. 2002. *Enchanted Feminism: The Reclaiming Witches of San Francisco.* London: Routledge.

Stone, Merlin. 1976. *When God was a Woman.* New York: Dial Press.

Thomassen, Bjørn. 2014. *Liminality and the Modern. Living Through the In-Between.* London: Routledge.

van der Veer, Peter. 2009. "Spirituality in Modern Society." *Social Research* 76(4): 1097–1120.

von Stuckrad, Kocku. 2005. *Western Esotericism: A Brief History of Secret Knowledge (translation of Was ist Esoterik? Kleine Geschichte des geheimen Wissens).* London: Equinox.

Wood, Matthew. 2009. "The nonformative elements of religious life: Questioning the "sociology of spirituality" paradigm." *Social Compass* 56(2): 237–248.

Woodhead, Linda. 2008. "Gender Differences in Religious Practices and Significance". In *The SAGE Handbook in Sociology of Religion*, edited by James A. Beckford and JayDemerathIII, 566–586. Los Angeles: Sage.

3 Healers, missionaries and entrepreneurs of the feminine

The secularization of contemporary women's spirituality

Chia Longman

Introduction

It has not gone unnoticed within the anthropology and sociology of religion that the vast majority of participants in new religious movements and new spiritualities such as Wicca, Goddess spirituality, feminist thealogy, Neo-paganism and 'New Age' have been female (Crowley 2011; Sutcliffe and Gilhus 2014). This trend largely dates back to the emerging spaces that allowed for more women-centred forms and expressions of ritual, religion and spirituality outside of the male-dominated traditional religions, in the wake of the last century's post-war counter-cultural movements in the West. In this period of increasing secularization, democratization and equal rights movements, second-wave feminists struggled against the subordination of women in all spheres of life, including the powerful hold of established 'patriarchal' religions on women's rights, their roles, bodies and experiences. While it has been noted that second-wave feminism for the most part was anti-religious and secular oriented (Aune 2011; Braidotti 2008; Llewellyn and Trzebia-towska 2013; Reilly and Scriver 2014), at the same time, many women active within their respective religious communities pushed for internal change towards more gender equality, while some others opted out, turning to new forms of post-patriarchal, gender-inclusive and female-oriented theology, religious and spiritual expression (Christ 1992; Reilly 2011).

As Fedele and Knibbe (2013) remark in their literature review on gender and spirituality in the predecessor to this volume, women appear to be especially attracted to the 'new spiritualities' that have developed further since this period. Not only do they offer alternative, non-hierarchical gender-equal belief models and ritual practices, but they also often involve a revalorization of 'femininity' through sacralizing female bodily processes and embodied experiences (including female sexuality, menarche, menstruation, maternity, menopause, etc.). Sociologists of religion like Sointu and Woodhead (2008) have explained this development in terms of the shift in gender role expectations over the past decades, especially among middle-class women, who, by tending to their personal spiritual selves, cope with the modern-day demands of combining professional work with more traditional feminized care work in the private sphere. Similarly, Trzebiatowska and Bruce (2013) argue that the 'gender gap' has nothing to do with women's 'inherent inclinations' towards the holistic spirituality milieu, but can be explained by the persistence of gender dualisms in social roles and ideologies of masculinity and femininity in contemporary society that is mirrored and then reinforced within the spiritual domain. Masculinity gains its meaning through its opposition to spirituality coded *as* feminine and catering to women's interests (such as practices related to wellbeing and healing), which Trzebiatowska and Bruce claim are already gendered in what stubbornly remains a gender dichotomous world. Hence one could argue that there seems to be more historical continuity than change in what gender historian Joan Scott (2017) calls the 'identification of women with/as religion'. Against the 'myth' that modernity and secularization would bring gender equality, Scott (2017, 25) shows how notions of differentiation have been intrinsic to the understanding of secularism in the West, being 'marked by a presumption of gender *in*equality'. Notwithstanding the fact that power positions in traditional religious institutions remain largely in the hands of men, the secularization process as a fundamentally sexed and gendered process continues to allocate women and femininity to the sphere of the religious *and* the realm of spirituality, opposed to men, masculinity and the secular, modern, rational public sphere; women, up to the present date, are on the whole 'more' religious and spiritual than men (Houtman and Aupers 2008; Vincett, Sharma, and Aune 2008).

However (as explained/referred to in the Introduction to this volume), debate abounds on the meanings of and differences between religion, spirituality, and the secular, and whether conceptual boundaries are attainable or desirable at all. For some, (new) spirituality might be conceived as a distinct, critical and alternative 'third way', opposing and different from, on the one hand, traditional religion and, on the other, scientific reason, disenchantment or secularization (Hanegraaff 1998; Houtman and Aupers 2007; Watts 2017; Woodhead 2010). Others argue that today in the West spirituality is one way or another part of religion (such as in 'personalized' religion, 'implicit' religion, and 'lived' religion), or suggest that it might in fact simply be 'religion' after all (Streib and Hood 2013; Harvey 2016; Aune 2015). Others have aligned the concept of spirituality with new terms such as 'non-religion' (Lee 2014), above 'new religion' and some, countering all of the above, argue those who identify as the so-called 'spiritual but not religious' (SBNRs) can simply be perceived as largely secular (Bruce 2017). A gendered perspective complicates these discussions further, precisely because women seem to be 'doing' something different to men, for example by incorporating (and 'fusing') new spiritual elements into mainstream liberal traditional religious identities and practices (Vincett 2008).

The focus of this essay is therefore not so much to seek additional or alternative explanations for what has been called the 'gender puzzle' (Heelas et al. 2005; Houtman and Aupers 2008) within the (religious-)spiritual domain, but rather to challenge some other less explored assumptions with regards to these analytical and conceptual divisions within the field of studies of women's spirituality based on recent empirical research in the Western European context. In order to make my case, I will apply what has been referred to as a more 'post-secular' perspective in gender and religions research, which involves reconsidering the empowering and agentic potentialities of religion/spirituality for women, in light of what, historically, has been a tense relationship between feminism and religion in Western modernity. Furthermore, post-secular critique does not merely respond to the 'failure' of the secularization thesis by emphasizing what some see as the persistence or resurgence of religion in modern society, but interrogates the seeming co-existence of ongoing secularization *and* religious revival. Post-secular thought also takes a step further by unpacking the way the dominant secular narrative in the first place frames 'religion' as its opposite, and aims at deconstructing related gendered binaries such as faith vs reason, private vs public, subjection vs freedom, and male vs female (Aune, Sharma, and Vincett 2008; Bracke 2008; Braidotti 2008; Braidotti et al. 2014; Graham 2012; Greed 2011; Longman 2008, 2018; Jakobsen and Pellegrini 2008; Korte 2011; Llewellyn and Trzebiatowska 2013; Nynas, Lassander, and Utriainen 2015).

My empirical focus is what I take to be the contemporary cultural 'mainstreaming' of women's spirituality in recent years, which, I will show, certainly shares features with women's participation in some of the more counter-cultural and marginal new religious and spiritual movements referred to above, but also diverts in some significant ways. I draw on field research and an analysis of excerpts from life story interviews across three neighbouring European countries (Belgium, the Netherlands and Germany) with women who are professionally active in cultivating and promoting 'the feminine' in the sphere of 'holistic spirituality', 'subjective-life spirituality' and what has also been referred to with a broader and more 'secular' term, as 'subjective wellbeing culture' (Heelas 2008; Heelas et al. 2005; Woodhead 2010). My fieldwork reflects what I believe is an increase in recent years of the local and global spread and marketization of 'female empowerment' among ritual workers, healers, life coaches, writers, trainers and consultants and at group and communal events such as women's circles, conferences, festivals and retreats, prompting women to re/connect with their 'femininity' as a source of strength and agency.

Firstly, based on my fieldwork results in which women's voices and self-descriptions serve as a starting point, and following up on some of the discussion above, I wish to question the secular–spiritual distinction that is sometimes assumed, and often remains under-theorized, with regards to women's spirituality/wellbeing culture today. Secondly, I maintain that my interviews with a variety of practitioners, who fulfil different roles – what I call 'healers, missionaries, or entrepreneurs of the feminine' – not only show how their intersectional identities and experiences elude simple categorizations in terms of the secular, the religious and the spiritual, but also challenge the often assumed class, age and ethnic homogeneity within the women's wellbeing milieu. Hence, my second objective is to challenge the presumption that although the women's spirituality market appears to mostly cater to educated middle-class white Western women (Crowley 2011; Houtman and Aupers 2008; Sointu and Woodhead 2008), this not only obfuscates the legacy of black, coloured, minority and non-Euro-American women's spiritualities (Alexander 2005; Delgadillo 2011; Facio and Lara 2014; Hooks 2000; King and Beattie 2005; Moraga and Anzaldúa 2015; Phillips 2006; Rayburn and Comas-Díaz 2008) and the current globalization of women's wellbeing-culture beyond the Global North (Ponniah 2018), but it also strongly simplifies what I encountered ethnographically in a Western European context.

Sites of women's spirituality and wellbeing: coaching, circles and festivals

The fieldwork on which this chapter draws serves as data for a larger ethnographic project on women's spirituality and wellbeing that was conducted between 2014 and 2017 in different regions of Belgium, the Netherlands and in the city of Berlin, Germany. I held in-depth interviews with 38 women who were active as, for example, organizers, workshop leaders, trainers, consultants, life coaches, therapists, healers, bodyworkers and ritual workers, and involved in developing discourses and practices of what they designate with terms such as 'women's or feminine power', 'women's leadership' or 'feminine presence'. Many women combined a number of these activities and some were also organizers of women's festivals where practitioners of the feminine come together during a larger yearly event at one location lasting one or several days, offering a variety of parallel workshops or sessions that aspire to cultivate the 'feminine' among their participants. Although content and style vary depending on the festival, they broadly engage with women's holistic wellbeing in relation to their mind–body–spirit (MBS), ranging from more thematic sessions revolving around, for example, relationships, bodily care and healthy living, to wisdom and creativity, self-confidence and awareness. Most workshops are experience-focused, including some form of exercise, handicraft, ritual, meditation or evocative story telling. Hence sessions at festivals might refer to 'soul healing', 'yoni yoga', 'pelvic self-care', 'womb blessings', 'sexual awakening', singing circles, family and foremother constellations, and more creative workshops such as Ayurveda cooking, mandala weaving, making Goddess amulets and singing, massaging, breathing, dancing sessions ranging from hula hoop to ecstatic movement and Bollywood- or belly-dancing. Other workshops are more geared to personal growth and development like 'saying yes to yourself' or 'inner leadership', and in more recent years titles have sprung up like 'entrepreneurism from your essence' and 'sexual healing after Me-Too'. Hence the offer is very much aligned with what has been identified as the current '*bricolage*' in MBS practices in the West, drawing on techniques from many 'Eastern' traditions to positive psychology

(Altglas 2014). Yet what they all share is an exclusive focus on the feminine, if not focused on the female body and bodily processes, then on themes such as 'The wild woman within' (see Plancke in Chapter 6), 'female essence', 'women's wisdom', 'Tantra for women', 'female archetypes', and so on.

By participating at different festivals in all three countries, I met and interviewed organizers and located other potential informants. Some of the festivals had been running for a number of years (held from once to several times a year), were of a large scale over two to three days attracting more visitors each year and up to several hundred participants. Others were more novel and/or smaller, ranging from 30–100 participants at a time. Festivals offer a forum for practitioners of the feminine to present their expertise and reach a larger audience of women who might be more unfamiliar with the women's 'spiritual' scene. They also function as networks among the work-shops' leaders and hence gave me an insight into the sense of a community of women active within the field within a particular city, region or country.

A second fieldwork site where I located participants was by visiting and contacting hosts of so-called 'women's circles', another increasingly popular yet under researched phenomenon across the globe, including in the countries in my study. Women's circles can be described as non-institutionalized, recurrent (often monthly) gatherings of a few hours at a time (day or evening, held at women's homes or rented spaces), for smaller groups of women to sit in a circle in order to come together and relax, meditate, share stories, partake in rituals, heal, nourish, and empower themselves. I similarly participated in and interviewed a number of circle organizers and have reported on the research results elsewhere (Longman 2018). Circles might also be held at fes-tivals; a larger circle often frames opening and closing sessions, and as a format it is often replicated in many of the workshops that take place. Women who lead and participate in workshops at festivals are often involved in circle movements themselves, which testifies to the connections between these activities and their organizer-participants.

Outside of locating my interviewees via the festivals, I also did internet searches for leaders of women's circles and femininity-focused coaching and workshops in all three countries; some of these worked more independently whilst others appeared more connected 'sister' femininity practitioners by being involved in a festival or transnational circle movement scene.

Spiritual awakenings, feminine awakenings

The women I interviewed varied in age from 27 to 60. The majority were white and had been born, raised and were currently living in Belgium, the Netherlands or Germany, although some had mixed race/ethnic and/or migrant backgrounds and some had travelled extensively. My sample included heterosexual, with a minority of lesbian and sexuality questioning, women. Some were single and childless (among which one was sologamous or 'self-married'); others were married or had partners and children (either biological, adopted or step-children in new family arrangements). Most women had enjoyed higher education (university or college), although a minority had only finished high school. Contrary to the dominant image of the women's spirituality milieu as catering to the 'middle class', I found that socio-economic class was more diverse, ranging from median middle-class income to more modest living levels due to part-time work, unemployment or sick leave. A minority was self-employed and professionally active as a coach or therapist in the wellbeing sector (either solely or next to another career and employment such as teaching, training, journalism, management); some were homemakers with breadwinning partners, others unemployed and living modestly off state support. My research site included both urban and more rural environments, depending on where I located interviewees. Perhaps not unexpectedly, I encountered more national and ethnic 'diversity' among practitioners and participants in urban surroundings, reflective of today's 'super-diversity' within many Western European cities (Vertovec 2007).

My interviews were open using a combination of the life story approach followed by addressing key topics in a more semi-structured way. As my initial enquiry during the conversations revolved around the way women had become involved in their current interests and activities in cultivating the feminine; different concepts and trajectories emerged from their narratives that appeared to defy simple categorizations in terms of the spiritual or the non-religious or the secular. While the majority had enjoyed some form of religious upbringing, they no longer identified as religious, by believing in and/or belonging to the tradition they were brought up in. Most came from a traditional Catholic or Protestant home, but had become unaffiliated, irreligious, non-religious or secular and/or no longer practising Christians, reflecting patterns of secularization among a large segment of the population in these north-west European countries (Lee 2014; Woodhead 2016). Some came from a religious minority, such as Evangelical, Orthodox Christian and Muslim backgrounds, but similarly had rejected or stood in a critical or ambivalent relationship with these traditions. Hence at first sight, as individuals active within the domain of holistic spirituality and subjective wellbeing culture, my interlocutors could be viewed as what has been referred by some in the scholarly literature as belonging to the category of 'spiritual but not religious' (SBNR). They had turned their back on institutionalized hierarchical religions towards more individualized, immanent and reflexive modes of 'life' and 'self'-focused experiences and holistic practices of mind, body and spirit, following what has been dubbed the 'subjective turn' in secular liberal modernity (Harvey 2016; Heelas 2008; Houtman and Aupers 2007).

However, with regards to their discursive positioning towards the concept of, and their identification (or dis-identification) with, 'spirituality' I ascertained a variety of patterns. While all interviewees had experienced some form of 'feminine awakening' during their life course which had ultimately led them to their interest in and entrepreneurism of the feminine, this could be analytically conceived as either 'spiritual' or more non-religious or secular. One group of my interlocutors had become interested in and was already actively engaged in various new spiritualities (e.g. shamanism, Reiki, druidism, Goddess Spirituality) at some point in their lives, which preceded their feminine awakening. During their 'spiritual journey', they then arrived at a point at which they started to question 'what being a woman really meant to them' – and/or were prompted by the women visiting their workshops, circles or coaching practices to do so.

For instance, when I interviewed her at her home, Phaedra was a married mother of two in her mid-thirties, who had graduated as a social worker, yet was now active as a coach and offered guided meditation, bodywork, family constellations, Reiki, shamanistic healing and 'moon mother work' in an attic space in her home decorated with an altar and floor cushions. Although most of her activities were open to all genders, like all the other practitioners I interviewed, the vast majority of her clients were female. For certain group sessions and workshops, however, she was more engaged in women-only spaces, including hosting women's circles, where I became a regular partici- pant over a two-year period. Phaedra told me how she had always been a sensitive and very open child, and first started getting involved in 'spirituality' as a student around the age of twenty, experimenting with yoga, bodywork and massage. She experienced becoming a mother in her late twenties as a profound and challenging period, and became attracted to shamanism, which had been 'a calling from the spirits for a long time', but then felt as 'too masculine-oriented'. At a certain point, through a friend, she came across a book on 'moon mother work', on the 'creative, sexual and spiritual gifts of the menstrual cycle' (Gray 2009), which she experienced as a real eye-opener as it brought her into touch with her 'cyclic self' and gave her more 'stability'. Together with the same friend, she followed a training with the book's writer, Miranda Gray, who is also a worldwide popular speaker and trainer on the female cycle in women's wellbeing culture today, and became a certified 'moon mother' to conduct 'womb blessing' ceremonies. Phaedra explained how thereafter, she experienced a calling to 'sit in a circle' which she couldn't seem to find in her hometown, and then decided to just start hosting regular circles herself, next to womb blessings using the circle format. Although Phaedra does not affiliate herself with any particular movement or organiza- tion, and has her own very particular way of organizing her circles, which include shamanistic elements such as visualizations and references to spirits and goddesses; as I experienced, the general structure and atmosphere was parallel to women's circles held elsewhere, including an interplay of relaxa- tion, ritual and story-sharing (Longman 2018; Leidenfrost 2012).

Hence Phaedra used notions of spirits and spirituality quite often in our talk; she was spiritually inclined from a young age, and besides mothering her main profession was her work as a spiritual practitioner, although she claimed it did not generate a decent income. She told me how at some point she experienced a spiritual calling to focus on the contemporary needs of women, who she felt 'long to make a connection' for which space is lacking in their daily lives, work, and in society. Both as individuals in her coaching work, and in a group setting such as the circle, Phaedra had learned that for women, this 'connection' which many people appear to have lost and crave for, for some women involves experiences of loss, in particular in relation to children, like abortion, miscarriage and young children who have died:[1]

> This is so essential to our female nature I think, that you can't miss it. It always hurts. And women solve it in the most diverse ways. But if there isn't really that connection, both with their selves, because I think most women come to find connection with themselves because they see themselves busy and do not recognize themselves anymore. So yes, connection, I think women come here because they are in search of connection. Or a place to make a connection with their pain. A place where that can just be... Something that doesn't exist anymore like mourning together. Because I think you should be able to do that. A place... and that I notice as well, that many women do not have that place. Not in time and not in space to be with their sadness.

Phaedra felt that although there was great need for 'connection' for both women and men, and she 'loved' them both equally, she felt women were in need of much healing, to reconnect with their femininity as a source of strength, and for a place to connect to each other in 'sisterhood'. As I will return to later, consistent with all my other interviewees, she saw the cultivation of the feminine within these spaces, beyond mere individual 'self-help', as a potential force that could lead to a better world. As regards her own practice, she felt the need to 'take it slow' and see what might come: "I'm not a business woman. I don't know much about that and it's not a must for me." The first circles and blessing ceremonies I visited, Phaedra did not ask for any fixed contribution and as a proponent of the 'gift economy' passed a pot around to participants to collect free contributions after a session. When I made a return visit to talk to her alone two years later, Phaedra claimed it was a financial struggle and she had switched to a fixed fee at a modest 15 euros, without excluding the participation of those women who might not have the financial means.

Phaedra's life story stands in contrast to that of Naomi, a mother, self-employed trainer, and women's festival and circle organizer in her mid-forties. Naomi has a degree in business administration, built a successful career at a large company while her husband was a stay-at-home father and claimed that she had a 'well-developed masculine side'. At a certain point, however, she felt that 'something was missing', became fed up with being the breadwinner and wanted to spend more time with her kids. She started attending more to 'how she felt in her body', and had a desire to explore her own femininity, which she claimed she had neglected. By participating in and organizing women's circles which evolved quite spontaneously, she told me, with a group of female acquaintances and friends, Naomi ultimately developed the need to 'bring more of this femininity into the world' by helping other women do so in their own personal and professional lives. One of her achievements, together with others, has been the development of a series of middle-sized weekend women's festivals (some 50 participants at a time) held twice a year over a five-year period. I became a regular and participated in four of these festivals including the closing tenth edition in 2017. When the festivals were still running, I asked Naomi to tell me how they started:

> You know, for me it is becoming clearer and clearer that what I want to do with the festival, that is to offer something for the... not something spiritual, not that... And also not exclusively women in a leadership position, but those women that are in an organisation context, who are looking for that: 'What is that feminine part here?' You know I'll never reach the women in leadership positions who are not concerned about this at all, they won't come to the festival, they'll claim, 'What do we need this for?' Nor for the spiritual women, who can find what they are seeking anywhere, by matter of speaking... But the women who are in those places... and really do not feel so well and do not know why, these women I want to reach... If someone like Mary (regular festival participant) can set up a pain clinic in the hospital she works, in a feminine way, whatever that might mean, then yes... isn't that fantastic? Or Christine, who is really high up in the police force, that she would succeed into bringing in some female energy?

Naomi explained to me how through developing and participating in circles and festivals, she was in a kind of experimental learning process of discovering what this 'female energy' could mean. Although she rejected the notion of spirituality to capture 'the feminine' and preferred a more 'grounded' approach, her understanding was consistent with what I encountered in my ethnography and interviews with others. She explained how she had discussed with one of her colleagues how to 'define' "putting something into the world in a feminine way"; she showed me a sketch of her preliminary 'model' of the feminine, a circle shape including the elements of 'slowing down', 'embodied living', 'organically connecting', 'the cyclical' and 'creating a nest'. For example, women's spaces like circles and festivals allow for women to 'slow down', step out of the daily rush, to start feeling rather than doing, "and then just to see what evolves, what new things creatively arise by themselves when you are in a women's group". Naomi also described the element of "reconnecting with your body":

> I have the feeling that when you are connected with... when you are living in your body, that the feeling is with women... that there is a lot of knowing in that body, yet that women cannot argue that very well. And if you ask, "Why is it like that?" Yes, then... I just know that it is like that... It's like that and I cannot give ten good arguments for that now, but... just to trust that. I have a colleague at a bank in a really high position, and she really has this, this sense of just 'knowing', and she

finds it terrible that she can never argue about it. So she tries… she says "Yes, and then I am in a meeting and then I see those men looking at me, and then I have to explain and then I don't have an explanation…" Yes, she is really struggling with that… And I have the feeling that it really is a thing for women that they just know and don't have to make arguments about it, just that their body already knows, and that is the way we should be heading, and that that should be enough…

Naomi thought of 'organically connecting' as something in opposition to 'planning', 'having a purpose' and the 'linear':

Feminine is that you have your goal in your body. So when you feel "Which way do I want go?" It's internal, it's not "there is a flag or the top of the mountain and I want to go to the top". But that there is more than that, it's about the desire of being able to see a much wider view. That there is more an internally localized purpose and that women meander towards it.

Similar to Phaedra, Naomi also referred to the cyclical, to the way in which:

Women are closely connected to life and death, and know that things do not always go in an upward trend. Sometimes it's good to consciously let things go so there will be room for something new, something else… Or that we don't have to see everything in terms of growth. You know the idea of the economy… That prosperity should always just grow and grow…

Finally, 'building a nest', for Naomi, refers to the spatial, to the way so much energy is 'lost' in, for example, landscape offices:

I find it terrible that so much energy is lost by not feeling ok in a certain place. I really need to have a good place, a warm place that when you come in you have the feeling… When I give trainings, I have to take care that the energy stays inside and I create a good energy for my group, and if the place already has that, then it becomes congruent and mutually strengthening, doesn't it? And I think that is something typical for women too. That women are sensitive to that. And you know, they are more into that carrying, taking care of a place, what they call 'holding space'.

Today, Naomi has set up a company that explicitly focuses on cultivating the feminine in women and men, "among leaders, in teams and in organizations". Together with colleagues she organizes women's networks, training modules, and inspirational speeches with the purpose of "feeding and strengthening the feminine, in co-operation with the masculine".

Although they sometimes strained to find words for what they meant by femininity, these kinds of associations resonated with what I learned from many of my interviewees. Although the intensity varied, what the practitioners of the feminine I encountered shared was that at some point in their biography a rupture occurred followed by an insight which they understood as a lack of the feminine in their personal lives, and more broadly in a masculine-oriented or dominated (or patriarchal) world. Sometimes it referred to what can be understood as more conventional feminine attributes such as 'softness' and 'gentleness'. But generally, I found that femininity was understood in very open, questioning, and sometimes more 'abstract' ways, stating it could mean or be associated with a 'large palette' of understandings and experiences, from 'experiencing through the senses', to 'being present', 'authenticity', 'vulnerability as strength', 'intention', 'intuition', 'knowing', 'boundaries', 'going inwards', 'desire', 'receptivity' and 'flowing instead of achieving'.

Consistent with some of the sexual and gender ideologies that have been propagated in other new spiritual and religious movements, in a social constructivist sense, femininity was therefore not seen to be necessarily, nor exclusively, determined by or linked to biological or physical sexual attributes or differences. Yet female embodiment, derived from subjective experience rather than societal expectations and media messages, was also felt as something that in a heavily masculinized world could no longer be overlooked or denied. The interviewed practitioners' vision of femininity was therefore both critical and affirmative. As I have argued elsewhere, in women's spirituality/ wellbeing culture, female embodiment is perceived to serve as a starting point, as a politics of location (Rich 2003) from which to question, explore, re-evaluate, desire and cultivate the feminine in an affirmative yet creative way, rather than as a fixed identity or essence (Longman 2018).

Thus Naomi and Phaedra – who I met independently and were not acquainted – were involved in similar activities such as coaching, circling, workshops and festivals. They employed, supported and promoted similar concepts and MBS rituals and techniques, and harboured a similar mission of healing and cultivating the feminine, within the individual woman, and within society and the wider world. Yet their approach, personality, education and professional background and biographical itinerary were markedly different. Phaedra's 'feminine awakening' evolved throughout what she explicitly identified and understood as a spiritual journey and she was more involved in 'healing' women to connect with their own femininity. In contrast, Naomi did not interpret her 'biographical disruption' (Bury 1982) during a successful business career in the secular world as marked by spiritual insight or experience, but rather as the recognition of the lack of femininity. Naomi was not oblivious to the women's spirituality market (and even recruited women's practitioners from this market to host workshops at the festivals she ran), but did not identify with it and consistently rejected the term, which she described as 'too wishy washy' for her feminine entrepreneurship, which she saw as a worldly endeavour. These different trajectories and positionings towards 'spirituality', I find, disrupt analytical boundaries between the spiritual and the secular, as similar experiences and practices of the 'feminine' related to women's wellbeing and empowerment seem to crosscut what might be conceived as otherwise separate domains. Furthermore, some practitioners, in their efforts to promote and 'mainstream' the feminine, consciously 'secularize' their practices, as I will show below.

Secularizing women's spirituality

In order, firstly, to illustrate further how women's spirituality becomes 'secularized', and, secondly, to point to the diversity among its practitioners in terms of their positioning with regards to religion, spirituality, class and ethnicity, I zoom in on one particular conversation I had which was a double interview with two women of different ethnic-national-religious backgrounds and ages, the female founders of a new women's festival in a large city, in a country neighbouring that of the interlocutors referred to in the previous paragraph. I had stumbled across these two women on the internet independent of each other in my search for local women who ran women's circles and were involved in coaching work related to the feminine. When I contacted them separately requesting an interview, their positive reply was that they both received my message and were happy to talk to me together about a new and unique one-day women's festival they were setting up.

Angela was in her early forties and, although she originated from Southern Europe, she was now settled in the city, where she had been living for more than eight years with her family. Her personal story was that she had 'a previous life' as a lawyer and owner of an international consultancy company until three years ago: "It was really a kind of a midlife crisis and I stopped doing the work that I used to do before. I almost had a burnout and then part of my recovery was to start going to women's circles and to get support from other women as well in a way that I never had before." Part of Angela's recovery, as she called it, was to spend time with women as she discovered she had been living her life 'through her male energy', which had caused her to crash. She started a monthly women's circle at her own home from which friendships and new acquaintances evolved, bringing her into contact with other 'spiritual women', from which the desire to set up a broader community, and now a festival, evolved. Her 'biographical disruption' and feminine awakening thus resonated strongly with that of Naomi mentioned in the previous paragraph.

However, opposed to both Phaedra's (spirituality precedes feminine awakening) and Naomi's journey (feminine awakening is seen as more secular than spiritual), for Angela, her feminine awakening coincided fully with her spiritual transformation, and she was much less reluctant than Naomi to use the word. Angela had been brought up in the Roman Catholic tradition but had lived a middle-class secular-liberal lifestyle as a successful professional career woman. However, the story of her working partner, who was my second interlocutor in the same conversation, was quite different. Sayira had previously met Angela at one of her women's circles, became a friend and is currently co-organizing the festival. She was 30 years old, had a partner but no children and, in contrast to Angela, proclaimed she had not at all reached "a point of midlife crisis" but had a very different life course that brought her to her current interest in "what it means to be a woman and be feminine". Besides the age difference, she reflected on how her mixed ethnicity, and having being brought up by a strict religious Muslim father, yet also having grown up surrounded by women (grandmother, mother and sisters), had a profound impact on her life and her desire to reconnect with the feminine:

> It feels so natural to me to be around women and to really develop intimate connections that last long years. So if anything I wanted to go back to that at some point, where we all went our own ways, and I realized at some point I have this not only with my blood-sisters but with sisters around the world; with women. It goes beyond just family.

Sayira was a trained teacher from another European country, but "entered the scene of Tantra and sensuality" when she moved to this city three years ago. She gave bodywork workshops, individual coaching and had also been hosting a women's circle for a year. Sayira had been brought up in a traditional religious household that associated femininity with modesty and shame, which led her sister and herself to

> a phase of rebellion in which becoming seductive or sensual or sexual was part of that; part of coming out of all of that repression. I think that that's definitely a big part of why it's important to me to be feminine and be a sensual and sexual woman. But it's not an extreme. It's finding a balance with it and I think a part of it is also maybe even reclaiming a power, which I didn't have as a child. At least I wouldn't say to any extreme but that's probably been part of the journey. It's kind of maybe finding the rights I always wanted for myself; the right to be me, kind of.

Like Phaedra and Naomi's narratives in the previous paragraph, the selected quotes of Angela and Sayira are mere excerpts of what are obviously more complex, rich and nuanced life trajectories than any conversation can convey. I do not intend to claim that they represent, but again, they do illustrate some of the diversity in the relation between feminine and spiritual awakenings among my interviewees. For some, their feminine awakening emerged as a part of a longer 'spiritual' journey; for others it coincided with their rise in consciousness of the feminine, for many of whom their identification with 'spirituality' was far less pronounced. Furthermore, as emphasized in the introduction above, whereas the development of women's spiritualities in the West has often been described as a reaction and viable women-centred alternative to traditional patriarchal religions, I would not apply this diagnosis to the vast majority of my participants. Having been brought up in a range from loosely to more orthodoxly religious, the majority was already 'secularized' in contemporary Western Europe and were seeking re-enchantment – through the feminine – in an already disenchanted world. Only for a minority did their feminine/spiritual awakening occur after and in breaking with a more religious traditional upbringing as illustrated in Sayira's story above. In this case, seeing the already diversified reality, which is multi-religious, multicultural or 'super-diverse' Europe today, this 'break' was not even with Christianity or Judaism as commonplace in the literature, but in this particular case with Islam. Hence this corroborates the point that my respondents were not homogeneous in terms of their ethnicity, nationality, class, age category nor life stance, ranging across the religious, non-religious and secular, particularly so among some of the younger interviewees, who had already been brought up in an environment that was post-Christian, super-diverse and/or were from a migration background.

Furthermore, as noted above, although one group of interviewees at a personal level did not 'disidentify' with the notion of spirituality, I often encountered that they 'secularized' their female empowerment practices. Hence, while some women's circles and festivals might openly use terms like 'Tantra' or 'Goddesses', others avoided such references. Such circles or festival workshops would similarly employ MBS techniques and rituals such as meditation, visualization, holding space and grounding, yet apart from very brief references to the sacred (such as Goddesses and the female divine), such terms might be omitted or avoided in both discursive, aesthetic and communicative aspects, often in order to reach out and appeal to a larger clientele. I asked festival organizer Angela about the spiritual element at their new festival:

ANGELA: Yes basically spirituality's part of it; also one of the things that we cannot fully define. It's there but it's also one of the things that we won't put in a programme. If you see the programme of the festival it doesn't say anything close to it. It was one of the taboo words we said, "Let's not use it because it's …"

CHIA: Was that a conscious choice?

SAYIRA: We wanted to reach out to women beyond the spiritual theme and the consciousness theme and to say it's about health, it's about your bodies, it's about your feelings and so we tried to avoid using words that normally just draw in those that are already doing the work for so long.

ANGELA: And that was part of our intention and it didn't work as well as we imagined but I think that's something we're going... I imagine we'll stick to it, like continue doing at least wanting to reach out to the mainstream audience... And I believe we're in that phase like, okay now we have developed it among ourselves and now I think a lot of us we are ready to reach out and include other women as well. And it will have an impact in society as well.

SAYIRA: For me the first thing is to give the so-called average woman a chance to just have a moment for herself to see what's important for me and to be given so many tools and just moments of interaction and reflection; everything that we're doing. And for so many women that's not part of their everyday life... They don't know what it means to have a minute of silence for themselves to just say "How am I feeling today?" And so for me it's I think if that happens we're creating some kind of impact or change to say "Hey, let's take care of ourselves so that we take care of each other". And so that in the bigger picture the world becomes a better place. I think every little step; every little action we take has some impact.

Although their 'secularizing strategy' did not attract the large numbers they hoped to have reached the first time; the movement is still going strong and at the time of writing a fourth festival has taken place in just two years' time.

Practitioners of the feminine: healers, missionaries, entrepreneurs

Throughout my research it became apparent that the field of female empowerment through the cultivation of the 'feminine' did not map onto, for example, a *sensu stricto* understanding of spirituality or what previously also been referred to as New Age (Hanegraaff 1998; Sutcliffe and Gilhus 2014). I encountered a growing and very diverse 'market' expressed in the number of books, websites, coaching, festivals and retreats on offer for women that has emerged over the past years. They propagate novel constructions of femininity, sociality and practice that sometimes do, and sometimes do not have 'spiritual' or 'religious' referents. Some refer to the 'Goddess' or the 'divine feminine' explicitly and others merely passingly or privately; for others using similar techniques, training schemes, rites and discourses of self-empowerment, this kind of symbolic referent, its accompanying ritual objects and imagery might be perceived as too 'wishy washy'. Nevertheless, what is offered and what is the main objective of the practitioners' mission is similar: the healing and empowerment of women by re/connecting to their personal 'feminine' self, their energy, sexuality, body and identity, which ultimately, might lead to the healing of society and of the world. So rather than limiting myself to one particular 'branch', which in any case would run against the very eclectic nature of women's spiritual/subjective wellbeing culture today, I have shown that despite the diversity among my interviewees in terms of their personal life journeys; and their very different positionings in relation to the 'spiritual' or more immanent and worldly orientation, the practices they embrace, the 'products' they might aim to sell, and the missions they preach are markedly alike.

In the scholarly literature, there has, of course, been some debate on the general slipperiness of the term 'spirituality' in relation to the way it has become increasingly mainstream and secular, with MBS practices such as mindfulness, yoga, and so on having entered the realms of nursing, health, education and business culture. Many of these can be considered to be either, and often simultaneously, leisurely, therapeutic and beneficial to mental and/

or physical health and wellness. Personal growth, self-development and positive psychology in (live or online) courses, coaching, workshops, lectures, books and newsletters can be added to this field of subjective wellbeing culture, and have even been dubbed 'secular spiritualities' (Fuller 2017; Heelas 2008; Lee 2007). Heelas et al. (2005, 84–88) distinguish spirituality or "the holistic milieu" from the broader realm of subjective wellbeing claiming the latter is "considerably more psychologized"; less "relational" (e.g. less intensive and 'face to face'); less focused on "nurturing the quality of personal subjective life per se" (e.g. towards institutional ends such as making better managers, educating pupils, etc.), and because it lacks "spirituality", which the authors then describe – perhaps indeed in a somewhat vague and 'wishy washy' way – as the "general sentiment" of "going deeper".

Yet from a post-secular perspective, my study of the femininity milieu challenges the tenability of these – already quite slippery – distinctions. At the same time, as Heelas (2008, 5) summarizes elsewhere, if "inner life spirituality" always involves some kind of sacralization of the self, drawing on "meta-empirical depths of life" or the "super empirical", then I believe that despite the omission or rejection of 'the spiritual' by some of my interviewees, from an analytical viewpoint, one could still argue that what they share is the very sacralization of the feminine (the feminine self, feminine essence, etc.) itself. For the inexplicable 'feminine' is attributed some kind of metaphysical or super-empirical status as a force or energy, within and outwardly; at the same time in a typically holistic sense it is also seen, experienced and 'known' as embodied, physical and grounded. As the ethnographic data shows, the 'feminine' is posed against the 'masculine', which, similarly in a very abstract sense, is understood in terms of, for example, rationality, control, profit, linearity, disembodiedness, and so on. Hence, one could argue that while the cultural mainstreaming of women's spirituality involves its 'secularization', at the same time the cultivation of the feminine also teases out the familiar differentiations of secular modernity that, as mentioned in the introduction, and Joan Scott (2017) in her work explains so eloquently, already rest on an inbuilt gender inequality. In an affirmative and simultaneously deconstructive sense, the work of femininity practitioners reveals the way, following the post-secular critique of the opposition between religion and secularism, the domains and concepts of the 'religious', the 'secular', and also the 'spiritual', are mutually co-constitutive.

As has also become clear in the interview excerpts and some of the above analysis, femininity practitioners across spiritual–secular divides are similarly not lacking in their visions in what some identify as the more relational, ethical, expressive and potential humanistic, empowering and emancipatory potential of the 'spiritual revolution' in post-traditional society (Heelas et al. 2005). By contrast, many critics have claimed that 'new spiritualities' merely serve the secular, psychological and highly superficial individualistic needs within capitalist consumer culture (Carrette and King 2005; Lau 2000). Especially the influx of 'psy discourses' into the sphere of self-help, therapy, life-coaching and personal growth has been lamented, arguing these 'technologies of the self' are the product of a neoliberal (and secular) governmentality that forecloses political critique and social change (Mäkinen 2014; Rose 1999). Critics of therapy culture (Furedi 2004; Illouz 2008; Salmenniemi and Vorona 2014) and more recently the 'wellness' industry similarly critique and often even mock the way the new moral imperative towards body and/or mind is directed at the cultivation and management of the happier, healthier, self, "where individual responsibility and self-expression are morphed with the mindset of a free-market economist" (Cederström and Spicer 2015, 4), hence suited to, rather than disruptive of, the demands of neoliberalism and late capitalism.

Both the field of holistic spirituality and wellbeing in which women are over-represented compared to men, and in particular those strands which cater specifically to them, have similarly been critiqued from a feminist perspective with regards to their, among others, neoliberal and gender and racial conservative character. Feminist researchers have expressed their critique of the dangers of gender essentialism and separatism, which is perceived as a notable strand within women-centred spiritual traditions. Especially with regards to what is subsumed under 'New Age', including Pagan, Goddess movements, it has also been noted how although 'New Age culture' in the West might offer white middle-class women modes of individual empowerment, it is also to be held accountable for the ways in which its content reproduces white privilege and cultural imperialism through the colonial and racial appropriation and commodification of, for example, Native American rituals, images and phantasies of sexualized, primitivist constructions of Oriental, African and prehistoric female archetypes or Goddesses (Crowley 2011; Eller 2000). There is also quite some feminist critique of the more secular realm of women's wellbeing, self-help and therapy culture for reproducing normative femininities and being complicit with a postfeminist version of the neoliberal self (Blackman 2004; Hochschild 1994; Kenny and Bell 2014; Salmenniemi and Adamson 2015). From within global consumer capitalism and neoliberalism has emerged a new kind of 'empowered' female subjectivity among white middle-class women involved in 'self-laboring' beauty politics and 'lean-in feminism', as entrepreneurs of the self (Elias, Gill, and Scharff 2017).

Much of what is subsumed under the 'wellness and happiness industry' geared to women can indeed be criticized on these terms, yet my study did not merely reveal women as neoliberal postfeminist dupes out for personal gain, but in a very somatic, practical and communal activist sense as critics and agents of the system in which they are subjects. It is therefore important to stress the many contradictions, diversities and – hopefully – increasing self-reflexivity among practitioners and participants within the women's spirituality/subjective wellbeing scene itself. For example, a recent report on 'global wellness' by a North American private institute, which includes a chapter called 'A New Feminist Wellness', claims that much of the 'wellness bashing' of a market that is largely pioneered and domineered by women, is simply misogynistic (Summit 2018). The writers claim that self-care does not necessarily preclude social engagement and empowerment and that the 'disturbing reality of white privilege' in the scene is increasingly being challenged by entrepreneurial women of colour. Yet at the same time the same report showcases women's co-working and wellness clubs and centres in major capitals of the West that are clearly geared to an affluent, multicultural 'global' elite. In a recent study based on participant observation in the world of professional elite women's networks, Fisher (2017) similarly critically analyses the emergence of 'a white corporate feminine spirituality' among the women she studied at an international women's managers networking conference.

However, it is interesting to note that the 'cultivation of the feminine' is increasingly appealing to women across class and ethnic differences in different sectors of society, and there remains research to be done from a more comparative, feminist perspective, in order to map and critically interrogate this diversity. Coincidentally, the corporate event referred to in the study above by Fisher took place at a grand hotel in one of the major European cities only six months before a much smaller women's festival I participated in at the rented space of a yoga centre in the outskirts of the same city centre. The festival organizers I interviewed (Angela and Sayira, referred to in the previous section) claimed they would be happy to break even, and also saw their event as an opportunity for the support and 'promotion' of other locally based femininity practitioners who were struggling to make a living – which I would like to add is a familiar pattern regarding the unpaid or badly paid care work many women, universally and across many differences, have performed historically and continue to perform to this day. What all of these femininity practitioners seem to share, as healers, missionaries and entrepreneurs, following a spiritual/secular awakening of consciousness and calling, is their response to what they see as a need among women (and some men) for embodied healing, resilience and agency from a sense of 'disconnection' in neoliberal secular society. While I find it crucial to take a critical perspective on the power hierarchies and inequalities this work might reproduce, my ethnographic research on a variety of practitioners shows how the demand and offer, or this desire and response of the feminine, cross-cuts parallel communities, and simultaneously eludes simple categorizations in terms of secular, spiritual, class and ethnic homogeneity.

Note

1   See also Anna Fedele's (2013) study of female spiritual pilgrims to French Catholic shrines dedicated to Saint Mary Magdalene. Pilgrims believe that Magdalene can help to heal 'wounds' related to their feminine side, such as physical and emotional pain and traumas such as sexual abuse, miscarriage, incest, etc.

References

Alexander, M. Jacqui. 2005. *Pedagogies of Crossing: Meditations on Feminism, Sexual Politics, Memory, and the Sacred.* Edited by Judith Halberstam and Lisa Lowe, *Perverse Modernities.* Durham: Duke University Press.

Altglas, Véronique. 2014. *From Yoga to Kabbalah: Religious Exoticism and the Logics of Bricolage.* Oxford: Oxford University Press.

Aune, Kristin. 2011. "Much less religious, a little more spiritual: The religious and spiritual views of third-wave feminists in the UK." *Feminist Review* 97(1): 32–55.

Aune, Kristin. 2015. "Feminist spirituality as lived religion: How UK feminists forge religio-spiritual lives." *Gender & Society* 29(1): 122–145.

Aune, Kristin, Sonya Sharma, and Giselle Vincett, eds. 2008. *Women and Religion in the West: Challenging Secularization.* Hampshire: Ashgate.

Blackman, Lisa. 2004. "Self-help, media cultures and the production of female psychopathology." *European Journal of Cultural Studies* 7(2): 219–236.

Bracke, Sarah. 2008. "Conjugating the modern/religious, conceptualizing female religious agency: Contours of a post-secular conjuncture." *Theory, Culture & Society* 25(6): 51–67.

Braidotti, Rosi. 2008. "In spite of the times: The postsecular turn in feminism." *Theory, Culture & Society* 25(6): 1–24.

Braidotti, Rosi, Bolette Blaagaard, Tobijn de Graauw, and Eva Midden, eds. 2014. *Transformations of Religion and the Public Sphere: Postsecular Publics.* New York: Palgrave Macmillan.

Bruce, Steve. 2017. *Secular Beats Spiritual: The Westernization of the Easternization of the West.* Oxford: Oxford University Press.

Bury, Michael. 1982. "Chronic illness as biographical disruption." *Sociology of health & illness* 4(2): 167–182.

Carrette, Jeremy R., and Richard King. 2005. *Selling Spirituality: The Silent Takeover of Religion.* London: Routledge.

Cederström, Carl, and André Spicer. 2015. *The Wellness Syndrome.* Cambridge: Polity Press.

Christ, Carol P. 1992. *Womanspirit Rising: A Feminist Reader in Religion.* San Francisco: HarperCollins.

Crowley, Karlyn. 2011. *Feminism's New Age: Gender, Appropriation, and the Afterlife of Essentialism.* Albany: SUNY Press.

Delgadillo, Theresa. 2011. *Spiritual Mestizaje: Religion, Gender, Race, and Nation in Contemporary Chicana Narrative.* Durham: Duke University Press.

Elias, Ana, Rosalind Gill, and Christina Scharff. 2017. "Aesthetic labour: Beauty politics in neoliberalism." In *Aesthetic Labour: Rethinking Beauty Politics in Neoliberalism,* edited by Ana Elias, Rosalind Gill and Christina Scharff, 3–49. London: Palgrave Macmillan.

Eller, Cynthia. 2000. "White women and the Dark Mother." *Religion* 30(4): 367–378.

Facio, Elisa, and Irene Lara, eds. 2014. *Fleshing the Spirit: Spirituality and Activism in Chicana, Latina, and Indigenous Women's Lives.* Tucson: University of Arizona Press.

Fedele, Anna. 2013. *Looking for Mary Magdalene: Alternative Pilgrimage and Ritual Creativity at Catholic Shrines in France.* Oxford: Oxford University Press.

Fedele, Anna, and Kim Knibbe. 2013. "Introduction: Gender and power in contemporary spirituality." In *Gender and Power in Contemporary Spirituality: Ethnographic Approaches,* edited by Anna Fedele and Kim Knibbe, 1–28. New York: Routledge.

Fisher, Melissa. 2017. "White corporate feminine spirituality: The rise of global professional women's conferences in the new millennium." In *Ethnographies of Conferences and Trade Fairs: Shaping Industries, Creating Professionals,* edited by Hege Høyer Leivestad and Anette Nyqvist, 43–63. Cham: Palgrave Macmillan.

Fuller, Robert C. 2017. "Secular Spirituality." In *The Oxford Handbook of Secularism*, edited by Phil Zuckerman and John R. Shook, 571–586. New York: Oxford University Press.

Furedi, Frank. 2004. *Therapy Culture: Cultivating Vulnerability in an Uncertain Age*. London: Routledge.

Graham, Elaine. 2012. "What's missing? Gender, reason and the post-secular." *Political Theology* 13(2): 233–245.

Gray, Miranda. 2009. *Red Moon: Understanding and Using the Creative, Sexual and Spiritual Gifts of the Menstrual Cycle*. Dancing Eve.

Greed, Clara. 2011. "A feminist critique of the postsecular city: God and gender." In *Postsecular Cities: Space, Theory and Practice*, edited by Justin Beaumont and Christopher Baker, 104–120. London: Continuum.

Hanegraaff, Wouter J. 1998. *New Age Religion and Western Culture: Esotericism in the Mirror of Secular Thought*. New York: State University of New York Press.

Harvey, Graham. 2016. "If 'spiritual but not religious' people are not religious what difference do they make?" *Journal for the Study of Spirituality* 6(2): 128–141.

Heelas, Paul. 2008. *Spiritualities of Life: New Age Romanticism and Consumptive Capitalism*. Oxford: Blackwell.

Heelas, Paul, Linda Woodhead, Benjamin Seel, Brinsolaw Szerszyinski, and Karin Tusting. 2005. *The Spiritual Revolution: Why Religion is Giving Way to Spirituality*. Oxford: Blackwell.

Hochschild, Arlie Russell. 1994. "The commercial spirit of intimate life and the abduction of feminism: Signs from women's advice books." *Theory, Culture & Society* 11(2): 1–24.

Hooks, Bell. 2000. *All about Love: New Visions*. New York: Perennial.

Houtman, Dick, and Stef Aupers. 2007. "The spiritual turn and the decline of tradition: The spread of post-Christian spirituality in 14 western countries, 1981–2000." *Journal for the Scientific Study of Religion* 46(3): 305–320.

Houtman, Dick, and Stef Aupers. 2008. "The spiritual revolution and the new age gender puzzle: The sacralisation of the self in late modernity (1980–2000)." In *Women and Religion in the West: Challenging Secularization*, edited by Kristin Aune, Sonya Sharma and Giselle Vincett, 99–118. Aldershot: Ashgate.

Illouz, Eva. 2008. *Saving the Modern Soul: Therapy, Emotions, and the Culture of Self-help*. Berkeley: University of California Press.

Jakobsen, Janet R., and Ann Pellegrini, eds. 2008. *Secularisms*. Durham: Duke University Press.

Kenny, Kate, and Emma Bell. 2014. "Irony as discipline: self-help and gender in the knowledge economy." *Social Politics: International Studies in Gender, State & Society* 21(4): 562–584.

King, Ursula, and Tina Beattie, eds. 2005. *Gender, Religion and Diversity: Cross-cultural Perspectives*. London: Continuum.

Korte, Anne-Marie. 2011. "Openings: A genealogical introduction to religion and gender." *Religion and Gender* 1(1): 1–17.

Lau, Kimberly J. 2000. *New Age Capitalism: Making Money East of Eden*. Philadelphia: University of Pennsylvania Press.

Lee, Helen. 2007. "'Truths that set us free?': The use of rhetoric in mind-body-spirit books." *Journal of Contemporary Religion* 22(1): 91–104.

Lee, Lois. 2014. "Secular or nonreligious? Investigating and interpreting generic 'not religious' categories and populations." *Religion* 44(3): 466–482.

Leidenfrost, Isadora Gabrielle. 2012. "Things we don't talk about: Women's stories from the red tent. PhD dissertation." School of Human Ecology: Design Studies, University of Wisconsin-Madison.

Llewellyn, Dawn, and Marta Trzebiatowska. 2013. "Secular and religious feminisms: A future of disconnection?" *Feminist Theology* 21(3): 244–258.

Longman, Chia. 2008. "Sacrificing the career or the family? Orthodox Jewish women between secular work and the sacred home." *European Journal of Women's Studies* 15(3): 223–239.

Longman, Chia. 2018. "Women's Circles and the Rise of the New Feminine: Reclaiming Sisterhood, Spirituality, and Wellbeing." *Religions* 9(1): 9.

Mäkinen, Katariina. 2014. "The individualization of class: a case of working life coaching." *The Sociological Review* 62(4): 821–842.

Moraga, Cherríe, and Gloria Anzaldúa. 2015. *This bridge called my back: Writings by radical women of color.* Suny Press.

Nynas, Peter, Mika Lassander, and Terhi Utriainen, eds. 2015. *Post-secular society.* New Brunswick: Transaction Publishers.

Phillips, Layli, ed. 2006. *The womanist reader.* New York: Routledge.

Ponniah, Ujithra. 2018. "Managing Marriages through 'Self-Improvement': Women and 'New Age' Spiritualities in Delhi." *South Asia: Journal of South Asian Studies* 41(1): 137–152. doi:10.1080/00856401.2017.1366682.

Rayburn, Carole A., and Lillian Ed Comas-Díaz. 2008. *Woman soul: The inner life of women's spirituality.* Praeger Publishers/Greenwood Publishing Group.

Reilly, Niamh. 2011. "Rethinking the interplay of feminism and secularism in a neo-secular age." *Feminist Review* 97(1): 5–31.

Reilly, Niamh, and Stacey Scriver, eds. 2014. *Religion, Gender, and the Public Sphere.* Vol. 30, Routledge Studies in Religion. New York: Routledge.

Rich, Adrienne. 2003. "Notes towards a politics of location." In *Feminist Postcolonial Theory: A Reader*, edited by Reina Lewis and Sara Mills, 29–42. New York: Routledge.

Rose, Nikolas. 1999. *Governing the Soul. The Shaping of the Private Self.* 2nd edn. London: Free Association Books.

Salmenniemi, Suvi, and Maria Adamson. 2015. "New heroines of labour: domesticating post-feminism and neoliberal capitalism in Russia." *Sociology* 49(1): 88–105.

Salmenniemi, Suvi, and Mariya Vorona. 2014. "Reading self-help literature in Russia: governmentality, psychology and subjectivity." *The British Journal of Sociology* 65 (1): 43–62.

Scott, Joan. 2017. *Sex and Secularism.* Princeton: Princeton University Press.

Sointu, Eeva, and Linda Woodhead. 2008. "Spirituality, gender, and expressive selfhood." *Journal for the Scientific Study of Religion* 47(2): 259–276.

Streib, Heinz, and Ralph W. Hood. 2013. "Modeling the religious field: Religion, spirituality, mysticism and related world views." *Implicit Religion* 16(2): 137–155.

Summit, Global Wellness. 2018. "Global Wellness Trends Report." Miami: Global Wellness Institute.

Sutcliffe, Steven J., and Ingvild Saelid Gilhus, eds. 2014. *New Age Spirituality: Rethinking Religion.* London: Routledge.

Trzebiatowska, Marta, and Steve Bruce. 2013. "'It's all for girls': Re-visiting the gender gap in new age spiritualities'." *Studia Religiologica* 46(1): 17–33.

Vertovec, Steven. 2007. "Super-diversity and its implications." *Ethnic and Racial Studies* 30(6): 1024–1054.

Vincett, Giselle. 2008. "The fusers: New forms of spiritualized Christianity." In *Women and religion in the West: Challenging secularization*, edited by Kristin Aune, Sonya Sharma and Giselle Vincett, 133–145. Aldershot: Ashgate.

Vincett, Giselle, Sonya Sharma, and Kristin Aune. 2008. "Women, religion and secularization: One size does not fit all." In *Women and Religion in the West: Challenging Secularization*, edited by Kristin Aune, Sonya Sharma and Giselle Vincett, 1–19. Aldershot: Ashgate.

Watts, Galen. 2017. "'Of' and 'for': studying spirituality and the problems therein." *Journal for the Study of Spirituality* 7(1): 64–71. doi:10.1080/20440243.2017.1290138.

Woodhead, Linda. 2010. "Real religion and fuzzy spirituality? Taking sides in the sociology of religion." In *Religions of Modernity*, edited by Stef Aupers, 31–48. Leiden: Brill.

Woodhead, Linda. 2016. "The rise of 'no religion' in Britain: The emergence of a new cultural majority." *Journal of the British Academy* 4: 245–261.

4 The sacred feminine in Mexico's Neopagan women's circles

Renée de la Torre and Cristina Gutiérrez Zúñiga[1]

For the past three decades, Mexico has seen the growth of *Neomexicanidad* (*Neomexicanism*), a hybrid creation that reinterprets the religious syncretism of indigenous Catholicism from a New Age perspective (De la Peña 2002). This spiritual movement incorporates esoteric and mystical elements to traditions from pre-Hispanic culture and certain existing indigenous expressions.[2] Neopagan ceremonies and ethnic rituals like temazcal baths, circle dances, vigils, marches, and sacred chants are part of this movement, as practices and mind–body techniques that promote the awakening of a cosmic awareness and a spirituality that emphasizes the sacred feminine. We are interested in analyzing how the meanings and symbols associated with Mexican national identity have been redefined in a New Age frame of reference, focusing particularly on three new dimensions: feminization, holistic spirituality, and its relationship to the secular world—and, more specifically, to the world of commerce. For this analysis, we will present an ethnography of several *Neomexicanidad* ceremonies organized by the Regina spiritual movement in two cities of Mexico, pondering the way in which the teaching of the rituals of the sacred feminine has translated into career opportunities for the women who are members of the movements and even led to pyramid funding schemes. As an alternative to religion, this gender spirituality (McGuire 2008) establishes ties to the secular world through different types of spiritually rooted activism that we will analyze here. In addition, we will examine how this has engendered a market for goods and services associated with alternative health with the symbolic plus of sacred femininity, part of a broader process of globalized spiritual commodification (Bowman 1999).

Regina: the epic book of the awakening of Mexican womanhood

The raison d'être and inspiration of Regina women's circles can be found in works by the author Antonio Velasco Piña, a follower of the Gran Fraternidad Universal (Great Universal Brotherhood). In the 1970s, the GFU helped spread New Age ideas across Mexico, especially yoga, vegetarianism, and Eastern spiritualities. In Velasco's novels, which combine fiction and non-fiction, the author seeks to reinterpret Mexico's most profound identity from a New Age perspective and recover the traditions and the formation of women's circles in order to awaken a new cosmic awareness.

The first movement associated with this trend appeared in 1988 after Velasco published a bestseller that tells the mythic tale of a real-life woman. For many people seeking spiritual alternatives, *Regina: 2 de octubre no se olvida* (Regina: Never forget October 2nd) (1987) has become an "epic book" (De la Peña 2012), used to justify beliefs that now inspire new rituals aimed at awakening Mexico's sacred feminine consciousness.

Regina tells the story of María Regina Teusher Krueger, a young Mexican woman who was killed during the student massacre on October 2, 1968, in Tlaltelolco. This date marks a before and after in Mexico's modern political history, a moment when protestors took to the streets to challenge the political system and the capitalist model of progress. It has turned into an emblem of leftist social movements that take to the streets each year on the anniversary of the massacre to chant "*Dos de octubre no se olvida*" ("Never forget October 2nd"). While the public views the massacre as an act of political repression or even a genocide directed at youth, Antonio Velasco Piña considers it a ritual sacrifice to awaken Mexico's spirituality.

The novel describes how the main character was set to work as a volunteer during the 1968 Mexico Olympics. Unlike the other students who were in Tlaltelolco to protest against the government, however, Regina was there making a ritual sacrifice to awaken the spirituality of deep Mexico. This nourished the millenarian belief of the cultural movement of *Mexicanidad*, a nationalist movement that appeared in Mexico in the 1960s.[3] This movement proposed that the treasures of pre-Hispanic civilization had been deliberately hidden for 500 years at the request of Cuauhtémoc, the last Aztec emperor, to preserve them and also resist Spanish colonization. The Prophecy of the Sixth Sun, which the movement subscribed to, predicted that at the end of these "suns" (time units on the Aztec calendar), the ancient splendor of Mexico would be restored. According to the novel, Regina was born on March 21, 1942, the day when the Age of Pisces gave way to the Age of Aquarius in the New Age imaginary (Ferguson 1981). In addition, Regina—whose name means "queen"—represents both the reincarnation of the last Aztec king, Cuauhtémoc, and a priestess in Tibetan Buddhism referred to as *dakini*.[4] In this way, Regina proved to be the link between the New Age and the prophetic millennial beliefs of the *Mexicanidad* movement, thus creating a Neo-Mexicanist myth.

The esoteric theories of the *Gran Fraternidad Universal* (Great Universal Brotherhood, GFU) are the basis for understanding the book.[5] According to these theories, the North–South axis will be dominant during the Age of Aquarius and it is the GFU's mission to unite the continent from Mexico to Peru through journeys based on the mass Hindu pilgrimage called Kumbh Mela (De la Peña 2002, 191), resignifying indigenous rituals at archeological sites across the continent to reactivate Mother Earth's *chakras*. Some followers of the *Mexicanidad* movement focused on a more nationalist ideology, convinced that the New Age would coincide with the Kingdom of the Sixth Sun God, whose dates correspond to the Age of Aquarius (De la Peña 2002). To back their argument of Mexico's greatness, they claimed that in spite of its geographical proximity to the United States, Mexico was still a great power because of the latent esoteric vibrations present at all of the continent's ceremonial centers and the rituals carried out there, all part of the "great [Latin American] culture" (Güemes 1984). According to Velasco, Regina herself also carried out such rituals, which were part of a transcendental mission to awaken a renewed planetary awareness at Mexico's *chakra* and redeem Mexico with the help of the ancient knowledge of the Tibetan lamas. As a child in Velasco's novel, Regina lives in China, where she becomes a disciple of Tagdra Rinpoche, a Tibetan monk who teaches her the Buddhist secrets to fulfill the mission of restoring sacred pre-Hispanic traditions (secret rituals to create vibrations) and, with this, start a movement for Mexico's spiritual awakening.

When she returns to Mexico in 1968 at the age of 20, Regina embarks on a search for the guardians of Mexico's Olmecan, Mayan, Zapotec, and Nahua traditions. These guardians confide in her, sharing the locations of the pre-Hispanic sites (like Teotihuacan) and the sacred routes that will liberate Mexico's energy. Regina orders the guardians of the hermetic tradition—generally, indigenous people or the *capitanes* (dance leaders) of the Concheros, a popular dance dating back to the colonial period—to allow youth and intellectuals from the "cosmopolitan" upper middle class to join the movement.[6]

After several ceremonies along the "sacred routes" of the archeological centers, Regina and her followers believe that they have awakened the energy of the Popocatépetl volcano (masculine consciousness) but still need to rouse Iztaccíhuatl (the female volcano, known as "the sleeping woman"). To achieve this, Regina has to sacrifice herself along with 400 of her followers, all of whom die during the slaughter at Tlatelolco on October 2, 1968. Through this act, the feminine spiritual awakening of Mexico begins (Velasco Piña, interviewed by De la Torre).

To summarize the connection between this book and recent spiritualities, many Mexican New Agers have been inspired by the book to reconcile their search for alternative spiritualities with their Mexican nationalism. On the other hand, the novel has given adherents of *Mexicanidad* a mystical and millenarian option to combine nationalist ideology with a spiritual project that offers a fringe benefit: it also appeals to non-Mexican spiritual seekers.

Regina circles: rituals to recover feminine spirituality

Beyond the historical accuracy of Regina's mystical biography, or the novel's *sui generis* spiritual interpretation of a national political event, the book has contributed to inventing a myth and a symbol. A powerful "archetype" has been identified that mobilizes rituals of *Neomexicanidad*, a hybrid spirituality that combines indigenous worldviews and rituals with Oriental techniques and knowledge (particularly Tibetan Buddhism).

Among her current followers, Regina is seen as a guide to recovering pre-Hispanic traditions like the Concheros dance and temazcal or sweatlodge and to participating in sacred rituals at archaeological sites believed to have powerful energy.[7] Yet it has also served as an inspiration for "Regina" women's circles, which meet to recover the sacred feminine.

In the words of one of the "grandmothers" who leads the Regina circles in Mexico City:

> Regina summoned a spiritual force. Today, she lives on through the voices of many women who responded to this call and who have bettered their spirit and their consciousness to offer their love and service. The only thing Regina asks for, urgently, is the awakening of Mexican consciousness. She is the loving face of many women who carry happiness within their hearts. Her message is universal and it has been manifested in different ways over time through different sacred feminine events.
>
> (Solís Gil 2003, 258)

For many Mexican women in the search of alternative spirituality, Regina has served as a model to rediscover the sacred side of their femininity. Women's circles began to form in 1988, twenty years after Regina Teuscher's "sacrifice" at Tlaltelolco and one year after the novel was published. One of the leaders refers to the message from Regina herself: "Women must form squared circles in order to help awaken Mexico's consciousness. The circle represents the shape of the energy and the square, its materialization on earth" (Solís Gil 2003, 59).

One of the traditions started by the Reginas is to meditate at the house where she lived her final days, located in the Mexico City neighborhood San Miguel Chapultepec. The house has become a shrine for the nascent spiritual movement. The Reginas have started many other traditions as well: walks along the sacred route to Teotihuacán to mark the changing of the seasons and awaken women's consciousness; the bell-ringing ceremony at the Catedral Metropolitana to reactivate the flow of harmonious life energy; pilgrimages or sacred marches to Tepeyac Hill, the ancient sanctuary of Tonatzín (which means "Our Mother" in Náhuatl and has been reinterpreted as "Mother Earth") represented by the statue of Our Lady of Guadalupe, a syncretic Mexican version of the Catholic icon. Every October 2nd, the Reginas hold annual celebrations at the house where Regina was born, Aldea de los Reyes, which is located at the foot of the Iztaccíhuatl volcano. Further on, we will describe one of these gatherings.

In Mexico, the Reginas have emulated their guide, seeking out the guardians of ancient traditions, joining traditional Concheros dance groups and even starting their own. The group was drawn to the traditional dances due to "their profound religiousness, their devotion to the saints and their rituals that pass onto them a millennial knowledge, making them the heirs of an ancient tradition that must be learned in order to renew the cosmic energy that traveled from Tibet to Mexico" (González Torres 2005, 171).

Unlike traditional Conchero dancing groups, which practice a popular version of Catholicism with elements inherited from pre-Hispanic traditions, the Reginas attribute a spiritual-esoteric meaning to the dance. Accordingly, they believe that the same route traveled during the traditional pilgrimages of different Marian devotions is a sacred feminine-human path that is reactivated through marching. They believe that their rituals serve as a sort of energy healing for the body of the earth, liberating its female energies (De la Torre 2012). In this way, a religious rite is transformed into spiritual activism, connected with causes defended by other secular social collectives in the public sphere.

It is the mission of initiates in the Regina circles to celebrate mystical rituals and sacred walks with the aim of awakening a new planetary consciousness based on feminine sensitivity. It is a holistic approach that combines the sacred development of self with therapeutic actions to heal the sacred geography of the earth's body.

Inside a Regina women's circle: Guadalajara[8]

The aim of women's circles is to recognize the positive aspects of femininity. Many different cultures and religions have circles, but Jean Shinoda Bolen, a popular author in the international spirituality movement who lives in California, believes that women have a "knack" for being part of such circles:

> Being in a circle is a learning and growing experience that draws upon the wisdom and experience, commitment, and courage of each one in it. [...] In a patriarchal climate, a circle of equals can be like an island of free speech and laughter. It makes us conscious of the contrast, through which we become aware if what we do to perpetuate the status quo, and how we can change it.
>
> (Bolen 1999, 15–17)

The premise for women's circles is to celebrate women's traditional skills—sewing, knitting, cooking, housekeeping, making flower arrangements, relating with nature—and recognize their potential to change patriarchal culture. Women's household tasks are valued in a new way but, more importantly, women are depicted as willing to cooperate with their peers, engage in equal partnerships, form a harmonious relationship with nature, and possess both an intuition and an inclination to nurture spiritual life (Ramírez 2017). By enhancing and even celebrating features like spirituality and the essence of a woman's character, women are encouraged to recognize and accept this reconnection with their feminine core.

The main activity of women's circles consists of informal meetings where women can discuss their concerns and personal issues with others. The meetings offer a place where they can realize what they have in common with other women, strengthen cooperative relationships, and generate trust and respect. According to Rosario Ramírez (2019), this process of support and reciprocity towards other women in the group is framed within the concept of *sorority*,[9] which becomes a way of relating to one's peers and of expressing alternative behaviors among women.

The members of the Regina women's circles are middle-class urban residents mainly, though not exclusively, from Mexico City; the groups have also expanded to other cities and on other circuits of holistic, therapeutic, environmental, and shamanic spiritualities.

Patricia Ríos, for example, was a disciple of Emilio Dias Porta's *Movimiento Mancomunidad Iniciática* Solar (an Indianist New Age offshoot of the GFU). After discovering Regina, Ríos did her initiation in the Lakota tradition as a woman of fire (a temazcal runner) and as a Conchero dancer. For her, the meaning of the rituals she leads is to create awareness of the sacred feminine. This means making feminine aspects sacred, aspects such as wearing skirts (to reconnect with the energy that emanates from Mother Earth) and braids, and placing renewed value on the traditional tasks of indigenous women.

In the 1970s, feminism developed as a social movement with ties to the left, demanding equal opportunities for both men and women while questioning the role of women in productive and reproductive labor (maternity and family). Later, feminism challenged the way femininity had been naturalized through religion, deconstructing the historic construction of its attributes (Lamas 1986). In the Regina movement, in contrast, femininity reclaims spirituality, creating a mystique around women's traditional roles, idealizing indigenous roles, and essentializing femininity through the uterus, its natural center and a source of energy. No attempt is made in the circles to revindicate women's dignity by insisting on their equality with men; instead, the aim is to emphasize the value of their spirituality, which makes them compatible with nature. Traditions are also important in the circles, to maintain each woman's ties to their ancestral lineage; and forms of feminine sociality are recovered based on the idea of the circle. The circle thus makes a contribution to femininity, differentiating women from men and empowering them to make human relationships more cooperative, fairer, and more horizontal. According to Rosario Ramírez, the contexts of the women's circles include: "the appropriation of discourses such as empowerment, the importance of the body as a sacred space and as a medium of expression and embodiment of the spiritual and, of course, the implications that these discourses have for the way the feminine is depicted" (Ramírez 2018, 254).

The premise of the groups developed for these purposes is a search for the transformation of women's consciousness and the circles are established as spaces capable of having an impact on society at large through the selective appropriation of spiritual discourses.

Due to the hegemonic masculinity of Mexican society, the women recognize the need to decolonize women's bodies, freeing them from taboos, prejudice, and patriarchal domination. In a certain sense, these point to a state of anomie (as used by Durkheim [1987], 1999), which explains the need among women to experience a change within. The idea is that this personal change of recovering self-esteem can have a social impact. The transformation of the role and the place that the feminine occupies in society represents a utopian horizon in which women's empowerment will forge a new harmony with the cosmos and more reciprocal relations associated with sorority. This also exists in other New Age/Neopagan women's movements (Pike 2001; Salomonsen 2002; Fedele and Knibbe 2013).

Approximately twelve women participate in the Regina women's circle that P.R. leads in Guadalajara. The circle meets every Thursday to talk, sew, and cook as ways to rediscover "the sacred feminine" that lies within all of them, a process in which the figure of Regina becomes a teacher and a sacred ideal. The circle's members are heterogeneous not only in their class origins but also in terms of the leadership tasks each has assumed (De la Torre and Gutiérrez Zúñiga 2011).

At the meetings, the women seek to find points in common with other women and discover and strengthen their abilities and feminine intuition. These are circles for personal growth that promote seeing the self as sacred (Heelas 1996) while invoking values associated with autonomy. From this perspective, we can observe how embodiment practices related to health, gender, nature, sexuality, emotion, and spirituality are a focus of the circles. Such practices can be found in the circle's narratives, the symbols of goddesses (archetypes), body rituals, circle dynamics, and Neopagan ceremonies that incorporate feminine elements of nature. Altogether, these symbolized and somatized activities gradually transform individual awareness of being a woman in the world and, in conjunction with this process, the limits imposed by society's dominant values shift to revindicate feminine strength in the face of patriarchy, capitalism, and colonialism. In this way, we can say that circles foster "gender spiritualities" (McGuire 2008, 159–161) that are geared to making, unmaking, and remaking the "selves" of their members through embodied rituals. The gender dimension, especially femininity, is at the core of the identity of the Regina women.

The circles do different ceremonies that connect members with feminine spirituality in nature, especially moon cycle rituals based on the recovery of the 13 moons (with 28-day cycles) that help realign women's hormonal cycles with cosmic time. Embodied rituals focused on nature's feminine essence or energy are somatic experiences, helping women to accept their biological functions, hormonal cycles, and associated emotional repercussions, concerns, everyday problems, feelings, and their own particular ways of thinking and acting in society.

These techniques and group dynamics aim to transform individual awareness of being and interacting in the world through somatic modes of attention, which Csordas defines as "culturally elaborated ways of attending to one's body in surroundings that include the embodied presence of others" (Csordas 1994, 138). Body rituals allow participants to somatize a new relationship with nature, which is now acknowledged as enchanted, with feminine energies, and with goddess archetypes (like Regina). This is achieved through rituals that allow bodily sensations to work as an intersubjective group medium, creating new perception and intuition as they interact with objects in nature that are now viewed as living and sensitive beings. The spirit attributed to these elements has a particular agency: it can be used to heal, to convey wisdom or to transmit energy.

The circles themselves are not therapies but they do incorporate certain dynamics of healing and personal empowerment. In principle, the holistic model of healing, whose importance has been emphasized in works by Meredith McGuire (1982, 2008), reinforces the notion of the inseparability of the subject as mind–body–spirit. This is experienced in the ceremonies of sacred temazcal, dance, songs, or circles focused on the fire or the full moon, generating a continuum between spirituality and therapy. As developed by Thomas Csordas, the therapy model uses a semiotic approach to ritual healing processes to produce a gradual experience of getting better (Csordas 1994). In this regard we can say that the feminine sacred Regina circles also foster a strong sense of group unity that connects the bodies, emotions, minds, social relations, and spiritual experiences of the individuals with the notion of a sacred feminine force. This force is seen as the awakening of the inner Goddess, who is associated with nature and the cosmos. The holistic vision experienced in rituals allows for somatization, creating "a holistic interpretative framework through which the cosmos becomes sacred when the self becomes sacred and projects of empowerment acquire the potential for transforming one's surroundings and attaining universal consciousness" (De la Torre 2013, 33). In addition, the holistic principle allows for a two-way connection between the individual (body–mind–spirit) and the cosmos (nature, cosmic energy, planetary vibrations), each of which is equally important for the analysis of these practices today.

The goal of the circles is to empower women, but this without ever questioning their gender roles. In the circles, all relationships are egalitarian and based on trust and dialogue. The belief is that individual change will lead to a social shift in gender relations but also to a spiritual change in harmony with feminine spirituality.

The circle periodically takes sacred journeys along the "feminine paths" (*nadis*, channels that connect the energy between the *chakras* or energy points) that go from the Zapopan Basilica to the Guadalajara Cathedral. Women come together for these marches when the seasons change, on the equinoxes and solstices. According to the Reginas, the sanctuary of the Virgen de Zapopan is one of the most important *nadis* (cf. *supra*) on Mexico's sacred map, a place where ritual activities help liberate the planet's energy flows. The group's personal work occurs within the space of the women's circles and this public ritual-demonstration fits within the holistic conception of the New Age, where the body's energy centers are aligned with those of the earth and, more specifically, women's energy is reconnected with that of Mother Earth.

To date, twenty-five marches under the sun have been organized along the women's path because, in the words of the coordinator, "It is critical for women to begin to exercise the role that awaits them in the next two thousand years" (P.R.D. in Ibarra 2002, 14). The marches are considered a purifying pilgrimage and a way to foster awareness among all the city's residents. "Just as a street sweeper comes out onto the avenue every morning to pick up the trash, we should raise awareness and plant the seeds of peace; it's very simple. The indigenous have been doing it since time immemorial" (Interview with P. R.D. by Ibarra 2002, 14).

The Regina women's circle in Guadalajara is also involved in social acti-vism. Here its activities reflect the core values of the Regina movement; that is, restoring the traditional importance of indigenous people and women, and defending nature. Their social activities have included environmental defense at Lago de Chapala; large concerts whose proceeds go to homeless children and young drug addicts; cultural promotion and community assistance at indigenous communities in Jalisco; managing a home for Wirárika indigenous people living in Guadalajara; and cooperation with the demands and protests organized by indigenous people like *Jornadas por la Paz y Dignidad* and *Caravanas Zapatistas.* Like the New Age, *Neomexicanidad* also generates what Heelas recently referred to as "spiritualities of life": spaces for subjective transformation and the resistance to materialism and to the dehumanization of contemporary life. On a small scale, such spiritualities are gradually fostering a humanist ethic of global dimensions that have broader acceptance than radical political movements (Heelas 2008). Far from a religiosity alienated from the world, *Neomexicanidad* gives a public face to social spiritual activism.

Ethnographic notes on Regina's vigil: a key event for understanding the network

Sacred times and spaces have sprung up around Regina. One example of this is the vigil ceremony that the Reginas organize every year at the house where the spiritual guide was supposedly born in Aldea de Los Reyes (near Ame-cameca, state of Mexico) on October 1. This march is followed by different sacred marches on October 2 to commemorate her sacrifice.

We attended the 2012 vigil, which attracted around a hundred people. Different spiritual activities took place during the vigil. Most of those attending wore white; women wore skirts; some wore embroidered ethnic garments; and the majority had a red scarf tied around their forehead (white symbolizes the spirit's purity and the red scarf, control of one's thoughts).

The vigil that year was held at a small seventeenth-century chapel, with many Conchero elements but also eclectic symbols and narratives. Outside the chapel, Mexican syncretism could be seen in a stone figure carved into a niche in the wall. According to the female leaders or "grandmothers" of the Regina movement, this figure represented the pregnant goddess. The grandmothers explained that an ancient fertility temple is buried beneath the Catholic chapel. It seemed as if the effigy had been intentionally placed in the niche to suggest the idea of a resurgence of ancient worship from beneath the walls of the Catholic temples, many of which were in fact constructed at the same locations (and with the very stones) of the temples of Mesoamerica's inhabitants. Their underlying presence symbolizes the awakening of the sacred knowledge of the ancient dwellers. The Virgen de Guadalupe is depicted on a painting located inside the chapel. She is worshipped as Our Mother Tonatzín.

Unlike other vigil ceremonies we have attended (see De la Torre 2012), at this vigil organized by the Reginas, the ceremony leader shared her tasks with the "grandmothers" in attendance. This sharing of responsibilities is a feminine attribute.

During the vigil, the visitors added the symbols and rituals of their own traditions and integrated them to the ceremonies of *Mexicanidad*, Lakota spirituality, and the Reginas movement.

Before the vigil, a "pre-Hispanic" circular dance (imitating the Conchero tradition) was done in the temple's atrium and a *Mexicanidad* ritual known as *siembra de nombre* (literally, name sowing, a kind of Aztec baptism) was done for three children. To form the holy sign or Nahui Ollin, which is done with flowers as prayers are chanted, the participants were invited to place flowers of different colors (in keeping with a Japanese tradition) and to form a new indecipherable shape, considered the creation of the collective unconscious. Some of the prayers had been created by the Reginas and spoke of awakening the sacred feminine: "We're a circle, a wheel of love that gives us peace." "Mark the hours to rouse all the women." "I'm a woman of the earth, dancing to the universe. I am a wild girl. I am a being of the wind. The goddess lives in me. I'm a woman of wind, water and fire." "I'm woman, I'm woman, I'm woman."

At the end, in keeping with the structure of Conchero tradition, a cleansing ritual was done. The sacred flower sticks that have been charged with the energies of the spirits and ancestors invoked during the ceremony are used for the cleansing. "Grandma Lulú" waved the stick and spoke to Regina's spirit: "Thank you for bringing us here and showing us your path." Then the initiation rites began for the new Regina followers, who swore to uphold the movement's six principles: develop an awareness of the sacred in relation to the cosmic order in the search for the unity of everything and one (holistic principle); discover and develop their feminine qualities; maintain their Mexican national identity; provide disinterested service for others; and show respect and love for nature (Mother Earth) and for diversity.[10]

In addition to the activities already described, the Regina women's circles have grown and expanded beyond Mexico's borders, integrating different circuits and acquiring different uses and meanings.[11]

There is a community in the Basque country of Spain called Amalurra, home to a community that seeks to recover feminine and community values. A hotel there offers meditation courses. The leader of this group worked hard to establish peaceful agreements between the Basque country and the Spanish government (Goicolea, 2002). Circles have also sprung up among the women in the Zapatista army in the state of Chiapas in the south of Mexico. The indigenous women in these circles are illiterate and do not speak Spanish but learned about the book through a person who knows how to read and another who translates for them. Regina has inspired them to revindicate women's traditional role in these indigenous communities, showing that "a revolutionary movement is not about killing people but about practicing community values." In Japan, a musical entitled *Regina, Cosmic Love* has been running since 2008. Here Regina inspired Japanese theater groups to recover their roots, remodeling their houses in traditional Japanese style and recovering their theater traditions (interview with Antonio Velasco Piña, 2008).

The sacred feminine and the creation of new "alternative" consumer styles

The discourse of the sacred feminine is not only religious but entails secular aspects related to alternative health, psychotherapies, and wellbeing services. It has generated a new circuit of centers, goods, and services where these alternative health and healing practices are offered while disseminating the movement's principles. While not all are associated with the Reginas, there is a clear continuity with the discourse and the sensitivity that the movement has promoted. The discourses and offering of services circulate among broader publics through a cultural industry and include literature on feminine spirituality, lunar calendars, and videos that are posted and reposted on social networks and websites. In addition, many of the leaders also promote the feminine spirituality of *Neomexicanidad* through courses, workshops, temazcal ceremonies, therapies, seminars, and spa-type rituals aimed at harmony and healing of the sacred feminine. Young guides of women's circles have worked with the Regina grandmothers to learn to lead experiential workshops, therapies, or rituals on secular circuits. Such knowledge is in turn offered at workshops and professional seminars in order to make these women's knowledge into a profes-sional credential, a way to make a living. Practitioners are known as "temazcal runners," "coaches," "therapists," "guides," or "consultants."

There are also endless alternative health options, including menstrual cups, herbal remedies, and nutritional supplements for breastfeeding or menopause; remedies and food products are based on seeds, flowers, and plants whose use dates back to pre-Hispanic times. These products and services not only involve consumption but also new ways of living inspired in the decolonizing of women's bodies, freeing them from allopathic medicine and gynecological-obstetric vio-lence. According to our informants, the products generate harmonious feelings with nature and the cycles and essence of femininity.

We can observe a new and rapidly consolidating demand for goods and services from a segment of women who seek to incorporate this sacred dimension of their being into their bodies, their everyday lives, and their relations. Within the global offer of "wellness," the specific nature of this particular selection stems from certain ideological features that are important to identify: this search for harmony and wellbeing stands in opposition to a world defined as patriarchal and capitalist and to contemporary forms of domination. Beyond the historic imposition of women's reproductive labor, this domination also includes the stereotypical hypersexualization of the feminine body through media images, identified as a powerful cultural matrix of multiple forms of violence. This wellness market is one of many emerging alternatives for being a woman.

The rise of a market of goods and services associated with the ritual reproduction of these feminine spiritualities can be inscribed in what Marion Bowman (1999) has defined as "globalized spiritual commodification," which also encompasses the formalized role of the ritual guide.

The teaching of certain knowledge, the ritual performance itself and the objects used in the ritual are goods and services presented as merchandise. It is thus important not only to note the commercial and anonymous nature of the act of the exchange but also the way this new commercial status strengthens this offer: commodification expands its circulation and provides multiple options for using, combining, and assembling the selection within a personal menu that is ultimately organized by the individual seeking the spiritual experiences (Gutiérrez Zúñiga 2008, 379–380).

The intermediation between the commercial and religious systems represents an important dynamic for understanding the myriad ways religion is manifested in late capitalism (De la Torre and Gutiérrez Zúñiga 2005).

One example that allows us to illustrate this aspect is the recent phenomenon of the so-called "Flower of Abundance" (also known as "The Loom of Abundance," "Women's Empowerment," and "Operation Abundance"), a pyramid moneymaking scheme that has spread through women's networks. This is a new version of the fraudulent Ponzi scheme,[12] which is as old as the U.S. postal service and has been launched under many different names using various discourses. This particular proposal consists of 15 people organized in four categories on a pyramid: the person who entered first is at the top and will receive the money followed by two people on the second level, four people on the third and eight people on the fourth and final level. These eight people, the last to have entered, give a certain amount of money to the person at the top of the pyramid in order to join. The person at the top then exits the scheme and the two people at the second level move to the top of two new pyramids while the rest move up one level. The eight original donors from the fourth level are also divided and move up to the third level of their respective pyramid. These are the people who must in turn recruit eight people to create the base of the new pyramid. Each person who enters the scheme gives their money with the hope of getting to the top and ending the cycle by receiving eight times more than she originally gave.

The financial authorities in many different countries have worked to put an end to these frauds each time a new one appears.[13] Here the particular case of "The Flower of Abundance" is of interest because it draws on the sacred feminine discourse to generate a version of the scheme aligned with this new sensibility, constructing a pyramid based on the value that "sorority" has come to represent for so many women. This new version of the pyramid has appeared under many names in various Spanish-speaking countries like Peru and Spain (2008), Argentina (2015) and Mexico (2016).[14]

The first noteworthy aspect is the depiction of this pyramid, which is shown as a flower or a loom. The geometric shapes suggest mandalas or even a Lakota dreamcatcher, as can be seen in figures that can be found with small variations on different websites.[15]

The second aspect involves the Neopagan elements used for the hierarchies of the pyramid: the four elements of nature, each assigned a function, that is, water (receive), earth (support), air (attract), and fire (give). Another important change in this scheme is that the ultimate objective is not simply multiplying one's money but for women to experience the "empowerment," "abundance," and "blessing" of women's solidarity. The loom is described as:

> a system of women's empowerment through financial abundance and internal growth; and a speedy course of learning and transformation to leave behind a mentality of need and embrace abundance. It's a group of women joined by mutual trust and their desire for a better life through common work.
>
> (http://visiontres.com/magazine/2016/06/24/los-telares-de-m
> ujeres-no-son-una-estafa-por-que/)

Messages of female motivation and empowerment are a key strategy for getting more women to join these gifting circles. Through the intensive use of social networks (Facebook, Twitter, and WhatsApp groups), the circles send out messages like "Recognizing that we are one, that you are me and I am you, gives meaning to support and sharing instead of competing with one another"; "The secret gifting group of Flower of Abundance is a circle of support and trust that teaches you what you can change to BE abundance" (from the "Flor de la abundancia Cancún" Facebook page); or personal messages of enthusiasm and affection from the group, covered by happy emoji (smiling faces, confetti, heart signs).

In the different versions of this scheme, other elements are added like the emphasis on women's solidarity to counter the individualist competition that characterizes the patriarchal and capitalist system. Another variant offers a more global approach that incorporates the fight against "the establishment" with a defense of nature, as can be seen in the following testimony:

> We have been taught that in order to have money, we must work from sunup to sundown and then pay our hard-earned money in taxes. Yet we have more and more things to worry about and less and less money. The establishment is playing us for fools.

We are entering the Age of Light. We are awakening from a spell that had been cast to keep us dormant. When there is unity, there is a connection, an awakening. Open your mind, don't judge, don't miss out on a way to benefit your life in every way.

Worry less about money and investing in solar panels, and instead live more consciously and connected to the earth. Support others and live a healthier life.

Abundance is about financial recycling: it's totally organic. It's about freeing us from that weight we're carrying around to focus on what really matters, which is our true home.

(Video testimony on the "Flor de la abundancia Cancún" Facebook page)

This case allows us to see how outside the specific realm of women's circles, the discourse of the sacred feminine is currently expanding and gaining a foothold in the dynamics of commerce.

Conclusion

Regina women's circles are ephemeral groups that women choose to join in order to experience profound transformations of the perception, value, and action associated with being a woman. The circles also lead women to experience shifts in their worldviews, values, biological dynamics (hormonal and menstrual cycles), relationships, professional lives, and work.

Although they promote an essentialized vision of femininity, their demands and utopias echo the discourses of postcolonial criticism. There is a staunch opposition to the foundations of contemporary society here, including the models of modernity, Christianity, neoliberalism, and patriarchy, all of which are perceived as having excluded women; the imposition of science over Eastern and indigenous knowledge and over techniques based on magic and sensitivity; an instrumental approach to nature as something to be exploited, as opposed to a living being; an opposition of body vs. spirit as opposed to a holistic conception of the two; the superiority of rational knowledge over intuition, and so on.

The impact of women's spirituality circles cannot be quantified but we can say that it is about more than mere subjective changes, small groups, or isolated communities. From a spiritual (but not religious) position, these circles contribute to the workings of an extensive network that has trickled into different secular circuits including alternative health, psychological therapies, non-governmental organizations, and cultural and environmental movements. The circles even offer an alternative for women's professional development as self-help group leaders or training for group guides, allowing them to develop a career (albeit without a degree) and earn a living. This has implications for women's empowerment in the areas of sales and customer service. Many of these women work as coaches at sales companies or in human resources departments. These spiritual practitioners are not new religious specialists but intermediaries between the religious and the secular.

In summary, Neopagan spiritualities like the *Neomexicanidad* movement of the Reginas are the seed of a renewed mystical feminism of postcolonial criticism. They promote holistic healing methods and represent new alternative ways for women to position themselves in the secular world while making their relationships more horizontal. Although they often reproduce stereotypes about women that have been deconstructed by feminists, these spiritualities are experienced as empowering; they engender ideas that allow women's value, nature, and spirituality to be reassessed in social spheres resistant to radical feminism. Unlike radical feminism, which has many points in comparison to secularism (see Aune, Chapter 1), the circles strive to offer a third option to the patriarchal authoritarianism of churches while revindicating both spirituality and gender. However, their essentialist conceptions of nature and of womanhood put them at risk of being trapped in their own biologism. In spite of rallying against materialism and capitalism, women's circles employ metaphors of magical energy flows and cosmic balance to refer to the exchange of money and work in a language that reinforces the most fraudulent version of the capitalist economic order.

Notes

1 We would like to thank Wendy Gosselin for her excellent translation of the original Spanish version of this manuscript.
2 *Neomexicanidad* is just one example of new forms of spirituality to emerge from a New Age-universalist reading of ethnic-indigenous traditions. See, for example, the study by Galinier & Molinié (2013) that proposes the terms "neo-Indian" and "mystical Indian"; on the Mayans, see Fahramand (2016); and for a Latin American vision, see De la Torre, Gutiérrez & Juárez Huet (2016).
3 According to Francisco de la Peña, *Mexicanidad* is "a revivalist, nativist and neo-traditionalist movement characterized by an emphasis on native elements, a reinvention of Pre-Hispanic traditions and a reinterpretation of the past. With a clear millenarian and prophetic component, *Mexicanismo* aspires to restore pre-Columbian civilization and the indigenous elements of national culture. Its ideological universe is inspired by an idealized reinterpretation of Mexico's pre-Hispanic past and the celebration of an archetypal image of the Indian. This is not an ethnic or an indigenous movement but a *mestizo* cultural phenomenon with strong urban roots" (2001, 96).
   One branch of the *Mexicanidad* movement came close to forming its own political party. Its principal impact has been on the world of culture, where it promotes the speaking of Nahuatl; awareness of the knowledge of the world that pre-Hispanic civilization had attained; the recovery of ancestral rituals; the reactivation of the *calpulli* (a sociopolitical unit among the Aztecs) and the decolonization of Mexican thought.
   Another branch evolved toward a more mystical and cosmopolitan version of *Mexicanidad* (Mexicanism), called Neo-Mexicanidad *(Neo-Mexicanism)*, interpreting the indigenous legacy from a New Age perspective (De la Peña, 2002). Neo-Mexicanism is "a syncretic circuit where movements of the spiritualist and esoteric current of Mexicanism, New Age networks, indigenous ceremonial communities and the Conchero dance all come together and are synthesized" (De la Torre and Gutiérrez Zúñiga 2011, 187).

4 This is the female name of *daka*, which usually refers to those who practice tantric yoga. In the Hindu and Buddhist tradition, the *dakini* is a feminine being with strong energy whose genealogy and role are complex. According to Simmer-Brown, "The dakini, in her various guises, serves as each of the Three Roots. She may be a human guru, a vajra master who transmits the Vajrayana teachings to her disciples and joins them in samaya commitments. The wisdom dakini may be a yidam, a meditational deity; female deity yogas such as Vajrayogini are common in Tibetan Buddhism. Or she may be a protector; the wisdom dakinis have special power and responsibility to protect the integrity of oral transmissions" (2002, 139–140). Anna Fedele documents references to this figure in the contemporary alternative spirituality among the Mary Magdalene pilgrims in France. See Fedele (2013).

5 The GFU was founded in Venezuela in 1948 by French astrologist Serge Reynaud de la Ferrière. The organization was the first to proclaim the values of the New Age of Aquarius in Mexico and different countries of Latin America. Its centers promoted the "Oriental" traditions of Hinduism and Buddhism's philosophy and the practices of meditation and vegetarianism, as well as Western esoteric trends (such as spiritism, Freemasonry, Gnosticism, Rosicrucianism, Christian esoterism, and theosophy) (García Medina 2010 and Gutiérrez Zúñiga 2015).

6 Though the author tells the story of Regina Teusher in the novel as if it were biographical, Regina's family has accused the author of creating a fictional character for the purposes of his bestseller, loosely based on Regina. The Mexican author Elena Ponatiowska met with the Teusher family to find out more about the young woman's life: she studied at the local German School and later at UNAM, not in China or Tibet. She wasn't born at the foot of the Iztaccihuatl Volcano but at the French Hospital, and on June 3, 1968 (not in March). She wasn't known as the "Queen of Mexico": her family nickname was Marietta and, most importantly, she didn't "offer herself" in a sacrifice to quench an absurd thirst for blood of ancient Aztec deities. As evidenced by the photograph of her corpse—part of her face destroyed by a bullet and a rictus of terror in her eyes—she was simply another victim of the student massacre (taken from http://amrtk.wordpress.com/, consulted on September 19, 2013). When asked about such inconsistencies, leaders of the Neo-Mexican movement like Alberto Ruz claim that it's irrelevant: what matters, they argue, is the spiritual movement that has sprung up around the figure of Regina.

7 According to the anthropologist Lourdes Arizpe, the term temazcal comes from the Nahuatl word *temazcalli* "comprised of *temaz* (steam, knowledge and bath) and *calli* (house)" (Arizpe 2009, 198). It is practiced by several of the groups that once inhabited Mesoamerica, each with its own name for the ritual,

which is *Inipi* for the Lakotas, *temazcalli* for the Otomi, *zumpul-ché* for the Mayans and *ñihi* for the Mixtec. The steam bath has survived as one of the therapy practices of folk medicine. Temazcal baths are now available as a cultural good, a body technique, and therapy within the vast global offering of alternative spirituality and as a neoshaman ritual in networks of neo-Indian spirituality (see De la Torre and Gutiérrez Zúñiga 2016.)

The Conchero dance has long been a practice in Mexican popular religiosity and represents "a form of parallel Catholic worship, involving many aspects of Pre-Hispanic religion" (González Torres 2006, 12). It is the syncretic result of a process of evangelization. As a ritual practice, the Conchero is part of a series of celebrations of devotional figures such as Christ, the saints and the Virgin Mary (under a range of titles). Drawing on a repertoire of chants, music, and dress, the Concheros organization has a hierarchical structure and strict discipline is demanded of members. The dance itself is an obligation to the deity and a mutual commitment to all Conchero groups. Like other traditional practices, the Azteca-Conchero dance has been displaced from its original context—the popular religiosity of Mexico—and used to reconstruct the memory of the nation and the predominant image of indigenous people in modern Mexico. In this process, the Mexicanism movement—and later, the Neo-Mexicanist movement—played fundamental roles. On the global circuits of alternative spirituality, the Conchero dance has become yet another holistic therapeutic practice (De la Peña 2002, 96; De la Torre and Gutiérrez Zúñiga 2011).

8 This section is based on ethnographic research conducted in the women's circle of the Guayabos community in Zapopan Jalisco. The decade of research (2005–2015) consisted of observing meetings, celebrations, and rituals, an ethnography of sensory registers and experiences at temazcal rituals and Concheros performances, interviews with leaders from the movement and with different members of the circles. The women's initials are used to maintain the anonymity of informants, though the names of the leaders whose biographies have been published are cited. For more information, see De la Torre and Gutiérrez Zúñiga 2011 and De la Torre 2012.

9 "Sorority is an ethical, political and practical dimension of feminism today. This term expresses the ethical-political principles of equality and parity among women. It is an alliance between women, promoting trust, support and reciprocal acknowledgment of one's authority. It is an experience among women that fosters a search for positive relations and an existential and political alliance, body to body, subjectivity to subjectivity with other women. It is about taking specific actions to help eliminate all types of social oppression, to foster mutual support, and to achieve gender power for a group of women and vital empowerment for every woman" (Lagarde 1997, 126).

10 These principles can be consulted in: http://ritualolmeca.ning.com/page/circulos-cuadrados-sagrados-femeninos-de-regina.

11 Fedele makes references to the influence of Conchero dancers and the Regina movement in feminine spiritualities in Spain (2013, 77–82).

12 See https://en.wikipedia.org/wiki/Ponzi_scheme, consulted on December 13, 2016.

13 See http://www.jornada.unam.mx/ultimas/2016/05/15/alerta-condusef-sobre-fraudes-en-tandas-o-piramides, consulted on December 13, 2016.

14 See https://es.wikipedia.org/wiki/Células_de_la_abundancia, consulted on December 13, 2016.

15 See for instance: https://www.perfil.com/noticias/sociedad/flor-telar-mandala-abundancia-estafas-que-se-reciclan-en-clave-feminista.phtml, consulted on October 23, 2019.

References

Aceves, Raúl. 1998. "Tlatelolco: los dos rituals." *Paréntesis* no. 48, Guadalajara Jal.

Arizpe, Lourdes. 2009. *El patrimonio cultural inmaterial de México: Ritos y festividades.* Mexico: Miguel Ángel Porrúa.

Bolen, Jean. 1999. *The Millionth Circle: How to Change Ourselves and the World.* Boston: Conari Press.

Bowman, Marion. 1999. "Healing in the spiritual marketplace: Consumers, courses and credentialism." *Social Compass* 46(2): 181–189.

Csordas, Thomas. 1990. "Embodiment a paradigm for anthropology." *Ethos: Journal of the Society for Psychological Anthropology* 18(1): 5–47.

Csordas, Thomas. 1994. "Introduction: The body as representation and being-in-the-world." In *Embodiment and Experience: The Existential Ground of Culture and Self,* edited by Thomas Csordas, 1–26. Cambridge: Cambridge University Press.

De la Peña, Francisco. 2001. "Milenarismo, Nativismo y Neotradicionalismo en el México actual." *Revista de Ciencias Sociales y Religión* 3(3): 95–113.

De la Peña, Francisco. 2002. *Los hijos del sexto sol*. Mexico: Inah.
De la Peña, Francisco. 2012. Profecías de la mexicanidad: entre el milenarismo nacionalista y la new age. *Cuicuilco* 19(55):127–144.
De la Torre, Renée. 2012. "Las danzas aztecas en la nueva era: Estudio de caso en Guadalajara." Cuicuilco: La mexicanidad y el neoindianismo hoy 19(55): 145–170.
De la Torre, Renée. 2013. "Religiosidades indoamericanas y circuitos de espiritualidad New Age." In *Variaciones y apropiaciones Latinoamericanas del New Age*, coordinated by Renée de la Torre, Cristina Gutiérrez Zúñiga and Nahayeilly Juárez Huet, 25–46. Mexico: CIESAS.
De la Torre, Renée and Cristina Gutiérrez Zúñiga. 2005. "La lógica del mercado y la lógica de la creencia en la creación de mercancías simbólicas." *Desacatos* 18: 53–70.
De la Torre, Renée and Cristina Gutiérrez Zúñiga. 2011. "La neomexicanidad y los circuitos New Age: ¿un hibridismo sin fronteras o múltiples estrategias de síntesis espiritual?" *Archives des Sciences Sociales de Religión* 153: 183–206.
De la Torre, Renée and Cristina Gutiérrez Zúñiga. 2016. "El temazcal: un ritual prehispánico transculturalizado por redes alternativas espirituales." *Ciencias Sociales y Religión/Ciências Sociais e Religião* 18(24): 153–172.
De la Torre, Renée, Cristina Gutiérrez and Nahayeilli Juárez Huet (eds). 2016. *New Age in Latin America: Popular Variations and Ethnic Appropriations*. Leiden: Brill.
Durkheim, Emile. [1987] 1999. *El suicidio*. México: Ediciones Coyoacán.
Ehécatl. 2012. Interview by Renée de la Torre and Cristina Gutiérrez, October 1.
Fahramand, Manéli. 2016. "Glocalization and Transnationalization in (neo)-Mayanization Processes: Ethnographic Case Studies from México and Guatemala", *Religions* 7(17): 1–19.
Fedele, Anna and Knibbe, Kim E. 2013. "Introduction: Gender and power in contemporary spirituality." In *Gender and Power in Contemporary Spirituality*, edited by Anna Fedele and Kim E. Knibbe, 1–27. New York: Routledge.
Fedele, Anna. 2013. *Looking for Mary Magdalene: Alternative Pilgrimage and Ritual Creativity at Catholic Shrines in France*. Oxford: Oxford University Press.
Ferguson, Marilyn. 1981. *The Aquarian Conspiracy: Personal and Social Transformation in the 1980s*. London: Routledge & Kegan.
Galinier, Jacques and Antoinette Molinié. 2013. *The Neo-Indians: A Religion for the Third Millenium*. Boulder: University Press of Colorado.
García Medina, Jesús. 2010. "De GFU a MAIS: La recuperación de la sabiduría ancestral indígena y la Nueva Era en Guadalajara 1967–2002." Master's thesis, CUCSH, Universidad de Guadalajara.
García Medina, Jesús and Cristina Gutiérrez Zúñiga. 2012. "La indianización de la nueva era en Guadalajara." *Cuicuilco* 19(55): 219–244.
Goicolea, Irene. 2002. "Regina en el país vasco." In *Regina y el movimiento del 68: Treinta y tres años después*, edited by Pablo Rulfo. Madrid: EDAF.
González Torres, Yolotl. 2005. *Danza tu palabra: La danza de los concheros*. Mexico: CONACULTA-INAH-Plaza y Valdéz.
Güemes, Odena. 1984. *Movimiento confederado restaurador de la cultura del Anáhuac*. Mexico: Cuadernos de la Casa Chata-CIESAS.
Gutiérrez Zúñiga, Cristina. 2008. "La danza neotradicional como oferta espiritual en la estantería exotérica new age." In *Raíces en movimiento: Prácticas religiosas tradicionales en contextos translocales*, edited by Kali Argyriadis, 363–392. Mexico: COLJAL-CEMCA-IRD-CIESAS-ITESO.

Gutiérrez Zúñiga, Cristina. 2015. "Gran Fraternidad Universal." In *Encyclopedia of Latin American Religions*, edited by Henri P. Gooren, 1–5. Cham: Springer International Publishing. doi:10.1007/978-3-319-08956-0_3.

Heelas, Paul. 1996. *The New Age Movement: The Celebration of the Self and the Sacralization of Modernity*. Oxford: Blackwe.

Heelas, Paul. 2008. *Spiritualities of Life: Romantic Themes and Consumptive Capitalism*. Oxford: Wiley-Blackwell.

Ibarra, Ricardo. 2002. "Entre el cielo y la tierra, la danza tradicional Mexicana." *Gaceta Universitaria*, 12: 14–15.

Lagarde, Marcela. 1997. *La política de las mujeres*. Madrid: Cátedra.

Lamas, Marta. 1986. "La antropología feminista y la categoría de género." *Nueva Antropología*, VIII: 173–198.

McGuire, Meredith. 2008. *Lived Religion: Faith and Practice in Everyday Life*. Oxford: Oxford University Press.

Pike, Sarah. 2001. *Earthly Bodies, Magical Selves: Contemporary Pagans and the Search of Community*. Berkeley: University of California Press.

PRD. 1994. Interview by Cristina Gutierrez Zúñiga, June.

PRD. 2002. Interview by Ricardo Ibarra.

PRD. 2005. Interview by Renée de la Torre, September.

Ramírez, Rosario. 2017. "Lo femenino resignificado: discursos y concepciones de lo femenino desde los círculos de mujeres." PhD diss., Universidad Autónoma de México Iztapalapa,

Ramírez, Rosario. 2018. "Expresiones femeninas de la Nueva Era: Los círculos de mujeres en México." In *Entre trópicos: Diálogos de estudios sobre Nueva Era entre México y Brasil*, edited by C. Steil, R. De la Torre and R. y Toniol, 243–267. Ciudad de México: CIESAS/COLSAN.

Ramírez, Rosario. 2019. "Espiritualidades femeninas: el caso de los círculos de mujeres." *Encartes: Revista digital multimedia*, 11(3), 144–162. Available at: https://ia801406.us.archive.org/16/items/encartesvol2num3/06-ramirez.pdf

Ríos Duggan, Patricia. 2002. "¿Qué significa para mí Regina?" In *Regina y el movimiento del 68: Treinta y tres años después*, edited by Pablo Rulfo, 89–104. Madrid: EDAF.

Salomonsen, Jone. 2002. *Enchanted Feminism: Ritual, Gender and Divinity among the Reclaiming Witches of San Francisco*. London: Routledge.

Simmer-Brown, Judith. 2002. *Dakini's Warm Breath: The Feminine Principle in Tibetan Buddhism*. Boulder: Shamblhala Publications Inc.

Solís Gil, Ana Luisa. 2003. "Regina y lo amoroso femenino por el despertar de la conciencia." In *Regina y el movimiento del 68: Treinta y tres años después*, edited by Pablo Rulfo, 57–72. Madrid: EDAF.

Velasco Piña, Antonio. 1987. *Regina: 68 no se olvida*. Mexico: Jus.

Velasco Piña, Antonio. 1993. *Cartas a Elizabeth*. México: Grijalbo-Círculocuadrado.

Velasco Piña, Antonio. 2008. Conference in presentation of his book *El retorno de lo sagrado*, 17 May.

Velasco Piña, Antonio. 2008. Interview by Renée de la Torre, May 17.

5 The (b)earth of a gendered eco-spirituality

Globally connected ethnographies between Mexico and the European Alps

Irene Becci, Manéli Farahmand and Alexandre Grandjean

Introduction

Within the field of research on contemporary spirituality various authors (Fedele and Knibbe 2013) have pointed out that although a certain discourse about the primacy and autonomy of the self predominates, social power dynamics still operate. Most of them are reproducing a certain gender order. Such findings were particularly insightful as they stressed the importance of including ethnographic approaches and contextualizing the discourses held. Observing and following spiritual practices leads one indeed to question a number of theoretically erected boundaries, such as the one between the secular and religion. When contemporary spiritualities deal with realms that are socially located as secular such as health or ecology, their study is particularly interesting. This is the case for the various practices we observed in very different sites such as in Maya revival networks in Yucatán, among Swiss ecospiritual movements claiming an "inner transition" and in an eco-esoteric community in Piedmont, Italy. Although these three sites we shall draw on in this chapter are very distant geographically, as well as in their size and configuration, we have chosen to discuss them side by side as they are globally interconnected by the circulation of actors and media. In that sense, they participate in a global framing of "spirituality" understood as part of a global ecological commitment, being "questing" or "counter-cultural" (Woodhead 2013), as they are aiming to change dominant gender relationships. Nevertheless, quite a few differences distinguish them, in particular with regard to their national political contexts and their positioning vis-à-vis "secular feminist agendas".

In all three sites, environmentalist or ecological concerns are linked with religious, (including spiritual and esoteric) views, approaches, practices or symbols, thereby challenging a certain secular view of ecology as mainly a technical subject. Moreover, this integration of religion and ecology also questions the dominant gender order. Indeed, through ritual actions linked to nature or cultural cosmological references to the earth, essentialized ideas about gender and the supposed values attached to it are emphasized. In each setting, notions and metaphors such as a "sacred feminine" (Fedele 2013) or the articulation of a gender polarity as a key to "harmonization" of, and "unification" with, nature were present in an idealized and smoothed form. Such idealizations of relationships are quite common among "New Age"[1] spiritualities, which join gender and ecological concerns (Frisk 2010). We contend that this influence of New Age inspiring languages and references at a global scale has a series of implications.

First of all, as Alejandro Frigerio (2013) and Jacques Galinier (2011) have thematized, New Age views nurture an ideological dimension of homogenization through images. Contrary to the narration line held by New Age discourses about the uniqueness of each individual combination, Frigerio has demonstrated that New Age hybridization is actually not infinite. Rather, it does not question power relationships but follows the dominant configuration. Moreover, by prioritizing the quest of an aesthetic harmony, it effects a "symbolical purification" as Jacques Galinier has demonstrated for the case of neo-Indian movements in Mexico (Galinier 2011, 32). Starting from these observations and reflections, we explore the question of whether these two processes also neutralize the subversive potential of the gender-challenging views in relation to ecology. We put the hypothesis forward that a global influence of New Age views is slowly making its way through the action of figures mediating between ecological activism and contemporary forms of spirituality, thereby putting a gloss on the dominant configurations of gender and power.

It is important to note that the three sites are situated in different contexts with regard to their level of insertion in New Age networks, as well as to secularization, politicization, and with respect to Western secular feminist agendas. We shall situate them only very briefly here. For our analysis it is helpful to mobilize Linda Woodhead's model on gender and power (2013) to conceive how these uses of a *gendered spiritual ecology* are fulfilling different strategies either to "confirm" or "challenge" gender roles in relation to their social location (mainstream/marginal). In this chapter, we shall explore how an essentialization of gender operates strategically within a transnational "spiritual" sub-culture, and ecological and feminist concerns are articulated varyingly whether they refer to the "secular" in Mexico (Yucatán), in the French-speaking part of Switzerland, or in Piedmont. These insights are based on the fieldwork of the respective authors, who have in some cases conducted cross-fieldwork.[2]

Below, we will first offer some conceptual clarifications of the different notions we use, such as gendered eco-spirituality and strategic gender essentialization, and then proceed to present the three sites we have studied ethnographically. In our Conclusion we discuss their similarities and differences.

Secular and spiritual ecology in global culture

Although ecology has started in the 1950s to be structured into an academic and therefore secular set of disciplines understood as "environmental sciences", as a wider concept it can be traced back to romantic criticism of industrialization and longing for "nature" as a wild, mysterious and "reenchanted" entity. This view of nature has had uninterrupted influence on contemporary spirituality movements

(Von Stuckrad 2002). However, the success of James Lovelock's (1972) metaphor known as the "Gaia hypothesis" is seemingly the turning point, enabling naturalistic ecological and holistic religious representations such as pantheism to encounter each other and form ecospiritual worldviews that came to be inserted into global New Age networks (Taylor 2010). At the same time, globalization has boosted the integration of transnational matters such as ecology, peace or women's rights in religious[3] discourses (Saint-Blancat 2001). It is the confluence of all these factors that has geared the emergence of global gendered eco-spiritual discourses. Despite their apparent similarity across various contexts, in practice they imply actually very different relations to a gendered social order. We therefore need to contextualize them.

During the 1990s in Latin America, awareness of ecological problems has been progressively integrated into the struggles of indigenous movements for the protection of natural resources and demanding agrarian reforms (MacKenzie 2017). For instance, in Mexico the Zapatista movement has mobilized pre-Hispanic myths in their political struggles (Bastos et al. 2013). The world-view conveyed by these myths rests primarily upon the notion of harmony with nature and the cosmos, complementarity between sexes and a certain approach to time employing cyclic calendars (Bastos and Cumes 2007). With the progressive diffusion of New Age in Latin America, we witness, near the end of the twentieth century, a reconfiguration of these identity movements. Anthropologists observe the development of groups in quest of "indigeneity" through a so-called New Age spirituality. These urban movements, mainly mixed-race, are supported by an idealized reinterpretation of the past and of millenarian representations. They call to return to a spirituality of the earth by restoring the indigenous cultures, considered to be the epicentre of a "new age", the age of *Quinto Sol* (De la Torre and Gutiérrez Zúñiga 2011, 2013; De la Peña 1999, 2001; Galinier and Molinié 2006).

In the European and Northern American contexts, ecological and environmental activism has been organized in two strands since the 1960s: a secular one and a religious one. The secular strand has been developed by a scientific transdisciplinary field of research and by Marxist and Third World critiques notably marked by *social and environmental justice* or anti-nuclear rationales. Religious institutions were rather absent from ecological debates during the institutionalization of environmental sciences. The hegemony of secular environmentalism was such that when, in 1967, historian Lynn White addressed an American Association for the Advancement of Science (AAAS) meeting with a radical critique of monotheistic traditions as the "matrix" of Western so-called "anthropocentric" culture at large, it created tidal waves of different reactions in the academic and religious spheres: either normatively trying to prove or reject Lynn White's thesis, or operating a "greening" of each world religion by enhancing specific textual and exegetic traditions (Berry 2003). Lynn White's hypothesis, as noted by Bron Taylor, fostered debates on religion and ecology, though former religious ecological critiques were silenced or elapsed (Taylor 2016). In the 1970s, religious – mainly Christian actors and arguments – reappeared in new forms within these ecological movements (Jenkins 2011; Deane-Drummond 2008). Meanwhile, counter-cultural spiritualities such as Neoshamanism, Neopaganism and cultural ecofeminism have structured their practices and beliefs around the central and sacralized figure of "nature" (Merchant 1980; Bloch 1998; Pike 2001; Taylor 2010).

Strikingly, in recent years, within both cultural contexts a certain notion of "spirituality" has come to blur the cultural divide between secularity and religion, especially through the notion of a *gendered ecology*. The conceptualization of the notion of contemporary spirituality contains, as Boaz Huss points out, a Christian Western European origin. In the second half of the twentieth century with the New Age appropriations of the term, "spirituality" has become a "new emergent cultural category" connected with the development of a neo-liberal ideology (Huss 2014). For Huss, this new semantic, shared by urbanized, upper- and middle-class people looking for inner fulfilment, intuitive and non-rational experiences, breaks with the earlier Christian view considering the spiritual world as opposed to the material one.

One could argue that since the 1970s "spirituality" has been integrated into secularity, focusing on the centrality of *body–mind–spirit* connection and promoting secular aims (social integration, professional success). With regard to the modern opposition between religion and the secular, "spirituality" is a new component transcending the historical dichotomy by integrating the two poles (the religious and the secular). This culturalist approach implies the acknowledgement that there are variations depending on the cultural and political context. The cultural turn valorizing authenticity, and a therapeutic religious experience (Rieff 1966) impacts on the way spirituality is seen with regard to religion. The distinction is not made according to clear and definite contents, as for instance doctrine versus subjectivity. As a matter of fact, as Nancy Ammerman's study has shown (Ammerman 2013), one and the same person can have different discourses about spirituality. The distinction is performative; that is, qualifying a practice or discourse as spiritual rather than religious means building up boundaries between a desirable and undesirable way to relate to ultimate questions.

In the following we articulate three sites we have studied ethnographically in order to show three different contexts where the notions of spirituality, religion, the secular and gender relate to each other in different ways. First, we will foreground the study of Maya revival movements in south-eastern Mexico. In a complementary perspective, two other sites situated around the two sides of the Alps will follow: the eco-esoteric community of "Damanhur" in northern Italy and the ecospirituality and "inner transition" movements in French-speaking Switzerland. A feature shared by all three sites – forming the basis of our analysis – is a form of social action that is gendered, spiritual and ecological at the same time but which does not connect to any historical feminist agenda, although not necessarily for the same contextual reasons. Moreover, all sites are connected to each other: the ecological activists in Switzerland refer to a supposedly Amerindian indigenous knowledge, and they also know and visit such places as Damanhur, which partly become a reference point for them.

Healing Mother Earth, healing the feminine: feminizing ecology within Maya revival networks of Mexico

In Mexico, "neo-Indians"[4] appeared in the public space following a celebration of the fifth centenary of the colonization in 1992, which unleashed disagreements all around Latin America. In neo-Indian ritual dedications to "Mother Earth", images and symbols play a major role. Thereby terrifying images of earth, a pre-Hispanic entity, devouring, monstrous and chthonic, demanding blood, sperm and other substances, are concealed and dissolved in those New Age aesthetics. These filtered images contribute to the creation of "aseptic cultural fictions" (Galinier 2011, 32), in agreement with the ideal of harmony which these movements seek. The role of world-view in indigenous movements is particularly important within women's movements in Mexico (Macleod 2011; Camus 2001; Sieder and Macleod 2009; Palencia and Patal 2003). For Morna Macleod, Maya world-views are a place of resistance, protest and redefinition of gender relations, a resource in women struggles for equity and emancipation (Macleod 2011). Yet today, more and more Mexican women, organized in networks of holistic practices, in particular therapeutic ones, are integrating neo-Indian images inspired by New Age and globalized neo-pagan spiritualities.

This is the case in south-east Mexico, in particular in Mérida (Yucatán). Women, mixed-race and Westerners dominate the holistic scene of Yucatán. Generally upper middle class, over forty and having pursued a higher education, mainly in applied or social psychology, they situate themselves in an "empowerment" dynamic and are simultaneously therapists, ceremony leaders and practitioners. Alongside their therapeutic-spiritual practices, most of them work in the field of social work and care.

In this region, inhabited by a considerable number of Mayas (Güemez Pineda, 2004), a spiritual subculture with a New Age sensibility has developed into a *Cultic milieu*, to use Colin Campbell's expression (2002), with more and more activities aiming at "healing" (yoga, tai-chi, reiki, meditation, tarot, massages, mediumship, Maya Kung Fu, Maya Yoga and even Maya osteopathy). Most of the techniques spread out from Mexico City, the progressive capital, offering a number of civil rights to gay people, towards the rest of Mexico where a secularized form of Catholicism has an important influence on issues relating to family and couples (Blancarte 2013, 137). This is especially true in Yucatán,[5] which is considered one of the states with the most conservative values and highest levels of violence (sexual and domestic) towards women.[6] Interestingly, its public space is flooded with holistic flyers, brochures and posters. Mystic tourism linked to the "2012 phenomenon"[7] (the end-of-the-world prognosis) between 1990 and 2010 contributed to the rise of this cultic milieu, despite the hostile context. In most cases, people interviewed said they felt, in the beginning, part of a very critical environment. They declare having suffered humiliation, both in family and work environments. They were forced to take a step back from hegemonic institutions in order to become independent neo-Mayas therapists, saying that evangelicals and Catholics stigmatize their holistic practices, considering them as deviant, sometimes demonical.

Among them, the majority of the women interviewed said they had to defy forms of patriarchal domination or had to negotiate with them to actually practise their spirituality. The women practising holistic-indigenous spiritualities are subjected to various forms of religious and social oppressions. They now move along this pre-established holistic local subculture where gender issues are at the crossroads of Maya pre-Hispanic values and the New Age topic of the "sacred feminine".

In Mexico, "women's movements" and "feminist movements", fighting against patriarchy and sexism, developed in the twentieth century (Masson 2009). Sabine Masson argues that the complexity of this issue in Mexico is particularly linked to divergent agendas: on the one hand, that of a feminism aiming at building a "radical otherness in relation to the patriarchy" and, on the other, the agenda of a women's movements aiming for a "policy of equality seeking their integration" (Masson 2009, 301). The claims are particularly linked to abortion rights, penalties and the fight against violence towards women (Masson 2009, 301).[8] Although several works have been dedicated to Mexican women and feminist movements, very few have considered women's actions within religious organizations and still fewer within holistic New Age networks. In those circles, the relation between women and ecology is a central issue. The way of connecting them is based on emancipatory discourses and syncretic references. We will see that they perform a particular idea of "femininity", in interaction with the so-called metaphor of "Mother Earth". They react to different social institutions, particularly medical and religious ones, and support gender equity through the use of spiritual/religious references. For them Mother Earth is a performative metaphor – an effect of a specific episteme.

When arriving at one holistic centre in Mérida (Yucatán) which is part of a Maya revival movement one can read the following message:

Que tu energía feminina sea honrada dignificada protegida, cuidada y respectada.
May your female energy be honoured, dignified, protected, cared for and respected.

Thirty-one-year-old MR is the director of this holistic centre. When interviewed, she, like other Mexican women of the healers' network, confided they had difficult lives behind them since they had been victims of sexual and domestic violence. The centre aims to provide psycho-spiritual support, courses in yoga, dance therapy, space for traditional midwives to practise, a rereading of the Maya Yucatec world-view, Mexica (Aztec) therapies, and other world cultures practices, such as qi gong.

Descending from a Maya grandfather, MR grew up in an urban context, in a family of Jehovah's Witnesses, with whom she says to have totally broken off to follow Maya elders. She comes from the Mexican middle class and graduated from higher education in applied social psychology. Yucatán has a close link with the history of women's movements in Mexico. In 1916, after the military phase of the Mexican Revolution, the first national feminist congress was held in this region, and it has strongly contributed to the women's right to vote at a national scale in 1953 (Labrecque 1987). But MR is critical of Yucatán mixed-race and Western varieties of feminisms. She considers them elitist, ethnocentric and conflict-ridden, and prefers the Maya world-view principles of duality, balance and complementarity.[9]

On 21 December 2014, a Maya ceremony honoured the winter solstice through the "reconnection with four elements and four directions". The ritual was organized by elders of the Maya Council of Mexico at Maria's holistic centre. MR is the first female member of this council, since men historically dominate this council.[10] The elders inaugurated the ceremony by playing their pre-Hispanic instruments. During the ritual, MR looked erased, passive. She never spoke up and was never invited to stand in the same row as the elders. Afterward, when questioned about this, she evoked the Maya notion of *complementarity*:

> They explained to me that in a ceremony, the women do all this work because their energy comes from the Earth, while for the men, their energy comes from the sun, but neither is worth more than the other. They are different, but they are not unequal. So I wondered to myself, "Let's see. I'd like to know more about this. What is going on?" And so, they told me what is so important: the Earth, water, fire, air. We cannot say that one is worth more than the others, but there is a clear difference in each of these elements.[11]

In this differentialist approach, women are assigned work connected with the Earth that is passive, internal, spiritual and invisible. Men, on the other hand, assume a more active and visible "material role" with fire, which is a symbol of the sky. This reading in terms of natural polarity structuring gendered positions during the ritual does not bring a radical transformation of power structuration within the Maya council of Mexico and in Mexico in general. Even if the complementarity legitimized, in practice, the invisibilization of women, they recapture symbolic power in the field of religiosity with the idea of a deep and special connection with Mother Earth. Therefore, if there is no revolution, there is a subtle change within the established gender order. In MR's case, gender structures organize her interpretation of the Maya ritual. The next interview's sequence illustrates this representation, underlying this privileged relationship between women and the Earth:

> [Talking about recapturing her lost femininity] So I was more involved in work with the Earth and the plants [...]. And I had to take off my shoes and sink my feet into the Earth to feel it – and what I felt all over again was my feminine side from the Earth. It takes care of you, it covers you, it is warm. And then I began to observe how it does everything for plants. And so how the Earth – how energy comes from the sun – the Earth doesn't fight with the sun! But it changes, it transforms everything. So I

said to myself, "Okay, I'm not going to fight." That's how it is with the Earth. And with the plants, too.

She then declared that this was the time when she decided to break up with the Mexican women's movement and the struggle for overthrowing power structure. This pattern, where mixed-race Mexican women, currently active in the field of holistic spiritualities, decide to break away from the narratives of second-wave feminists because of their radical anti-patriarchal vision aiming to make profound changes, is recurrent in the interviews given. Women prefer to incorporate a discourse of gender equality in complementarity, meaning a differentialist vision of gender roles integrated in a feminist spiritualized discourse ("women have to find their place at an energetic level").[12]

In this interview sequence with MR, a therapeutic dimension in the ecological relationship is added in a "care" relation between women and the Earth. This reinforces the idea of women's privileged status with Earth, a spiritualized element described in the language of "energies". This idealized and privileged relationship contrasts with the classic representation of earth in Mexico, and especially in the Mexica traditions, where the goddess Nahua Coatlicue, associated with the Earth, with life and death, revival and fertility, mother of seasons and agriculture, is represented as a hideous-looking female figure, a monster with a huge head covered in scales, two rounds, deep-set eyes, and a mouth with four large fangs and a forked tongue (Taube and Miller 1993). In both cases, we observe a connection between "woman and earth". However, the classic representation of Earth emphasizes monstrosity, whereas the neo-Mayas narratives emphasize a more romantic and positive association between women and Earth, throwing out death and destruction. This sends us back to the ideological dimension of New Age and the role of image manipulation in the process of homogenization of indigenous spiritualities (Galinier 2011). This idea of harmony also contrasts with the history of the relations with Earth and natural resources in Mexico, a source of conflicts since colonization.

The symbolic appropriation of the Mother Earth image by Mexican women here has the emic function of helping to "find one's *lost* femininity" since the Spanish invasion. Reconsidering the relationship to Mother Earth in terms of the masculine/feminine duality is a response to *machismo* within Mexican society and to the traditional, dominant structures of Catholic institutions in the Yucatán. In this perspective, the vision behind this symbolic appropriation joins indigenous Latin American's women trend considering that sexism and patriarchy are external phenomena, products of colonization, and that the only way to overcome them will be the appropriation of endogenous heritage in a decolonizing perspective (Masson 2009, 313).

To sum up, in this site, re-imagining gender among women in the cultic milieu of Yucatán is informed by a religious and social critique; self-actualization and the search for one's authentic self in connection with Mother Earth are prioritized. Christianity is considered responsible for the current catastrophic situation of women's inequality. Finally, the notion of religion is rejected in favour of the notion of spirituality, eliminating the need for inter-mediaries to come into contact with the sacred. This is in line with what Anna Fedele finds in her research on alternative pilgrimages and the Goddess movement in Europe (Fedele 2013), termed feminist spiritualities.

Gendering ecology, practising spirituality north and south of the Alps

The forms of spirituality practised in Mexico as we just described display a simi-larity with what we found in two sites in Switzerland and Italy, just north and south of the Alps: the practice of gendering *ecology* through a differentiation which does not imply an *essentialized* self but "principles" and "energies" everyone is assumed to carry within themselves. However, the differences with regard to the social and political contexts, as well as to the social locations of the actors claiming this *gen-dered spiritual ecology*, have to be taken into account for an analysis of the *power structuration* at work in these different sites (Becci et al. 2015). We shall start with the "inner transition" movements in French-speaking Switzerland as they present salient connection points to the Mexican site. Finally, the presentation of the eco-esoteric community of Damanhur will bring a different insight into the "New Age" circulation of gendered values.

"Inner transition" movements in French-speaking Switzerland (Romandie) and the promotion of a gendered spiritual ecology

In 2014 we started to follow grassroots ecological activists in urban Romandie – a region of Switzerland marked historically by Protestant Christianity but having institutionally different regimes of churches and state relations – who were con-structing a network around a narrative in favour of an "inner transition". Their ideas were inspired by Rob Hopkins' *Transition Towns* (started in 2006) and by the *Colibri movement*, launched by the French agroecologist Pierre Rabhi (also in 2006). With the notion of "inner transition" they reunite two usually well-separated views on ecology: a religiously connoted ecospirituality and a rather secular ecopsychology (Macy 2008). The frontiers between these two views are blurred precisely through the use of the term "spirituality" as a new cultural category (Huss 2014). In these movements structured and federated by several associations and faith-based NGO hubs, the necessity that everyone undertakes a process of self-evaluation of one's deep (inner) beliefs in order to reconnect to "nature" is emphasized. This "inner transition" is supposed to enable individuals to reconsider their values and then engage more efficiently into collective actions oriented toward what some call a "change of paradigm" (Egger 2017, 12) or the "Great Turning" (Macy 2008, 24).

When these movements started spreading in French-speaking Switzerland around 2012, the main spokespersons making reference to "inner transition" and "ecopsychology" were men. However, in the last two years, several women have become speakers of these "inner transition" movements, adding an emphasis on the sacredness of the feminine with regard to what they refer to as an indigenous framework. A case in point is Marianne Grasseli Meier, a speaker we followed for a while in local circles of ecospirituality, who has been active as a music therapist and has become an inspirational writer and ritual master in her retirement. In her latest book she calls women the "guardians of the Earth" (2018) in a way that is similar to what we described above for the Mexican site. Since the network is not homogeneous, we shall concentrate on one of the key speakers of this discourse about "inner transition" in Switzerland, Michel Egger, comparing him with Marianne Grasseli Meier.

Michel Egger, an energetic man in his late fifties, was educated as a sociologist and a journalist and converted to Orthodox Christianity as an adult. After working for 15 years as a political lobbyist for a faith-based NGO, he gained recognition in the environmental milieu through publishing three books, the first one specifically on ecospirituality and the subsequent two on ecopsychology (2012, 2016, 2017). These two notions both imply a transformational approach to the ecological "selves", notably through numerous rituals inspired by Joana Macy's "work that reconnects" (2008). Interestingly, Michel Egger has not abandoned one notion for the other; he rather situationally mentions ecospirituality or ecopsychology in his speeches. Depending on his audience, he either frames his approach as being inserted in a religious or in a more secular realm. When questioned about this oscillation he told us: "I do not have the impression to betray my cause while trying to meet the 'other' where he stands, and speaking a language he can therefore understand."

He is also known as a zealous promoter of "inner transition" approaches in festivals and conferences. Indeed, he was commissioned in 2016 to constitute a Laboratory for Inner Transition by a Protestant faith-based NGO, Pain pour le prochain. With this institutional status, his work is eventually to promote within associations, NGOs, corporations and public services what he calls the *path of the meditating-militants*, an integrative approach mixing up alter-globalization militancy as well as rituals inspired by religious and spiritual rationales (body and eye contact, visualization exercises, theological exegesis, etc.). Being in the "holistic field" as well as within the boundaries of a more institutional religiosity, Egger conveys a "toolkit" to quote him, hence aiming at a "change of paradigm" which is supposed to "change the system" externally.

Within this network, we have followed and recorded for about two years various public conferences, publications and have conducted a series of formal and informal interviews with Egger. It is mainly in his writings that a *gendered spiritual ecology* is explicitly presented. His first book, *La Terre comme soi-même* (2012), depicts the necessity of an "inner change" through Christian resources and theologies. He claims that "inner change" cannot operate unless human beings accept that "inner attitudes correspond, in fact, with essential qualities that are part of the feminine within" (our translation, 2012, 273). Largely drawing on gender stereotypes, in his texts attitudes such as "welcoming", "intuition", "cooperation", "understanding", "concreteness" and "deductive skills" are associated with feminine values. These values are to be enhanced as they are according to him an "antidote" that enables a positive balance with masculine values such as "competition", "analytic intelligence", "abstract rationality", "domination" and a "spirit of conquest" (2012, 273).

Still, according to Egger's writings these gendered values are to be found both in men and women.[13] Following his theological interpretation and biblical exegesis, God created men and women in its image (Gn 1.27). In his theological synthesis, Creation and "inner transition", "misericord" – the act of mercy – are conceived as the "other feminine face of God, the motherhood dimension of the Father" (2012, 269). References to oriental notions also appear in Egger's work. This is for us a second indication that his endeavour is also a mediation work between religious tradition and new forms of spirituality. For him, "To live fully, is to enter the dance and the everlasting interpenetration of masculine and feminine, of yin and yang" (2012, 273, our translation). He maintains this idea of a "gender polarity" in his further books centred on ecopsychology (2017, 45) as well as on his website.[14]

Interestingly, though Egger is not framing and addressing his books and conferences solely to women as in Marianne Grasseli Meier's case (2018, 18), they both share common references to emblematic French-speaking and Anglo-Saxon authors active in the field of "inner transition" and contemporary spirituality such as Starhawk and Joana Macy. In both sites the feminine and the masculine are perceived as "principles" or "energies" one has within. This is a common feature found along "New Age" global views. Yet, how are these views enacted by different social actors? In Egger's case, we wonder whether this discourse aims at *neutralizing* the gender issue in a "tactical" sense (see Woodhead 2013) as these principles are not necessarily framed in the narrative of a "lost femininity". As a writer and inventor of ecospiritual rituals in her early sixties, Marianne Grasseli Meier gets her inspiration both from Michel Egger and from what she calls Amerindian traditions, and addresses women directly (2018). She builds her teachings on her personal biographical experience which is composed of a migratory background, family separations and urban life but which in her narrative never refers specifically to the feminist struggles that took place in her city. She considers that in a feminist perspective, women are warriors while for her, they should rather be guardians. For her, ecospirituality turns into a more cultural ecofeminism either "questing" or being "counter-cultural" with regard to mainstream gender claims about abortion or equal civil rights. Having said this, the two figures are, as in the Mexican site, not intersecting with secular and so-called emancipatory feminist agenda and ways of struggling such as street demonstration, political lobbying, academic symposium, legal battles, etc. (Becci and Grandjean 2018).

Gender polarity in an eco-esoteric community in Piedmont

In Piedmont, only about 40 kilometres north of Turin, a community considered by some as an eco-village or by others an esoteric or a New Age "inspirational community", has reunited hundreds of members since the 1980s around one spiritual utopia (Palmisano and Pannofino 2014) which revolves around the reintegration of the pieces of a primordial androgynous being. Within the larger frame of a culturally Catholic country, Turin is known for being also among the most religiously pluralist cities in Italy (Berzano 1997). Founded in 1975 by a former salesman, Oberto Airaudi and other members of the esoteric circle he had animated in Turin called Horus, Damanhur is organized as a federation of communities and regions, has its own currency and is strongly present in local political life (Stanley 2000; Cardano 2015; Zoccatelli 2016). In the 1970s, the founders – all Italians from a middle-class background – bought some land in this rather remote mountainous area where some industries had shut down, spurring emigration, to exercise more freely their activities such as agriculture, the construction of instruments to make music with plants, develop alternative medical practices, hold parapsychological meetings, and so on.

We shall here concentrate only on what relates to ecology and gender in this site. Damanhur is known as an eco-village because of practices and actions supporting bio-diversity, recycling, sustainable production of energy (solar), ecologically sustainable construction and maintenance modes of the buildings based on local resources (including the recycling of the water used in the toilets), and because of the members' sacralizing relation to nature (e.g. communication with trees and plants) (Cardano 1997). Visitors come from all over the world to spend some time here, visit the sacred woods or the temple, among them also Michel Egger, one key figure in the Swiss ecospiritual network. Damanhurians base their cosmological beliefs, among other aspects, on a dualistic split between the feminine and the masculine. According to their creation myth, these two forces have emerged from the mythical primal being which was androgynous and represented perfection. These "feminine" and "masculine" essences or forces can, for Damanhurians, be variably present within men and women. Because of this utopian view of gender relations, Damanhur appeared as a place where women had an emancipated role to play (Introvigne 1996). Equality between men and women was affirmed and women's authority encouraged in some respects, such as women placed at the head of the domestic units – ironically still confirming a gendered division of labour. For some members, the argument of gender equality was a strong motivating factor for joining (Cardano 2015, 183).

The rules and thinking within the community have varied across time and seem to become fluid when observing the members' practices. Ecological concerns co-exist unquestioned with the practice of using vans to accompany visitors around the area or the consumption of meat based on the idea that plants have the same value as animals and all reincarnate anyway. The community's principles that rule daily life depend on the knowledge shared by members, according to their internal organizational order given by a series of initiations.

One of the aspects that especially attracts public attention is an underground temple which remained secret until 1992.[15] This structure is called the "Temple of Humankind" and is composed of seven halls connected by 150 metres of corridors. Figurative creativity is highly valued within the community and seen as one way through which spirituality develops, following the example of the leader, who is also celebrated as a painter and writer. Each hall has been attributed a specific function. On the community's website, one can find the description of the halls of the temple. We will concentrate on the hall called "The Hall of Water":

> Dedicated to the feminine principle and the female divine forces, this hall has the shape of a chalice, a symbol of receptivity and welcoming ... This Hall is available for meditations on the life cycles, in preparation for childbirth, to reawaken profound memories, and to enter into contact with one's feminine essence. Because of its extraordinary acoustics, it is an ideal place for singing and composing music.[16]

The knowledge about the temple and some of the founder's teachings are still enveloped in an aura of secrecy. As Georg Simmel wrote, "secrecy secures ... the possibility of a second world alongside the obvious world, and the latter is most strenuously affected by the former. Every relationship between two individuals or two groups will be characterized by the ratio of secrecy that is involved in it" (1906, 462). When we entered into contact with Damanhurians we clearly experienced that we were outsiders to the secrecy surrounding the temple and the founder's teachings. When we visited the temple the answers to our questions were often vague or allusive. Practically all paintings and representations were about men and women in stylized, idealized bodies. The answers seemed confusing to us, in particular because they did not seem to fit with the practices we observed. For instance, in one of the rooms, a huge woman is painted half naked, symbolizing what our guide called "The feminine inside of us". She went on saying that this "is the key for our battle for a better humanity – fighting with smiling, joy, optimistic vision".

In her discourse, the guide constantly stressed that the feminine and the masculine are "of course" not equivalent to men and women, but in all the paintings and statues, the masculine was represented by male bodies and the feminine was represented by female bodies, both in a physically idealized way. All the paintings portray these figures in a natural environment, surrounded by plants and animals, reflecting the analogies created between the human, animal and vegetable world through the renaming of the members when joining the community. When approaching the community as an interested person one meets an "apostle", a person assuming this function officially for the community. From what we could observe, it is mostly young women, who spoke Italian and English fluently, who took this role. It is also the women who are most visible on the community's website. Men were rather present when it came to giving lectures about the significance of rituals and Damanhurian doctrines. Also the way women and men were dressed seemed to us quite close to other populations outside of the community in the Piedmont region. Masculinity does not seem to be at stake physically, though this quest for unity and "reunification" between the masculine and the feminine is often thematized (Becci, et al. 2019). An illustration of the way in which a narrative of gender polarity is maintained is to be found in the only guesthouse present in the area of Damanhur, the Principe d'Oro, whose owners are members of the community. The history of the restaurant is told to the customers in a brochure and on the walls as the "Legend of the Golden Prince".[17] It tells the ambiguous narrative of a Golden Prince – probably the restaurant owner who is portrayed in the main room as an idealized medieval white knight – and of his "Dame" who had been kidnapped and went through a journey of metamorphosis to finally be "reunited on December 21st, 2012" and then "open their House to all Travelers and Pilgrims [...] to help them to become One whit [sic] any other Being. One with All Universe ...". Another example is the practice of labyrinths installed all over the site. In the "sacred grove", these labyrinths have different meanings according to what they are supposed to "activate", such as defending from insomnia or digestion troubles. One is particularly striking; it is the labyrinth of gender polarity. While crossing the lines is forbidden in every other labyrinth, in this one it is on the contrary recommended to do so in order to harmonize the masculine and the feminine within.

According to Damanhurians, because at the origin there was an androgynous being, the ideal to reach is to balance the feminine and the masculine within ourselves. The separation of the feminine and the masculine "would create the old story, the battle, we are in a time where the feminine principle is in balance with the masculine so and ... it's not men and women of course, it's the masculine inside of each one of us, it's the work to do inside of us. And the feminine can help us because the feminine can help us to produce this oneness", as one guide told us. In Damanhur, feminine and masculine are not located in different parts of the body, but "inside of each one of us" and there they have "to be in balance". When questioned about the values that these two poles represent, the answer is quite straightforward: "the feminine principle contains the following values: beauty, love, sweetness, container, order". Masculine values are "action, exploration, courage, will, movement". For Damanhurians, the masculine generates the universe, "from the masculine principle, from its belly comes the force of creation", while the woman in the paintings "is the container – she is also pregnant". The representations of pregnancy are very idealized, not alluding in any way to feminist concerns such as health and social issues linked to it.

As it is common for esoteric thinkers to build polar views opposing for instance spirit to matter, so Damanhurians "are always in the duality" which they unite/ bring together through metaphors such as: "two but one" (Runggaldier, E. 1996). Notions such as "diversity" and "plurality" are omnipresent in their rhetoric, linking up with secular discourses, but then seem to always be brought down to some form of polarity. Interestingly, in the world-view and esoteric teachings of this community, there is no such thing as Mother Earth. Rather the opposite, the Hall of the Earth, for instance, also part of the temple, is described as celebrating "our planet, nature, and the masculine principle, which is active and fertile".[18]

This discourse of openness and diversity clashes, however, with a practice of canalization: here the hall is said to remind the visitor of each person's "responsibility to preserve life and diversity, and to actively engage in promoting the sustainability of the earth". Moreover, the hall

> helps one to access the ancestral memory of our species, and it allows a
> profound contact with the element fire, with the forces of the earth, and

with the intelligence of the planet. It may also be used for dancing and contacting the body. Because of its acoustics, it is a beautiful space for playing music and singing.

While the planet is male in the room dedicated to earth, there is, however, also a feminized way to refer to it. According to Damanhurians, humans co-exist in a "spiritual ecosystem" with "forces" and various forms of "intelligence", which are physical and "subtle", living in different worlds they call the "Mother Worlds",[19] probably situated elsewhere than in or on our planet. The natural world serves here as an inspiration about how to look for ways to contact the forces in those other worlds. Interestingly, when it comes to plants, gender boundaries are crossed. For example, in the sacred woods Damanhurians particularly honour the oldest tree, an oak. Its name is Diamantel and in most languages used they refer to it as a "he", stating, however, that Diamantel is the matriarch (Palombo, 2017). In particular, this last example shows that the link to ecology can bring with it contradictions in the views on masculine and feminine.

Conclusion

To wrap up the insights we can gain from the joint study of these settings, we may say that the tendency to mobilize *naturalized* and *gendered* organic metaphors and gender values reflects a proximity to New Age views at a global scale (Frisk 2010). A worldwide spiritual subculture fosters, through transnational networks, images such as the "sacred feminine", the quest for a "lost femininity", the notion of "gender complementarity" and "harmony with nature", the latter being perceived as a feminine entity. Important differences do, however, exist between the settings.

The Mexican and the Swiss "inner transition" settings illustrate that the discourses and rites expressing a masculine/feminine complementarity essentialize gender differences. To consider the masculine and feminine to be essentially different, however, does not imply that men and women are considered to be essentially different. They both contain masculine and feminine values in varying amounts internally, but externally, in terms of their appearing conformity to mainstream gender roles, this does not lead to more gender-fluid expressions of identity. One interesting innovation in the community rules in Damanhur is, for instance, to view heterosexual couples as committed only for a limited time with the option to renew their commitment. Children grow within the units (nuclei) and their education is shared more widely than by their natural parents. During their teenage years they can even join a community of only teens where they learn independence. On the other hand, the division of labour within the community seemed quite conventional: women were dedicated to jobs of care and reproduction while men were occupied at production sites. In the light of these innovations, it is even more striking to see an oversimplification and essentialization of gender in the visual and creative work done at Damanhur. This essentialization seems to fix a social order that otherwise could be confusing.

The ethnographic study in Mexico illustrates, in contrast, that a gendered dualist perspective can become a strategy for rethinking, in harmonious terms on a broader scale, the power structures between gender and nature within what has been labelled "strategic essentialism" (Carlassare 2016; Hache 2016). To consider women as close to nature, is in this view no longer a weakness but a strength as nature itself is revalorized. The representation of what is called "nature", "Gaia" or "earth" is abstract and idealized as a harmonious, nurturing entity, needing care but also as a realm where feelings, sensitivity, sensoriality and representations of "authenticity" can be expressed and precisely "reclaimed".

In the three sites the gendered representation of the relation with natural elements (men with fire/women with earth) becomes what has been observed as a *strategic essentialism* (Becci and Grandjean 2018) through the integration of structural aspects. However, a number of elements distinguish the sites: while in Yucatán, the discourse surrounding Mother Earth seeks to reinterpret gender relationships by invoking the pre-Hispanic value of complementarity and the Earth acts as a performative metaphor for more harmonious and decolonized gender relations, in Switzerland and Piedmont, the visual and discursive essentialization of gender seems to counterbalance some of the gender challenging organizational and rhetorical innovations of the group. MR recognizes the authority of the elders and accepts the traditional order, but she searches to improve these structures from what we might call a spirituality of "quest", with reference to Linda Woodhead's typology (2013).

Through such strategic essentialism, a gendered representation of the relationship with natural elements aims at redefining power relations while distancing from surrounding feminist rhetorics (radical liberal, indigenous and mixed-race feminisms). Although MR's natural metaphors reify a binary conception of gender (masculine/feminine),[20] the eco-spiritualized rhetoric underlines a social critique and a critique of religion.

While the Mexican and Western European settings are linked by processes of transnationalization of New Age spiritualities, their reterritorialization implies socio-cultural differences. As we saw, in Mexico religion has a different place than in Western Europe, due to its interweaving with the political field. Our observations in Alpine Europe have shown that spirituality does not oppose the secular but integrates it through arts and ecology. In a social universe marked by postcolonial struggles and a strongly patriarchal Catholicism and Evangelicalism,[21] women's holistic neo-indigenous spiritualities take on a militant flavour. If feminist standpoints generally denounce religious production and culture as a factor of women's subordination and oppression, here, although a possible regulative use of gendered interpretation of rituals (strengthening stereotypes), the solstice ceremony is a space of negotiation of power relations at a symbolic level, even if in practice women had to remain silent and in the background during the ritual.

In the Western European regions, the observed practices remained far from the concrete struggles feminists have carried out. In that sense, we prefer to qualify the observed processes as *gendered spiritual ecology* since ecofeminism is not a category they claim for themselves. Ecofeminism is seen as the result of Western colonial secularism, whereby the emancipation of women can only occur outside of religion (cf. for instance Badinter 2003). In this sense, these ecological spiritual gendered practices and discourses question secularity as the ideal modern way of life without claiming a return to religion. Rather, through the notion of "spirituality", the road is opened for the construction of a new relation to secularity, ecology and religion at the same time. This innovation is not, however, accompanied by any emancipatory feminist agenda.

There is no doubt that in these settings an *essentialization* of gender roles and values is at work. However, they are not presented as essentialist: men and women as entities are not different by "nature" or "culture". We hence analyse this approach as a *neutralization* of gender that occurs at least in texts and discourses. Gender inequalities and power structuration are not being presented as an issue to struggle with or against. Neutralizing gender in a non-essentialist approach enacts the ideal of symmetrical gender relationships. The problematics related to binary gender representations have already been pointed out extensively by all the studies nurturing a queer approach. Our analysis simply intends to highlight some of these issues in a rarely studied field, the one emerging out of the combination of various religiously motivated actors in the frame of ecological activism.

Notes

1 In this text we use "New Age" as a "meaning matrix", a frame of "holistic reinterpretation" based on a specific millenarist world-view, involving the succession of a new era down here (see De la Torre and Gutiérrez Zuñiga, 2013).

2 Manéli Farahmand has conducted research in Mexico as part of her doctoral work (2012-2018) following a multi-sited ethnographic research approach (Marcus 1995). The observations and interviews made in Switzerland were part of the research project "Religion and Spirituality: The New Fuel to Energy Transition ?" (2015–2018), held by Irene Becci, Christophe Monnot and Alexandre Grandjean and funded by the Volteface program (University of Lausanne). All the authors have been involved in the Damanhur fieldwork. Irene Becci started with an exploratory fieldwork in 2016 and in June 2017 we all spent three days there together with a dozen students and colleagues as part of a pedagogical project on gender and new rituals funded by the University of Lausanne. A few months later, Alexandre Grandjean participated in a night long meditation in the Temple under the label of "Contact with the cosmos". We share a similar qualitative and ethnographic approach mobilizing interviews.

3 In this text we take the position of using "religious" or "religion" as an inclusive notion to refer also to the domain that in current common sense is considered as "spiritual" (see Wood 2010; Huss 2014).

4 Neo-Indianism is an urban phenomenon, which constructs a culture on the mirror handed by Westerners and a "symbolic appropriation of the past" (Molinié and Galinier 2006, 19).

5 According to the national census on belief and religious practices in Mexico, published by RIFREM – comparative analysis conducted in 2016 – contemporary religious changes strongly affect the south and southeast Pacific regions, including the region of this chapter (Yucatán) (Hernández, Gutiérrez Zuñiga and De La Torre 2017). The configuration of the Mexican southeast religious field from the end of the twentieth century

may be approached from the perspective of pluralization. This region knows a reduction in the percentage of self-identified Catholics, and a growth of Protestant evangelicals, Pentecostal churches and the category "no denomination".

6　Here data were collected through biographic open-ended "narrative interviews" (Bertaux and Kohli 1984).

7　That is, the end-of-the-world prognosis and messages about a supposedly Maya calendar which generated a number of important transnational events and alternative neo-Indian pilgrimages.

8　All translations from Spanish to English are by Manéli Farahmand.

9　According to Landy Santana Rivas (2003), in the pre-Hispanic Maya cosmology, supernatural entities, people, natural elements were a mix of masculine and feminine, there was a complementarity of opposite poles that constituted a cycle with the alternation of great forces of life, in dual unities (no life without death, no light without darkness) (Santana Rivas 2003, 49). In this dualist conception, gender identities move in an ever-changing continuity where the defining factor is the maintenance of balance. Some pictorial representations of the classic period suggest this complementary ideology where the differences of gender are based on the differences of actions and not on inherent biological characteristics. This representation was part of an elitist political construction, the complementary duality feminine/masculine, mother/father, was the language in which the Maya elites maintained control and reproduced power.

10　The Council is embodied by the Association Kuch kaab Yéetel J-Men Maaya'Ob (in Spanish: Consejo de Ancianos y Sacerdotes Mayas), whose executive committee sits in Mérida. The association was created in the 2000s. It aims to coordinate meetings of continental native representatives, working for the "development and promotion of Maya Culture values". It also celebrates local ceremonies and fight against "any form of cultural discrimination and economic marginalization of Maya people". The sources result from the official document of the Council, received in Mérida during their General Assembly, on 21 December 2014.

11　Interviewed on 22 December 2014 at her Center.

12　For criticism of feminism within neo-pagan movements and New Age movements, see Salomonsen (2002) and Fedele (2013); for the notion of lost feminine, see Fedele (2012, 59) and Eller (1993).

13　We never observed any ethnographic situations with Michel Maxime Egger in which such a "gender complementarity" was enacted."

14　http://www.trilogies.org/blog-notes/ecologie-interieure-56. Accessed on 5 April 2017.

15　Without telling anybody outside of the community for years, members had "carved several rooms out of the Alpine rocks" but a former leader exited the community and filed a lawsuit. Different government officials and authorities ordered the destruction of the temple since it was not respecting local building laws or violating zoning regulations. "Academic and artistic voices were raised in its support and public opinion swung behind Damanhur. The move against the temple was blocked", finally (Introvigne 1996) and the community was able to pay the fines and continue the construction. See also Merrifield (1998).

16　https://www.thetemples.org/en. Accessed on 25 August 2017.

17　To read the full legend and see the portrait: http://principedoro.com/la-leggenda-del-principe-doro/. Accessed on 8 November 17.

18　https://www.thetemples.org/en. Accessed on 25 August 2017.

19　www.damanhur.org/en/research-and-experimentation/the-plant-world. Accessed on 28 June 2018.

20　To the question we asked about the position of queer and transgender people during rituals – if they have to work with earth or fire – she answers they have the freedom to choose to work with the element with which they identify the most.

21 According to the national poll about belief and religious practices in Mexico published by the RIFREM in 2006, Mexico has 85 percent Catholic affiliation and 8 percent Evangelical (Hernández Hernández, Gutiérrez Zuñiga and De la Torre 2017).

References

Ammerman, Nancy. 2013. "Spiritual But Not Religious? Beyond Binary Choices in the Study of Religion." *Journal for the Scientific Study of Religion* 52(2): 258–278.

Badinter, Elisabeth. 2003. *Fausse route*. Paris: O. Jacob.

Bastos, Santiago and Aura Cumes. 2007. *Mayanizacioón y vida cotidiana: La ideología multicultural en la sociedad guatemalteca*. Texto para debate. Guatemala City: FLACSO-CIRMA-Cholsamaj.

Bastos, Santiago, Engel Tally, and Marcelo Zamora. 2013. "La reinterpretación del oxlajuj b'aqtun en Guatemala: entre el new age y la reconstitución maya". In *Variacones y apropiaciones latinoamericanas del New Age*, edited by Renée De la Torre, Cristina Gutiérrez Zuñiga, and Nahayeilli Juárez Huet, 309–336. México D.F.: Centro de Investigaciones y Estudios Superiores en Antropología Social.

Becci, Irene, Manéli Farahmand, and Alexandre Grandjean. 2015. "Power and Gender Structures in Contemporary Spirituality and Cosmovisions." *Ethnografia e Ricerca Qualitativa* 1: 156–169.

Becci, Irene, Manéli Farahmand, and Francesca Prescendi. 2019. « *Actes de terrain* ». *Saisir le genre à travers des nouveaux rituels: le cas de Damanhur*, Working Paper no. 15, ISSR, Université de Lausanne.

Becci, Irene and Alexandre Grandjean. 2018. "Tracing the Absence of a Feminist Agenda in Gendered Spiritual Ecology: Ethnographies in French-Speaking Switzerland." *Antropologia* 5(1): 23–38.

Berry, Evan. 2003. "Religious Environmentalism and Environmental Religion in America", *Religion Compass* 7(10): 1–13.

Berger, Peter L. and Thomas Luckmann. 1966. *The Social Construction of Reality: A Treatise its the Sociology of Knowledge*. New York: Anchor Books.

Bertaux, Daniel and Martin Kohli. 1984. "The Life Story Approach: A Continental View." *Annual Review of Sociology* 10: 215–237.

Berzano, Luigi (ed.). 1997. *Forme del pluralismo religioso*, Turino: Il Segnalibro.

Blancarte, Roberto. 2013. "Droits sexuels, catholicisme, sécularisation et laïcité au Mexique". In *Normes religieuses et genre. Mutations, resistances et reconfiguration XIXe-XXIe siècle*, edited by F. Rochefort, 137–150. Paris: Armand Colin.

Bloch, Jon. 1998. "Alternative Spirituality and Environmentalism." *Review of Religious Research* 40(1): 55–73.

Campbell, Colin. 2002. "The Cult, the Cultic Milieu and Secularization." In *The Cultic Milieu. Oppositional Subcultures in an Age of Globalization*, edited by J. Jeffrey Kaplan and H. Lööw, 12–25. Walnut Creek: AltaMira Press.

Camus, Manuela. 2001. "Mujeres y mayas: sus distintás expresiones." *INDIANA* 17 (18): 31–56.

Capone, Stefania. 2010. "Religions 'en migration': De l'étude des migrations internationales à l'approche transnationale." *Autrepart* 56(4): 235–259.

Cardano, Mario. 1997. *Lo specchio, la rosa e il loto: Uno studio sulla sacralizzazione della natura*. Roma: SEAM.

Cardano, Mario. 2015. *Pannofino Nicola, Piccole apostasie: Il congedo dai nuovi movimenti religiosi*, Bologna: Il Mulino.

Carlassare, Elisabeth. 2016. "L'essentialisme dans le discours écoféministe." In *Reclaim: Recueil de textes écoféministes*, edited by E. Hache, 219–341. Paris: Cambourakis.

Deane-Drummond, Celia. 2008. *Eco-theology*. London: Darton, Longman and Todd.

De la Peña, Francisco. 1999. "Le mouvement de la mexicanité ou l'invention de l'autre néo-tradition: millénarisme et imaginaire indigène." Doctoral dissertation in Ethnology. Paris: EHESS.

De la Peña, Francisco. 2001. "Milenarismo, nativismo y neotradicionalismo en el México actual." *Ciencias Sociales y Religión* 3(3): 95–113.

De la Torre, Renée. 2005. "La teología ecofeminista en América Latina." *Revista Querens Ciencias Religiosas* 6(16): 22–29.

De La Torre, Renée and Cristina Gutiérrez Zuñiga, eds. 2007. *Atlas de la diversidad religiosa en México*. El Colegio de Jalisco, Jalisco. México D.F.: Centro de Investigaciones y Estudios Superiores en Antropología Social.

De La Torre, Renée and Cristina Gutiérrez Zuñiga. 2011. "La neomexicanidad y los circuitos new age. ¿Un Hibridismo sin fronteras o múltiples estrategias de sintesis espiritual?" *Archives de sciences sociales des religions* 153: 183–206.

De La Torre, Renée and Cristina Gutiérrez Zuñiga. 2013. "Introdución." In *Variacones y apropiaciones latinoamericanas del New Age*, edited by R. De la Torre, C. Gutiérrez Zuñiga, and N. Juárez Huet, 13–27. México D.F.: Centro de Investigaciones y Estudios Superiores en Antropología Social.

Egger, Michel Maxime. 2012. *La Terre comme soi-même: Repères pour une écospiritualité*. Genève: Labor et Fides.

Egger, Michel Maxime. 2016. *Soigner l'esprit, guérir la terre*. Genève: Labor et Fides.

Egger, Michel Maxime. 2017. *Ecopsychologie: Retrouver notre lien à la terre*. Archamps: Editions Jouvence.

Eller, Cynthia. 1993. *Living in the Lap of the Goddess: the Feminist Spirituality Movement in America*. New York: Crossroad.

Farahmand, Manéli. 2016. "Glocalization and Transnationalization in (neo)-Mayanization Processes: Ethnographic Case Studies from Mexico and Guatemala." *Religion* 7(2). http://www.mdpi.com/2077-1444/7/2/17.

Fedele, Anna, 2012. Gender, sexuality and religious critique among Mary Magdalene pilgrims in Southern France. In *Gender, Nation and Religion in European Pilgrimage*, edited by Willy Jansen and Catrien Notermans, 55–70. Farnham : Ashgate.

Fedele, Anna. 2013. *Looking for Mary Magdalene: Alternative Pilgrimage and Ritual Creativity at Catholic Shrines in France*. Oxford: Oxford University Press.

Fedele, Anna and Kim Knibbe, eds. 2013. *Gender and Power in Contemporary Spirituality: Ethnographic Approaches*. New York: Routledge.

Frigerio, Alejandro. 2013. "Lógicas y límites de la apropiación New Age: donde se detiene el sincretismo." In *Variaciones y apropiaciones latinoamericanas del New Age*, edited by R. De la Torre, C. Gutiérrez Zuñiga, and N. Huárez Huet, 47–67. México D.F.: Centro de Investigaciones y Estudios Superiores en Antropología Social.

Frisk, Liselotte. 2010. "Globalization: A Key Factor. Contemporary Religious Change." *Journal of Alternative Spiritualities and New Age* 5, i–xiv.

Galinier, Jacques. 2011. "Le montage des autochtonies: Translocalisation de la Terre Mère dans le New Age amérindien." *Topique* 114: 23–34.

Galinier, Jacques and Antoinette Molinié. 2006. *Les Néo-Indiens: une religion du IIIe millénaire*. Paris: Odile Jacob.

Grasseli Meier, Marianne. 2018. *Le réveil des gardiennes de la terre Guide pratique d'écothérapie*. Paris: Le Courrier du Livre.

Güemez Pineda, Miguel. 2004. "Consideraciones sobre la lengua Maya de Yucatán." *Palabra en Flor*, órgano Informativo de la Acadamia de la Lengua y Cultura Mayas de Quintana Roo, A.C., Quintana Roo, Felipe Carillo Puerto 3(2): 6–7.

Güemez Pineda, Miguel, 2008. "La lengua maya en el contexto sociolinguistico peninsular". In *Yucatán ante la Ley General de Derechos Linguisticos de los Pueblos Indígenas*, edited by Esteban Krotz 115–148. México, D.F. : Instituto Nacional de Lenguas Indígenas.

Hache, Émilie. 2016. "Introduction: Reclaim ecofeminism!" In *Reclaim: Recueil de textes écoféministes*, edited by E. Hache, 13–57. Paris: Cambourakis.

Hernández Hernández, Alberto, Cristina Gutiérrez Zuñiga, and Renée De la Torre. 2017. "Encuesta Nacional sobre Creencias y Prácticas Religiosas en México. Informe de resultados." Informe de resultados. México: Red de Investigadores del Fenómeno Religioso en México (RIFREM).

Introvigne, Massimo. 1996. "Damanhur: A Magical Community in Italy." In *New Religious Movements: Challenge and Response*, edited by Bryan Wilson and Jamie Cresswell, 183–194. London: Routledge.

Huss, Boaz. 2014. "Spirituality: The Emergence of a New Cultural Category and its Challenge to the Religious and the Secular." *Journal of Contemporary Religion* 29(1): 47–60.

Jenkins, Willis. 2011. "Ecological Management, Cultural Reform, and Religious Creativity." *Union Seminary Quarterly Review* 63: 1–17.

Labrecque, Marie-France. 1987. "Les femmes et le mouvement féministe mexicain." *Indiens, paysans et femmes d'Amérique latine* 11(2): 95–106.

Lovelock, James. 1999. *La Terre est un être vivant, l'hypothèse Gaïa*. Paris: Flammarion.

MacKenzie, C. James. 2017. "Politics and Pluralism in the Círculo Sagrado: The Scope and Limits of Pan-Indigenous Spirituality in Guatemala and Beyond." *International Journal of Latin American Religions* 1(2): 1–23.

Macleod, Morna. 2011. *Nietas del fuego, creadoras del alba: luchas político-culturales de mujeres mayas*. Guatemala City: FLASCO.

Macy, Joanna and Molly Young Brown. 2008. *Ecopsychologie pratique et rituels pour la Terre: Retrouver un lien vivant avec la nature*. Gap: Editions le Souffle d'Or.

Marcus, George E. 1995. "Ethnography in/of the World System: The Emergence of Multi-Sited Ethnography." *Annual Review of Anthropology* 24 : 95–117.

Masson, Sabine. 2009. "Genre, race et colonialité en Amérique latine et aux Caraïbes. Une analyse des mouvements indigènes et féministes." In *Le sexe du militantisme*, edited by O. Filleule and P. Roux, 299–317. Paris: Presses de Sciences Po "Académique".

Merchant, Carolyn. 1980. *The Death of Nature – Women, Ecology and the Scientific Revolution*. San Francisco: HarperCollins.

Merrifield, Jeff. 1998. *Damanhur: The Real Dream*. London: Thorsons.

Palencia, Tania P. and H. Magzul Patal. 2003. *Généro y cosmovisión maya*. Guatemala City: Prodessa.

Palmisano, Stefania and Nicola Luciano Pannofino. 2014. "Damanhur, An Exemplary Utopia: An Analysis of the Public Identity of a New Religious Movement Online." *International Journal for the Study of New Religions* 5(1): 27–50.

Palombo, Silvio. 2017. *Un Tempio nel Verde: Cos'è e cosa rappresenta il Tempio Bosco Sacro*. Vidracco: Damanhur con te.

Pike, Sarah M. 2001. *Earthly Bodies, Magical Selves: Contemporary Pagans and the Search for Community*. Berkeley: University of California Press.

Rieff, Philip. 1966. *The Triumph of the Therapeutic: The Uses of Faith after Freud*. Chicago: University of Chicago Press.

Runggaldier, Edmund. 1996. *Philosophie der Esoterik.* Stuttgart: Kohlhammer.

Saint-Blancat, C. 2001. "Globalisation, réseaux et diasporas dans le champ religieux." In *La globalisation du religieux*, edited by Jean-Pierre Bastian, Françoise Champion, and Kathy Rousselet, 75–86. Paris: L'Harmattan.

Salomonsen, Jone. 2002. *Enchanted Feminism: The Reclaiming Witches of San Francisco.* London: Routledge.

Santanas Rivas, Landy. 2003. "La construcción del género en la cultura maya. " *Revista de la Universidad Autónoma de Yucatán* 225(47): 46–59.

Sieder, Rachel and Morna Macleod. 2009. "Género, derecho y cosmovisión maya en Guatemala." *Descatos* 31: 51–72.

Simmel, Georg. 1906. "The Sociology of Secrecy and of Secret Societies." *American Journal of Sociology* 11(4): 441–498.

Stanley, Alessandra. 2000. "Baldissero Canavese Journal: New Age Commune Is into Crafts and Time Travel." *The New York Times*, 26 July, online: http://www.nytimes.com/2000/07/26/world/baldissero-canavese-journal-new-age-commune-Is-into-crafts-and-time-travel.html

Taube, Karl and Mary E. Miller. 1993. *The Gods and Symbols of Ancient Mexico and the Maya. An Illustrated Dictionary of Mesoamerican Religion.* London: Thames & Hudson.

Taylor, Bron. 2016. "The Greening of Religion Hypothesis (Part One): From Lynn White, Jr and Claims That Religions Can Promote Environmentally Destructive Attitudes and Behaviors to Assertions They Are Becoming Environmentally Friendly." *Journal for the Study of Religion, Nature and Culture* 10(3): 268–305.

Tucker, Catherine and Adrian Ivakhiv. 2012. "Intersection of Nature, Science, and Religion: An Introduction." In *Nature, Science, and Religion: Intersections Shaping Society and the Environment*, edited by C. Tucker. Santa Fe: SAR Press.

Von Stuckrad, Kocku. 2002. "Reenchanting Nature: Modern Western Shamanism and Nineteenth-Century Thought." *Journal of the American Academy of Religion.* 70(4): 771–799.

Wood, Matthew, 2010. The sociology of spirituality: reflections on a problematic endeavor. In *The New Blackwell Companion to the Sociology of Religion*, edited by Bryan Turner 267–285. Oxford: Wiley-Blackwell.

Woodhead, Linda. 2013. "Gender Differences in Religious Practice and Significance." *International Advances in Engineering and Technology* 13: 58–85.

Woodhead, Linda, Paul Heelas et al. 2005. *The Spiritual Revolution: Why Religion Is Giving Way to Spirituality.* Oxford: Blackwell.

Zoccatelli, Pierluigi. 2016. "All the Heavens in your Hands: Oberto Airaudi and the Art of Damanhur." *Nova Religio: The Journal of Alternative and Emergent Religions* 19(4): 145–162.

Interviews

MR, 22 December 2014, Mérida, Yucatán, Mexico.
MR, 17 January 2015, Mérida, Yucatán, Mexico.
Guide – Damanhur, 7 June 2017, Piedmont, Italy.
ME, various meetings and interviews, winter/spring 2016–17.
MGM, various meetings and interviews, winter/spring 2017/18.

6   Re-enchanted selves

An ethnography of wild woman workshops in Belgium

Carine Plancke

Introduction

In the last decades, religion scholars have increasingly abandoned the thesis that, with the advent of modernity, religion would fade away and be replaced by secularism (Casanova 1994; Berger 1999). As a matter of fact, the contemporary salience of religious movements and new spiritual practices around the globe has discredited the idea that religion is disappearing in the modern world, making the straightforward narrative of progress from the religious to the secular no longer acceptable. With it, Max Weber's equation of modernity with disenchantment has come to be questioned. In Weber's view, because of the modern process of intellectualization, the role of magic to control mysterious, unpredictable forces has disappeared, since we can in principle control everything by means of technology and calculation (Weber 2004, 12–13). This confidence in the victory of rationalism in modern human beings has been called into question. Michel Maffesoli, in particular, suggests that the generation of spaces of (re-) enchantment where non-rational aspects of the self are invoked is a typical phenomenon in our contemporary late modern/postmodern society rather than being alien to it. In his book *The Reenchantment of the World* (2007), Maffesoli states that contemporary Western society is currently undergoing a deep transformation in which the control of a strong and confident self is no longer the norm. He evokes "a return of mystery" (2007, 79), of "primitive forces" (2007, 102), sensed in a "shift from rationalism to sensualism" (2007, 105) and in the presence of a "vitalist impulse that links up the material and the spiritual" (2007, 41).

The notion of the post-secular (Habermas 2008) is commonly used nowadays to signify the failure of the secularization narrative. It can be questioned, however, whether this means that something has irrevocably changed in our society after a phase of secularization. This seems to be implied by Maffesoli's account of our inherently re-enchanted postmodern world as one that radically breaks with a previous rational one. Jenkins (2000, 12), however, claims that disenchantment has never totally arrived or, at best, has proceeded unevenly. Alongside the imperialism of formal-rational logics and technical processes, the history of modern Europe has all along seen a subversion of these by a diverse array of oppositional (re-)enchantments, even though the latter are particularly striking in our current times. In this view, the post-secular principally means a more nuanced position and detailed gaze of the researcher than was possible some time ago (Utriainen 2011, 421). This position rests on the view that, rather than an achieved reality, modernity is a project that aims at institutionalizing a number of principles, one of which is secularism (Asad 2003). Hence, the very construction of the notion of "the secular" does not exist without its counterpart "the religious". This means that the secular and the religious – and hence also disenchantment and enchantment – are mutually determined and intertwined with each other (Asad 2003; Jakobsen & Pelligrini 2008; Moberg, Granholm & Nynas 2012; Ingman et al. 2016).

The need to reassess the secularization thesis critically becomes especially evident when one takes into account gender and uses women's experiences as the standpoint from which to examine secularization. Feminist scholars have shown that Max Weber's thinking, which is foundational for this thesis, reveals male bias (Bologh 1990). The advent of a secular political world was a male endeavour dependent on the continuing existence of a feminine domestic world where religion remained important. The fact that women are numerically dominant in new spiritualities, while leaving the churches, attest to their continued religiosity and underscores the relevance of assuming the coexistence of the religious and the secular (Vincett, Sharam & Aune 2008, 15). In this essay, I advance that, just as secularization theory needs to be gendered (Woodhead 2008), the study of disenchantment and re-enchantment has to integrate a gendered perspective. A crucial condition for the disenchantment of the universe in Western modernity was the development of a new sense of self: one that is no longer open, porous and vulnerable to a world of spirits and powers but one that is bounded or "buffered" (Taylor 2007). It is precisely with regard to this issue of the boundedness of the modern self that it is necessary to take gender into account. Linda Woodhead (2008) advances that the constitution of the rational, autonomous, self-assertive subject of ideal secular modernity was never imposed on women in the same way as on men since the feminine remained associated with affect, care, other-orientedness and relationality. The continued need for women to provide care for others and be receptive to their needs, and the strong association of the feminine with the non-rational, prevented them from developing to the same degree as men did a strongly bounded self. This can also explain why women are so numerous in new spiritualities, which favour experiences of re-enchantment.

New spiritual movements value a relational ethos where what matters is caring and sharing, being trusting and listening without judgements in a non-competitive atmosphere so that affect-laden reciprocal bonds can develop (Heelas 2008, 120). The kind of self that is aimed at in this way is not the autonomous, rational self of modern secularism. These movements regard intuition highly (Hanegraaff 1996, 221; Heelas 1996, 5) and strongly oppose narrow-minded rationality, countering in this sense "positivistic iron-cage tendencies" (Heelas 2008, 3). The self is here not just a locus of reason and autonomy, but a sacred entity that is part of the larger cosmos (Heelas 1996).

It is an "unbounded self" (Heelas 2008, 2), which is open to a realm beyond the strictly rational and hence to experiences of enchantment. The latter are deliberately sought for by turning to premodern or non-Western worldviews and traditions seen to harbour an authentic spirituality the modern West has lost.

The workshops I will deal with in this essay, by centring on the theme of the wild woman, explicitly situate themselves within this mindset. They take place in a natural environment deliberately removed from urban, industrial or high-tech settings. While intended for women who are fully part of contemporary Western society, they aim to help them (re)discover their "inner wild woman", which they have supposedly lost in their lives as modern women, as well as to reconnect with the wildness of nature. "Wildness" refers here to all that is spontaneous and unplanned – what breaks through the patterns of ordinary functioning and does not follow rational reasoning and/ or (self)imposed logics or norms. Hence, becoming a wild woman entails an opening up to being moved by unexpected forces, both within and without, affects, longings, pains but also natural phenomena, the wind, rain, the full moon and possibly a realm of spirits or divine beings. Because of this orientation, the workshops have the potential to induce experiences of re-enchantment among the participants and a sense of self that is not closed off to its environment.

Simultaneously, however, the need to remain in close contact with one's true self is highlighted in the workshops. This double movement, towards the relational, on the one hand, and towards the self, on the other, will be interpreted in light of Eeva Sointu and Linda Woodhead's thesis (2008) that holistic spiritualities are helpful for present-day Western women in dealing with two contradictory demands: to be for oneself and to be for others. This will allow to give a gendered reading of Heelas' account of the self in new spiritual settings and hence of the phenomenon of re-enchantment. As Crowley suggests (2011, 3), Heelas seems not to envisage that for women the sacralization of the self can be liberating in itself since they have struggled to have a self all along. In this view, re-enchantment for women rests on a double movement: going beyond the closed-off self but also preventing a complete sacrifice of the self. Following the description of the case study, I will mainly explore the movement beyond the bounded self. In the section after that I will show how becoming more open and relational is balanced with an emphasis on the very fact of having a self. I will especially show how the participants' life trajectory and life-stance, whether oriented towards self-affirmation or rather towards caring for others, helps to understand which tendency is most accentuated.

The essay is based on ethnographic research I started in 2013 on women's spirituality in Belgium, the Netherlands and the UK. As a case study, I will use one specific wild woman workshop from Belgium I participated in three times and for which I conducted in-depth interviews with the conveners and about 20 participants. This extensive study will allow me to show in detail the proceedings of the retreat and the way it affects the participants. I will outline the discourse that guides the workshops, describe the practices that are designed to lead to a reconnection with so-called lost spirituality and true femininity,[1] and develop actual instances of re-enchantment related by interviewed participants as experiences of moving beyond a bounded, rational and/or socially normative self towards a relational self in tune with oneself and human or non-human others.

Case study of a wild woman workshop[2]

The workshop presented here as a case study is a three-day retreat that took place in summer on the property of an ecological community. The space comprised a main building and a few acres of land with a mixture of permaculture gardens, wild vegetation, trees and a small pool; it also housed some yurts and a caravan. Participants slept either in their own tents, in one of the yurts or on the wooden floor of a space in the main building in which, for the occasion, a small altar had been erected with an Indian goddess statue,[3] flowers and goddess cards. The group consisted of two conveners, An and Nathalie,[4] and around 10 participants, all women, with ages ranging between 25 and 65, although most were between 35 and 45. The fee for the retreat was 240 euros plus accommodation and food costs (about 150 euros). An and Nathalie were both active in the wellbeing counselling sector for individuals and groups. In organizing the workshop, they drew on a range of inspirations belonging to the broad field of contemporary spiritualities. Besides emotional bodywork, Shamanism and Goddess Spirituality, tantra was the main source of inspiration. While they had become acquainted with these practices through participating in other courses and gatherings, they did not simply assemble copied exercises for their workshop. The retreat was born in an experiential way: Nathalie had a vision that she needed to facilitate women's groups and saw An, whom she knew already, as her partner for realizing that. When they discussed the idea, one of the themes that emerged was the wild woman. In order to give the project concrete realization, they gathered on a warm summer day in the garden of one of their homes and started embodying the wild woman, which they interpreted as letting their authentic selves and spontaneous impulses live. They then selected from the practices they had explored in this way and set up the programme.

   On the first day of the workshop, after everyone had arrived, a welcome ritual was held. We gathered barefoot in the garden within a circle of trees. After a moment of silence, attending to our breath and feeling the earth, An started playing a shamanic drum and invoked the goddesses of the four elements (earth, water, fire and air) as well as the goddess that resides in each woman: Babayaga, the wild woman goddess. She then blessed the circle by igniting a piece of aromatic charcoal and spiralling it in front of each woman with the words, "And for your wild woman." After this ritual opening, Nathalie invited us to welcome ourselves in the space, to feel the earth, the wind, the rain (if there was any) and to start to move the body slowly as it felt good. She put on some music and suggested that, if it felt OK, we start dancing and move in contact with someone else. We were then invited to say our names and a word about how we felt. This moment of presentation was followed by a brief session of information. An and Nathalie explained that they did not have a fixed image of the wild woman, but rather equated it with "letting the vital flow exist, being spontaneous, being open to the unpredictable, going into the unknown, letting go of structures, etc.". They then asked us to share our answer to the question "Where do I withhold my wild woman?" with a partner, without giving comments or judgements. Before lunch, some practical information was provided. We were divided into three groups – water, earth and fire – and each group received tasks related to its chosen element.

The afternoon was devoted to the "kundalini[5] exercise", accompanied by music from 5Rhythms founder Gabrielle Roth. One woman knelt on all fours, breathing continuously (i.e. without a break between inhalation and exhalation). When she felt the impulse, she started moving her hips and then her spine in an undulating way, making sounds as they arose, and gradually coming to a standing position. All along, her partner for the exercise helped her by exerting pressure with the thumb, index and middle fingers on her sacrum. The aim of the exercise, as explained by An, was to "find a pure, authentic energy, a primitive power" and "to connect again with our past when we still walked on all fours, before we were civilized and had all kinds of norms". This was followed by a creative exercise with clay prepared during the break by the earth and water women. We were given the option to make something with clay, play with it, throw it at each other, or do anything else we felt like doing. The evening consisted of a goddess visualization in the yurt. While seated in a meditative pose or lying down, Nathalie invited us to visualize how we passed through a hole into a huge tree, descended through its roots into the earth, met our wild goddess, gave her a gift, received one in return and then went back to the earth through the roots of the tree. The day ended with a gathering around the fire built by the fire women.

The second day started with sound improvisations in the yurt. The idea was to make sounds as they emerged: either in our own hands, held as a cup, in the hands of a partner, or towards a place on our body touched by a partner. Subsequently, some grounding and tension-release exercises in a circle outside introduced the major exercise: the lioness salutation. The aim of this exercise was to get into the sensation of being a catlike animal, expressing it through movement and sound by following spontaneous impulses in the body. The exercise took place outside in the grass. We started from a circular configuration on all fours. We first spent some time on our own, exploring, and then An invited us to begin interacting with each other according to the prevailing mood: affectionate, seductive, challenging or assertive. After a small break, An and Nathalie playfully suggested there was a mud pool we might go in naked. This resulted, two times, in throwing mud and/or massaging each other with it; another year, in sacredly honouring our bodies, each woman went to the middle of the pool in turn while the others blessed her body by stroking it with mud.

The afternoon was set up as a space for more personal exploration of the wild woman. After a sharing circle, during which each woman could relate her experiences and express how she was feeling in a non-judgemental sphere, An asked us to write down our answers to the following questions:

1   What is your image of the wild woman?
2   How can you connect to this wild woman?
3   What can you do right here to live this wild woman?

Small groups were then formed of women with similar views on how to realize their wild woman, and each group concretely enacted the vision by attending to each member in succession. Ways of living the wild woman that I observed included body painting, nakedness, massage, dance, touch, playing in the mud, improvising on instruments, creating a ritual around a fire and dressing up in unusual clothing, such as Native American-style or tiger-motif garments. The day ended with another gathering around the fire prepared by the fire women, this time in a more ritualized way. Nathalie asked us to take a small stick and throw it in the fire while stating an intention to let go of something and let something new come. The thing to be released was, for instance, one's self-image as "the nice girl" or negative, diminishing views of oneself.

The last day started with dancing to music we had brought, followed by a temple ritual for which we donned white clothes. The ritual was led by Nathalie and took place in the yurt or in a circle of trees decorated with orange, reddish and pink veils. The Indian goddess statue was removed from the altar and placed in the middle of the space, and a previously prepared list of meditative, instrumental music from India played in the background. We gathered in threes and took a mat or mattress, decorating it with cloths we had brought. Two women took on the role of priestesses, serving as a channel for the goddess. First, they made a *namaste* – a bowing gesture with the palms of the hand pressed together in front of the chest – to each other and to the third woman. They then purified the latter woman, who lay down on the mattress, by gently stroking her using a sponge and warm, perfumed water and circling her with incense. Then, by touch, words or other gestures, they conveyed the quality the woman wished to receive from the goddess (as she has communicated to them beforehand). For instance, if wishing to receive the quality of firmness in delineating boundaries, the priestesses applied a rather firm touch to her body. If lightness was wished for, they stroked her with a feather. After a final *namaste*, the roles were switched. Afterwards, we went silently into the surrounding nature. The afternoon ended inside the circle of trees with some dancing, a final sharing circle and a last dance to the song "Totally Wild and Absolutely Free" by Miten and Deva Premal.

Enchanting experiences of participation

The conveners interpreted the theme of the wild woman as a relinquishing of habitual structures – both societal norms and habitual patterns in one's life. The aim of the retreat was to release the security given by the known order and go into the unknown; its guiding principle was said to be spontaneity and the ability to feel natural impulses in the body in order to give flow to a vital energy that links the human to others and to the environment. In this sense, the workshop was situated in the critique of rationality and the bounded self, typical for new spiritualities, and intended to awaken feelings of interconnectedness. In the in-depth interviews I conducted with participants, experiences of going beyond a closed self towards a connected self were abundant and were also those that left a deep imprint. They entailed a new, affectively powerful experience of the cosmos as being active, alive and sentient and conveyed a quality of enchantment.[6] In Taylor's view (2007), disenchantment goes with the replacement of a cosmos of spirits and forces by a mechanistic universe.[7] This seemed to be countered in the related experiences. The following excerpt, in which Karen recalled the kundalini exercise, literally shows the advent of this porous self and the ecstatic experience it causes:

> I felt all kind of things coming open. Something really happened in me. [...] I felt something awakening, something old, not just sexual energy, although I also felt that, but an opening of every pore, as if every pore became receptive to feel. You don't feel that easily. That is why I also found it very beautiful and intimate to see how that awakened in L. [her partner in the exercise] and to witness that. [...] Afterwards, we both felt so ecstatic. We started to walk and hug the trees. Really, we were totally high off ourselves, and we started dancing and gently rocking. Really, I did not need anything else, and then I arrived at the weeping willow and, really, the earth was there, I was one with the earth and the earth was there to love me. Every tree sensed differently, but it all opened up so much. I was like a flower. And L. was like that as well.

Karen referred to the opening of the pores, suggesting the breakdown of the buffered self and the advent of a more porous one. This went along with strong ecstatic feelings through which her relationship with her partner in the exercise, as well as with the trees and the earth, was felt as responsive and mutually adjusted. In using the image of the flower, Karen even suggested that she was becoming like nature. In an interview with Elke about the clay exercise, she recounted a similar experience of erasure of the border between human and non-human, attributing the position of subject to the latter category. Elke had interpreted the exercise as a playful naked clay battle outside in the rain with a few other women in the group. Since the water hose did not work for them to clean themselves off, she had the idea to roll in the wet grass:

That was definitely the most pleasant thing I have ever done in the garden. Rolling like that in the grass in the rain. I absolutely enjoyed that. [...] It felt fresh, but not cold. To lie in the grass and see the air, you saw the clouds, you saw all the green around you and the rain falling on you, so fresh. I really had the feeling, "Well, that is it now to be grass."

This possibility of imagining how the grass must experience its life was absolutely new for Elke, as she subsequently told me. The free exercise of enacting one's own wild woman particularly stimulated the imagination as a way to discover novel ways of relating to the environment and to realize hitherto unrealised aspects of oneself. This exercise, more than the others, encouraged the participants to go beyond habitual patterns and, hence, opened up new horizons. Emma, in imagining her wild woman, had the following vision:

I had the image of how I was standing on a hill near a tree while singing and how my song moved the whole world, affected the whole world, in waves. We actually found a small hill there with a tree on it. But then, I did feel some shame to really do it. First I closed my eyes, because I found it embarrassing to let myself go into that vision while people were watching me. But afterwards they told me that it was so beautiful. That moved me so deeply. It was not a real song, just sounds. First hesitant and then very powerful.

What is striking in these excerpts is that the experience of a loss of neat boundaries between the I and the surrounding world and the advent of a possibility of encounter, of communication or of exchange with other beings was experienced as something out-of-the-ordinary and was accompanied with emotional intensity or resistance. Wouter Hanegraaff's (2003) discussion of enchantment in reference to the concept of participation as a tendency of the human mind which is denied in mainstream Western culture is instructive in this regard. In proposing the notion of participation, Hanegraaff draws on Lucien Lévy-Bruhl who associated this concept with mystical and prelogical modes of thinking – where a being can be simultaneously itself and something else – and opposed it to the principle of causality. While Lévy-Bruhl (1910), in his original formulation, tended to overemphasize the connection between participation and "primitive" cultures, on the one hand, and between causality and "modern" culture, on the other, he increasingly came to recognize that participation constituted a primary and irreducible human constant (Lévy-Bruhl 1949, 131, 164–165, 188). Adopting the latter understanding, Hanegraaff (2003, 374) suggests that participation can be seen as an affective stratum in human thought and action, which is analogical rather than logical and which he also refers to as "spontaneous animism". Instrumental rationality is another, opposite, universal tendency of the human mind. This view allows Hanegraaff to reframe the question of disenchantment in terms which make sense of the continuous resurgence of experiences of participation in present-day societies. Disenchantment is then defined as "the social pressure exerted upon human beings to deny the spontaneous tendency of participation, by accepting the claims of a culturally established ideology according to which instrumental causality amounts to a worldview capable in principle of rationally explaining all aspects of reality" (Hanegraaff 2003, 377). Starting from this view, Hanegraaff argues that the establishment of instrumental causality as an ideology during and since the eighteenth century provoked the establishment of a Romantic counter-ideology based upon participation; and that such an ideology of participation has now established itself as a dominant social narrative, for instance in contemporary spiritualities.

The studied retreats focused on the trope of the wild woman were embedded in this counter-ideology that romanticizes a premodern, so-called primitive mode of relating to nature. This facilitated women to actually have experiences that can be qualified as participation inasmuch as they manifested an affect-laden tendency to become like another being and feel a belonging to the larger universe. The resistance or anxiety this experience evoked or the avowed difficulty to feel it attests to its denial in contemporary society. The workshops precisely aimed to overcome this social dismissal by appealing to a so-called spontaneous, intuitive tendency for relatedness beyond a closed-off self, which was supposed to be present in each woman. This very tendency was seen as feminine and linked to the female self as a relational self which is never completely closed off from others and the environment. In the next section, I will more clearly focus on the issue of gender. I will highlight the gendered reading of the intuitive and authentic way of being and relating that was sought for and felt to be (re)discovered during the workshop in terms of a specifically female power. In particular, I will show the gendered dimension of the way the relational self as an expression of this feminine way of being is accessed and developed in the workshops by tracing a link with women's social position in contemporary Western society. This will facilitate a more complex reading of the thesis according to which new spiritualities favour a move beyond the bounded, autonomous self.

Rebalancing the self-in-relation

In interviews with participants of the workshop, the search for a reappraisal of the feminine, in its authentic strength, was a recurring aspect. It was present in the interview I had with Elke who, in narrating her motivation to sign up for the retreat, expressed the need she felt to access a feminine power in a world dominated by men and the desire to get out of being stuck in achievement-oriented and rational thinking. She told how the weekend taught her to follow her intuition rather than rational thoughts. This came about in an interaction with the goddess in a quite unexpected manner. Having ignored her longing to sleep in the yurt, reasoning that this was too "alternative" for her, she decided to sleep in the communal space and did not revise that decision since she felt that once she had decided something she had to logically stick to it.

I slept right near the altar. I had the feeling – it is strange – but I dreamt that the goddess who was there on the altar kept me awake. I slept very bad and then I woke up and looked straight into that statue "ouou [expression of anger], I want to sleep". And again. [...] That goddess symbolized the inner fight to let go off things [= patterns, preconceived thoughts]. [...] I also learned that being a woman is meaningful in itself. Before it was just: you are either a man or a woman but you all have to do the same things. If you are pregnant, you should not complain. Giving birth should go as fast as possible so you can get to work again. All that kind of rationality.

This reappraisal of feminine difference and the access to a more feminine dimension in her self which she associated with following intuition and which became concrete in the relation to the goddess was most powerfully experienced during the temple ritual.

That ritual was very special to me. Because it was one of the first times that I was completely in service to someone else. My thinking was not there, and I was just – well, it sounds bad – an empty shell in the service of someone else. Judgements or prejudices were not there at that moment. It was only: I do what I feel. At that moment it was just with my heart. I really had the feeling: the goddess who is in charge of this, I am just a means for her. And that is it. [...] I was like a part of the divine. If I say this, it sounds like, "Oh" [said in a self-deprecating tone], but it was just like that. I had that feeling. A lot of love also. No judgement, a feeling of unity, of caring, a feeling of protecting the person who was lying there. It was very serene. No complexity. It was what it was.

The way in which Elke described her experience of the ritual shows that it was uncanny and new for her. She feared disapproval, especially when she conveyed the feeling of being overtaken by and partaking in something beyond herself, presumably since this strongly defies the ideal of an autonomous self. She told me how after the ritual she went outside and sat near the extinct fire looking over the fields in a deeply peaceful mood of surrendering to all that is. The experience had a strong impact on her life. She felt compelled to move away from an exclusively rational and "linear" way of thinking and to regularly go to the woods to find a similar sensation of belonging to a larger whole. This allowed her in a next workshop to follow more easily her intuition and her longing for moving beyond an entirely mastered way of being without perceiving it as strange. She even decided a few months after the retreat to change jobs and to quit her former employment, which she labelled as "feminist" and which entailed helping migrant single mothers to become self-sufficient by managing their lives in rational and efficient ways.

Whereas Elke very much stressed the movement towards a more open self that gives over control and lets itself be guided by its intuitions, Marleen's experience revealed a movement towards self-assertion and a relatedness that is balanced in terms of giving. The kundalini exercise particularly allowed her to feel a perfect adjustment to and exchange with her partner which deeply moved her:

> I remember I was so attuned to her energy that I started to cry, just because of the emotion that it gave. It was crazy. The fact that it was such a match, that I was able to give her that, that I had that feeling, that I was moved and that, because of that, she could also give me a lot. It was a very intense experience.

Later on in the workshop she felt compelled to strongly affirm herself no longer in terms of giving but in terms of just being and receiving:

> I remember when we could dance to our favourite music. I remember also that, the whole time, I held my arms up in the air. I still know very well why. It had to do with the sternum, something that had to come free and I still remember how, the whole time, I held my arms up in the air. My arms just had to go up. Complete freedom. Straighten your back, your breasts forward and just receive. That song [the one she had brought to the workshop to dance upon the last day], when I had discovered it, it was so true. My interpretation is that it is about our being imprisoned in society, what they make of us, that we are so far from our nature. [...] After the workshop, I had made a kind of small altar in my room. But with our renovations it is not there anymore. I also had discovered a small shop where I had found a card with a woman wearing a long dress, in the forest and she stands with her arms upwards amidst the trees [...] Still now if I look at that card, it still does that to me. Oh, it is so, so myself that I meet there. I remember. Once I needed something and I opened the cupboard and I saw it. Immediately it was again "voum" [sudden affect that emerges]. Oh, my card. No, if ever it would go really bad with me, and I see that card, I am sure that immediately it will be better. It is the core of my being, which gets me going.

While the first excerpt reveals a wish to depart from the bounded, male, autonomous self of Western secular society, this excerpt rather shows a reaction against a sacrificial, always giving female self. This difference between the two women can be traced back to their background and stance in life. Elke told me how she grew up with a feminist mother who pushed her towards independence and self-reliance. Her job and her life situation as a childless woman in her late thirties also highlighted these principles. The workshop strongly instigated her to let go of these views and to enter a more intuitive mode of being experienced as a surrendering to alterity and to love. Marleen, on the other hand, was a nurse with two small children and spoke several times of how care was the most important thing in her life now and evoked in this the example of her mother. While, after a trip in India to learn ayurvedic massage, she had decided to quit her job as a nurse to start her own massage practice, she again gave up this longing after meeting her husband and having two children. For Marleen, the retreat – for which she did not sign up herself since it was gifted to her by her mother – was a moment of reconnecting with this passion. It entailed the rediscovery of a possibility of a balanced and seemingly perfectly attuned giving and an affirmation of her own self as a pure, free being which is part of nature.

According to Eeva Sointu and Linda Woodhead (2008), women, particularly middle-class women, in contemporary Western societies are forced to negotiate two different modes of selfhood: the feminized, immanent "self for others" and the masculinized, transcendent "self for itself" (Sointu and Woodhead 2008, 271). In their view, holistic spiritualities allow women in modern Western society to deal with this key dilemma they face between "living life for oneself" and "living life for others" (Beck & Beck-Gernsheim 2002). Tensions can be negotiated between their task to be caring and other-oriented and the drive to be autonomous and self-centred. In synthesizing this view, Woodhead (2008) stresses that spiritualities move on a spectrum from the self-in-*relation* where relationality prevails to the *self*-in-relation where the self is stressed. This is also what seemed to happen in the discussed workshops. Most of the participants were women who had received a relatively high degree of education and went out working, often while combining it with household duties and child care. The two excerpts just discussed reveal how, in the workshops, a relational self was sought for which maintained a balance between relationality and selfhood in correspondence to each woman's situation. More narratives among those interviewed stressed the need for relationality, I assume, since the very act of choosing to participate in and to pay for a three-day retreat just for oneself, entails a privileging of selfhood. Women whose lives are mainly defined by care for others, were not as numerous and, hence, the focus on self-affirmation to counter self-sacrifice was less present in the interviews. The fact that Marleen did not sign up herself for the retreat but accepted it as a gift confirms this. The advantage of including this kind of narrative is precisely that it reflects that, while re-enchantment for present-day Western women definitely entails a moving beyond a bounded self, it also relies on the possibility of being someone, of actually having a self.

Conclusion

This chapter has argued for the need to develop a gendered perspective on disenchantment and re-enchantment. With regard to disenchantment and the view that modernity entails the triumph of the rational, autonomous and bounded self, it was suggested that women's experiences might have been different since, as previous studies have argued (Woodhead 2008), they remained associated with care and other-orientedness. This entailed that they probably never experienced disenchantment as dramatically as men and hence remained open to these experiences, as their high presence in new spiritual movements also suggests. Secondly – and this was the main object of the essay – it was shown, through an ethnographic study of wild woman workshops, that re-enchantment relies on participation as a movement beyond the bounded self, as has been generally argued, but also presupposes a sense of actually having a self, which historically has not been as easy for women as for men. It is especially for taking into account this dimension that a gendered analysis proved useful.

A gendered perspective is further fruitful to understand what re-enchantment precisely entails. Maffesoli strongly highlights the fusional dimension of enchantment. It is about finding "communal ecstasies" (2007, 50) and a "fusional ambiance" (2007, 107). In his book *The Time of the Tribes* (1988), mass society is presented as that which allows enchantment as a move beyond individualism towards a feeling of group fusion. This view does not correspond to the one I encountered in the studied retreats, since a loss of self is not aimed at. Sointu and Woodhead (2008, 267) make a similar observation when comparing the contemporary predominantly holistic spiritualities with male Romantic expressivism, held to be the basis for current movements of re-enchantment (Maffesoli cited in Mirande 2008, 67) and the move beyond the instrumental, rational self (Taylor 2007, 507). Compared with some earlier forms of spirituality closer to the Romantic spirit, such as theosophy, in present-day spiritualities there seems to be little or no desire to merge the self into some greater whole, or to dissolve individuality into oneness. Rather, there is an attempt to reconcile individuality with relationships in a way that can do justice to both. This difference is gendered according to Sointu and Woodhead. Mostly women are involved in contemporary spiritualities. They are committed to a vision of "authentic selfhood-in-relation", rather than to either autonomous individualistic selfhood on the one hand, or to the loss of individuality in experiences of sublime self-transcendence on the other. The last two interview excerpts that were discussed in this essay reveal this kind of vision, where in link with the specific life situation either relatedness or selfhood is stressed.

Finally, these interviews also made me aware of how the experience of a balanced, relational self results in the development of a new understanding of femininity, similarly to what Chia Longman (2018) describes with regard to women's circles in Belgium. For Elke, the movement beyond logical thinking and the rational self entailed a distancing from what she labels as feminism without, however, resorting to a conservative feminine position. She changed job and decided to go and live together with her partner but this did not entail the taking up of the role of the traditional housewife. Her dismissal of feminism is especially connected to a typically postfeminist view on feminism as unfeminine and an imitation of male behaviour (Genz 2009; McRobbie 2009; Scharff 2012). Marleen at the end of the interview told me that once her children were older and she could leave the caring a bit more, she definitely would take up her passion for ayurvedic massage again. She has not decided to abandon the typically feminine caring role but already projects a way to balance it with a more autonomous search for her own path. This confirms that new forms of spirituality are not necessarily incompatible with a sense of empowerment for women – whether framed in feminist terms or not – as Braidotti (2008) has suggested and other ethnographic research on contemporary spirituality has convincingly shown (Salomonsen 2002; Bowman 2004; Pike 2004; Magliocco 2004; Rountree 2004; Coleman 2009; Trulsson 2010; Fedele & Knibbe 2013; Kieft 2014). This study even hints at how the experience of (re-)enchantment, which is at the core of these spiritualities, can become a source of power for women, inasmuch as it revitalizes them by giving a feeling of participation in a shared cosmic energy that both moves the self beyond its limits and brings it to its very core.

Notes

1 Elsewhere (Plancke 2020), I develop how an appeal to cultural alterity is a crucial means used in these workshops for redefining femininity.
2 While using similar imagery and having similar aims, workshops with the wild woman as their theme can be organized in very different ways according to the inspiration of their conveners. In another tantric- and shamanic-inspired wild woman workshop I participated in, the main activity involved a sweat lodge modelled on Native American traditions and conceived of as the womb of Mother Nature. Participants were invited "to give to her their stuck emotions and patterns" and "to rejuvenate with the elements" by rubbing themselves with the earth of the lodge. In a final exercise meant to further induce transformation, participants were invited to go successively in small groups to a nearby pool to leave behind what they deemed necessary, to the garden in order to ask the help of the nature spirits, and to an adjoining lake where they could make a representation of their *yoni* (Sanskrit for female sex) with natural materials as an expression of their sacred femininity. The second part of this exercise particularly induced experiences of enchantment: one woman reported, for instance, that she felt how a tree waved towards her with its branches, and another described how, leaning on a strong tree, she suddenly had a vision of a circle of women protecting her and heard a voice that said, "Embrace yourself."
3 More specifically it was a statue of the goddess Parvati. However, this was not mentioned in the workshop and I did not hear anyone asking for it. The statue was rather used as symbol for a generic goddess.
4 All names are pseudonyms.
5 The concept of kundalini, borrowed from yogic practice, refers to an energy that lies at the bottom of the spine and can rise up like snake along the different energy centres called chakras.
6 Sarah Pike recounts similar, yet more radical, experiences of re-enchantment, the development of porous boundaries between humans and other species and what she calls a "rewilding of the human self" (Pike 2017, 119).
7 For a more detailed discussion of the presented workshops in reference to Taylor's view on modernity, see Plancke (2019).

Acknowledgements

This research has been funded by the Flanders Research Foundation (FWO) under grant number FWOOPR2017000501. I would like to thank Chia Longman, director of the Centre for Research on Culture and Gender at Ghent University, for her willingness to supervise and support this research project. Furthermore, I am thankful to the workshop participants and conveners for having agreed to share their views and experiences with me.

References

Asad, Talal. 2003. *Formations of the Secular: Christianity, Islam, Modernity.* Stanford: Stanford University Press.

Beck, Ulrich and Beck-Gernsheim, Elisabeth. 2002. *Individualization: Institutionalised Individualisation and Its Social and Political Consequences.* London: Sage.

Berger, Peter (ed.). 1999. *The Desecularization of the World: Resurgent Religion and World Politics.* Grand Rapids: Eerdmans.

Bologh, Roslyn W. 1990. *Love or Greatness: Max Weber and Masculine Thinking – A Feminist Inquiry.* London: Unwin Hyman.

Bowman, Marion. 2004. "Procession and Possession in Glastonbury: Continuity, Change and the Manipulation of Tradition." *Folklore* 115(3): 273–285.

Braidotti, Rosi. 2008. "In Spite of the Times: The Postsecular Turn in Feminism." *Theory, Culture & Society* 25(6): 1–24.

Casanova, José. 1994. *Public Religions in the Modern World.* Chicago: University of Chicago Press.

Coleman, Kristy. 2009. *Re-riting Woman: Dianic Wicca and the Feminine Divine.* Lanham: Altamira Press.

Crowley, Karlyn. 2011. *Feminism's New Age: Gender, Appropriation and the Afterlife of Essentialism.* Albany: SUNY Press.

Estes, Clarissa. 2008 [1992]. *Women Who Run with the Wolves. Contacting the Power of the Wild Woman.* London: Rider.

Fedele, Anna and Kim Knibbe. (eds). 2013. *Gender and Power in Contemporary Spirituality.* New York: Routledge.

Genz, Stephanie. 2009. *Postfemininities in Popular Culture.* London: Palgrave Macmillan.

Habermas, Jürgen. 2008. "Secularism's Crisis of Faith: Notes on Post-Secular Society." *New Perspectives Quarterly* 25(4): 17–29.

Hanegraaff, Wouter J. 1996. *New Age Religion and Western Culture: Esotericism in the Mirror of Secular Thought.* Leiden: Brill.

Hanegraaff, Wouter J. 2003. "How Magic Survived the Disenchantment of the World." *Religion* 33(4): 357–380.

Heelas, Paul. 1996. *The New Age Movement: The Celebration of the Self and the Sacralization of Modernity.* Oxford: Blackwell.

Heelas, Paul. 2008. *Spiritualities of Life: New Age Romanticism and Consumptive Capitalism.* Oxford: Blackwell.

Ingman, Peik, Tehri Utriainen, Tuija Hovi and Måns Broo. 2016. "Introduction: Towards More Symmetrical Compositions". In *The Relational Dynamics of Enchantment and Sacralisation. Changing the Terms of the Religion versus Secularity Debate*, edited by Peik Ingman et al., 1–24. Sheffield: Equinox.

Jakobsen, Janet R. and Ann Pellegrini. 2008. "Introduction: Times like these". In *Secularisms*, edited by Janet R. Jakobsen and Ann Pellegrini, 1–35. Durham: Duke University Press.

Jenkins, Richard. 2000. "Disenchantment, Enchantment and Re-Enchantment. Max Weber at the Millenium." *Max Weber Studies* 1(1): 11–32.

Kieft, Eline. 2014. "Dance as a Moving Spirituality: A Case Study of Movement Medicine." *Dance, Movement & Spiritualities* 1(1): 21–41.

Lévy-Bruhl, Lucien. 1949. *Carnets.* Paris: Presses Universitaires de France.

Lévy-Bruhl, Lucien. 1960 [1922]. *La mentalité primitive.* Paris: Presses Universitaires de France.

Longman, Chia. 2018. "Women's Circles and the Rise of the New Feminine: Reclaiming Sisterhood, Spirituality and Wellbeing." *Religion* 9(1), 9. doi:10.3390/rel9010009

Maffesoli, Michel. 1988. *Le temps des tribus: Le déclin de l'individualisme dans les sociétés de masse.* Paris: Mérdiens Klincksieck.

Maffesoli, Michel. 2007. *Le réenchantement du monde: Une éthique pour notre temps.* Paris: Editions la Table Ronde.

Magliocco, Sabina. 2004. *Witching Culture: Folklore and Neo-paganism in America.* Philadelphia: University of Pennsylvania Press.

McRobbie, Angela. 2009. *The Aftermath of Feminism: Gender, Culture and Social Change.* Los Angeles: Sage.

Mirande, Yves. 2008. "Le retour du romantique." *Sociétés* 4(102): 61–68.

Moberg, Marcus, Kennet Granholm, and Peter Nynäs. 2012. "Trajectories of Post-Secular Complexity: An Introduction." In *Post-Secular Society*, edited by Peter Nynäs, Mika Lassander and Terhi Utriainen, 1–25. New Brunswick: Transaction Publishers.

Pike, Sarah. 2004. *New Age and Neopagan Religions in America.* New York: Columbia University Press.

Pike, Sarah. 2017. *For the Wild: Ritual and Commitment in Radical Eco-Activism.* Oakland: University of California Press.

Plancke, Carine. 2019. "Engendering Liminality: The Experience of Re-Enchantment in Wild Woman Workshops." *Social Compass* 66(3): 418–434.

Plancke, Carine. 2020. "Re-Envisioning Female Power: Wildness as a Transformative Re-Source in Contemporary Women's Spirituality." *Nova Religio* 23(3): 7–30.

Rountree, Kathryn. 2004. *Embracing the Witch and the Goddess: Feminist Ritual Makers in New Zealand.* London: Routledge.

Salomonsen, Jone. 2002. *Enchanted Feminism: The Reclaiming Witches of San Francisco.* London: Routledge.

Scharff, Christina. 2012. *Repudiating Feminism: Young Women in a Neoliberal World.* Farnham: Ashgate.

Sointu, Eeva and Linda Woodhead. 2008. "Spirituality, Gender and Expressive Self-hood." *Journal for the Scientific Study of Religion* 47(2): 259–276.

Taylor, Charles. 2007. *A Secular Age.* Cambridge, MA: The Belknap Press of Harvard University Press.

Trulsson, Åsa 2010. *Cultivating the Sacred: Ritual Creativity and Practice among Women in Contemporary Europe.* Lund University: Lund Studies in History of Religions.

Utriainen, Terhi. 2011. "The Post-Secular Position and Enchanted Bodies." *Scripta Instituti Donneriani Aboensis* 23: 417–723.

Vincett, Giselle, Sonya Sharma and Kristin Aune. 2008. "Introduction, Women, Religion and Secularization: One Size Does Not Fit All." In *Women and Religion in the West: Challenging Secularization*, edited by Kristin Aune, Sonya Sharma and Giselle Vincett, 1–22. Aldershot: Ashgate.

Weber, Max. 2004. "Science as a Vocation." In *Max Weber: The Vocation Lectures*, edited by David Owen and Tracy B. Strong. Translation by Rodney Livingstone. Indianapolis: Hackett Publishing Company.

Woodhead, Linda. 2008. "Gendering Secularization Theory." *Social Compass* 55(2): 189–195.

7 Gendering the spiritual marketplace

Public, private, and in-between

Laurel Zwissler

Introduction

The concept of "the spiritual marketplace" is one result of particular conceptions of secularism, in which religious participation becomes optional and specific religions are personal choices. In North American public space, hard-policed tensions between secularity and religion in the public sphere nonetheless allow a third category of "spirituality" to flourish. The category of spirituality highlights the fuzziness of the public/private split and ambivalences about where religion is supposed to fall in the divide. Further, the concomitant construction of personalized spirituality is grounded in notions of consumption as liberating and a sign of personal agency.

In the West, the division between public and private spheres historically relegated all non-economic transactions to the private, the traditionally feminine domain (Weintraub 1997; Reilly 2014). Yet the market also intervenes in intimacies, with domestic consumption symbolizing care-taking and affective attachment to family; that is, women's moral value. The contradictory messages of domestic consumption as both a moral virtue and as a frivolous, even corrupting practice in its required engagement with the outside world, create a historically familiar problem for women, caught in the middle as conduits between the public, in this case the market, and the private, in this case home and heart.

This project brings analysis of these historical trends together with fieldwork on a major fair-trade organization in the USA and Canada, Ten Thousand Villages, that works with volunteers, predominantly women. I draw on ethnographic work with stores in Toronto, Canada (2011–2012), and ongoing fieldwork with the flagship store in Ephrata, Pennsylvania (summer 2014 and 2015).[1] In this chapter I investigate how participants negotiate between their loyalty to the Christian values that founded the project, and the organization's current desire to compete in a secularized retail market.

Spirits of the market

Scholars continue to disagree on the definition and practical effects of secularization. Philosopher Charles Taylor (2007) offers three options for conceptualizing modern secularization: 1) religion retreats from public space and politics into the private sphere; 2) private belief and practice decline; or, 3) as a result of the above, religious belief becomes one available option, in contrast to the common default of non-belief. In contrast to secularization models that envision public space as emptied of religious discourses and practices, sociologist Peter Berger (2014) argues that contemporary secularity is actually constituted by experiences of religious pluralism. When people are free not to "default" to Christianity, public space opens up to multiple religious and non-religious options. However, as anthropologists Asad (2003) and Mahmood (2016) demonstrate, constructions of secularity and religious pluralism remain predicated on distinctly Protestant Christian assumptions about what constitutes both religion and the public sphere, historically built in explicit contrast to Islam and other religions in colonial contexts.

Competing definitions of secularism continue to drive political conflict on the ground. In the US context, defensive evangelical Christian groups tack between claiming unfair exclusion from public space, based on Taylor's first definition above, and claiming a right to public presence via equating secularization with religious plurality, as in Berger's formulation, of which they claim rightful part (Connolly 2010). Especially relevant to discussions of religion and consumption, the "war on Christmas," supposedly re-exposed each year in the US, mobilizes rhetoric of Christians as persecuted religious minorities deserving of protection in a religiously plural nation state (Castelli 2007; Norton and Summers 2011). Apparently unaware of the long history of Puritans fighting against the celebration of Christmas, based on concerns of both revelry and commercialism (Nissenbaum 1997; Bartuneck and Do 2011), evangelicals today invoke notions of founding fathers and Christian nation in their arguments for mandating the dominance of Christmas in retail spaces. Specifically objecting to some retailers' changes in customer service practices, away from greeting patrons with "Merry Christmas" and towards phrases like "Happy Holidays" (Olsen and Morgan 2009), some Christian-right communities portray the displacement of the once-hegemonic Christian holiday into a religiously plural space, one inclusive of numerous religious and civic holidays, as an attack. Interpreting their experience of reduced privilege as systemic oppression, evangelical communities seek government and social protections as persecuted minorities.

However, conservative Christian groups often abandon the minority-status strategy when their activism, demanding protection under rubrics of pluralism, is poised to result in actual religious diversity. As one cartoonish example among many, the fight to keep a monument of the Ten Commandments in front of the Oklahoma State Capitol, despite its blatant mixing of religion and government business, was nearly abandoned after the Satanic Temple sued to display a goat-heated statue of Baphomet to "complement and contrast" the Christian monument. The Universal Society of Hinduism also followed with a petition to place a statue of the Ramayana's monkey god, Lord Hanuman, nearby (Resnick 2014; Perez-Pena 2015). Ten Commandments proponents regrouped and now hope to specify that only Christian monuments may be displayed on state property, despite clear violation of the national constitution, and so the conflict remains ongoing.[2]

While the Baphomet anecdote and the "war on Christmas" agitation throw the tensions into relief, the place of Christianity within public space continues to be confusing for many, including those who do not identify with politicized evangelical Christianity. Ten Thousand Villages stores, interweaving a foundational Christian history, an ongoing social justice mission, and secular retail practices, provide an example of spaces in which secularism's ambivalences coalesce. As individuals negotiate their roles within the social space of the stores they must also engage categories of religion and secularity.

Ten Thousand Villages

Ten Thousand Villages is over 70 years old. Founded by American Mennonite Christian, Edna Ruth Byler, in 1946, Villages' projects were originally focused within the Mennonite community. This was largely because pre-existing social networks facilitated its early goals. A well-known story recounted often by Villages participants relates that Byler vacationed in Puerto Rico and met a women's sewing collective. Impressed with their embroidery, but shocked by the poverty she encountered on the island, she brought some of their handiwork back home, to see if she could get a better price for the women's products. Initially selling to family, friends, and fellow church members, Byler's informal distribution networks grew rapidly and developed into an international non-governmental organization, originally directed by the Mennonite Central Committee (MCC), a disaster-relief organization. However, today Villages now operates as an independent partner to the MCC, and is no longer an explicitly Mennonite organization.[3]

At its base, Villages' underlying Mennonite Christian values challenge what philosopher Phillip Goodchild (2009) has called the "theology of money." Goodchild criticizes the illusory construction of the public sphere as morally empty, even as profit is held to trump ethical concerns, thus slyly claiming its own moral superiority. In other words, capitalism constructs a regime of truth (Foucault 1995 [1977]) that makes it impossible to raise ethical objections to business practices, because the only legitimized scale of value is money. Fair trade offers an alternative worldview, in which the labor conditions under which an object was made affect its price. The consumer is ethically responsible for the wellbeing of the people who created the objects they purchase (Zwissler 2017).

The cosmology of interconnection posited by fair-trade organizations invokes religious values and is deeply, though often implicitly, gendered. Villages quotes Byler on its website, "I'm just a woman trying to help other women" (Ten Thousand Villages). Just as Byler's life example illustrates, women in the developed world are encouraged to help women in the developing world through integrating conscious consumerism into their management of domestic space. Such messaging echoes Victorian rescue relations and moralized gender complementarity: women are burdened with informally mitigating damages caused by the systemic inequalities of formal economic, religious, and political systems. However, it also draws on feminist care ethics, offering creative alternatives to traditional neoliberalism.

Customers have varying levels of knowledge about the individual stores and their overarching organization; therefore, they may or may not be familiar with the underlying Mennonite values or identify with the denomination. To a lesser degree, this varying level of engagement and religious affiliation is mirrored among the store employees and volunteers. Despite origins within a faith community, and despite the high numbers of volunteers and supporters with religious affiliations, the stores tacitly present themselves as secular. The aid they offer is not articulated in religious terms, although individual employees, volunteers, suppliers and customers frequently interpret their roles in the organization from within their own religious worldviews.

Sandra, manager at the store where I did the most sustained participant-observation in Toronto, said that many of their volunteers come from a wide range of religious backgrounds. In my work there, I have spoken with volunteers who are conservative evangelical Christian, mainline Christian, ISKCON members,[4] Buddhist, Mennonite, and religion-friendly atheist. Participants also shared stories of working with Muslim and contemporary Pagan volunteers. Religious diversity is something Sandra tries to be conscious of as a manager. She laughed as she told me about discussing this occupational challenge with her boyfriend. He works in corporate banking and was surprised to hear about this aspect of her job, juggling people's comfort levels with each other's religions. She repeated, "He said, 'That's not like the corporate environment at all. That stuff doesn't come up.' But it does, they just don't recognize it."

In contrast, my fieldwork with the flagship store in Ephrata revealed a very different religious world. Because it operates in the tight-knit world of Lancaster County, Pennsylvania, where the Mennonite Central Committee began, some staff, but especially volunteers and many customers, at the Ephrata location tacitly assumed that the store was Mennonite space. In my interviews, it became very clear that even those who did not identify with the denomination, culture, or ethnicity themselves nonetheless assumed that everyone else around them was Mennonite.

Ten Thousand Villages, as an organization built on but also trying to trans-cend specific religious values, must further grapple with challenges of plural-ism. If diverse religions are included in store space, that means that "Christianity" will be visible in company with other religions. In my field-work, it became clear that exactly what that visibility entails is a source of continuous negotiation.

First, given that the foundational Christianity from which the organization was built, Mennonite, is a minority denomination within the US, and given that supplier artisan groups often practice other types, the "Christianity" represented in store space actually comes in multiple forms; it becomes more appropriate to talk about "Christianities" in this context. Second, there is the challenge of trying to represent religions equally in store space when the political reality is that they are not actually on equal footing in a US context. In a Christian-dominant culture, Christianity often overtakes and crowds out everything else. Lastly, in practice, when Christian participants take issue with images or practices from another religion, they assume the right to override the plurality of the space in the name of orthopraxy. As much as the organization strives to uphold pluralism and accessibility, on the ground this becomes complex, especially because Villages relies on volunteers and long-term community partnerships, many of which are tied up with churches, both Mennonite and otherwise. One strategy for reconciling Christianity in the context of religious pluralism is a shift to the language of spirituality.

For example, in talking with Phoebe, long-time manager at another American store, about other participants' concerns over whether or not the stores are Christian space, she said,

> I can easily see how that could happen in any of our stores, but for us [in her store] it's clearly a spiritual space. There's a big difference between spiritual and religious. The comments we get most frequently from customers who come in are, "Ah I just love how it feels in here," "Oh, it's so calm in here," "Oh, it's so lovely in here," "Oh, it smells so good in here." ... So, I think the fact that the products we sell are made with love ... that creates a certain atmosphere, so yeah, it's definitely a spiritual space.

For Phoebe, the language of spirituality is a means to get around conflicts over religion and, instead, to emphasize a universally accessible experience of peace and contentment.

Gendering spirituality

The term "spirituality" has gendered connotations. As I have argued elsewhere (Zwissler 2018), if the struggle between secularization and religion is understood as a struggle between two traditionally patriarchal institutions, "church" and "state" in Western cultural contexts, then it makes sense that women and other marginalized communities may have little interest in the contest. Regardless of which institution has the upper hand in a given moment, women remain disempowered, objects rather than subjects (Scott 2011). In their conflicts, proponents of each side align the other with femininity through accusations of irrationality and reactivity, but concurrently accuse each other of oppressing women through sexism (Jakobson and Pellegrini 2008). In the midst of the dichotomy, the category of spirituality provides an alternative "third space" from which non-dominant groups, including women, can launch critiques of the institutions of secular state and religious authority, and from which they can imagine alternative distributions of power.

Disengagement from traditional forms of authority helps explain the decentered nature of contemporary spirituality in both practice and discourse. Generally eschewing single doctrines or leaders, broader spiritual communities are often diffuse and flexible.[5] Various labels, such as *bricolage* spirituality (Wilcox 2002; Magliocco 2004), spiritual creatives (Weible 2013; Badone 2008), or New Age (Hanegraaff 2007; Bender 2010; Zwissler 2011), describe methods of adopting and combining previously separate religious elements, rituals, terms and symbols into personal cosmologies. Emphasizing personal spiritual development and healing as key to improving the world around each individual, these spiritual techniques are adopted by non-institutionally aligned practitioners (e.g. Gilmore 2011; Bowman 2013), participants in new religious movements, such as contemporary Witchcraft and Paganism (e.g. Fedele 2013; Zwissler 2016a, 2016b), and members of more established religious traditions (e.g. Luhrmann 2012).

The practice of discovering, sorting and choosing elements from across religious traditions lends itself to the concept of a "spiritual marketplace." However, it is important to note that in their formulations scholars, such as sociologists Ellwood (1997) and economists Ekelund, Hébert, and Tollison (2006), approach the concept of a spiritual marketplace as a collision of competing coherent denominations and world religions. In these analyses, scholars present the spiritual marketplace as a metaphorical space of specific, whole traditions vying for members, rather than one of individual elements, removable from the historical and cosmological contexts of particular religious traditions. In this theoretical form, the spiritual marketplace is the venue in which prepackaged traditions compete for adherents.

However, in complicating formulations sociologists, such as Wuthnow (1994) and Roof (1999), treat religious identity as a dialectic of institutional templates and individual choices. Bender (2010), Gilmore (2011), and Bowman (2013) document ways that contemporary spiritual practitioners feel free to detach elements from specific religious traditions or cultural contexts without adopting related worldviews wholesale. Instead, practitioners create their own cosmologies out of hand-selected pieces, a process by turns celebrated by scholars as progressive resistance against hegemonic institutions and criticized as flippant cultural appropriation.

As practitioners curate their own worldviews out of chosen parts of others, their practices connect to broader cultural trends that emphasize the shopping experience as one of self-empowerment and expression (e.g. Cambell 1987; Graeber 2001). In the same way that a shopper may pick and choose clothing and decorative items to best construct a sense of self, so too can a practitioner select religious elements with which to construct a spiritual sense of self. In fact, these two activities, physical shopping and spiritual self-fashioning, are often combined simultaneously (Bowman 2013).

The potentially subversive power of spirituality to resist traditional institutions does not go unchallenged. Popular discourse criticizes spirituality's liberating/emancipatory claims in several ways. Here I will highlight two angles of such criticism that also align with traditional dismissals of women within Western culture. The first criticism is that personalized spirituality is immoral and selfish. The second criticism is that personalized spirituality is too easily co-opted by consumer culture, literally aligning its potentially alternative messages with "business as usual".

The first set of concerns deals with spirituality as selfish and not community oriented. From one of the earliest scholarly dismissals of individualized religiosity as self-absorbed, Bellah et al.'s (1985) criticism of "Sheila" and her Sheilah-ism (see also Wilcox 2002), non-institutionally aligned spirituality has regularly been met with disdain by scholars. Scholarly suspicion parallels criticism leveled by churches and other religious institutions; that alone should give pause to scholars engaged in the academic study of religion. Just as Braude (1997) demonstrates that the "feminization" thesis of American religion is, in fact, a theological argument grounded in Protestant concerns yet disguised as social science, so too is the tendency to blame the rise of non-aligned spirituality on self-centered women (Fedele and Knibbe 2013). Relatedly, Sointu and Woodhead (2008) argue that much of the critical backlash against spirituality is a reaction against messages that women should direct energy to self-care, rather than deplete themselves by exclusively caring for others (see also Knibbe 2013). The division between individual women's desires to promote their own wellbeing and the socially expected labor of caring for others also parallels divisions between feminist and backlash movements in the West (Zwissler 2018).

The second set of criticisms aimed at personalized spirituality is that it is easily subsumed into the market economy, thereby subverting its claims to challenge traditional institutions and encouraging, in the words of Donaldson, "psycho-spiritual collecting," rather than real, transformative work (2001). This line of criticism also branches into two related discussions. The first branch focuses on a concern that personalized spirituality is an extended form of the lazy self-indulgence associated with consumer culture, as discussed in the next section. The second branch focuses on ways that, in the pursuit of self-actualization, spiritual practitioners may unthinkingly perpetuate oppressions, such as racism and colonial exploitation, through cultural appropriation. If spiritual consumers do not reflect upon their own positions of privilege – often white privilege and middle-class socio-economic status, as well as first-world positionality – then it is easy for their do-it-yourself spirituality to continue to silence already marginalized cultures from which they "borrow" (Zwissler 2011).

The critique of cultural appropriation is especially significant in the North American social context in which legacies of racism are so salient and yet so obfuscated. However, it is also important to acknowledge ways that this type of criticism can just as easily be weighed against more established religions, and yet is not, even as religious institutions are arguably much more instrumental in creating and maintaining those very oppressions, based in colonial histories of racism. Precisely because of its diversity and its lack of interest in institutional authority, further compounded by its feminized connotations, personalized spirituality becomes an easy target for criticisms that apply all across societies that are based in inequalities. In other words, personalized spiritualities may perpetuate and exacerbate oppressions that exist across the cultures of which they are a part, but it is inaccurate to insist that they are solely responsible for them or to pretend that getting rid of non-institutionalized spirituality will actually solve those inequalities. It is also difficult not to see some forms of these criticisms, when leveled by more established religions against non-aligned spirituality, as a way of avoiding reflection on their own complicities or as attempts to deflect criticism from themselves (Zwissler 2016a).

Gendering consumption

The concept of a spiritual marketplace draws not only on inherently gendered categories of secularization versus institutionalized religion, but also on implicitly feminized concepts of consumption. As Gauthier, Woodhead and Martikainen write in discussing a lack of scholarly attention, "As has been the case with popular culture and mass media, consumption has been deemed trivial, superficial and debased ..." (2013, 23). For all the emphasis on (white) male subjectivity as comprised of and enacted through exercising choices, women and other marginalized communities are suspected of not being able to handle choices in practical or properly moral ways. Some of the most contentious political issues in the American context continue to revolve around freedom of choice over intimacy and embodiment: rape; birth control, including whether or not to terminate a pregnancy; sexual orientation; even which bathroom to use in public spaces. The political frames for these moral panics are set largely by white, heterosexually identified men (Puar 2007). Because shopping and consumption involve issues of choice – what to buy, where to buy, from whom to buy, how much to pay, whether to purchase on credit or save up – they invoke gendered and sexualized tensions.

The activity of shopping has historically been a discursive space to socially process conflicts over women's power in the home and in the public sphere. A rare realm of overlap between the private (female) space of the home and the public (male) space of the economy, women's shopping for domestic products, such as food, clothing, and decorative goods, brings the public and private into direct contact, highlighting the artificiality of their separation and thereby exacerbating tensions between them as ideals (Loeb 1994). Further, because women's domestic consumption has traditionally used economic resources supplied by men, it also induces androcentric social concerns about a lack of patriarchal control. Kowaleski-Wallace (1997, 3) writes, "Female consumption is a kind of depletion that 'eats up' everything in its path, laying waste to what men would otherwise preserve. It becomes symbolically emasculating when it demands the sacrifice of male resources." Men turn over their money to women so that currency might be transformed into the comforts of home. However, in giving their money, men are afraid of also handing over power and control, their very headship, along with it.

The stereotype of the "shopaholic" is one example of the association of women's shopping with irresponsibility and emotionality (e.g. Kinsella 2001; for analysis, see Jubas 2010, 138–156). Even when adopted as a humorous self-identity by women themselves, it reflects social sanction. Another stereotype that reflects misogynist concerns about female consumption as well as racism is the "Welfare Queen" (Foster 2008), who exploits not an individual man's resources, but that of the entire nation, in her pursuit of unearned comfort and luxury items. These stereotypes further demonstrate ways that consumption is not only gendered, but also raced and classed (Williams 2006).

Scholars focusing on consumer behavior have suggested underlying motivation as a way to subdivide the goals and experiences of shopping. Consumer behavior researchers refer to the categories of "utilitarian" and "hedonic" shopping practices (e.g. Hirschman and Holbrook 1982; Babin, Darden and Griffin 1994). Utilitarian shopping focuses on procuring necessary items and is supposed to be a purely instrumental exercise. Hedonic shopping practices focus on the emotional effects that procuring particular objects creates for the purchaser; it is driven by desire. Clearly, analysis itself creates this division; a single shopping experience may involve elements of both practicality and pleasure.

It is also not happenstance that utilitarian modes are generally correlated to men and hedonic are correlated to women (Tifferet and Herstein 2012). Gendered socialization encourages men to view shopping as "women's work" and therefore a potentially demeaning chore (Dholakia 1999; Otnes and McGrath 2001), whereas socialization encourages women to view shopping as empowering, fun, social, and a mode for self-transformation (Alreck and Settle 2002; against generalizing, see Otieno, Harrow, and Lea Greenwood 2005). Even as these subdivisions of shopping behavior reflect cultural assumptions about who is responsible for shopping and who is supposed to enjoy shopping, they also draw on moralistic categories. "Hedonism" is generally understood as self-serving and irresponsible: bumping up against Weber's Protestant ethic (1995), money used to purchase non-utilitarian items is money not invested (though see Cambell 1987).

In a cultural world of gendered dichotomies, shopping and consumption are feminized and juxtaposed to masculinized values of supply and production. Capitalist societies need consumers to spend money, but individual households need their consumer spending to be disciplined and rational. As Kowaleski-Wallace discusses, Victorian culture "projected onto the female subject both its fondest wishes for the transformative power of consumerism and its deepest anxieties about the corrupting influence of goods" (1997, 5). These tensions erupt in contradictory stereotypes targeting women. Women must spend money to care for their household, but just the right amount, in just the right way (Elisha 2011). They must not pursue fashion to the detriment of thrift, but they must also remain attractive and keep their loved ones respectable. Domestic shopping can be a moral minefield for women, in which both spending and not spending produce gender-performance failure.

Unfaithful women

Tensions over the moral value of consumerism are especially salient in Villages' corporate training efforts, directed at sales people, and in the trainees' reactions to them. Based on the results of multiple marketing surveys, corporate leadership has developed customer character profiles, such as the Duty-Bound Shopper, the Caring Emotional Giver, and the Seasonal Stalwart. Reflecting the demographic reality that the majority of the stores' customers are women, the profiles are feminized. At the annual store manager conference, in a session on "Understanding Your Customer", the trainer explained the construction of these different profiles, but then zeroed in on one, in particular, the elusive Happy Treasure Seeker (Brown 2013 also discusses). Corporate feels that the stores do well with other profiles, but that the "HTS" is a relatively untapped demographic for them and, therefore, the key to expanding sales. It remains implicit, but at times the rhapsodizing about the HTS suggests that connecting with this type of shopper is the key to keeping Villages in business.

Ah, but the composite Happy Treasure Seeker is promiscuous. She shops at many hip stores and fair-trade is not her driving concern; she just wants unique, but very "on-trend" items. Unlike the loyal customer base that Villages has developed over decades, shoppers who prioritize fair-trade items and simply choose the best of the available store selection, HTS will not buy unless she absolutely loves something. If she loves it, however, she will spend freely.

The attitude that organization members should do everything they can to court this type of shopper seemed to perplex the store managers in the training. As one said to me after, "I don't understand why we're chasing this imaginary shopper when we have loyal customers who understand our projects." More general anxiety over the labor involved in producing sales is directed at the imaginary Happy Treasure Seeker who, unlike many of those being trained to serve her, has much expendable income and capricious aesthetic, rather than moral, tastes. In other words, a difficult market is given an imaginary young, female form, against which employees react with confusion.

Notions of loyalty and disloyalty are directly shaped by consumer research discourse. As discussed above, in pursuing goals of understanding and potentially redirecting socialized behavior, rather than deconstructing its origins in systems of power, consumer research literature reinforces stereotypical assumptions about different social demographics. In the case of Villages' customer profiling, desire for the spending money of the HTS mixes with frustration that it must be so hard-earned. Reactions to this teasing, constructed profile replicate gendered stereotypes. Members of Villages want women to be faithful to the store, to spend money on gifts and the occasional personal treat, but become critical of the kind of consumerism that trendy shopping, a potentially lucrative business for them, represents.

Home economics

Paralleling customer demographics, the majority of Villages' employees and volunteers are middle-aged and white, but they are also women. The signs produced by the marketing department feature smiling artisans, a majority of whom are people of color and also women. In perusing a physical store or visiting the website, customers can learn about the artisan collectives that make the products they are browsing, see pictures, and read personal stories. The objects themselves are almost entirely home furnishings, beauty products, and food, consumer goods generally associated with domestic space and, therefore, women.

The environment of Villages stores is coded as domestic space in several ways. As Phoebe, manager, described her role, "The spiritual thing about the store to me is, it's almost like you're welcoming people into your home." The items available for purchase are overwhelmingly for home use. Stores are subdivided into sections formulated around the areas of a typical middle-class home, including kitchen, dining, living room, and bedroom, as well as additional sections for food and bath products. Clothing for sale is predominantly designed for women, with occasional items for children.

Volunteers are encouraged to direct customers shopping particularly for men to a few specific items, such as an eyeglasses holder and a chess set, with the underlying message that most of the stores' products would appeal more directly to women. Phoebe, the store manager who describes the stores as spiritual, finds the presumptions behind these customer service practices frustrating. She said, "The opinion persists, 'We don't have anything for men.' And I'll say to people, 'The men in my family are 24, 36, and 62, so they're a wide range, they all pretty much like everything in here.'" She summed it up, "My opinion is that men love beautiful things just as much as women do and I believe that we do not pay enough attention to that." As she knows, Phoebe's perspective is not widely shared.

Beyond having a volunteer and staff base almost entirely comprised of women, Sandra and Carrie, as management, reinforced the sense of the Toronto store as a feminized, domestic space in several additional ways. When customers arrived, those of us working the sales floor greeted them by asking if they would like a cup of the fair-trade coffee we always had brewing in the back. If they preferred tea, we plugged in the electric kettle. Several times a week, volunteers would bring home-made food into the break room to share. When customers lagged, we would talk about recipes or send someone down the street for lattes.

Sandra and Carrie would often consult with volunteers about what food items they should open for customer sampling and then decide based on what we were ourselves in the mood to nibble. One particularly trying morning, after the storefront window had been smashed overnight by some teenagers, requiring Sandra to come in at 4 a.m. to oversee the police report, clean-up, and supervise replacement, Carrie declared that we all needed a special treat.

She opened an especially expensive box of chocolate-peppermint wafers for "sampling." In an empty, just-opened store, we gathered together around the chocolate, sipped our coffee, and soothed each other's nerves with conversation.

The marking of stores as domestic space goes beyond the physical layouts, products, and staff practices and continues into the mission of the organization itself. As Villages constructs an ethics of interconnection, it does so in a largely feminine world, in which women are helping women. This construction by turns mobilizes current feminist discourses about global sisterhood and feminist care ethics, making the "other" into an intimate (Noddings 2003; Held 2006). However, it also invokes long traditions of women in the West rescuing women in the developing world (Loomba 2005). Further, it tasks women with lessening the harms of global systems through domestic consumption practices.

Critics argue that fair trade correctly identifies problems caused by global capitalism, but, rather than taking on the system itself, suggests minor tweaks within it (Zwissler 2017). Leveraging consumer power within a capitalist system means maintaining its structures and redeploying, rather than undoing, its power dynamics (Doane 2010). Privileged women, and some men, are being asked to soften the damage that the larger systems of their privilege cause in the first place. Yet, particular fair-trade projects do indeed change specific women's lives and sometimes whole communities. Nonetheless, in the same way that Villages' economic practice accepts capitalist models even as it tries to mitigate their harm, it also accepts some Western gender models, even as it strives to help women artisans in the developing world. By connecting the purchasing power of Western women with the productive labor power of women artisans abroad, Villages creates ethical relationships out of links in the supply chain.

Proper and improper relationships

The ability of material objects to represent ethical connections and blur the cultural boundaries between people also materializes metaphysical dangers for some store workers. Sandra, the Toronto manager, told me that certain objects used to go missing from the sales floor, only to turn up months later, stashed in strange places in the storage basement. It wasn't random: items that would go missing included Tibetan Buddhist prayer flags (an item no longer carried by the company) and singing bowls.

She suspected that the more conservative, evangelical Christian employees would deliberately disappear the items because they objected to them on religious grounds. Sandra's way of dealing with the issue, after a few times of simply returning the items to the floor without comment, was to announce a general policy that they needed to keep better track of inventory. Privately, however, she addressed the individuals she knew were up to the shenanigans and simply told them it had to stop: no judgment, no denial, but it can't happen anymore. I myself never experienced such mysteriously missing items, so my impression is that the issue had resolved by the time I was working in the store.

This concern, the danger that the wrong kinds of objects can open up the wrong kinds of connections, actually fits well in the larger scheme of fair-trade cosmology. Consumer items obtained through unfair trade and exploitation carry with them *negative* ethical currency. As a college friend used to say, "There's blood in your tea." When combined with particular kinds of dualistic Christianity, this view can expand from the equity of the labor involved in producing the item, to the religious purpose of the item, or even the religion of the person *creating* the item. In other words, non-Christian religions taint certain physical objects. In a rather surprising way, then, fair trade becomes compatible with spiritual warfare theology.[6]

Carrie, the Toronto assistant manager and a new Christian, told me that she and long-time volunteer, Deborah, were especially concerned about the singing bowls and, when they were alone in the store sometimes, they would pray over them. She said, "We just ask God that he would bless them, that they would only sing songs that praise him and nothing else." The presence of Buddhist religious objects causes anxiety for certain staff, anxiety that is somewhat managed by bringing these objects back within a Christian frame through focused prayer, asserting theological authority over them. In the Ephrata store, there were similar tensions over items, such as a decorative three-legged pottery pig from Peru, which one employee believes draws on a tradition of Indigenous magic and is therefore not Christian, Thai carvings of the Buddha, and a CD, no longer stocked, from the Philadelphia Gay Men's Choir.

I want to stress that these concerns were unique to a select few individuals; most staff and volunteers enjoy the eclecticism of the different items in the store and many stressed to me how important it is to them that Villages and the MCC do not proselytize to the people they help in the developing world. Moreover, to emphasize her view that the store she manages is a spiritual space, Phoebe shared a story of meeting an artisan from the Philippines, who puts hand-made cards into their plastic sleeves to be shipped to North American stores. The artisan told Phoebe that she puts a blessing on every card as she processes it, hoping for good things for the person who buys it. To be fair, based on the dominant religion in the Philippines, odds are high that this artisan is Roman Catholic, but her story demonstrates that the same potential for metaphysical connection that unsettles Carrie and Deborah warms Phoebe's heart.

Anxieties about policing the spiritual influences of objects in the store parallel concerns that women must police the home to protect it from the untoward influences of the outside world. Drawing on Victorian domestic ideals (Hartnell 1996; Moore 2015), the home, as a traditionally feminine domain, is idealized as free from the Douglasian dirt of politics and the flow of history (Douglas 2005; Scott 2011). As strict separation between home, community, and world becomes increasingly untenable, a nostalgia for this imagined refuge underlies many contemporary discourses: political, religious, and economic. In this sense, concerns over the wrong kind of religious plur-alism invoke traditions of women's boundary-keeping roles relating to domesticity, which remain consistent with other ways the stores and their mission are tacitly feminized.

Conclusion

The concept of a "spiritual marketplace" has largely been invoked to describe religious choice in a secularizing culture; however, the term can also be rede-ployed to describe spaces in which consumption is linked to spirituality. It is this latter sense that is most prominent in the context of Ten Thousand Villages. Founded on Mennonite values and supported by communities that still embrace them, in its efforts to bring more money to disadvantaged artisans abroad, Ten Thousand Villages must promote consumption and model its stores on other retailers, making itself legible and appealing to non-Mennonite consumers. In other words, it has to appear secular, at least in the sense of being religiously plural. Customers find "exotic" items on shelves, produced in far-off places, some of which connect to non-Christian religious ideas and practices. For some Villages members, the openness of the organization to religious diversity is a metaphysical threat that needs to be controlled in order to keep the store, the staff and the customers safe from unwholesome, spiritual influences. While the stores' religious plurality unsettles particular staff, others embrace the language of spirituality to construct a more inclusive space, in which the organizations' traditionally Christian values can remain, co-existing with products and ideas from other religions. Participants' negotiations between religious purity and relational ethics occur in a cultural context in which both spirituality and con-sumerism are feminized.

Villages provides an opportunity to explore ways that a non-profit, originally based on explicitly Christian values, negotiates with secular markets, volunteers, and consumers at the same time that it tries to keep religious participants happy and engaged. Layers of communication variously emphasize or obfuscate Christian codes of salvation, mission, and charity. Such ethical cosmologies, which historically have been, and sometimes continue to be, explicitly articulated as religious, invoke metaphysical interconnection and mutual responsibility, concepts that Villages now strives to reframe, not as exclusively Christian, but as secular and, therefore, universal. Thus, Ten Thousand Villages offers an oppor-tunity to observe broader cultural tensions over gender, secularization, and religion as they play out within a particular "spiritual marketplace".

Notes

1 All participants have been assigned pseudonyms.
2 The State House of Representatives passed a measure in April 2016 offering Oklahoma voters a chance to amend the state constitution to allow state funds or property to be used towards religious purposes, which would allow the Ten Commandments to return

to the Capitol, unthreatened by the need for equal recognition of other religions (Mayer 2016). It was defeated, but a new bill, calling for another public vote, was reintroduced and has passed the state house (Querry 2017).

3 It is worth noting that this is a recent shift for Ten Thousand Villages, which completed a change from being wholly owned by the MCC to a partnership in 2012. The process was outlined on the website, http://www.tenthousandvillages.com/about-history/. Accessed November 7, 2011.

4 The International Society for Krishna Consciousness is a form of Hinduism that missionizes to the West. Members are often referred to as "Hare Krishnas" because of their public performances of mantras.

5 Of course, specific spirituality communities often form around particular teachings and teachers. Knibbe (2013) persuasively argues that the criticism of religious institutional authority within spiritual communities can obfuscate existing hierarchies.

6 On evangelical spiritual warfare, see Cuneo 2001; Luhrmann 2012.

References

Alreck, Pamela and Robert B. Settle. 2002. "Gender Effects on Internet, Catalogue and Store Shopping." *Journal of Database Marketing & Customer Strategy Management* 9(2): 150–162.

Asad, Talal. 2003. *Formations of the Secular: Christianity, Islam, Identity.* Stanford, CA: Stanford University Press.

Babin, Barry J., William R. Darden, and Mitch Griffin. 1994. "Work and/or Fun: Measuring Hedonic and Utilitarian Shopping Value." *Journal of Consumer Research* 20(4): 644–656.

Badone, Ellen. 2008. "Pilgrimage, Tourism and the Da Vinci Code at Les-Sainte-De-La-Mer France." *Culture and Religion* 9(1): 23–44.

Bartunek, Jean M. and Boram Do. 2011. "The Sacralization of Christmas Commerce." *Organization* 18(6): 795–806.

Bellah, Robert N., Richard Madsen, William M. Sullivan, Ann Swidler, and Steven M. Tipton. 1985. *Habits of the Heart: Individualism and Commitment in American Life.* Berkeley, CA: University of California Press.

Bender, Courtney. 2010. *The New Metaphysicals: Spirituality and the American Religious Imagination.* Chicago: University of Chicago Press.

Berger, Peter. 2014. *The Many Altars of Modernity: Toward a Paradigm of Religion in a Pluralist Age.* Berlin: De Gruyter.

Bowman, Marion. 2013. "Valuing Spirituality: Commodification, Consumption and Community in Glastonbury." In *Religion in Consumer Society: Brands, Consumers and Markets,* edited by François Gauthier and Tuomas Martikainen, 207–224. Farnham, UK: Ashgate.

Braude, Ann. 1997. "Women's History Is American Religious History." In *Retelling U. S. Religious History,* edited by Thomas Tweed, 87–107. Berkeley, CA: University of California Press.

Brown, Keith R. 2013. *Buying into Fair Trade: Culture, Morality and Consumption.* New York: NYU Press.

Cambell, Colin. 1987. *The Romantic Ethic and the Spirit of Modern Consumerism.* New York: Blackwell.

Castelli, Elizabeth A. 2007. "Persecution Complexes: Identity Politics and the 'War on Christians.'" *Differences: A Journal of Feminist Cultural Studies* 18(3): 152–180.

Connolly, William E. 2010. "Belief, Spirituality, and Time." In *Varieties of Secularism in a Secular Age*, edited by Michael Warner, Jonathan Van Anterpen, and Craig Calhoon, 126–144. Cambridge, MA: Harvard University Press.

Cuneo, Michael W. 2001. *American Exorcism: Expelling Demons in the Land of Plenty.* New York: Doubleday.

Doane, Molly. 2010. "Relationship Coffees: Structure and Agency in the Fair Trade System." In *Fair Trade and Social Justice: Global Ethnographies*, edited by Sarah Lyon and Mark Moberg, 229–257. New York: NYU Press.

Dholakia, Ruby Roy. 1999. "Going Shopping: Key Determinants of Shopping Behaviors and Motivations." *International Journal of Retail & Distribution Management* 27(4): 154–165.

Donaldson, Laura E. 2001. "On Medicine Women and White Same-ans: New Age Native Americanism and Commodity Fetishism as Pop Culture Feminism." In *Women, Gender, Religion: A Reader*, edited by Elizabeth Castelli and Roseamond C. Rodman, 237–256. New York: Palgrave.

Douglas, Mary. 2005 [1966]. *Purity and Danger: An Analysis of the Concept of Pollution and Taboo.* New York: Routledge.

Ekelund, Robert B. Jr., Robert F. Hébert, and Robert Tolleson. 2006. *The Marketplace of Christianity.* Cambridge, MA: MIT Press.

Elisha, Omri. 2011. *Moral Ambition: Mobilization and Social Outreach in Evangelical Megachurches.* Berkeley, CA: University of California Press.

Ellwood, Robert. 1997. *The Fifties Spiritual Marketplace: American Religion in a Decade of Conflict.* New Brunswick, NJ: Rutgers University Press.

Fedele, Anna. 2013. *Looking for Mary Magdalene: Alternative Pilgrimage and Ritual Creativity at Catholic Shrines in France.* New York: Oxford University Press.

Fedele, Anna and Kim Knibbe. 2013. "Introduction: Gender and Power in Contemporary Spirituality." *Gender and Power in Contemporary Spirituality: Ethnographic Approaches*, edited by Anna Fedele and Kim E. Knibbe, 1–27. New York: Routledge.

Foster, Carly Haydan. 2008. "The Welfare Queen: Race, Gender, Class, and Public Opinion." *Race, Gender & Class* 15(3/4): 162–179.

Foucault, Michel. 1995 [1977]. *Discipline and Punish: The Birth of the Prison*, translated by Alan Sheridan. New York: Vintage.

Gauthier, François, Linda Woodhead and Tuomas Martikainen. 2013. "Introduction: Consumerism as an Ethos of Consumer Society." In *Religion in Consumer Society: Brands, Consumers and Markets*, edited by François Gauthier and Tuomas Martikainen, 1–24. Farnham, UK: Ashgate.

Gilmore, Lee. 2011. "DIY Spiritual Community: From Individualism to Participatory Culture." In *Media, Spirituality and Social Change*, edited by Stewart M. Hoover and Monica Emerich, 37–46. New York: Continuum.

Goodchild, Philip. 2009. *The Theology of Money.* Durham, NC: Duke University Press.

Graeber, David. 2001. *Toward an Anthropology of Values: The False Coin of Our Own Dreams.* New York: Palgrave.

Hanegraaff, Wouter J. 2007. "The New Age Movement and Western Esotericism." In *Handbook of the New Age*, edited by Daren Kemp and James R. Lewis, 25–50. Boston: Beacon.

Hartnell, Elaine. 1996. "'Nothing but Sweet and Womanly': A Hagiography of Pateore's Angel." *Victorian Poetry* 34(4): 457–476.

Hirschman, Elizabeth C. and Morris B. Holbrook. 1982. "Hedonic consumption: Emerging concepts, methods and propositions." *Journal of Marketing* 46: 92–101.

Jakobsen, Janet R. and Anne Pellegrini. 2008. "Introduction: Times Like These." In *Secularisms*, edited by Janet R. Jakobsen and Ann Pellegrini, 1–35. Durham, NC: Duke University Press.

Jubas, Kaela. 2010. *The Politics of Shopping: What Consumers Learn about Identity, Globalization and Social Change.* Walnut Creek, CA: Left Coast Press.

Held, Virginia. 2006. *The Ethics of Care: Personal, Political, Global.* New York: Oxford.

Kinsella, Sophie. 2001. *Confessions of a Shopaholic.* New York: Dell.

Knibbe, Kim. 2013. "Obscuring the Role of Power and Gender in Contemporary Spiritualities." In *Gender and Power in Contemporary Spirituality: Ethnographic Approaches*, edited by Anna Fedele and Kim Knibbe, 179–194. New York: Routledge.

Kowaleski-Wallace, Elizabeth. 1997. *Consuming Subjects: Women, Shopping, and Business in the Eighteenth Century.* New York: Columbia University Press.

Loeb, Lori Anne. 1994. *Consuming Angels: Advertising and Victorian Women.* Oxford: Oxford University Press.

Loomba, Ania. 2005. *Colonialism/Postcolonialism.* London: Routledge.

Luhrmann, Tanya M. 2012. *When God Talks Back: Understanding the American Evangelical Relationship with God.* New York: Vintage.

Magliocco, Sabina. 2004. *Witching Culture: Folklore and Neo-Paganism in America.* Philadelphia: University of Pennsylvania Press.

Mahmood, Saba. 2016. *Religious Difference in a Secular Age: A Minority Report.* Princeton, NJ: Princeton University Press.

Mayer, Anna. 2016. "Oklahoma House Passes Resolution Giving Potential to Ten Commandments Monument." *Oklahoma Daily.* http://www.oudaily.com/news/oklahoma-house-passes-resolution-giving-potential-to-ten-commandments-monument/article_a6eedfb4-08c2-11e6-a548-ef6f26f1ec11.html Accessed June 23, 2016.

Moore, Natasha. 2015. "The Realism of the Angel in the House: Coventry Patmore's Poem Reconsidered." *Victorian Literature and Culture* 43(1): 41–61.

Nissenbaum, Stephan. 1997. *The Battle for Christmas: A Cultural History of America's Most Cherished Holiday.* New York: Vintage.

Noddings, Nel. 2003 [1984]. *Caring: A Feminine Approach to Ethics and Moral Education.* Berkeley, CA: University of California Press.

Norton, Michael I. and Samuel R.Summers. 2011. "Whites See Racism as a Zero-Sum Game That They Are Now Losing." *Perspectives on Psychological Science* 6(3): 215–218.

Olsen, Richard K. and Julie W. Morgan. 2009. "Happy Holidays: Creating Common Ground in the 'War on Christmas.'" *Journal of Religion and Popular Culture* 21(3): 1–21.

Otieno, Rose, Chris Harrow, and Gaynor Lea Greenwood. 2005. "The Unhappy Shopper, a Retail Experience: Exploring Fashion, Fit and Affordability." *International Journal of Retail & Distribution Management* 33(4): 298–309.

Otnes, Cele and Mary Ann McGrath. 2001. "Perceptions and Realities of Male Shopping Behavior." *Journal of Retailing* 77(1): 111–137.

Perez-Pena, Richard. 2015. "Oklahoma Removes Ten Commandments Monument." *New York Times.* http://www.nytimes.com/2015/10/07/us/oklahoma-removes-ten-commandments-monument.html?_r=0. Accessed June 23, 2016.

Puar, Jasbir K. 2007. *Terrorist Assemblages: Homonationalism in Queer Times.* Durham, NC: Duke University Press.

Querry, Kimberly. 2017. "Bill That Would Allow Ten Commandments Back at the Capitol Passes Oklahoma House." KFOR-TV. http://kfor.com/2017/03/22/bill-that-would-allow-ten-commandments-back-at-the-capitol-passes-oklahoma-house/. Accessed March 30, 2017.

Reilly, Niamh. 2014. "Introduction: Religion Gender and the Public Sphere: Mapping the Terrain." In *Religion, Gender and the Public Sphere*, edited by Niamh Reilly and Stacey Scriver, 1–17. New York: Routledge.

Resnick, Giddeon. 2014. "Who Are the Satanists Designing an Idol for the Oklahoma Capitol?" *The Atlantic.* http://www.theatlantic.com/politics/archive/2014/02/who-are-the-satanists-designing-an-idol-for-the-oklahoma-capitol/283567/ Accessed June 23, 2016.

Roof, Wade Clark. 1999. *Spiritual Marketplace: Baby Boomers and the Remaking of American Religion.* Princeton, NJ: Princeton University Press.

Scott, Joan Wallach. 2011. "Sexularism: On Secularism and Gender Equality." In *The Fantasy of Feminist History*, 91–116. Durham, NC: Duke University Press.

Sointu, Eeva and Linda Woodhead. 2008. "Spirituality, Gender and Expressive Self-hood." *Journal for the Scientific Study of Religion* 47(2): 259–276.

Taylor, Charles. 2007. *A Secular Age.* Cambridge, MA: Belknap.

Ten Thousand Villages. n.d. "About Us." http://www.tenthousandvillages.com/about-history/. Accessed November 7, 2011 and April 28, 2017.

Tifferet, Sigal, and Ram Herstein. 2012. "Gender Differences in Brand Commitment, Impulse Buying, and Hedonic Consumption." *Journal of Product & Brand Management* 21(3): 176–182.

Weber, Max. 1995 [1905]. *The Protestant Ethic and the Spirit of Capitalism*, translated by Talcott Parsons. Los Angeles: Roxbury.

Weible, Deana L. 2013. "Blind in a Land of Visionaries: When a Non-Pilgrim Studies Pilgrimage." In *Missionary Impositions: Conversion, Resistance, and Other Challenges to Objectivity in Religious Ethnography*, edited by Hillary Crane and Deana Weibel, 93–108. Lanham, MD: Lexington Books.

Weintraub, Jeff. 1997. "The Theory and Politics of the Public/Private Distinction." In *Public and Private in Thought and Practice: Perspectives on a Grand Dichotomy*, edited by Jeff Weintraub and Krishan Kumar. Chicago: University of Chicago Press.

Wilcox, Melissa M. 2002. "When Sheila's a Lesbian: Religious Individualism among Lesbian, Gay, Bisexual, and Transgender Christians." *Sociology of Religion* 63(4): 497–513.

Williams, Christine L. 2006. *Inside Toyland: Working, Shopping, and Social Inequality.* Berkeley, CA: University of California Press.

Wuthnow, Robert. 1994. *Sharing the Journey: Support Groups and America's New Quest for Community.* New York: Free Press.

Zwissler, Laurel. 2011. "Pagan Pilgrimage: New Religious Movements Research on Sacred Travel within Pagan and New Age Communities." *Religion Compass* 5(7): 326–342.

Zwissler, Laurel. 2016a. "In Memorium Maleficarum: Contemporary Pagan Mobilizations of the Burning Times." In *Emotions in the History of Witchcraft*, edited by Laura Kounine and Michael Ostling, 249–268. London: Palgrave.

Zwissler, Laurel. 2016b. "Witches Tears: Spiritual Feminism, Epistemology, and Witch Hunt Horror Stories." *The Pomegranate: International Journal of Pagan Studies* 18 (2): 176–204.

Zwissler, Laurel. 2017. "Markets of the Heart: Negotiating Economic and Ethical Values at Ten Thousand Villages." In *Anthropological Considerations of Production, Exchange, Vending and Tourism*, edited by Donald C. Wood. Research in Economic Anthropology, Volume 37. Bingley: Emerald Publishing.

Zwissler, Laurel. 2018. *Religious, Feminist, Activist: Cosmologies of Interconnection.* Lincoln, NE: University of Nebraska.

8 "God wants spiritual fruits not religious nuts"

Spirituality as middle way between religion and secularism at the Marian shrine of Fátima

Anna Fedele

The streets of Fátima were getting more and more crowded with pilgrims every day as the celebrations for 13 May 2016 drew closer. I had finally scheduled my first formal interview for a research project focusing on pilgrimage, gender and lived religion to coincide with the occasion of the celebrations of the centenary of the apparitions of Our Lady of Fátima (2016–2017). Although I had already talked with Beth on several occasions, I was a bit worried about the development of the interview. I expected to be confronted with a different scenario from those I had encountered during earlier fieldwork among Mary Magdalene pilgrims for my dissertation (2013a). Although the Mary Magdalene pilgrims I had accompanied came from a Christian (mostly Catholic) background and visited Catholic shrines dedicated to Saint Mary Magdalene or holding 'Black Madonna' statues (Fedele 2013b), they were influenced by Goddess spirituality, generally considered themselves spiritual but not religious and tended to describe everything in terms of energy. Beth, on the other hand, was a militant Catholic from Northern Ireland. She had organized pilgrimages from Ireland to Fátima as well as to other Marian apparition sites in Europe for many years and had links with the World Apostolate of Fátima (formerly called Blue Army of Fátima).

As I often do, I tried to break the asymmetry inherent to ethnographic interviews by sharing also personal feelings and experiences. Answering Beth's question about my favourite spots in Fátima, I explained how much I loved the area close to *Aljustrel*, the village of the three visionaries. To my great surprise, Beth answered approvingly: "I see, you are more a spiritual person than a religious one!" As I would gradually discover, this was only the tip of the iceberg and I would meet many Catholic pilgrims from different countries who described themselves as spiritual but not religious. Building upon findings about the religion/spirituality divide in the companion volume to this book, as well as in texts by other authors, who have argued for a more nuanced approach regarding this dichotomy, this chapter explores how the pilgrims' spirituality relates to religion but also to secularism.

In the last few decades, religious studies scholars have analysed the growing number of people who describe themselves as 'spiritual but not religious'.

According to this dichotomy, spirituality is seen as a positive term, associated with personal contact with divine forces, attained through practices that require little or no external mediation from gurus, priests or other authoritative figures. Although there may be variations depending on local contexts, there seem to be some features commonly related to spirituality. Spirituality tends to be seen as non-hierarchical and gender equal, empowering people in terms of gender but also, in a more general sense, allowing the individual to connect with his or her own inner authority and power, often described as the (Inner) Self. Religion, on the other hand, is perceived in rather negative terms, as a hierarchical and age encrusted authority structure that disempowers the individual by imposing figures such as priests as mediators between the individual and the divine. Criticism of religion usually focuses on monotheistic religions and more specifically on Christian religions (e.g. Klassen 2001; Sointu and Woodhead 2008; Fedele and Knibbe 2013).

Initially believed to be used mainly within alternative spirituality movements (Heelas and Woodhead 2004), this spiritual/religious dichotomy was also soon discovered to be in use among those observing traditional religious beliefs and practices (Fedele and Knibbe 2013; Ammerman 2013). So far scholars have paid little attention to the ways in which the spiritual/religious binary is gradually being assimilated by Catholics. This chapter aims to start filling this lacuna, analysing how an increasing number of Catholic pilgrims in Fátima prefer to describe themselves as spiritual rather than religious and teasing out what they mean by 'spiritual'.

The analysis of culturally constructed discourses related to spirituality can provide a window on the underlying social meanings that shape contemporary religious and spiritual, as well as secular, domains. Like other authors in this volume (Zwissler, Knibbe), I found that in Fátima people seem to use spirituality to describe a middle way between religion and secularism. Drawing on Nancy Ammerman's analysis of the spiritual but non-religious in the United States (2013), I show that by calling themselves spiritual, the pilgrims draw a moral boundary between themselves and what they consider as a sort of religious, immoral enemy. Moving some steps further, I argue that the pilgrims also create a bridge towards secularism, strategically using a spiritual *lingua franca* they feel can be acceptable both for those representing Catholic local institutions and for secular institutions or viewpoints. Spirituality offers the pilgrims a language, which they perceive as being more acceptable to secularism and to non-believers without invalidating their belonging to Catholicism.

By using this distinction, pilgrims are not only adopting a different descriptive position but also engaging in political work. Catholic pilgrims in Fátima challenge certain positions adopted by the Vatican, in general, and the local Church, in particular, and embrace what they perceive as more secular values, especially those related to feminism, such as gender equality and the freedom of sexual orientation. This distinction between spirituality and religion implies an important and spreading criticism towards gender related topics, such as female exclusion from priesthood or the celibacy of priests, which pilgrims often identified in our conversations as the possible reason for the widespread scandals related to paedophilia within the Catholic Church. The distinction between spirituality and religion should not, therefore, be underestimated as simply a fleeting trend or shift in language, but understood as an expression of discontent towards religious institutions, as well as an effort of dialogue with the secular sphere.

Methods and literature review

My research in Fátima is part of a five-year project funded by the Portuguese Foundation for Science and Technology, "Fátima, one century after the apparitions: Pilgrimage, gender and lived religion" (2015–2020). In 2016 I also joined HERILIGION, an international and interdisciplinary research project investigating the intersections of religion and heritage in different European countries funded by the European Hera programme.

As a passionate ethnographer, I believe that long-term fieldwork is essential to grasping the complexities and constantly changing features of religion as lived (Orsi 2006; McGuire 2008). For this reason, after spending some weeks in Fátima in April and May 2016 and on subsequent occasions from August 2016 onwards, in March 2017 I settled in Fátima with my daughter, Maya, who attended the kindergarten there while I did intensive fieldwork until the end of October 2017. In 2018, I made shorter visits during May and October, as well as staying for two months in July and August to undertake follow-up interviews and observe changes in the ceremonies and devotion of the inhabitants of Fátima after the celebrations of the centenary (2016–2017) were over. I had informal conversations with residents of Fátima and my language skills allowed me to speak with pilgrims from different countries in Europe, the Americas and Asia. Like my earlier research, the compilation of life stories was particularly useful for understanding not only the worldview and ritual practices of the pilgrims, but also their evolution over time and their connection with the cultural and social background. Using the 'layered life stories' method (Fedele 2020b), whenever possible, I kept in touch with the pilgrims and interviewed those whose profiles I found more relevant after some months had passed. This allowed me to gain insight about their evolving religiosity and to see how they related changes in their life with their pilgrimage. Layered life stories are especially valuable for understanding those who describe themselves as spiritual but not religious. This is because they allow us to observe the pilgrims' religious backgrounds and the ways in which they have gradually distanced themselves from them. But before we explore the pilgrims' use of spirituality further, let us first review what scholars have said about the spiritual but not religious so far.

Since the 1990s "spirituality" has increasingly been used by social scientists as an analytical category that represents an alternative to organized "religion". This trend was closely related to theories about the decline of religion and its increasing privatization (Berger 1969; Bellah et al. 1985). Drawing on statistical data in America and in Europe indicating that a growing number of people identified as religious rather than spiritual, at the beginning of the new century several authors proposed this dichotomy as a useful analytical tool for analysing contemporary religiosity. Some even spoke of a "spiritual revolution" (Heelas and Woodhead 2004) where religion would give way to spirituality.

Drawing on Talal Asad's analysis of secularism and religion as two inter-connected realities (2003), reciprocally creating each other, Fedele and Knibbe proposed to see religion and spirituality as two interconnected reali-ties that mutually constitute each other. They advocated for an "anthropology of 'the spiritual' as a category that in recent years has emerged as a significant 'other' of the category of religion and that should be studied bearing in mind local and cultural specificities taking into account also its relationship with the secular" (2013, 7). In a publication of that same year, Nancy Ammerman used qualitative data emerging from a wide project in the United States to analyse the "moral boundary work" done by those who prefer to identify as spiritual rather than religious. She observed that this distinction was made, although in different ways, by members of traditional religions as well as by those with a more secular approach. In both cases, being "spiritual" implied marking a boundary from "religion" considered as an immoral enemy. Ammermann concludes that "political and not descriptive work is being done, that people are engaged in moral boundary work (Lamont 1992), setting out distinctions that allow status comparisons based on qualities judged as virtuous" (Ammerman 2013, 275).

Although certain scholars continued to consider the religious/spiritual distinction as analytically useful for their scholarship (e.g. Houtman and Aupers 2006), others picked up the new direction proposed and focused increasingly on what people meant when they said that they were spiritual, without assuming that this necessarily meant that they did not belong (or no longer belonged) to a certain religious group (e.g. Aune 2015; Zwissler 2018).

During research on pilgrims influenced by Goddess spirituality visiting Catholic shrines related to Saint Mary Magdalene or holding "Black Madonna" statues in France (2013a), I was mainly confronted with women (and some men) with a Catholic background. The vast majority of them described themselves as spiritual but not religious and harshly criticized religion, especially Catholicism, for being patriarchal, hierarchical and misogynistic. However, it was difficult to determine whether they had ceased being Catholic, since Catholic rituals, figures and texts still played a very important role in their lives. Even if they came from different countries (Italy, Spain, United Kingdom, United States), they all used what I described as a common 'grammar', drawing on Elisabeth Claverie's study of Medjugorie (2003). The pilgrims' 'energy grammar' (Fedele 2013a) allowed them to translate Catholic symbols, figures, buildings and rituals in a way that neutralized their negative aspects and transformed them into something perceived as empowering. The concept of energy was so central and wide-spread that in a more recent publication (2018) I proposed 'energy pilgrims' as an umbrella term to describe the increasing number of spiritual travellers who visit both Catholic shrines and places related to other religious traditions from the past and present (e.g. Egyptian or Mayan pyramids, Stonehenge, etc.) – sites of energy seen as empowering and healing 'power places' (Fedele 2014, 2018; see also Bowman 1993; Ivakhiv 2001; Rountree 2006).

Very often the translation process from religion to spirituality among Magdalene pilgrims implied an inversion of meanings and attributes in the literal sense of the term, turning things upside down. Just to give a quick example, Saint Mary Magdalene, usually described as a sinner saved by Jesus – a symbol of the dangers and sins related to the female sex – became a priestess of the Goddess, personifying the sacrality of sexuality and the wisdom of women who had helped Jesus to fulfil his mission. As a kind of female equivalent of Jesus, Mary Magdalene and the energy emanating from her and from the places related to her, provided a positive reference model for women, "reversing Eve's curse" (Fedele 2014). This construction by opposition is very common in contemporary forms of spirituality and emerged in several of the chapters contained in the companion volume (2013). As in a sort of magical mirror, spirituality reverses all the evils of religion, with all the problems and dependencies this strategy entails (Fedele 2013a, 2013b, 2019; Fedele and Knibbe 2013).

The religion the Magdalene pilgrims rejected was very different from the religion being practised by those affiliated to religious institutions and described by anthropologists (Fedele 2013a). Furthermore, the spirituality described as a sort of antidote to the evils of religion is also practised by members of established religions (Fedele and Knibbe 2013). As Ammerman observes, the "spirituality" being endorsed as an alternative is at least as widely practised by those same religious people as it is by the people drawing a moral boundary against them. Hence, "researchers should not take the rhetoric as a guide for understanding either spirituality or religion *per se*" (2013, 275). In a similar vein, we will see that the religion criticized by Catholic pilgrims in Fátima is an abstract construct that served as a moral enemy for the creation of their own, different, spirituality.

The visions in Fátima and the development of a pilgrimage shrine

Marian apparition shrines are arenas for the creation of competing discourses (Eade and Sallnow 1991) and the narratives about the visions are complex and constantly evolving in close relationship with the historical and political context (e.g. Christian 1996; Claverie 2003). Fátima is no exception and Portuguese authors, in particular, have analysed the gradual transformation of Fátima from a contested local apparition site during the First Portuguese Republic into a vibrant pilgrimage site under the Salazar regime (Fernandes 1999; Barreto 2002; Reis 2007) and, finally, to a centre of global Catholicism (Cadegan 2004; Duque 2017; Franco and Reis 2017). The initial short descriptions of the apparitions given by the visionaries in 1917 vary considerably from the elaborate version provided by the main visionary, Lucia, in her memoirs written between 1936 and 1942 (see, for instance, Torgal 2011, 2017). The development of the narratives around the Fátima visions is particularly long because the last of the so-called "secrets of Fátima" that have been, and still are, at the centre of much speculation and controversy, were only revealed in 2000.[1]

For reasons of brevity I will introduce here only the narrative offered to visitors through the official leaflet distributed by the Sanctuary, through its website, and by the most popular books about the shrine and its origins. Most of the pilgrims I encountered, knew little about the secrets of Fátima nor did they know precise details about the apparitions or the visionaries when they arrived. They knew bits and pieces about the apparitions but were mostly interested in experiencing a place where Our Lady had appeared. Those pilgrims who were the most informed and interested in the historical details, controversies and prophecies, usually belonged to groups organized by specific associations dedicated to spreading the devotion to Our Lady of Fátima.

In 1916, while they were tending their sheep close to the village of Aljustrel, Lucia (aged 9) and her two cousins Francisco (8) and Jacinta (6), saw on three occasions an angel, twice at a place called Loca do Cabeço (now more commonly known as Loca do Anjo) and once at the well in the garden of Lucia's family (now Poço do Anjo). On 13 May 1917, the 'three little shepherds' saw a lady dressed in white while pasturing their sheep at the Cova da Iria.

Figure 8.1 Loca do Cabeço

Figure 8.2 Chapel of the apparitions (capelinha), Cova da Iria

This first apparition of what was later discovered to be Our Lady of the Rosary was followed by monthly apparitions at the same place on the 13th day of June, July, September and October. On 13 August, the shepherds were questioned by the local authorities in Ourem, and that month the visions occurred on 19 August at a place not far from Aljustrel called Valinhos.

During the last apparition on 13 October, Our Lady performed "a miracle so that all could believe", known as the "Miracle of the Sun", in the presence of a multitude of people.

Before it gradually became one of the most popular Marian pilgrimage shrines in the world, Fátima was a small village clustered around a parish church. What is known today as Fátima consists of three different places: a) the original village called Fátima; b) Cova da Iria, the main apparition site, situated some kilometres away, which gradually developed into a town only after the apparitions; c) the village of Aljustrel, where the three visionaries lived.

Elsewhere (Fedele 2017), I have distinguished between two areas – "first zone Fátima" and "second zone Fátima". I mention them here briefly because I found that these two areas are closely related to the religion/spirituality divide:

1   In the first zone, at the Cova da Iria, we find the most important places of devotion that are promoted and strictly controlled by the local religious authorities – the chapel of the apparitions, the basilica of Our Lady of the Rosary, the basilica of the Holy Trinity and what is more generally known in Portuguese as *recinto de oração* (praying area). This part is supervised by guards and during the main celebrations also by volunteers like local volunteer

Figure 8.3 Valinhos

guards, the *servitas* (mostly coming from outside Fátima), and Scouts. It represents the threshold of all that is related to 'religion' and its representative, the 'Church', and is often simply identified in Fátima as 'the Sanctuary'.

2   The second zone is larger and closer to nature. It is located close to Aljustrel and encompasses a) the houses of the shepherds; b) the two apparition sites of the angel in 1916; c) Valinhos, the place of the apparition of Our Lady on 19 August; d) the Way of the Cross that connects Cova da Iria with Aljustrel.

Almost all pilgrims I met agree that the chapel of the apparitions (*capelinha*) is the most important place. Here is where they most feel the presence of Our Lady or, in other terms, where the presence of the divine, sometimes described as energy, is strongest. However, many pilgrims also observed that it was difficult to experience a sense of communion with the divine in the *capelinha* because of the presence of so many people there, the ongoing celebration of masses in different languages and the strict control exercised by the local religious authorities. Several pilgrims, therefore, preferred the second zone where they could pray on their own and enjoy the silence and peace. This second part is where I observed mostly the presence of groups involved in different forms of contemporary spirituality. People meditating, chanting mantras, making offerings in nature, leaving texts related to the Goddess, and so on.

As we saw at the beginning of this chapter, when I told Beth that I liked the zone of Aljustrel, she interpreted this as evidence that I was a spiritual rather than a religious person. Other pilgrims whom I met during my frequent strolls to Aljustrel confirmed Beth's distinction and described their experiences of communing with the divine in the second zone (Fedele 2017), referring to it as a "more spiritual" place or a place where there was "more spirituality and less religion".

But what do Catholic pilgrims mean when they speak of spirituality? How does this relate with religion and why is this distinction important for them?

"People feel different things when visiting apparition sites – I think it depends on their level of spirituality"

During the interview that opens this chapter, Beth described Fátima as a place that was different from the increasingly empty churches in Ireland: "When we (the Irish pilgrims in her groups) were all back home we were all able to pray in a much deeper, spiritual, sense than the moment before we came to Fátima". She added: "When you went back home you felt drawn to come back ... Every time you come you feel renewed, and you always feel a lovely spiritual feeling".

Beth also added that if I was to understand pilgrims to Fátima, I needed to speak with Barbara, who had been accompanying Irish groups to this and other Marian shrines for a long time. An energetic lady in her late fifties, Barbara was used to speaking about Fátima and had read many books and also visited other shrines in that area.[2] After telling me about her life and her visits to officially recognized as well as other Marian apparition sites in Ireland and Continental Europe, Barbara started to describe her special devotion to Our Lady of Fátima and her personal way of being a good Catholic. She observed: "you know, God wants spiritual fruits not religious nuts". Surprised by this further, spectacular appearance of the spiritual/religious divide, I asked Barbara to explain what she meant. "The religious nuts are all spiritually sick, they are all ... they are overdosed. They have taken in too much religion, they are unbalanced. We need them to be levelled. So we get the religious nuts up here".

To explain this overdose of religion better, Barbara told me the following story she had once heard from a priest. A couple of Catholics are driving through the countryside towards the church to attend the Sunday mass when they see some people with a broken-down car. Instead of stopping to help them, the couple drives on because otherwise they will miss the Sunday mass and this will represent a sin. In Barbara's words the couple are religious nuts because they only follow the rules and are unable to understand that according to Jesus' message it is much more important to help those in need rather than attend Mass on Sunday. As Barbara said: "they got the faith wrong" – they were "spiritually sick" and unable really to encounter the divine and experience joy and peace.

During the following months, I would hear similar stories taken from everyday life about apparently devout Catholics practising a shallow religion, unable to decide when it was important to "follow the rules" and when it was more important to "follow the heart" and help others rather than arriving at the next pilgrimage stop in time to pray the rosary or attend Mass.

Barbara urged me to write in my book about Fátima that the spiritually sick people were cured in Fátima and that this kind of cure was in fact one, if not the main, specific feature of Fátima: "Lourdes is for the (physically) sick and here it is the spiritual sickness of people that gets cured".

The idea that Fátima is a particularly important place in terms of spirituality emerged also in comments by a substantial number of other pilgrims coming from different countries. Sometimes, these pilgrims also made a comparison with Lourdes in similar terms to Barbara. As one Italian pilgrim put it: "In Lourdes you see religion, in Fátima you can see, live and share the spirituality of the people." When I asked him to say more, he explained that religious people just follow the rules and go to Mass or light a candle because this is what they have learned to do. Spiritual people may do similar things but they have a profound devotion and manage to feel the presence of God. According to him, the Portuguese pilgrims in Fátima, in particular, clearly embodied this kind of spiritual, more real approach, whereas in Lourdes the devotion of the French and other visitors appeared more formal and, in some ways, shallow. This distinction is very similar to the comments made to Nancy Ammermann by "spiritual" informants concerning the hypocrisy and empty rituals involved in religion (2013). Religion has become a sort of umbrella term for elements that are criticized and viewed as immoral or "unbalanced", as Barbara put it. Spirituality stands for a sort of inverted or re-balanced religion that has been purged of its problematic features.

Not all pilgrims who had been to Lourdes were critical of this French shrine. However, when a comparison with Lourdes was considered important by my interlocutors, usually Fátima emerged as the moral winner, representing lively spirituality as opposed to a shallow religion.[3]

In some cases this reference to spirituality was also accompanied by the use of the term energy to describe the special feeling of divine presence that the pilgrims experienced in Fátima. After learning about my research, Elettra, an Italian woman in her early forties whom I met in my Italian hometown, described her visit to Fátima in 2017 thus: "The energy inside the apparition chapel is very powerful. I visited Fátima with a friend who is (Russian) Orthodox and she felt the same. As soon as you enter you can feel how powerful it is." The term 'energy' was most often used by Brazilian pilgrims, who insisted on describing themselves as Catholic and often criticized the growth of evangelical churches in their home country. On rare occasions I found Catholic pilgrims who were strongly critical of the New Age and alternative spiritualities. One of them reacted negatively when I used the term 'energy' referring to things I had heard from other pilgrims and he subsequently sent me links to articles about the danger that the New Age represented for Catholics.

So far we have seen that the way in which the spiritual/religious divide is used by pilgrims in Fátima is not so different from what I have observed among Magdalene pilgrims or what is reported in Ammerman's study (2013). Religion emerges as a moral enemy that pilgrims need to distance themselves from and their spirituality is constructed in opposition to religion. Following Talal Asad's analysis (2003) of the ways in which the religious and the secular mutually constitute each other, we can observe that a similar phenomenon happens with religion and spirituality (Fedele and Knibbe 2013). But how does spirituality relate to the secular in Fátima?

Gendering the entanglements of religion, spirituality and secularism

After initial interviews in May 2016, I started paying increasing attention to the ways in which the pilgrims used the word 'spirituality'. I also checked whether they described themselves as spiritual rather than religious and when and how this differentiation process occurred. I gradually observed that the dichotomy emerged especially during conversations with pilgrims who supposed that, being a researcher, I might be critical of their devotion or sceptical about the truth of their religious experiences. They tried to use expressions that they perceived as more 'neutral' and acceptable for what they assumed to be a 'secular' observer representing a secular institution (a university). When I asked about their visit to Fátima, they often started using words that did not belong to a Christian or, in this case, Catholic discourse, such as holy, blessed or sacred. They used a more neutral language like "the place is very powerful", "there is something special going on" or, in some cases, even "the energy of the site is special". Like Elettra above, to prove their point further they often added that sceptical people in their group, or those who were Christian but not Catholic, had also perceived this special feeling or power.

As we kept talking and they gradually realized that I respected their faith and was open to hearing their experiences, they started using more "Christian" expressions, such as "I felt God's grace there" or "I could perceive the presence of God". When they started using these expressions I often felt that they did so hesitantly, testing my reaction. Only when they found that I did not appear to be shocked or to react critically to their observations with scepticism, they kept using this more "religiously marked" discourse. Sometimes, towards the end of our conversation, they even added that they usually did not talk about these kinds of experiences to people who did not belong to their Catholic community or did not clearly share their devotion, because they had been criticized or ridiculed by friends or colleagues.

During formal, semi-structured interviews I deliberately left the more "political" questions that could potentially intimidate or upset my interlocutors towards the end. These were questions about their position regarding female priesthood, homosexuality and the possibility of priests marrying. The distinction between spiritual and religious frequently emerged when the pilgrims wanted to distance themselves from the restrictions imposed by the Vatican concerning gender or sexual orientation. The majority, both male and female, was in favour of female Catholic priesthood and the priest's right to marry. A few refused to take a position saying that they respected those who disagreed with the official position of the Vatican but they did not have a clear-cut opinion on these issues. The great majority of them also did not believe that homosexuality should be considered a problem or that homosexuals should be excluded from the Catholic community.[4] Those who expressed their concerns about homosexuality usually belonged to international conservative groups such as the World Apostolate of Fátima or national conservative groups such as the Italian Comunione e Liberazione.

Justifying the fact that their personal opinion diverged from the Vatican's position, the pilgrims commented that they had "their own spirituality", they were "spiritual persons" or belonged to a local parish led by a priest, who was "very spiritual", unlike most priests who had "lost touch with spirituality" or were only concerned about "worldly issues". Some others did not use the term spirituality but explained that they had their own, personal kind of religion, or their own way to live their faith. Some pilgrims openly criticized both "the Sanctuary" and the Vatican for being too strict and narrow minded and sometimes also for being too much interested in accumulating money rather than redistributing it to those in need (see also Gemzöe 2000).

Marian apparition sites like Fátima or Lourdes attract millions of pilgrims every year and contribute to the revitalization of contemporary Catholicism, a religion that is facing the emptying of churches and a constant drop in vocations. The Vatican is increasingly confronted with criticisms related to gender and sexuality, such as its position concerning contraception, abortion and LGBTQI rights or acts of paedophilia committed by priests that have increasingly come to public attention. Catholic pilgrims are aware of these ongoing debates and the Irish and Italian pilgrims were particularly concerned about the international scandals related to paedophilia. Especially Northern Irish pilgrims often felt judged and excluded in their home countries because of their religious belonging. Portuguese pilgrims, on the other hand, were used to hostility on the part of those in their social environment who saw Catholicism as linked with the Salazar regime and/or related it to a rural and backward Portugal that needed to be secularized in order to be completely modern.

Catholic pilgrims in Fátima have learned to use the spirituality/religion dichotomy in a creative way to avoid being criticized and ridiculed by non-believers or sceptical people in their social environment, or when confronted with Vatican positions related to gender and sexuality that are widely criticized in the media and public opinion. Like the informants described by Laurel Zwissler in Chapter 7, for the pilgrims "the language of spirituality is a means to get around conflicts over religion and, instead, to emphasize a universally accessible experience of peace and contentment". Spirituality language allows people to criticize both religion and secularism without having to renounce being a Catholic. Through this approach, the pilgrims resist the hegemony of Catholic institutions and assert their right to create their own way of being Catholic.

With their creative approach and their religious criticism the pilgrims also challenge the widespread assumption that, especially in terms of gender and sexuality, religion is conservative and opposed to progressive secularism (Cady and Fessenden 2013; Aune et al. 2017). Increasingly, women and sexuality take centre stage in discussions about the necessity to create solid secular bases for nation states. In these discourses, secularism emerges as liberating women from the restricting and disempowering influences of religion. Recent scholarship has challenged this positioning, showing that secularism is related to historical legacies that are far from being only emancipatory and oriented towards gender equality (Scott 2017), and that religion can be empowering in terms of gender (e.g. Dubisch 1986 ; Mahmood 2005). Spiritual language offers a strategy that allows pilgrims to extricate themselves from this binarism and to engage with religion and secularism in a creative way. Although in some cases pilgrims in Fátima had positions that were opposed to that of secular feminists (in their position against abortion, for instance), a fine-grained analysis of their discourses shows that in order to understand the ways in which they live their devotion in terms of gender, we need not only to tackle the values that are usually associated with religion and secularism, but also to explore how these two categories are intertwined with a third one, that of spirituality.

Conclusion

Building on the findings in the companion volume (Fedele and Knibbe 2013), in this chapter I have approached religion and spirituality not as analytical categories but rather as interrelated phenomena for study. This distinction may be somewhat fuzzy but it is an important one for people in today's world and should be studied and problematized in relationship with secularism. In line with Ammerman (2013), I showed that through the use of this distinction, pilgrims in Fátima are not only adopting a different descriptive position but are also engaging in political work, by challenging certain positions of the Vatican, in general, and the local Church, in particular. Moving some steps further, I analysed spirituality as a form of religion that is more acceptable to secularism, showing that through the translation of religion into spirituality, a language appears that is less religiously charged and, therefore, more easily accepted by non-believers. Something similar has also been observed by Kim Knibbe (Chapter 9) among spiritual practitioners in the Netherlands and by

Laurel Zwissler (Chapter 7) among women belonging to a Mennonite association working in fair-trade shops in the United States. More research needs to be done to analyse the role played by this kind of mediating spirituality language not only among Christians worldwide, but also among native religions in Africa (e.g. Steyn 2003) and Latin America (e.g. Galinier and Molinié 2006) that are increasingly influenced by contemporary spirituality.

Since John Eade and Michael Sallnow's groundbreaking work on Christian pilgrimage sites as arenas for competing discourses (1991), many other ethnographic studies of pilgrimage sites (e.g. Dubisch 1995; Tweed 1997; Frey 1998; Badone and Roseman 2004; Hermkens, Jansen and Notermans 2009) have described the divergences between religion as lived and the religious discourses we find in religious texts or hear during official religious ceremonies. Scholars have analysed the complex ways in which pilgrimage is changing and adapting to contemporary social shifts and, in a recent edited volume, Simon Coleman and John Eade (2018) invited pilgrimage scholars to go beyond the religious/secular distinction and explore also the political and economic dimension of pilgrimage (Reader 2014). Pilgrimage shrines represent privileged sites on which to study the ways in which the religious, the spiritual and the secular mutually influence and create each other, and it would be interesting to explore how these entanglements play out in other global Catholic shrines, in shrines belonging to non-Christian traditions and especially in inter-religious shrines (Albera and Couroucli 2012; Bowman 2012).

As we have seen, in Fátima the distinction between religious and spiritual emerged in particular when discussing issues related to gender and sexuality and allowed the pilgrims to voice their discontent. Scholars interested in exploring the increasingly important role that gender and sexuality play whenever religion is accused of preventing human freedom (Cady and Fessenden 2013; Amir-Moazami 2016), as well as those exploring the production of secular bodies and emotions (Hirschkind 2011; Scheer, Fadil and Johansen 2019), could profit from an approach that takes into account also the ways in which spiritual language is complicating the scenario and is increasingly used as a *lingua franca* to navigate between religion and secularism.

This text has only scratched the surface of the ways in which spirituality and its language are influencing how religion and secularism co-create each other. More research is needed that takes spiritualities seriously without forgetting the importance of gender and sexuality for those who describe themselves as spiritual but not religious.

In memoriam

I dedicate this chapter to the memory of my father, Gianfranco Fedele (1931–2020). He was a passionate intellectual who witnessed firsthand the revolutions in China, Cuba and Portugal with both commitment to the cause and a critical view of the flawed outcomes. In difficult situations, he quoted to me Fidel Castro's motto: we "have to transform a defeat into a victory".

Notes

1 Other authors have analysed the ways in which devotion to Fátima has been relevant in different international political contexts (e.g. Perry & Echeverría 1988; Zimdars-Swartz 1991; Scheer 2006).
2 I have kept details about Beth and Barbara deliberately vague in order to protect their identity.
3 Having been to Lourdes myself and having read ethnographic accounts (Eade 1991; R. Harris 2008; A. Harris 2013), I know that the complex and multi-layered ways in which pilgrims experience that shrine cannot be easily reduced to a shallow religion. The relationship and competition between Lourdes and Fátima is a wide-ranging and fascinating topic that cannot be fully explored here.
4 The fact that the pilgrims knew me as an unmarried woman, living in Fátima with her daughter, while her partner was working abroad, may have influenced the pilgrims' answers. Especially their answers in terms of their position in favour of women's access to Catholic priesthood, since they probably assumed that I was against this kind of gender inequality within Catholicism.

Acknowledgements

Research for this essay was mainly funded by FCT/MCTES (the Portuguese Foundation for Science and Technology) as part of the strategic research plan of the Centro em Rede de Investigação em Antropologia (UID/ANT/04038/ 2013) and as part of my activities as an FCT investigator (IF/01063/2014). This project has also received funding from the European Union's Horizon 2020 research and innovation programme under grant agreement No. 649307. I would like to thank José Mapril, Maria Cardeira, Antónia Lima, Mafalda Sousa, David Soares, Oscar Salemink, Irene Stengs, Paulo Fontes, Alfredo Teixeira, Teresa Toldy, Helena Vilaça, João Leal. Special thanks go to Monique Scheer, William A. Christian, Clara Saraiva and Tiago Pires Marques who participated in an expert meeting on the centenary of the apparitions in Fátima I organized at the ISCTE-IUL in December 2017. John Eade and Kim Knibbe provided useful comments to an early version of this text. At the Rectory of the Sanctuary of Fátima I am particularly grateful to Marco Daniel Duarte, André Melicies, Sonia Vazão and Frederico Serodio. Last but not least, I am grateful to all the pilgrims who generously shared their experiences with me.

References

Albera, Dionigi and Maria Couroucli. 2012. *Sharing Sacred Spaces in the Mediterranean: Christians, Muslims, and Jews at Shrines and Sanctuaries*. Bloomington, IN: Indiana University Press.
Amir-Moazami, Schirin. 2016. "Investigating the Secular Body: The Politics of the Male Circumcision Debate in Germany." *ReOrient* 1(2): 147–170. https://doi.org/10. 13169/reorient.1.2.0147.
Ammerman, Nancy T. 2013. "Spiritual But Not Religious? Beyond Binary Choices in the Study of Religion." *Journal for the Scientific Study of Religion* 52(2): 258–278.

Asad, Talal. 2003. *Formations of the Secular: Christianity, Islam, Modernity.* Stanford: Stanford University Press.

Aune, Kristin. 2015. "Feminist Spirituality as Lived Religion How UK Feminists Forge Religio-Spiritual Lives." *Gender & Society* 29(1): 122–145. https://doi.org/10. 1177/0891243214545681.

Aune, Kristin, Mia Lövheim, Alberta Giorgi, Teresa Toldy and Terhi Utriainen. 2017. "Introduction: Is Secularism Bad for Women? La Laïcité Nuit-Elle Aux Femmes?" *Social Compass* 64(4): 449–480. https://doi.org/10.1177/0037768617727464.

Badone, Ellen and Sharon R. Roseman. 2004. *Intersecting Journeys: The Anthropology of Pilgrimage and Tourism.* Champaign, IL: University of Illinois Press.

Barreto, Jose. 2002. *Religião e Sociedade: Dois ensaios.* Lisboa: Imprensa de Ciencias Sociais.

Bellah, Robert N., Richard Madsen, William M.Sullivan, AnnSwidler and Steven M. Tipton. 1985. *Habits of the heart: Individualism and Commitment in American Life.* Berkeley: University of California Press.

Bender, Courtney. 2010. *The new metaphysicals: Spirituality and the American religious imagination.* Chicago: University of Chicago Press.

Berger, Peter L. 1969. *The sacred canopy.* Garden City, NY: Anchor Doubleday.

Bowman, Glenn. 2012. *Sharing the Sacra: The Politics and Pragmatics of Intercommunal Relations Around Holy Places.* New York: Berghahn Books.

Bowman, Marion. 1993. Drawn to Glastonbury. In *Pilgrimage in Popular Culture,* edited by I. Reader and T. Walter, 29–62. *Pilgrimage in Popular Culture.* London: Macmillan.

Cadegan, Una M. 2004. "The Queen of Peace in the Shadow of War: Fátima and U.S. Catholic Anticommunism." *U.S. Catholic Historian* 22(4): 1–15.

Cady, Linell and Tracy Fessenden, eds. 2013. *Religion, the Secular, and the Politics of Sexual Difference.* New York: Columbia University Press.

Christian, William A. 1996. *Visionaries: The Spanish Republic and the Reign of Christ.* Berkeley, CA: University of California Press.

Claverie, Elisabeth. 2003. *Les Guerres de la Vierge: Une Anthropologie des Apparitions.* NRF Essais. Paris: Gallimard.

Coleman, Simon and John Eade, eds. 2018. *Pilgrimage and Political Economy: Translating the Sacred.* New York: Berghahn Books.

Dubisch, Jill. 1995. *In a Different Place: Pilgrimage, Gender and Politics at a Greek Island Shrine.* Princeton: Princeton University Press.

Duque, João. 2017. *Fátima: uma aproximação.* Prior Velho: Paulinas.

Eade, John. 1991. "Order and Power at Lourdes: Lay Helpers and the Organization of a Pilgrimage Shrines." In *Contesting the Sacred: The Anthropology of Pilgrimage,* edited by John Eade and Michael J. Sallnow, 51–76. Champaign, IL: University of Illinois Press.

Eade, John and Michael J. Sallnow, eds. 1991. *Contesting the Sacred: The Anthropology of Christian Pilgrimage.* New York: Routledge.

Fedele, Anna. 2013a. *Looking for Mary Magdalene: Alternative Pilgrimage and Ritual Creativity at Catholic Shrines in France.* New York: Oxford University Press.

Fedele, Anna. 2013b. "'Black' Madonna versus 'White' Madonna: Gendered Power Strategies in Alternative Pilgrimages to Marian Shrines." In *Gender and Power in Contemporary Spirituality: Ethnographic Approaches,* edited by Anna Fedele and Kim Knibbe, 96–114. New York: Routledge.

Fedele, Anna. 2014. "Energy and Transformation in Alternative Pilgrimages to Catholic Shrines: Deconstructing the Tourist/pilgrim Divide." *Journal of Tourism and Cultural Change* 12(2): 150–165.

Fedele, Anna. 2017. "Pellegrinaggio, topografia sacra e religione vissuta a Fátima." In *Annali di Studi Religiosi*, 83–95, https://books.fbk.eu/media/uploads/files/Fedele.pdf

Fedele, Anna. 2018. "Translating Catholic Pilgrimage Sites into Energy Grammar: Contested Spiritual Practices in Chartres and Vézelay." In *Pilgrimage and Political Economy: Translating the Sacred*, edited by Simon Coleman and John Eade, 112–135. New York: Berghahn Books.

Fedele, Anna. 2019. "Spirituality and Gender" in *The Routledge International Handbook of Spirituality in Society and the Professions*, edited by Bernadette Flanagan and LaszloZsnolnai, 135–141. London: Routledge.

Fedele, Anna. 2020a. "Walking Pilgrimages to the Marian Shrine of Fátima in Portugal as Democratic Explorations." In *Reassembling Democracy: Ritual as Cultural Resource*, edited by Jone Salomonsen, Michael Houseman, Sarah M. Pike and Graham Harvey. London: Bloomsbury.

Fedele, Anna. 2020b. "Capturing Lived Religion through Layered Life Stories." Working paper. https://www.academia.edu/42015799/Capturing_Lived_Religion_Through_Layered_Life_Stories

Fedele, Anna, and Kim Knibbe. 2013. "Introduction: Gender and Power in Contemporary Spirituality." In *Gender and Power in Contemporary Spirituality: Ethnographic Approaches*, edited by Anna Fedele and Kim Knibbe, 1–27. New York: Routledge.

Fernandes, António Teixeira. 1999. *O confronto de ideologias na segunda década do século XX: à volta de Fátima*. Porto: Afrontamento.

Franco, José Eduardo, and Bruno Cardoso Reis. 2017. *Fátima: lugar sagrado global*. Lisboa: Circulo de Leitores.

Frey, Nancy L. 1998. *Pilgrim Stories: On and Off the Road to Santiago, Journeys Along an Ancient Way in Modern Spain*. Berkeley, CA: University of California Press.

Galinier, Jacques, and Antoinette Molinié. 2006. *Les néo-Indiens: Une religion du IIIe millénaire*. Paris: Odile Jacob.

Gemzöe, Lena. 2000. *Feminine Matters: Women's Religious Practices in a Portuguese Town*. Stockholm: Department of Social Anthropology, Stockholm University.

Gemzöe, Lena. 2014. "Every Minute Out There: Creating Ritual among Swedish Pilgrims to Santiago de Compostela." *Journal of Ritual Studies* 28(2): 65–75.

Harris, Alana. 2013. "Lourdes and Holistic Spirituality: Contemporary Catholicism, the Therapeutic and Religious Thermalism." *Culture and Religion* 14(1): 23–43. https://doi.org/10.1080/14755610.2012.756411.

Harris, Ruth. 2008. *Lourdes: Body and Spirit in the Secular Age*. London: Penguin.

Heelas, Paul and Linda Woodhead. 2004. *The Spiritual Revolution: Why Religion Is Giving Way to Spirituality*. Malden, MA: Blackwell.

Hermkens, Anna-Karina, Willy Jansen and Catrien Notermans. 2009. *Moved by Mary: The Power of Pilgrimage in the Modern World*. Farnham: Ashgate.

Hirschkind, Charles. 2011. "Is There a Secular Body?" *Cultural Anthropology*. Wiley Online Library. Accessed 26 March 2019. https://anthrosource.onlinelibrary.wiley.com/doi/abs/10.1111/j.1548-1360.2011.01116.x.

Houtman, Dick, and Stef Aupers. 2006. "The Spiritual Revolution and the New Age Gender Puzzle: The Sacralisation of the Self in Late Modernity (1980–2000)." In

Centre for Rotterdam Cultural Sociology (*CROCUS*). http://hdl.handle.net/1765/7576.

Ivakhiv, Adrian J. 2001. *Claiming Sacred Ground: Pilgrims and Politics at Glastonbury and Sedona*. 1st edition. Bloomington, IN: Indiana University Press.

Klassen, Pamela E. 2001. *Blessed Events: Religion and Home Birth in America*. Princeton Studies in Cultural Sociology. Princeton: Princeton University Press.

Knibbe, Kim E. 2013. *Faith in the Familiar: Religion, Spirituality, and Place in the South of the Netherlands*. Leiden: Brill.

Lamont, Michele. 1992. *Money, Morals, and Manners*. Chicago: University of Chicago Press.

Linell, Cady, and Tracy Fessenden, eds. 2013. *Religion, the Secular, and the Politics of Sexual Difference*. New York: Columbia University Press.

Mahmood, Saba. 2005. *Politics of Piety: The Islamic Revival and the Feminist Subject*. Princeton, NJ: Princeton University Press.

McGuire, Meredith B. 2008. *Lived Religion: Faith and Practice in Everyday Life*. Oxford: Oxford University Press.

Orsi, Robert A. 2006. *Between Heaven and Earth: The Religious Worlds People Make and the Scholars Who Study Them*. New edn. Princeton, NJ: Princeton University Press.

Orsi, Robert A. 2010. *The Madonna of 115th Street: Faith and Community in Italian Harlem, 1880–1950*. 3rd edition. New Haven, CN: Yale University Press.

Perry, Nicholas and Loreto Echeverría. 1988. *Under the Heel of Mary*. London: Routledge.

Reader, Ian. 2014. *Pilgrimage in the Marketplace*. New York: Routledge.

Reis, Bruno Cardoso. 2007. "Historiografia sobre Fátima." In *Enciclopédia de Fátima*, edited by Carlos Moreira Azevedo and Luciano Cristino, 245–252. Estoril: Principia.

Rountree, Kathryn. 2006. "Performing the Divine: Neo-Pagan Pilgrimages and Embodiment at Sacred Sites." *Body & Society* 12(4): 95–115. https://doi.org/10.1177/1357034X06070886.

Scheer, Monique. 2006. *Rosenkranz und Kriegsvisionen: Marienerscheinungskulte im 20. Jahrhundert*. Tübingen: Tübinger Vereinigung für Volkskunde e.V.

Scheer, Monique, Nadia Fadil and Birgitte Schepelern Johansen. 2019. *Secular Bodies, Affects and Emotions: European Configurations*. London: Bloomsbury Publishing.

Scott, Joan Wallach. 2017. *Sex and Secularism*. Princeton: Princeton University Press.

Sointu, Eeva, and Linda Woodhead. 2008. "Spirituality, Gender, and Expressive Selfhood." *Journal for the Scientific Study of Religion* 47(2): 259–276. https://doi.org/10.1111/j.1468-5906.2008.00406.x.

Steyn, Christina W. 2003. "Where New Age and African Religion Meet in South Africa: the case of Credo Mutwa." *Culture and Religion* 4(1): 67–158.

Torgal, Luís Filipe. 2011. *O sol bailou ao meio dia: a criação de Fátima*. Lisboa: Tinta-da-China.

Torgal, Luís Filipe. 2017. *Fátima, a (des)construção do mito*. Coimbra: Palimage.

Tweed, Thomas A. 1997. *Our Lady of the Exile: Diasporic Religion at a Cuban Catholic Shrine in Miami*. New York: Oxford University Press.

Zimdars-Swartz, Sandra. 1991. *Encountering Mary: From La Salette to Medjugorje*. Princeton, NJ: Princeton University Press.

Zwissler, Laurel. 2018. *Religious, Feminist, Activist: Cosmologies of Interconnection*. Lincoln, NE: University of Nebraska Press.

9 'A merely private activity'

Spiritual consumerism as a way to transform gendered relationships to secular and religious authorities

Kim E. Knibbe

Introduction

The Netherlands, late 1990s. I was a student at VU University of Amsterdam and had decided to study a phenomenon that to many people seemed quite ridiculous: the spiritualist medium Jomanda. She had enjoyed a quick rise in popularity and fame from the mid-nineties onward, helped by a media-savvy husband who promoted her via what are called 'gossip magazines' (*Privé*). In more highbrow and 'serious' media, however, she provoked mostly ridicule and accusations of quackery. Opinion leaders were quick to condemn the phenomenon as a resurgence of medieval superstition that we had supposedly left behind. Several things fascinated me: her seeming imperturbability in the face of the storm of critique she faced, the fact that she was able to draw thousands of people every weekend from all over the country, and the nature of the critique that she, but also her visitors, faced. This critique was not only in the vein of accusations of medieval superstition, but also, strangely, seemed to centre on matters of taste and class: her visitors were consistently described as low-educated, badly dressed, gullible, provincial and mostly female and middle aged. One newspaper recounted the goings-on at a healing service with distaste, ending with a description of a woman who had fallen onto the floor in what she thought was a 'trance' (inadvertently) showing her big underpants. Jomanda herself was also ridiculed for her appearance: big hair, a dramatic blue gown and gold sandals. This lack of respect and even ridicule was also typical of conversations that arose whenever my colleague and I mentioned that we were doing research on Jomanda: reactions ranged from laughter, to lectures about how she was only doing it to rake in money. The accusation that she was exploiting people's vulnerabilities for her own financial benefit was another persistent refrain of critiques against her. To enter the healing services, one had to buy a ticket, and at the entrance one could buy water that had been energized by Jomanda (when I pointed out to critics that one could have water energized for free by putting a bottle in front of the radio during Jomanda's weekly broadcast, this of course segued nicely into a headshaking disbelief at this level of medieval superstition). They seemed to be a distorted and commercialized versions of Catholic practices (using Lourdes water, for example).

In short, to the Dutch secular elites, the phenomenon of the popularity of Jomanda was an anomaly, which might be surprising in modern times, but ultimately not dangerous. Later, when commercial broadcasting services developed, the supernatural became a much more regular topic, but in the 1990s it was still a surprise to many intellectuals that people were actually interested in this topic. Indeed, the topic of many newspaper columns, when they did not ridicule the phenomenon, was a reassuring argumentation about why her popularity was destined to decline: the lower classes and women were destined to follow the same developmental path as the more educated, and male, population had followed towards a more enlightened and modern worldview.

Puzzle and argument

So why, then, in the face of all that ridicule and secular dismissal did people go to Jomanda's healing services, not once but many times? And was she indeed just a temporary blip in a mostly secularizing evolution of Dutch culture? Her popularity was already declining at the time of our research, but we found that the phenomenon of Jomanda was part of a larger landscape of spiritual(ist) practitioners with a long, persistent, although largely ignored, history in the Netherlands, both among elites and among lower classes. Later, during the research for my PhD thesis on religious change in the Netherlands I picked up these questions again, as I observed that, while church pews had emptied dramatically since the 1970s, the religious and spiritual landscape had become much more pluralistic but also more commercial, following the logic of a marketplace, sometimes literally through so-called 'paranormal fairs'. Although spiritual consumers themselves often critique this commercial character, it does persist and work in some way. In other publications, we have described the processes of meaning-making in the context of Jomanda, and how people are induced to resignify their life-story and their ailments through the performative practices of the healing rituals (Knibbe and Westra 2003).

In this contribution, I wish to zoom in on the forms of ridicule and critique that Jomanda, her visitors and other spiritual practitioners face in order to bring into view the ways that spiritual practices relate to the secular frames of which they are a part. As Giselinde Kuipers and other humour researchers have shown, ridicule flags important rifts and inequalities between groups, and can give important insights into structures of a society (Kuipers 2008; Friedman and Kuipers 2013). If this is true, this throws into even starker relief the question I posed above: why go to Jomanda or other spiritual entrepreneurs, if it only earns you ridicule and scorn? Somehow, it must be empowering as well, but how? And what, exactly, are the implicit understandings on which secular critics draw, in ridiculing these phenomena? How do these understandings divide groups and elevate some groups above others?

To address these questions, I will go into some aspects of the structural location of the people I conducted research with, both visitors of Jomanda and spiritual practitioners in the landscape of spiritual societies and para-normal fairs that I researched later. Secondly, as indicated in the summary of the scorn and critique of Jomanda above, it might be worthwhile to go into the structural location of the category of spirituality as a set of practices, ideas, networks and institutions in the context of the Netherlands. In the final part of the chapter, I will go into three biographical narratives of women of different backgrounds to address the puzzle outlined here in the introduction: how can we understand that people frequent commercialized contexts of spiritual practitioners, despite the scorn and ridicule that this elicits in hege-monic elites? Based on long-term participation in these contexts, I came to understand people's interest mainly in terms of how it enabled them to transform gendered personal relationships with their partners and immediate family, as well as, more importantly, their (gendered and classed) relationship to religious and secular authorities. Like Zwissler (in Chapter 7) I came to understand the consumerist 'marketplace' character of spiritual services and objects in a different way, namely as an arena of exploration for developing new ways of relating to both secular and religious sources of authority and reshaping personal relationships.

The secular–religious–spiritual landscape of the south of the Netherlands

Between 1999 and 2004, I conducted research on contemporary spirituality in several contexts, mainly in the south of the Netherlands. Until the late 1960s, this area was overwhelmingly Catholic. Like the other 'pillars' of Dutch society, the Catholic pillar was characterized by very strong interlocking networks of organizations and institutions that together enmeshed peoples everyday lives from cradle to grave. Dechurching, when it set in, was extre-mely rapid. Historians and sociologists have argued that the secularization of Dutch society, and in particular in the Catholic areas, was in fact brought about internally, within these pillars. And indeed, within the Catholic pillar, clergy deliberately made room for the rise of a professionalized, university-educated class of specialists (Simons and Winkeler 1987; Kennedy 1995). Simultaneously, the liberalization within Dutch Catholicism threw many people on the level of local communities into confusion: priests were no longer automatically celibate, their children no longer automatically had to go to church and confession, people were told to follow their own conscience. Later, a counter-reaction sponsored by a policy of appointing neo-con-servative bishops occurred, which only accelerated dechurching: people did not want to 'turn back the clock' as they called it (Knibbe 2013).

This background of dechurching and the rise of secular sources of author-ity is important to place the linked phenomena I will discuss here, based on ethnographic research conducted in the years 1999 and 2001–2002, both heavily influenced by spiritualism, but preferring the label 'spiritual'. The first ethnographic research concerned the context of Jomanda, a medium who drew on spiritualist practices to create a link between this world and what she called 'the other side'. She drew thousands of people to her 'healing services' in the mid-nineties. At the time a colleague and I conducted research she was already less popular. The crowd usually consisted of frequent visitors, and some hangers-on and first-time visitors. The second context where I carried out long-term fieldwork is that of so-called 'spiritual societies' in the south of the Netherlands. Before Jomanda became famous, she toured this network of spiritual societies. The groups have different names sometimes, but descend loosely from the local chapters of the spiritualist society established in the nineteenth century after a visit from the famous spiritualist Daniel Douglas, Home to the Dutch Royal Family. Originally an interest of the cultural and societal elites, today these societies are mostly populated by people of lower-middle-class or working-class background. In the south of the Netherlands, interest in this type of spirituality had to be kept away from the public eye due to the strong influence of the Catholic church. However, dechurching has enabled these groups to come out into the open since the late 1980s, and at the time I was doing research in the early 2000s, their meetings were advertised on the free calendar given out by the municipality, where the bingo nights and church services were also announced.

In these spiritual societies, members come together to develop their own spirituality, practise their paranormal gifts on each other and listen to other members or guest speakers on topics such as tarot card reading, dream interpretation and the power of pyramids. On some nights, a medium or paragnost would exercise his or her gifts. These nights were open, and usually drew quite a crowd of people who usually had quite a difficult time for one reason or another. This could be related to the passing away of a loved one, or it could be related to relationship troubles, life crises, traumatic experiences or, although rarely, work crises. I met women who were searching for their purpose in life after having had a career in hospitality services, or as a mother and housewife. I met men who had suddenly been confronted with their own history of abuse in Catholic boarding schools. I also met many divorcees, and the odd lonely and shy man who was protectively adopted by some of the women.

The reason I call them 'spiritual societies' is that they can all identify with the term 'spiritual'. At the time of my research, the term 'spiritualist', or in Dutch, 'spiritist', had become discredited. Thus, Jomanda advertised herself as a 'medium', which seems to confirm a lineage associated with spiritualism, but did not want to identify as a spiritualist. Similarly, many of the members of a spiritual society branded themselves as a magnetist, but slowly evolved towards becoming a reiki master. Thus, while spiritualism has deep historical roots in the Netherlands, the practices and ideas previously associated with this term slowly migrated to become subsumed under the broader eclectic umbrella of 'spirituality'.

Structural location of people engaging with spiritual practices

The people frequenting the contexts of these societies and paranormal fairs were different from the middle-class, urbanized women often encountered in other research on spirituality in the Netherlands and other Northern European countries. Rather, the women, and some men, that I encountered lived in the more provincial areas of the Netherlands (villages or unremarkable provincial towns), and often had no more than elementary school or high school education. In the cases where they did have a higher education, they had often had to give up their career to focus on raising children or caring for sick family members, or had suffered a serious life crisis related to business failure, depression or trauma (this was more often the case for men).

The south of the Netherlands is a region that was heavily Catholic, certainly during the time the women and men I encountered grew up. Since their childhood, however, Catholic Netherlands secularized rapidly, creating strong generational differences. The visitors of Jomanda embodied the historical shift from a society dominated by the authority of a Catholic clergy, by definition set apart from the people through their celibacy and special status as dispensers of the sacraments, to a society dominated by secular authorities of university educated professionals, often equally distant and incomprehensible (on the special status of priests and how this changed, see Knibbe 2013, chap. 3).

Many visitors, despite their diversity, had in common the following characteristics with regard to their relationship to authority and sense of their own status. Many of the women had an awkward relationship with paid work, which in the Netherlands as in many other societies, has become a primary source of identity, status and recognition. As I have analysed in other publications, many of the women had been raised in a context where a Catholic view of family life required women to be the 'angel in the home', to be always ready with a smile, to sacrifice themselves for the wellbeing of others (Knibbe 2012; Fedele and Knibbe 2016). Whatever one may think of this ethos, managing to embody this ideal was a source of pride for women and earned them recognition from their environment. As Hochschild, as well as many philosophers focusing on care and ethics, notes, the practice of caring has a very low status, is taken for granted, usually unpaid or paid very little, and is overwhelmingly carried out by women (Hochschild 2003). Whereas the religious world women grew up in valued their work in the private domain, the secular world that emerged later devalued it.

The individualization of Dutch society, the increasing emphasis on the emancipation of women understood in terms of their participation in the labour market, in combination with the decline of Catholicism during their lifetime, thus presented women with an impossible tension between two sets of standards: they had focused their life on caring for others, but the framework in which such work was seen as valuable had become devalued, stale and marginal, while the new standards for validating the self through a professional identity were simply out of reach (Knibbe 2012; Fedele and Knibbe 2016; c.f. Sointu and Woodhead 2008).

Furthermore, many women, and also the men, had fraught relationships with religious authorities and institutions. In the Catholic context they grew up in, relations with the divine were very firmly in the hands of the priest. Especially in Limburg, the sacraments of baptism, marriage and the Eucharist were employed very effectively to enforce a particular morality that was very much focused on ensuring 'chastity' and chaste sex: sex that took place within the bounds of heterosexual marriage and did not in any way hinder the primary aim of sex, namely procreation (according to the papal encyclical Castii Connubii; Knibbe 2013, chap. 2). Priests were trained to inquire into the status of a marriage in the confessional, and there are many reports of women who were denied absolution because they had indicated that they did not want sexual relations anymore with their husband, and/or did not want to have more children. Concerning baptism and burial, several women told harrowing stories of mothers who gave birth to children that were stillborn or died before baptism. Unbaptized children were buried outside the graveyard, often women did not know where (Knibbe 2011).

At the same time, their low educational level put people at quite some distance from 'secular' sources of authoritative knowledge: science, professionals such as teachers, doctors and civil servants, public intellectuals, the world of highbrow media. The continuing importance of local dialects reinforces this distance: when I was conducting my research there, often the only way I was able to talk to people was by having someone familiar with them reassure them that I was from the region and that I could understand the dialect (although I did not speak it). Greeting people in the street in Dutch never elicited a response. Historically, there is a deep suspicion towards 'the Dutch', who, it is assumed, do not understand the people of Limburg, ignore their interests and who are arrogant, loud and ignorant. Therefore, anyone who speaks Dutch, rather than the local dialect, is assumed to not be able to understand them.

Without going into this too deeply, it can be concluded that this context predisposes both women and men to have a fraught relationship with both religious and secular authority. Where it concerns religious authorities, they have been taught that it is there, concerned with the intimate details of their lives, necessary for their spiritual salvation both on earth and after death, and that they might be denied access to this salvation at any moment for reasons that often had to do with their sexual and gendered conduct. Where it concerns secular authority, an unbridgeable divide is assumed based on language, history and the assumed myopia of educated Dutch professionals.

Against this background, the allure of spiritual practices where one might establish a personalized connection to the divine becomes more understandable. Even though this might be scorned by others, and people themselves might scorn others seeking out spiritual healers they considered charlatans, the challenge to navigate the minefield of commercialized spiritual practices on offer to tap into something that did make sense to them was taken up and felt to be invigorating and interesting, honing ones critical and spiritual abilities.

To understand how people were scornful of the spiritual marketplace but at the same time drawn to it, we now turn to the question of the structural location of spirituality.

The location of spirituality in the Netherlands

Although 'spirituality' is a term that is often used by the people I did research with, it is usually not very well defined and a very wide variety of practices are associated with it. In the introduction to the previous volume that Anna Fedele and I edited, we argue that the category of spirituality is always formed in relation to a particular understanding of religion, or more specifically, especially in the context of my research and that of Fedele, the Catholic church (Fedele and Knibbe 2013). Spirituality always seems to refer to individual practices, and usually establishes an individual relationship with the divine, often envisaged as located within, i.e. the divine self. New Age, Paganism, meditation, shamanism, healing practices, yoga, mediumistic practices and many other practices and bodies of ideas may all fall under the umbrella of spirituality. Boundaries between these bodies of thought and practices seem very fluid, and rules are de-emphasized in favour of feeling whether a particular practice or idea works for you. That does not mean that there are no boundaries at all. As many have pointed out, there is a certain underlying logic that mediates traffic between these ideas and practices, and closes off traffic with certain religious contexts, such as Pentecostalism and Evangelicalism, or the more exclusive forms of Catholicism.

In the sociology of religion, a lot of ink has been spent exploring the gender puzzle of religion: the fact that although religious contexts are often led by men, they are usually numerically dominated by women. Where it concerns spirituality, the consensus has often been that spiritual contexts empower women, a claim that is often made by spiritual practitioners themselves in relation to what is called 'religion' (Woodhead 2007; Sointu and Woodhead 2008). However, as Fedele and I have pointed out, this assumption needs to be researched, rather than taken for granted (Fedele and Knibbe 2013). Here, I would like to delve a little deeper into the structural location of spirituality, and specifically the contexts where I conducted research. In line with the aims of this volume, I will do this in relation not only with religion but also in relation to the secular, with spirituality as the third category of a gendered triangle.

As noted in the introduction, spirituality is often seen as even more private, individualized and decentralized and, at least in some forms, feminine than religion. What does this mean, then, in terms of the structural location of spirituality? Some of the first sociologists who concerned themselves with spirituality saw this as an outcome of the increasing narcissism of American culture (Lasch 1978; Bellah et al. 1985). The self as divine, no explicit rules to adhere to, how could that not be narcissistic? The term that was invented for this in retrospect seems especially misogynistic: Sheilaism. Yet, as Sointu and Woodhead have pointed out, a very different interpretation emerges if one takes into account the fact that it is very often women who get involved into spirituality: many forms of spirituality validate the qualities that women have been raised to embody, of care, while promoting the idea of finding their own direction in life, in line with their own internal subjectivity, rather than aligning with external standards that create impossible dilemmas (Sointu and Woodhead 2008).

In the Netherlands, this critique was echoed to some extent, also in scholarship on spirituality. More often, the eclectic and unserious character of spiritual practices was critiqued. However, most prominent in the years I conducted this research was the criticism of the unscientific and therefore ridiculous claims of spiritual practitioners. Whenever I discussed my research, people assumed that spiritual practitioners such as, most prominently, Jomanda, were in it for the money and that those who 'believed' them were stupid. Therefore, they jumped immediately to the next question, whether Jomanda believed in it herself or not. There was no room for doubt in the public debate on Jomanda, or aura readers, mediums and paragnosts more generally: they are taking advantage of gullible, dumb, superstitious and often sick people. For example, Jomanda was invited several times to participate in public, televised debates where she was attacked for giving people false hope, and her claims of miraculous healings occurring during her services. Her accusers were sometimes medical doctors, but more often public intellectuals. In the face of the apparent sincerity of Jomanda they felt it was their duty to point out that we should leave such medieval superstitions behind. Later, she was accused and prosecuted because it was believed that she kept people away from medical care. She was never convicted though, which did not surprise me since she was always very careful to emphasize that people should continue to seek medical help in case of illness.

Summarizing, there are several aspects to the structural location of the people attending spiritual events and engaging in spiritual practices that make them an easy target for ridicule: their provinciality, low education, gendered life choices or life crises and, most of all, their claim to follow their own feelings and intuition in matters that have traditionally been the domain of male religious authority and now are the domain of secular (and still usually male) professional authority. Furthermore, the unscientific character of the claims of spiritual practitioners, the assumed narcissism, commercial character and medievalism of a belief in miracles attributed to spirituality further contribute to the ridiculousness of both the practitioners and the practices in the eyes of secular elites.

Finding oneself

So how can spirituality be a resource for transforming gendered relationships in family life, and in relating to secular and religious authority? How can the much-maligned phrase of 'finding oneself' be understood in terms of the gendered negotiation of people's life paths? And how can this be understood in the light of the equally much-maligned commercial character of the spiritual marketplace? In this section, I will go into several life stories to explore these questions.

Let me start with Marja, who I encountered as a visitor of Jomanda. She visited Jomanda quite often, although her husband and her son thought that this was ridiculous. When I interviewed her, she was in her 50s. She had finished elementary school, but not high school because her mother fell ill. She had been planning to take up nursing as a profession, but instead became the unpaid nurse to her mother. When her mother died, after 10 years, it seemed too late to go into nursing. Besides, she found a man who would provide for her, so she fell in with the accepted path in life, which meant she became a housewife. They had one son, for whom she cared until he was 18. When I visited her, she was alone in a large house in a residential neighbourhood where houses are built far apart. A good neighbourhood, but also very quiet. Her husband usually did not come home until late at night, so she was mostly alone during the day. Her son did not want to talk to her anymore (the reason was unclear, but I can imagine that she might have come across as needy). In short, she felt that life had passed her by and that the people she had always cared for had abandoned her.

In the past few years, she had been suffering intense pains that could not be explained. Finally, she had decided to visit Jomanda and after the first time, kept going to the healing services regularly. Through her visits, she started searching for the larger pattern in her life, to make sense of the missed chances, broken and dead relationships and intense loneliness of her current life. Jomanda, and especially the way she stood up to the ridicule of opinion leaders in the public sphere, gave her some strength and courage. The thought that 'the other side' really exists, that there was a divinely ordained purpose to her life, also helped, although she had not yet figured out what this purpose was. To her, visiting Jomanda and spiritual healers was a secret source of strength and healing. She was hopeful that somehow she would be able to find her way to a better, more meaningful life.

Another woman, Roos, had given up her professional life as an art historian to care for her husband, who suffered from schizophrenia. After 15 years of caring, he died and she had no idea how to continue her life: her whole life had been bound up in caring for him, but also in the notion that this was a worthwhile activity, that self-sacrifice was a virtue. Now that he was dead, how could she live a virtuous life? She had no professional life anymore, and was estranged from her family. Through engaging in spiritual practices, she was feeling her way to a renewed sense of self. Interesting here was that, in contrast to Marja, Roos slid back and forth between a metonymical understanding of the spiritual and a metaphorical understanding. Whereas to Marja the notion that the 'other side' is real, and concerned with your life, was extremely important, Roos switched codes several times during our conversations and interview, was more widely read and could talk about her connection to the other side both in terms of its tangible reality, where signs and messages were pieces of something bigger and unseen, and in terms of metaphor, where the whole notion of the other side was much more ephemeral, simply a way of talking about abstractions such as the meaning of life, in more concrete terms.

A third woman, Marcia, had always worked as a nurse and never married. She had a Catholic background as well, although she had fallen away from religious engagement a long time ago. She had come to visit Jomanda through her concern for her dog. After she retired, her dog had become her most significant companion. When he fell ill, she tried everything to find a cure, including taking him, or a picture of him when he was too ill, to Jomanda. Jomanda encouraged this, telling people that they could take pictures of their loved ones, including pets. During the healing services, people would put these pictures under their chair at Jomanda's signal, and while they were under the chair, Jomanda stated that 'the other side' would work on the people or animals depicted. After the dog died, she felt she was able to continue and round off the relationship with her dog through the sense-making the context of Jomanda provided her.

For these women, the factual reality of the other side was important although, as noted, Roos could switch codes and make this more of a psychological notion. For Marcia, the notion that there really was another side was something that she only came to terms with because of the illness and death of her dog. The notion that everything is preordained is very important, as is the notion that any kind of relationship is there to teach you something. Anyone you meet, including animals, may be linked to your life's purpose, and may have played a role in previous lives. People are thought to reincarnate many times, and be reborn each time with a particular blueprint for their lives, including the challenges they have to face and the lessons they have to learn.

Although living very different lives, they have several things in common: they grew up with a Catholic ethos that emphasized the virtue of care and self-sacrifice, within a taken-for-granted gendered role division. Furthermore, they had all three experienced the feeling of being left empty-handed after a lifetime of taking care of others, with very little in the way of fulfilling relationships and recognition to show for it. From this position, all three found their way to Jomanda and other spiritual practitioners.

Commercial relationships

While the commercial character of the spiritual landscape was maligned both by insiders and outsiders, it is quite a dominant and pervasive characteristic of the ways spiritual practices, goods and services are encountered, and deserves further analysis. As Campbell already argued long ago, if the Protestant ethic is linked to capitalism, the Romantic ethic, browsing, daydreaming and figuring out what clothes or items best expresses one's true authentic self, is what informs consumerism (Campbell 1987). The commercial character of the relationship between service providers on the spiritual marketplace and the women browsing in it also affords a welcome anonymity and looseness in the relationship to those who claim to have authority on spiritual matters, and those who seek insight. In view of the structural position both of the service providers, such as Jomanda, and those who used her services and those of others, the commercial character of this relationship needs to be interpreted through a biographical and gendered lens. So let's take a look at the ways these relationships are commercial: to attend a healing service, one had to buy a ticket of 10 guilders, which would now be the same amount in euros. To go to a private session with a healer, paragnost or tarot reader costs a lot more, something like 30 to 50 guilders per session. At paranormal markets, one could try out someone's services for a price of between 10 to 15 guilders. These paranormal markets were organized on a commercial scale since the 1990s, but were often reviled by both visitors and practitioners as harbouring many charlatans. However, most of the people I spoke to had frequented these paranormal markets before they settled on a particular person with whom they established a more personal relationship. This relationship, although a practitioner might know a lot about someone's life, is also transactional: you pay for someone's time. In the context of spiritual society I attended, the topic of the relationship between practitioners and client was often discussed. Too much dependency was frowned on, and I recorded several horror stories of mediums or paragnosts who made people dependent on them. All practitioners emphasized the importance of a client learning to recognize their own intuitions and act on them. They encouraged clients to feel if their services were 'right' for them, and assured them that they would not hold it against them (although the moral high ground was then usually found in saying that a client was 'not ready' for the high-quality spiritual insights they had to offer).

Interestingly, in the context of Jomanda, the relationship is even more impersonal. Most people never speak to Jomanda directly. Ultimately, the relationship that is established is between an individual and 'the other side'. This may become personalized, in the form of the conviction that a deceased family member or friend may act as a guide, but more often this was quite impersonal, involving the conviction that unnamed 'beings of light' help us along here on earth, operate on us and guide us to live out the blueprint of our life. Through attending to signs, one could learn to recognize this guidance. Here especially, there was a fine line between becoming too dependent and expectant of signs from the other side (which can always be interpreted in many different ways) and simply being attentive and open while following one's own intuition.

This direct relationship with the other side and one's own (moral) intuitions is quite remarkable if one takes into account the Catholic background of these women, where they had been taught to defer to the priest in all spiritual matters. The fact that it can be mediated through a relationship that theoretically can be terminated at will if a client does not want the services anymore is also significant. Discussing the quality of mediums and paragnosts, what level of spiritual energy they were tapping into, and how evolved they were spiritually were all important topics in the informal moments around the meetings of the spiritual societies, as well as Jomanda's healing services. Critical discernment was a crucial skill to develop. This is quite different from the uncritical acceptance of authority most women (and lower class men) grew up with in the south of the Netherlands. Dutch Catholicism in the time that these women grew up (post-Second World War) was very much focused on getting all areas of life under the auspices of the church, including people's intimate lives.

Therefore, the fact that a relationship between a practitioner and a client can be initiated and terminated by a client may be less a sign of commercialization to be lamented, and much more a quite radical and daring reformation of the relationship to religious and secular sources of authority on the part of these women. Often, women still relied on mediums to provide them with answers, but gradually, through becoming more involved and discerning in the spiritual marketplace, they started to pride themselves on being able to separate the authentic from the fake, the sensationalist from the true, the manipulative from the refined spiritual practitioner. Rather than the institute of the church with all its weight of morals and history behind it, all its requirements of a life lived in a certain way, these women could search for answers to their questions in a direct way and expect the kind of answers that a priest could never give. Furthermore, the answers to be expected combined the weight of the supernatural with another source of authority, namely that of science: auras can be pictured, energies can be measured, deceased doctors have more refined techniques than living ones. Both in the context of Jomanda, and in the context of spiritual societies, 'proof' was considered crucial. As Hanegraaff has shown, spiritualism could be considered the most 'positivist' of the esoteric branches that sprung up in the nineteenth century, and the emphasis on proof exercised by people like Arthur Conan Doyle could be observed among the visitors of Jomanda, but also in the spiritual society (Hanegraaff 1996). At the same time, among higher educated women, the scientific backing was less positivist and more psychological, ensuring that at all times they could exchange their language of signs from the other side to a language of significance and psychological integration through symbols, in line with the trend also observed by Hanegraaff (2000).

Furthermore, the commercial character of spiritual services fit well with framing their engagement with spirituality as a private activity and a personal choice, an activity that should not concern anyone. In the case of Marja, both her husband and her son dismissed her interest in the spiritual, and this was not unusual. However, in other cases I found that both wife and husband developed an engagement with spiritual practices, sometimes also involving their children, relatives and friends.

Conclusion

In this chapter I have aimed to show how the structural position of both the women who frequent spiritual contexts and these spiritual contexts themselves is quite marginal in relation to secular intellectual elites. Yet, through providing access to sources of religious and scientific authority through a commercial relationship, these contexts may provide a secret source of empowerment that is crucial in redefining the self in relation to a family context, one's path in life, or one's deceased family members. The commercial character allows for a shift in the balance of power between the seeker and the provider that should be understood within the gendered biographies of the women involved. Furthermore, the commercial character allows for a piece-meal and gradual integration of particular ways of seeing things, particular spiritual practices and significant items into the private sphere of these women, rather than the wholesale dedication that is demanded by becoming a 'member' of a church.

Rather than creating narratives lamenting the 'takeover of religion by the commercial forces of spirituality' (Carrette and King 2005) or seeing the popularity of spirituality as a sign of the increased narcissism of our times, or the inability to appreciate tradition or submit to any kind of authority, I hope that I have been able to show that it is important to pay attention to the conjuncture of structural positions and biographical moments that cause people to seek out help in these domains. A gendered reading of the position of religion, spirituality and women's lives may provide one with very different insights into the significance of spirituality in our societies and the ways they enable women to mediate the tensions of a society where those who have dedicated their life to caring work in the private domain, guided by a gendered Catholic ethos where this kind of work has a certain standing and recognition, can no longer count on much recognition, company or appreciation in the current secular valuations of their life. Furthermore, it enables a recognition of the ways a relationship with commercialized spiritual services allows women to reformulate their relationship to both religious and secular authorities.

References

Bellah, Robert N., Richard Madsen, William M. Sullivan, Ann Swidler, and Steven M. Tipton. 1985. *Habits of the Heart: Individualism and Commitment in American Life.* Berkeley, CA: University of California Press.

Campbell, C. 1987. *The Romantic Ethic and the Spirit of Modern Consumerism.* Oxford: Blackwell.

Carrette, Jeremy R., and Richard King. 2005. *Selling Spirituality: The Silent Takeover of Religion.* Abingdon: Routledge.

Fedele, Anna, and Kim Esther Knibbe, eds. 2013. *Gender and Power in Contemporary Spirituality: Ethnographic Approaches.* London: Routledge.

Fedele, Anna, and Kim Esther Knibbe. 2016. "From Angel in the Home to Sacred Prostitute: Unconditional Love and Gendered Hierarchies in Contemporary Spirituality." In *Contemporary Encounters in Gender and Religion*, edited by Lena Gemzöe, Marja-Liisa Keinänen and Avril Maddrell, 195–216. Cham: Springer/Palgrave Macmillan. http://link.springer.com/chapter/10.1007/978-3-319-42598-6_9.

Friedman, Sam, and Giselinde Kuipers. 2013. "The Divisive Power of Humour: Comedy, Taste and Symbolic Boundaries." *Cultural Sociology* 7(2): 179–195.

Hanegraaff, Wouter J. 1996. *New Age Religion and Western Culture: Esotericism in the Mirror of Secular Thought*. Leiden: Brill.

Hanegraaff, Wouter J. 2000. "Het Einde van de Hermetische Traditie." Universiteit van Amsterdam.

Hochschild, Arlie R. 2003. *The Commercialization of Intimate Life: Notes from Home and Work*. Berkeley: University of California Press.

Kennedy, James. 1995. *Nieuw Babylon in Aanbouw: Nederland in de Jaren Zestig*. Amsterdam: Boom.

Knibbe, Kim. 2011. "Secrets, Gossip and Betrayal: Doing Fieldwork on the Role of Religion in Moral Orientation in a Dutch Catholic Province." *Fieldwork in Religion* 6(2): 151–167.

Knibbe, Kim. 2012. "An Ethnography of a Medium and Her Followers: How Learning Takes Place in the Context of Jomanda." In *Meister Und Schüler in Geschichte Und Gegenwart: Von Religionen Der Antike Bis Zur Modernen Esoterik*, edited by Almut Barbara Renger, 383–398. Göttingen: V&R unipress.

Knibbe, Kim. 2013. *Faith in the Familiar: Religion, Spirituality and Place in the South of the Netherlands*. Leiden: Brill.

Knibbe, Kim, and Iti Westra. 2003. "Van Ongeloof Naar 'Zeker Weten': Betekenisgeving En Legitimatie in de Context van Het Fenomeen Jomanda." *Sociale Wetenschappen* 46(2): 75–93.

Kuipers, Giselinde. 2008. "The Sociology of Humor." *The Primer of Humor Research* 8: 361–398.

Lasch, Christopher. 1978. *The Culture of Narcissism: American Life in an Age of Diminishing Expectations*. New York: Norton.

Simons, Ed, and Lodewijk Winkeler. 1987. *Het Verraad Der Clercken: Intellectuelen En Hun Rol in de Ontwikkelingen van Het Nederlandse Katholicisme Na 1945*. Baarn: Arbor.

Sointu, Eeva, and Linda Woodhead. 2008. "Spirituality, Gender, and Expressive Selfhood." *Journal for the Scientific Study of Religion* 47(2): 259–276.

Woodhead, Linda. 2007. "Gender Differences in Religious Practice and Significance." In *The Sage Handbook of the Sociology of Religion*, edited by James Beckford and Jay Demerath, 550–570. Los Angeles: Sage.

10 Is yoga a girl's thing?

A case study on working-class men doing yoga in jail

Mar Griera

Introduction

Most of the empirical research on holistic spirituality has been carried out among white middle-class, middle-aged women living in Europe and the US. This is not a coincidence. According to the literature (Heelas et al. 2005; Houtman and Aupers 2007; Fedele and Knibbe 2013), the growth and expansion of holistic spirituality has been especially successful among women of a mature age living in middle- and upper-class areas. Men seem to have been less affected by the 'spiritual revolution' and there are almost no studies focused on male and holistic spirituality. However, this might be changing since holistic spirituality is also gaining presence among males. For this reason, as Linda Woodhead (2007b) puts forward, the study of spirituality and masculinity demands urgent attention for the comprehension of contemporary processes of religious change.

This chapter is a first step towards filling this lacuna. The aim is to develop a sociological understanding of the ways in which holistic practices find their place in a working-class male-dominated environment, and about how they contribute to refashioning conceptions of masculinity. Based on an extensive fieldwork among kundalini yoga students in two male penitentiary institutions in the area of Barcelona, the chapter particularly focuses on three independent questions: How does yoga get legitimated, and become popular among men in prison? To what extent does the practice of yoga have spiritual implications in the context of the prison and how is it positioned vis-à-vis the religious–secular categories? And in what ways, if so, can spirituality contribute to fostering new understandings of masculinity?

As I will explore more deeply in the following pages, the body, and work on the body, is the principal means by which yoga is made meaningful and becomes a legitimated practice in the eyes of male inmates in the context of a prison. However, the impact of yoga practice goes beyond its physical effects. The regular practice of yoga, and the subsequent involvement into the holistic milieu, entails the acquisition of new languages related to the care of oneself and others and attention to emotions that blur traditional working-class conceptions of masculinity. Yoga is described as a 'secular practice' with no relation to religion but rather tied to spirituality. The chapter explores these new narratives and practices of masculinity that, in turn, play a strategic role in prison since they hold an affinity with the spiritual therapeutic culture that is gaining credibility among penitentiary authorities and staff.

As I already mentioned, this chapter is based on extensive fieldwork carried out in two penitentiary institutions, one high-security prison and one remand institution. The fieldwork was not initially designed as focused on questions of masculinity but on understanding the phenomenological experience of doing yoga in prison, and on the institutional opportunities and constraints of undertaking spiritual activities in a 'total institution'. However, the empirical data gathered have been re-examined with a view to analysing gender and power dynamics, and reflecting on the transformation of conceptions of masculinity in the context of yoga practice in prison.

Masculinities, spirituality and penitentiary institutions: theoretical premises

The theoretical framework of this chapter derives from the cross-fertilization among three different research subfields: masculinities in prison, gender and religion, and spirituality in penitentiary institutions. I will start by briefly underlining the main questions that emerge from each of these subfields when enquiring into the role of yoga in mediating notions of masculinity in prison. Then, I will move to the empirical case.

Masculinities in prison: state of the art

Most of the recent literature on masculinities in prison "has drawn attention to the relationship between gender and crime, more specifically concluding that cultural constructions of masculinity are correlated with crime and that male prison culture reifies hyper masculinity" (Karp 2010, 63). There is an academic consensus in identifying penitentiary cultures as privileging traditional forms of hegemonic masculinity, and in characterizing prisons as a fertile ground for the reproduction and maintenance of aggressive forms of manhood.

This is mainly explained by two factors. First, men entering prison are dispossessed of socially accepted forms of power such as money, education or status (Evans and Wallace 2008). As Jewkes argues "in prisons, the deprivation of such items [...] associated with the inability to purchase them with a 'man's wage' – emasculates the individual and attacks his sense of self-worth" (Jewkes 2005, 58). In a way, this extreme dispossession makes men more attracted to hypermasculinity repertoires such as aggressive or intimidating behaviours, the use (and abuse) of physical strength or the denigration of alternative forms of masculinity. Second, what has been called the 'prison code', historically rooted in hegemonic (and aggressive) conceptions of masculinity, seriously hinders the emergence of new models of masculinity.

Moreover, the fact that the fear for personal safety becomes one of the major 'pains' associated with imprisonment and that this fear is usually prevented by looking for peer group respect and a reputation for aggressiveness (Jewkes 2005; Evans and Wallace 2008) makes the emergence of alternative notions of masculinity especially difficult. As Evans and Wallace note in their research on masculinities in prison, "Even when your personal viewpoint has been truly transformed, the social policing of masculine codes is sufficiently strong to mean that you keep these views secret most of the time" (2008, 502). Thus, literature makes clear that penitentiary institutions are not favourable contexts for the reshaping of traditional forms of masculinity but rather the contrary. However, then, in this light, the popularity of yoga in the prison context becomes even more intriguing, and several questions arise: How do inmates perceive the practice of yoga and its compatibility (or not) with prisons' masculine regimes? How are practices such as singing mantras or lying in the floor with the eyes closed made plausible in the prison context? To what extent does the practice of yoga shape new understandings of manhood?

Religion and gender: what about masculinity?

Paul Heelas and Linda Woodhead, in their research in Kendal (UK), found that around 80 per cent of the practitioners, members and clients of the holistic milieu were female. Years later, Woodhead observed that this was "one of the most striking findings of the research" and added "This was a finding which we struggled to explain [...] we felt rather like explorers taking slow and tentative steps into relatively uncharted territory" (Woodhead 2007a, 115). Heelas and Woodhead were not the first ones to emphasize the overwhelming presence of women in the holistic movement, nor were they the last. However, they – and especially Woodhead in her later articles (2007a, 2007b) – sharply point at the need to take gender on board when researching the transformations of religion and spirituality in contemporary society. Ursula King notices that in recent years "a remarkable paradigm shift has occurred, especially among younger religion scholars, so that gender-critical analyses have globally spawned an impressive range of new research in a relatively short time" (2008, 120). Two distinct areas have been especially fertile in producing innovative works on religion and gender: research on holistic spiritualities and studies on Pentecostalism. This is not coincidental; both religious/spiritual movements have undergone a process of feminization in quantitative but also in qualitative terms. In both movements, women have played a role as main cultural carriers of the 'spirit' in a Weberian sense, and as catalysts for the movement's expansion. Initially, scholars mainly examined the growing prominence of women in Pentecostal and holistic spiritual circles through the question of the empowering or disempowering capacity of these movements. This dualistic – and highly political – approach strongly influenced initial research on gender and religion and encapsulated the debate in such a way that the final assessment of the capacity (or not) of religion to empower women hid other crucial aspects (Cazarín and Griera 2018). However, recent research has provided a more nuanced account of the relationships between gender and religion, especially by showing the complex interplay between religion, gender and power in contemporary societies (Fedele and Knibbe 2013; Burchardt 2017). New research has shown how religion and gender operate in a dense web of power relations and social configurations, which makes it necessary to critically discuss processes of social construction of gender in relation to the contexts in which they develop. In this regard, while holistic spirituality and Pentecostalism may become creative sources from and through which new models of femininity and masculinity emerge, they may also contribute to the appearance of more subtle gender power dynamics. These conclusions become especially relevant when researching spirituality in prison, since they show the importance of taking the singularity of the prison context into account when considering the role of spirituality in transforming dominant conceptions of masculinity. To what extent, can the prison setting become a 'magnifying glass' (Beckford and Gilliat-Ray 1998) of wider societal developments in relation to spirituality and masculinity? Or how can one void gender dynamics getting masked when doing research in the hyper-masculinized setting of the prison 'total institution'? These considerations take especial saliency due to the scarcity of previous research on spirituality and masculinity, which complicates the comparison between the world inside and outside prison.

The religious, the secular and the spiritual in penitentiary institutions

In recent years, there has been a growing interest in research on the role of religion in public institutions (Cadge et al. 2017, and especially in prisons (Beckford and Gilliat-Ray 1999; Béraud et al. 2016; Martínez-Ariño et al. 2015). Public institutions have been identified as crucial sites for exploring the transformation of religion in contemporary societies. As Cadge and Konieczny put forward

> studying religion in secular organizations allows us to examine closely how the tension between the disestablishment of religion and its free exercise affects social life not only at the level of public institutions but also in the everyday lives of people who practice religion, as well as those whose identities include a negative stance toward religion
>
> (2014, 555)

However, research on public institutions not only offers us interesting insights about the deployment and impact of secularization processes but also about the consequences and challenges brought by processes of religious diversification. The processes of de-establishment of traditional churches, and of religious diversification, are the major trends faced by public institutions in Europe nowadays and most research has been devoted to these two topics (Beckford and Gilliat-Ray 1999; Furseth 2003; Furseth and Kühle 2011; Michalowski 2015). Nevertheless, there are an increasing number of publications that mention the growing relevance of spirituality in public institutions. In this regard, Becci and Knobel (2013) show the emergence of what they call "grey zones" in prisons, which are characterized by the appearance of religious expressions that lie beyond formal religious membership and that are located at the margins of official expressions of religiosity. Most of these 'liminal' religious expressions are read, and expressed, in terms of spirituality and not of religion. Wendy Cadge (2012), in her research on US hospitals, also points out the increasing relevance of spiritual practices that resist being considered along traditional religious lines. In a similar fashion, in many countries we are witnessing a process of professionalization of 'spiritual chaplains', who do not identify themselves with any official religious tradition and who consider their job as lying beyond these categories (De Groot 2010). To my consideration, two of the most interesting elements that emerge from this still very preliminary research area are the following: first, there seems to be a silent encroachment of spiritual activities in public institutions. A growth that is largely ignored or unnoticed both by scholars and institution managers. This institutional invisibility is related to the fact that usually the penetration of these spiritual activities in public institutions follows a bottom-up route, being diffused through low-profile workers such as nurses in hospitals or social educators in prisons (Griera and Clot-Garrell 2015b; Griera 2017). Second, in terms of regulation these activities usually lie in no-man's-land and are not inserted into the legal-bureaucratic apparatus regulating religion. In this chapter, it becomes especially relevant to ask whether the practice of yoga might be considered as belonging to the 'spiritual field' in prison, and to understand how it is framed by the different actors. Additionally, and in the light of the whole volume, we might consider to what extent the spiritual domain holds an independent position vis-à-vis religion, and what this tells us about the contemporary configurations of power in the religious-secular dynamics.

Case study: masculinities, yoga and spirituality in penitentiary settings

Contextual and methodological considerations

In the autumn of 2011 I went to a male penitentiary centre, located in Barcelona city, to interview a social educator working there. At that time, I was involved in a research project focused on analysing the accommodation of religious diversity in prisons and hospitals (Griera and Clot-Garrell 2015b). While walking through the prison I saw a placard in one corridor announcing yoga classes for inmates. I asked the social educator about it and he told me that yoga was a very popular activity in the prison context. I tried to investigate a bit more, but he just told me that this was an activity taught by volunteers and with no relation at all with my research on religion. Some months later, one of my colleagues, Anna Clot-Garrell, went to do fieldwork in another penitentiary institution in the outskirts of Barcelona. There she also found that yoga was a popular activity offered to inmates and taught by volunteers. Additionally, she also learned that yoga was not the only holistic activity being offered to inmates but also reiki, sofrology, tai chi and Ho'oponopono, among others. Afterwards, we discovered that the emergence and popularity of 'spiritual activities' was not a phenomenon limited to these two cases but was part of a more general trend (Becci and Knobel 2014; Griera and Clot-Garrell 2015a, 2015b). These initial findings brought us to more systematically explore the growth of holistic spiritualities in prison settings in Catalonia. We interviewed several volunteers, social educators and psychologists from five different prisons in Catalonia and we confirmed that holistic spirituality was on the rise within public institutions. We identified reiki and yoga as the most extended and institutionalized practices, the others more marginal. We discovered that these practices were usually offered by holistic volunteers who wanted to 'give back' what their spiritual journey had brought them (Clot-Garrell and Griera 2019). These practices counted, in most cases, on strong support from the staff, especially from the 'social' staff (psychologists, social educators, leisure instructors). Penitentiary staff considered all these practices as belonging to the 'secular' domain; thus, they were not regulated by the strict rules governing religious organizations in prisons (Griera and Clot-Garrell 2015a). However, in a more-or-less fashion, most of the prison staff interviewed acknowledged the spiritual dimension of these activities. Even, in several cases, the interviewees used a highly connoted holistic spiritual language, speaking of 'energy', angels, karma or synchronicity while describing these practices and justifying their importance in the prison context. We also found out that some social educators and psychologists were themselves carrying out 'holistic practices' with inmates, such as a social educator who organized a ritual of the solstice, another leisure instructor teaching reiki to inmates and many others using meditation or yoga techniques in their therapeutic sessions. The spiritual character of these practices was unproblematized by our interlocutors. Prison staff interviewed marked a clear boundary between the spiritual and the religious domain. Any possible links of these spiritual activities with religion were strongly denied, even if in some cases the links were rather evident, such as in the case of a Brama Kumaris group teaching raja yoga or when inviting a lama to give a talk on 'spiritual growth'. The categorization of certain practices as religious or secular also has legal and regulatory implications, which might explain why there is a strong denial of the religious character of spiritual activities. If these same activities were labelled as 'religious', it would have been more difficult to carry them out in prison, to include them in the leisure programmes or to make them available for all the inmates. Likewise, discursively, our interlocutors identified spirituality as compatible with the secular regime governing the prison while assessing the benefits of these practices in therapeutic terms by using 'scientific' arguments. They talked very differently about religion – and especially about minority religions – which in some cases were considered a 'suspicious' presence that had to be accepted in the name of freedom of religion but also had to be strictly regulated. The growing presence of religious minorities was problematized by some of our interviewees, while holistic activities went unquestioned (Griera and Clot-Garrell 2015a) and fitted under the appearance of normality (Goffman 1971).

For methodological and comparative reasons (see Griera 2017) we focused on the analysis of the practice of kundalini yoga in penitentiary institutions. The research project was designed around three objectives. First, to examine the role, significance and effects of yoga for inmates practising it. Second, to put the institution at the centre, and explore the conditions that enabled the emergence, legitimacy and dissemination of yoga in penitentiary settings. Third, to focus on yoga volunteers and analyse the increasing relevance of the 'culture of giving back' (Koch 2015) in the holistic milieu.

The fieldwork was done in three different phases. First, I did an exploratory fieldwork in a high-security prison where volunteers were organizing a yoga quarantine which consisted of 40 days of yoga practice (2 hours per day) with a group of 15 inmates (July–August 2013). Second, together with two other researchers, we did intensive fieldwork in a three-month intensive yoga course organized by a yoga NGO in a remand prison (June–July 2014). Third, I did intensive fieldwork in the second yoga quarantine being organized in the first prison (June–July 2015). Fieldwork consisted of participant observation, informal and formal interviews with inmates, staff and yoga volunteers, and surveys with inmates. In addition, follow-up interviews and observations were done during 2016 and 2017.

Inmates participated in the yoga courses on a voluntary basis and following the courses had no direct penitentiary benefits. The selection of the inmates was done by the prison social educators according to different criteria: disciplinary issues, previous knowledge of yoga, compatibility with other leisure activities and compatibility with the other inmates participating in the group. In each of the three cases, there was a long waiting list of inmates since volunteers and penitentiary staff decided to limit the number of participants. In the quarantine, the group was mixed in terms of gender (70 per cent male, 30 per cent female); in the case of the course organized in the remand prison, there were only males. The courses were organized by a Yoga NGO (World PREM) devoted to promoting yoga to socially excluded persons. Most of the volunteers were trained in kundalini yoga, and there was an almost equal distribution between male and female volunteers.

Most of the inmates participating in the research had a previous knowledge of yoga. Apart from these intensive courses, all the Catalan prisons offer weekly yoga courses to inmates, also taught by volunteers. Thus, the majority of the inmates participating in the intensive courses were already participating in these weekly classes. Therefore, most of them, especially in the high-security prison, already had a good command of yoga and, in some cases, they were advanced students with years of practice behind them. The yoga practised in prison belongs to what has been labelled as modern yoga, which covers

> those disciplines and schools that are, to a greater or lesser extent, rooted in South Asian cultural contexts and more specifically draw inspiration from certain philosophies, teachings, and practices of Hinduism. These teachings and practices, by virtue of exportation, syncretic assimilation and subsequent acculturation processes, have now become an integral part of (primarily) urban cultures worldwide.
>
> (De Michelis 2008, 19)

In this context, the practice of yoga is neither a practice directly transplanted from Hinduism or Sikhism, nor is it framed in terms of a religious activity. It is rather a global phenomenon conceived as a secular expression although, simultaneously, there exists a tacit – and sometimes explicit – acknowledgement of its spiritual character (Smith 2007). This spiritual character is especially visible in Kundalini yoga.

Yoga, men and the body in prison

In my first interview with one of the yoga teachers, Amaya, she expressed what many others manifested again later: that yoga was very popular among men in prison, in opposition to the norm outside the prison walls. Simultaneously, in the same interview, Amaya showed her frustration because a yoga course that was going to be developed in a maternal care unit in a female prison was cancelled due to the lack of interest of inmates in participating. She showed surprise and stated, "Before, I would have never imagined that yoga would had been more attractive to jailed males than to mothers. It is shocking. I can't really explain this." In later conversations, different explanations were offered by Amaya and other yoga volunteers to make sense of the failure of yoga courses in the penitentiary maternal care unit. From a sociological point of view, I am not able to provide an answer to Amaya's puzzle but it is interesting to highlight the implicit conceptions about who should be the 'natural' target of yoga courses. As another yoga volunteer, Joana, told me once: "You know, it is very shocking to see all these big men with all these tattoos and their criminal histories in a prayer position singing mantras: I would have never imagined this before." For Joana, who works as a yoga teacher in 'female-only' gyms, it was a surprise, but also a challenge, to teach yoga to male inmates in prison. However, at the same time, she pointed out that "it is also very rewarding, you know, all this masculine energy is very powerful and you can feel this in the class". While addressing gender issues most of the volunteers relied on preconceived spiritual notions of the 'masculine' and the 'feminine' and associated them with notions of strong/soft, sun/moon, rigidity/fluidity among others. The masculine and the feminine are constructed as ideal-types, which are both present (but in different proportions) in men and women. From their point of view, masculine and feminine energy might be creative sources for the self but, if not dealt and cultivated properly, might be also destructive. The prison is perceived by yoga volunteers as a space 'saturated' with male energy in need of healing and balance.

However, not only the volunteers commented on gender issues. Miguel, one inmate who has been practising yoga in prison for more than six years now, right at the beginning of the interview told me the following: "Keep in mind that we are where we are and for many [*the practice of yoga*] it is nonsense, or something for young ladies ..." He was not the only one who pointed out that the prison environment was apparently not conducive to activities such as yoga, and who also manifested that, initially, inmates have to overcome many 'resistances'. These 'resistances' are expressed through the production of feelings of shame or embarrassment. Manel, another inmate, commented: "In the first lessons the singing of mantras made me laugh and feel very stupid." As Thomas Scheff (1988) argues, feelings of shame or embarrassment might work as mechanisms of social conformity and as regulatory emotions for disciplining the self. In this case, the feeling of embarrassment when practising yoga emerges because it defies the 'normal' behaviour code in a male prison, and yoga practice is perceived as susceptible to being sanctioned by male peers. However, most of the interviewees coincide in stating that these feelings of shame usually disappear early on and, as Manel also expressed, "after a while, you don't care".

The first and most basic mechanism that inmates use for confronting embarrassment is to render yoga rational through the lenses of the masculinity codes. This excerpt from Miguel's interview is telling:

> While I'm working, in the kitchen, sometimes I do yoga exercises in the break since I need to stretch my body and feel better again ... at the beginning many of my fellow workers laughed and made fun of me. However, then, I decided to bet them to be in plank pose for a while. I won. Then, I bet them again with other asanas, I always won. So, then, they stopped laughing at me.

Yoga is then legitimated as an activity to contribute to building physical strength.

As stated by several researchers, the physical body has a crucial relevance in the context of the prison. The work on the body helps to build an appearance of hardness – which might be crucial for inmates' survival. As Martos-Garcia et al. state, drawing on Bourdieu, "physical prowess and fighting ability provide a form of physical capital that can be converted to social and cultural capital within the prison environment" (2009, 80). But also, to keep one's body fit becomes a strategy for fighting the pains of imprisonment, and especially for softening the deteriorating effects of imprisonment being inscribed in the body (Wahidin 2002). Many of the participants in the yoga course, and especially those with long-term sentences, expressed their fears about the harsh impact that prison might have on their bodies and their perception that yoga might counteract them. This can also explain, although not fully, why yoga is much more popular than meditation in the prison context. However, most of the interviewees stated that through yoga they have also learned about the relevance of improving inner strength, not only physical strength. As one inmate avowed: "At the beginning I thought that yoga was very easy but then I started to understand that this does not only require physical strength but, above all, mental and inner strength. Gradually I got to know how to use this strength that I have in my interior and to be able to control it. Then, I gained in serenity."

Looking for freedom: spirituality, transcendence and yoga

When asked how to deal with shame or embarrassment, Juan, another inmate, stated: "well, when you feel that this really works for you, you forget these fears and you stop feeling ridiculous". As in many other holistic spiritual practices (Cornejo 2012; Fedele and Knibbe 2013) the final reason used to explain their involvement in the practice is that it 'works for them'. When asked more specifically, this is generally elaborated in terms of well-being. Yoga is considered a vehicle to produce well-being at three different levels: physical (reducing body pains), psychological (lowering anxiety and stress) and spiritual (fostering transcendence and fullness). The well-being is conceived as starting at a very physical level and most inmates acknowledge that the improvement of physical well-being was the chief perceived benefit when they started to learn yoga. However, the interviews also show that inmates do positively correlate the performance of yoga's body movements with psychological well-being expressed in terms of inner peace, better self-control, anxiety reduction or emotional stability. These results go in line with most of the research on yoga done from an experimental-science perspective (Bilderbeck et al. 2013; Rocha et al. 2012). However, from a sociological perspective, what is interesting to examine is how well-being is conceptualized, produced and experienced in the specific context of the prison, and how this production relates with broader political, social, and religious processes.

As Erving Goffman put forward decades ago in his book *Asylums* (1961), prisons are total institutions, hybrid social forms, where "a large number of individuals in the same situation, isolated from society for an appreciable period of time, share a formal daily routine in their confinement" (1971 64). When entering a total institution, the individual is submitted to processes of self-mortification such as isolation from the outside world, the limitation of his autonomy, procedures of depersonalization and, especially, the loss of control over their privacy and intimacy (Goffman 1971; Nizet and Rigaux 2005) To a certain extent, the 'success' of yoga in prison is closely related with the fact that it can serve to counteract the impact of self-mortification processes at different levels. On the one hand, yoga creates spaces of calmness in the middle of the chaotic, dirty and noisy prison environment. The aesthetics of the yoga class, the music, the mats, the incense and the volunteers' white clothes create an atmosphere that is perceived as symbolically transgressing the prison order. The transgression is elaborated in the following terms: while prison spaces are perceived as threatening and full of aggressiveness, the yoga class is viewed as a calm and safe space where emotions can be showed and gestures of friendship (among inmates but also, especially, between volunteers and inmates) are displayed. An atmosphere that helps to put the reality of prison in parentheses for a while. It is not by coincidence that the time dedicated to relaxation and meditation is one of the most valued moments for inmates as it offers them an opportunity for introspection, providing a 'safe' and silent context where inmates can feel intimacy – or 'inner peace' as one inmate put it – with themselves, which is not easy to find in the crowded environment of the prison.

In the academic literature on prisons, several authors have identified the existence of 'emotional zones' (Crewe 2014) or 'sanctuaries' (Johnson 1987), which are considered 'sheltered spaces' in between 'front stage' and 'backstage' domains (Goffman 1971). Yoga classes might also be interpreted in this light, as 'sanctuaries' or special 'emotional zones'. These sheltered spaces allow for broader emotional registers and are perceived by inmates as "safe places" where you "can take off your mask" (interview). Through the practice of yoga, participants regain control over their private space – and to what Goffman (1971) termed the 'territories of the self' – and get access to what is perceived as the 'authentic self'. In this regard, another inmate in the final survey after the second quarantine wrote: "what surprised me the most is how we showed our vulnerability and how we were receptive to love". This atmosphere offers a counterpoint to the generally hyper-masculinized space of the prison and opens the door to the expression of a broader register of emotions which go beyond the traditional masculine repertoires.

On the other hand, yoga is perceived by inmates as a vehicle to experience transcendence and fullness. The scenography and 'altered' symbolic order of the yoga class seem to contribute to create an emotional and sensory context conducive to experiences of transcendence. As I more fully developed elsewhere (Griera 2017), the concept of the "finite province of meaning" (Alfred Schütz 1973) is appropriate for explaining inmates' experiences when doing yoga. From a socio-phenomenological perspective, at some moments in life we might experience that ordinary reality is transcended and we enter into a different layer of reality governed by a different temporal order, involving a specific tension of consciousness and imbued with a particular tone of feeling. This is the entrance to a "finite province of meaning", and the practice of yoga, together with meditation and the singing of mantras, may trigger the crossing to this new reality space. These hold some similarities with what Csikszentmihalyi (2000) identified as "flow experiences" or Smith named as experiences of "connection with oneself" (Smith 2007). In many cases, these experiences are interpreted as 'spaces of freedom', which become especially meaningful in the prison context. To a certain extent, the relief of the prison stress that the physical exercises produce, together with the self-confidence gained when they are able to master their own bodies, is what offers these inmates opportunities to experience transcendence and "be free despite being in prison" (interview).

Looking for meaning: masculinity, holistic spirituality and narratives of hope

To get introduced into yoga consists not only of learning how to practise a group of asanas (yoga poses) but also of acquiring a certain knowledge, vocabulary and manners. Yoga classes involve the transmission of certain ideas that, step by step, are gaining ground in an inmate's approach to life. My most surprising initial discovery was that inmates were using a highly spiritual language when expressing what yoga meant to them. Even those belonging to other religions were using a narrative impregnated with holistic spirituality notions such as energy, karma or synchronicity. It was also interesting to find out that many of the conversations at the beginning and end of the classes had a spiritual tone. Sometimes the class served as a space for talking about spiritual books or films (from Paulo Coelho, to the Bhagavad Gita or the film Phi) and, at other times, a comment made by the instructor during the class on a spiritual matter fostered conversations and reflections afterwards. In the survey, one inmate wrote "before, when I heard the word yoga what came to my mind was relaxation, now it is knowledge", which reveals that their conception of yoga goes beyond considering it as a particular type of sport.

To some extent, and using a socio-phenomenological approach again, we might say that the practice of yoga entails the acquisition of a spiritual "stock of knowledge" (Schütz 1973) that provides a new perspective for self-understanding and also some concrete rules about how to orient one's life. There is a pragmatic side to the knowledge acquired, which might help inmates in the concrete organization of living, but also a more religious-philosophical one that provides them with new symbolic resources to narrate and make sense of their lives. The following excerpt from an interview nicely expresses this multi-sided characteristic of yoga:

> Yoga connects me with the divinity. Years ago, I smoked marihuana, I have also taken drugs [...] and with yoga I have felt similar sensations. However, this is not a drug, this is not false, this is not hypocritical, and this is not happening because someone else is giving me drugs. This doesn't come from outside. This comes from inside of me, it comes from my own serenity, and I feel happy with myself [...] I feel happy, and I am able to understand my context, I see how things really are [...] and I say to myself, I feel so good!

The practice of yoga may foster transcendence but also become a tool for reinterpreting one's life through the spiritual 'stock of knowledge' that is gradually being acquired. In the interviews, it was easy to capture how inmates' own personal trajectories were reinterpreted through the lens of holistic spirituality. Ideas about karma were used to explain their previous decisions or circumstances (the ones that brought them to prison) while suffering was made meaningful as a necessary condition to acquire wisdom. Even, in some cases, inmates drew a parallel between the prison and a temple, thus giving new meaning to their imprisonment: "To be here may also be an opportunity. This is like a temple and you need to be strong, and train and discipline your body, your mind and your soul."

Their suffering was incorporated into a narrative of hope that was mostly organized through the following plot: while their previous life was guided by a 'suffering and confused self', now, in their prison time, they had the opportunity to discover their inner and authentic self and acquire the necessary wisdom to live in harmony with the universe. Difficulties are 'proofs' in the path towards balance and wisdom. Thus, there is a process of reinterpretation of their own biographies, which may also have an effect on shaping their conceptions of manhood.

Four elements emerge as having an impact on their conception of what it means to be a man. First, there is a process of reinterpretation of what it means to be a 'strong man'. As I already briefly mentioned, their yoga practice might foster a new understanding of strength by putting the focus on the 'inner' strength. Thus, there is not a complete break with hegemonic conceptions of masculinity, since the idea of being strong still plays a major role in defining what a man should be. However, from this perspective, what is especially valuable – and difficult to obtain – is inner strength. Second, through their involvement in the spiritual universe, the idea that there is an 'inner self' to which one may accede if liberated from suffering and confusion might also have an impact on conceptions of masculinity. From this perspective, aggressiveness and attitudes of physical abuse are read as signs of weakness and as 'masks' that hide the 'true self'. To be able to take one's mask off (or at least to be aware that there is a mask that is hiding something more valuable) is considered as a symptom of wisdom and courage. In many of the interviews, violent attitudes were read as part of the 'false' self, while more positive and conciliatory attitudes were considered as 'signs' from their authentic inner self. I do not have enough data to prove whether their behaviour in fact changed in their everyday life in prison. However, what we observe is that at least the yoga class offers them a stage in which to show this calmer, kinder and more emotional self. Third, and related to the former, it is important to consider the role of the yoga class as a sanctuary (Johnson 1987) or as an 'emotional zone' where inmates might perform differently without the risk of being sanctioned. On some days, in the yoga class, and especially in the high-security prison, there were inmates that started to cry or to show emotional signs while practising. These kinds of emotional expressions usually generated signs of solidarity and friendship, and most of the fellow inmates expressed that they had also had a 'breakdown' at some point in the yoga class. However, it was also clear that outside the yoga class inmates might be sanctioned if expressing their emotions in public. One day, after one inmate started to cry loudly, another inmate went there to solace him and said: "Cry. Cry as much as you can here. Don't worry. This is safe. But then, breathe, stop, and don't let them [the others, the ones not belonging to the class] see you crying." As also Karp (2010) shows in her work on therapies on masculinity in prison, the existence of a 'safe space', where different emotional registers are permitted, is crucial to start to develop more positive understandings of manhood.

Finally, it is also interesting to see how the acquisition of a spiritual narrative might provide new hope for the future. This might be at the philosophical level, by giving meaning to their prison situation as a learning point in their spiritual journey, but also in some cases in more practical terms. Many of the inmates, and especially in the high-security prison, expressed the will to become yoga teachers once outside prison or even already became yoga teachers in their prison galleries by teaching other inmates. Through yoga, then, they start a process of self-reinvention, which also usually entails some changes in modes of dressing, walking and acting. This is illustrated by a discussion during the first quarantine, when a group of inmates asked the yoga teacher if she could bring them yoga clothes. When she told them that you can do yoga in all types of clothes they were not satisfied, and they asked for 'real' yoga clothes. For some of them, and especially for those with many years of practice ahead, their involvement in the yoga class might become a form of refashioning their identity. To a certain extent, the lack of symbolical and identity resources to distinguish oneself while in prison makes inmates more susceptible to use the few available resources – in this case, yoga – as a form of distinction from other inmates, and also from their previous self.

Conclusion

The research on new spiritualities in the prison setting defies the traditional portrayals of holistic spirituality: mainly female oriented, middle class, fostering only self-cultivation and being disseminated through the market and the private sphere. The case of yoga in prison shows how holistic spirituality also penetrates public institutions and is gaining ground in working-class male-dominated environments. The 'carriers' (cf. Weber) of these practices are holistic volunteers with the aim to 'give back', which transcend the classic stereotype of the 'New Ager' as a narcissistic and hedonist individual.

In institutional terms, there are several reasons that explain the success of yoga in prison (see Griera and Clot-Garrell 2015a) but in this chapter it is particularly relevant to stress the affinity between the therapeutic shift on conceptions of rehabilitation and holistic spiritualities. Currently, penitentiary settings are also amidst a change regarding ideologies of rehabilitation and therapy (Crewe 2011a; Malventi and Garreaud 2008), in line with the increasing hegemony of therapeutic discourses (Illouz 2008). In this context, the success of holistic spirituality might be explained by the fact that it works in consonance – and it reinforces what Rieff (1966) named the "triumph of the therapeutic" or what Illouz has called the "transnational language of selfhood" (2008). As Sherry and Kozinets (2007) point out, the spread of the 'culture of authenticity' coincides with the rise of expressive individualism and with the spread of the therapeutic ethos and of 'reflexive spirituality'.

The institutionalization of a holistic milieu in prisons follows a bottom-up approach: it emerges from the initiative of volunteers, is promoted by workers and is tolerated by penitentiary authorities. In most cases, penitentiary staff promoting these practices are also themselves practitioners, clients or members of the holistic spiritual milieu, and share a social and cultural affinity with yoga volunteers. When justifying the role of these activities in prison, its religious character is totally denied. Their promoters are able to mobilize a non-religious frame to justify their presence in public institutions, and they are successful in doing so because holistic spirituality is inscribed in the secular normativity and is gaining hegemony as a 'secular' technology of the self. The practice of yoga might be interpreted as a technology of the self, since it allows "individuals to effect by their own means or with the help of others a certain number of operations on their own bodies and souls, thoughts, conduct, and way of being, so as to transform themselves" (Foucault 1988). The practice of yoga also offers inmates an embodied acquisition of therapeutic language and facilitates new meaning plots for refashioning the narrative of their biographical trajectories. Yoga gives them access to a particular stock of knowledge based on oriental spiritualities, positive psychology and syncretic elements which offer them resources to adapt the presentation of their biographies to contemporary hegemonic conceptions about the rehabilitated self. The acquisition of these narrative repertoires becomes a powerful tool for reinventing their biographies and facing the future, but also for generating proximity with the social staff (psychologists, social educators, instructors). Through yoga and their involvement in the holistic universe, these inmates adopt a middle-class therapeutic/spiritual language, which helps them to better perform the role of the 'rehabilitated' self in the context of the prison and to adapt to the requirements of the increasingly therapized penitentiary context. To a certain extent, the study shows that the practice of yoga can perform similar results to that of religion in prison (Johnson 2002), namely transformation, self-discipline and hope. However, the main difference between the religious and the spiritual field in prison is that, while religion is perceived as a separated and clearly demarcated area, spirituality appears to be conflated with the secular realm. Spirituality is not considered as contradicting the secular ethos and is thus easily incorporated as belonging to the therapeutic dimension of prison, while this is not so in the case of religion.

References

Aupers, Stef and Dick Houtman. 2006. "Beyond the spiritual supermarket: The social and public significance of new age spirituality." *Journal of Contemporary Religion* 21: 201–222.

Becci, Irene and Brigitte Knobel. 2013. "La diversité religieuse en prison: entre modèles de régulation et émergence de zones grises (Suisse, Italie et Allemagne)." In *Quand le religieux fait conflit: Désaccords, négociations ou arrangements*, edited by Anne-Sophie Lamine and Nathalie Luca, 109–122. Paris: La Découverte.

Beckford, James and Sophie Gilliat-Ray. 1998. *Religion in Prison: Equal rites in a multi-faith society*. Cambridge: Cambridge University Press.

Béraud, Celine, Claire de Galembert, and Corinne Rostaing. 2016. *De la religion en prison*. Rennes: Presses universitaires de Rennes.

Bilderbeck, Amy, Miguel Farias, Inti A. Brazil and Sharon Jakobowitz. 2013. "Participation in a 10-week course of yoga improves behavioural control and decreases psychological distress in a prison population." *Journal of psychiatric research* 47 (10): 1438–1445.

Burchardt, Marian. 2017. "Saved from hegemonic masculinity? Charismatic Christianity and men's responsibilization in South Africa." *Current Sociology* 66(1): 110–127.

Cadge, Wendy. 2012. *Paging God: Religion in the halls of medicine*. Chicago: University of Chicago Press.

Cadge, Wendy and Mary Ellen Konieczny. 2014. "'Hidden in plain sight': The significance of religion and spirituality in secular organizations." *Sociology of Religion* 75(4): 551–563.

Cadge, W., M. Griera, K. Lucken and I. Michalowski (2017). Religion in public institutions: Comparative perspectives from the United States, the United Kingdom, and Europe. *Journal for the Scientific Study of Religion* 56(2), 226–233.

Cazarin, Rafael, and Mar Griera. "Born a pastor, being a woman: biographical accounts on gendered religious gifts in the Diaspora." *Culture and Religion* 19.4 (2018): 451–470.

Clot-Garrell, Anna, and Mar Griera. "Beyond Narcissism: Towards an Analysis of the Public, Political and Collective Forms of Contemporary Spirituality." *Religions* 10.10 (2019): 579.

Cornejo, M. 2012. "Religión y espiritualidad,¿ dos modelos enfrentados?.Trayectorias poscatólicas entre budistas Soka Gakkai." *Revista Internacional de Sociología* 70(2), 327–346.

Crewe, Ben. 2011a. "Depth, weight, tightness: Revisiting the pains of imprisonment." *Punishment & Society* 13(5): 509–529.

Crewe, Ben. 2011b. "Soft power in prison: Implications for staff–prisoner relationships, liberty and legitimacy." *European Journal of Criminology* 8(6): 455–468.

Crewe, Ben, Jason Warr, Peter Bennett, and Alan Smith. 2014. "The emotional geography of prison life." *Theoretical Criminology* 18(1): 56–74.

Csikszentmihalyi, Mihaly. 2000. *Beyond Boredom and Anxiety*. San Francisco: Josey-Bass.

De Groot, K. 2010. "The institutional dynamics of spiritual care." *Revista de Estudos da Religião*, 10(1), 21–28.

De Michelis, Elizabeth. 2008. "Modern yoga: History and forms." In *Yoga in the Modern World: Contemporary Perspectives*, edited by Mark Singleton and Jean Byrne, 17–35. New York: Routledge.

Evans, Tony, and Patti Wallace. 2008. "A prison within a prison? The masculinity narratives of male prisoners." *Men and Masculinities* 10(4): 484–507.

Fedele, Anna and Kim Knibbe. 2013. *Gender and Power in Contemporary Spirituality: Ethnographic Approaches* (Vol. 26). New York: Routledge.

Foucault, Michel. 1988. "Technologies of the self: A seminar with Michel Foucault." Paris.

Furseth, Inger. 2003. "Secularization and the role of religion in state institutions." *Social Compass* 50(2): 191–202.

Furseth, Inger, and Lene Maria van der Aa Kühle. 2011. "Prison chaplaincy from a Scandinavian perspective." Archives de sciences sociales des religions 153(1): 123–141.

Goffman, Erving. 1961. *Asylums: Essays on the social situation of mental patients and other inmates.* Harmondsworth: Penguin.

Goffman, Erving. 1971. *Relations in Public: Microstudies of the social order.* London: Allen Lane.

Griera, Mar. 2017. "Yoga in penitentiary settings: Transcendence, spirituality, and self-improvement." *Human Studies* 40(1): 77–100.

Griera, Mar, and Anna Clot-Garrell. 2015a. "Doing yoga behind bars: A sociological study of the growth of holistic spirituality in penitentiary institutions." In *Religious Diversity in European Prisons*, edited by Irene Becci and Olivier Roy, 141–157. Cham: Springer International Publishing.

Griera, Mar, and Anna Clot-Garrell. 2015b. "Banal is not trivial: Visibility, recognition, and inequalities between religious groups in prison." *Journal of Contemporary Religion* 30(1): 23–37.

Heelas, Paul, Linda Woodhead, Benjamin Seel, Bronislaw Szerszynski, and Karin Tusting. 2005. The Spiritual Revolution: Why religion is giving way to spirituality. London: Blackwell.

Houtman, Dick, and Stef Aupers. 2007. "The spiritual turn and the decline of tradition: The spread of post-Christian spirituality in 14 Western countries, 1981–2000." *Journal for the Scientific Study of Religion* 46(3): 305–320.

Illouz, Eva. 2008. *Saving the Modern Soul: Therapy, emotions, and the culture of self-help.* Berkeley: University of California Press.

Jewkes, Yvonne. 2005. "Men behind bars: 'Doing' masculinity as an adaptation to imprisonment." *Men and Masculinities* 8(1): 44–63.

Johnson, Robert. 1987. *Hard time: Understanding and reforming the prison.* Pacific Grove, CA: Brooks/Cole Publishing.

Johnson, Robert. 2002. "Assessing the impact of religious programs and prison industry on recidivism: An exploratory study." *Texas Journal of Corrections* 28(1): 7–11.

Karp, David R. 2010. "Unlocking men, unmasking masculinities: Doing men's work in prison." *The Journal of Men's Studies* 18(1): 63–83.

King, Ursula. 2008. "Spirituality and gender viewed through a global lens." In *Religion, Spirituality and the Social Sciences: Challenging marginalization*, edited by Basia Spalek and Alia Imtoual, 119–136. Bristol: Policy Press.

Koch, Anne. 2015. "Competitive charity: A neoliberal culture of 'giving back' in global yoga." *Journal of Contemporary Religion* 30(1): 73–88.

Malventi, Dario and Álvaro Garreaud. 2008. "Curar y reinsertar el fenómeno de la deslocalización terapéutica en el engranaje penitenciario. " *Revista Espai en Blanc*, 3–4. Available online at: http://espaienblanc.net/?page_id=1692

Martínez-Ariño, Julia, Gloria García-Romeral, Gemma Ubasart-González, and Mar Griera. 2015. "Demonopolisation and dislocation: (Re-)negotiating the place and role of religion in Spanish prisons." *Social Compass* 62(1): 3–21.

Martos-Garcia, Daniel, José Devís-Devís, and Andrew C. Sparkes. 2009. "Sport and physical activity in a high security Spanish prison: An ethnographic study of multiple meanings." *Sport, Education and Society* 14(1): 77–96.

Michalowski, Ines. 2015. "What is at stake when Muslims join the ranks? An international comparison of military chaplaincy." *Religion, State & Society* 43(1): 41–58.

Nizet, Jean and Natalie Rigaux. 2005. *La Sociologie de Erving Goffman*. Paris: La Découverte.

Pagis, Michael. 2010. "From abstract concepts to experiential knowledge: Embodying enlightenment in a meditation center." *Qualitative Sociology* 33(4): 469–489.

Rieff, Philip. 1966. *The triumph of the therapeutic*. New York: Harper.

Rocha, Kliger Kissinger Fernandez, et al. 2012. "Improvement in physiological and psychological parameters after 6 months of yoga practice." *Consciousness and Cognition* 21(2): 843–850.

Scheff, Thomas J. 1988. "Shame and conformity: The deference-emotion system." *American Sociological Review* 53(3): 395–406.

Schütz, Alfred. 1973. *Collected Papers I: The problem of social reality*. Edited by Mark Natanson. The Hague: Matinus Nijhoff.

Sherry, John and Robert Kozinets. 2007. "Comedy of the commons: Nomadic spirituality and the Burning Man festival." *Research in Consumer Behavior*, 11, 119–147.

Smith, Benjamin R. 2007. "Body, mind and spirit? Towards an analysis of the practice of yoga." *Body & Society* 13(2): 25–46.

Van Klinken, Adriaan. "Male headship as male agency: An alternative understanding of a 'patriarchal' African Pentecostal discourse on masculinity." *Religion and Gender* 1(1): 104–124.

Wahidin, Azrini. 2002. "Reconfiguring older bodies in the prison time machine." *Journal of Aging and Identity* 7(3): 177–193.

Woodhead, Linda. 2007a. "Why so many women in holistic spirituality?" In *A Sociology of Spirituality*, edited by Kieran Flanagan and Peter Jupp, 115–125. Aldershot: Ashgate.

Woodhead, Linda. 2007b. "Gender differences in religious practice and significance." In *The Sage Handbook of the Sociology of Religion*, edited by James Beckford and Jay Demerath, 550–570. Los Angeles: Sage.

11 "Things I do are manifestations of love"

Queer religiosities and secular spirituality among Montreal Pagans

Martin Lepage

Since the 1980s, contemporary Paganism in the province of Quebec, Canada, has enabled women, lesbian, bisexual, and heterosexual, as well as gay men, to reconcile sexual diversity with a need for spirituality or religious life (Adler 1986; Charbonneau 2001; Dufresne 2004; Griffin 1999; Hurteau 1993; Kraemer 2012; Luhrmann 1989; Magliocco 2004). Wicca, for instance, has offered a fertile alternative to the Catholic Church, especially in regards to normative popular—and very negative—discourses on religion in Quebec (Charbonneau 2008; Gagnon 2003). Much research has shown how such religiosities have flourished in a context where Christian authority had lost dominion over people's sexual lives and expressions of sexual identities (Heelas 2008; Heelas and Woodhead 2005; McGuire 2008). But few have explored the relationship, in terms of categories, between religion and spirituality, as they are part of a larger social debate, around power, agency and normativity, pertaining to gender and sexual identities.

Today, LGBTQ identities are very much at the edge of research in social studies and humanities. Following the lineage of Simone de Beauvoir (1949), Michel Foucault (1976), Judith Butler (1990, 1993), Eve Kosofsky Sedgwick (1990), and Teresa de Lauretis (2007), queer theory has become a liberatory project pertaining to academia as well as social justice in general. According to queer theory, gender is a social construct based on the imposed iterative performance of certain types of behaviors and labels dividing men and women on the basis of biological distinction (Dorlin 2008). The category of "sex" itself is gendered, the body being conceived, perceived, controlled, and portrayed in all social spheres, and it is very much rooted in patriarchal hierarchies that marginalize women and sexual minorities as less, deviant, or dangerous. As we are still witnessing today, individuals who do not conform to the gender binary continue to be victims of rejection and violence, subject to threats and death. Some of them, who enjoy an easier, often wealthier way of life, try to use their platform to send a message of acceptance and to educate Westerners about non-binary identities. With that said, their impact is greatly moderated by the force of social norms which keep prescribing the gender binary and heterosexuality as the natural model and as ideal exclusive essences. Understood as such, the power they deploy, the agency they enact, can only be measured in relation to the pervasiveness of cisnormativity and heteronormativity (Guilhaumou 2013; Dorlin 2008).

This chapter will explore the ways in which contemporary Paganism inter-
sects specifically with the experience, from childhood on, of queer individuals
from Montreal, Quebec. This research illustrates how queer Montreal Pagans
perceive their own spirituality in relation, mostly, to Quebec's alleged secularization after the Quiet Revolution in the 1960s and 1970s, which history
will first be problematized vis-á-vis sexual diversity. Furthermore, it will
examine the ways in which queer Montreal Pagans understand and integrate
negative perceptions of religion in general, a notable marker of Quebec
"secular" society. Quebec population is very much aware of those (not so)
new gender and sexual identities, but the multiplication of discourse coming
from the different sub-groups of the LGBTQ community often results in
confusion, erasure, or appropriation of conflicting political issues and stances
(Chamberland et al. 2009; Lamoureux 1998). This chapter also questions the
construction of queer identities as it is greatly facilitated by contemporary
spiritualities, understood not as separate from religion, but in conscious
dynamics with different types of social norms in established religion, in alternative spiritualities, as well as in the gender binary.

Secularism in Quebec: spirituality after the Quiet Revolution

Understanding the process of secularization in Quebec and in Canada
requires the articulation of secularization and *laicité* or laicity, two concepts
which stem from conflicting influences in terms of separation of Church and
State. Historically, Quebec's stance on freedom of religion and religious
practice has been either very discreet or non-existent in writing. Quebec's
secularization process has been, and continues to be, torn between Imperialist
and French models. The former model of secularization describes a gradual
loss of social and cultural purpose for religion as a normative reference for
moral values and behaviors, as well as worldviews (Milot 2004, 29). The latter
understands secularization as aimed directly at the lawful separation of
Church and State, in addition to a step back of religion in sociocultural space.

The issue of secularization is very much alive in the Canadian province of
Quebec. In fact, scholars often argue about different things when it comes to
the separation of State and Church in Quebec (Milot 2004; Taylor 1991).
There are even still debates about the legitimacy of secularization and *laicité*
in Quebec, as some municipal government officials, for example, continue to
put forward Catholic rites and symbols during procedures in smaller cities.
Consequently, an extensive commission on *accomodements raisonnables* or
"reasonable accommodation" was ordered in 2007 by Quebec Prime Minister Jean Charest, and led by philosopher Charles Taylor and sociologist
Gérard Bouchard. The ultimate goal of this commission was to determine
what religious symbols and rites from different religious traditions, namely
Christian and Muslim, among many, were allowed, and to what extent, in
the public sphere.

Moreover, an important part of the research on the results and consequences of secularization in Quebec focused on education (Estivalèzes and Lefebvre 2012). There is still much debate about religion in public schools, one aspect of it being the *Ethique et Culture Religieuse* curriculum, which aims at teaching religion to elementary and high school students in a non-biased way, from an ethical and cultural perspective. There are still many questions as to whether this program is having effective and positive results in regards to the "vivre-ensemble" and prescribed attitudes toward religious and cultural diversity.[1]

The process of secularization started in the province of Quebec after what historians call the *Révolution tranquille*, French for the "Quiet Revolution". This period, from 1960 to the beginning of the 1970s, designates a time of particular turmoil in Quebec's sociopolitical and religious panorama which ended the *Grande Noirceur* ("Great Darkness"), the postwar period during which, for better or for worse, schools and medical facilities, mainly, were closely intertwined with the Catholic Church. Following the industrial revolution, a major baby boom was somewhat orchestrated by religious leaders as a tactic to strengthen the Church together with the nation. During the years of Duplessis, a Quebec prime minister who implemented very conservative politics from 1944 to 1959, a feeling of revolt was brewing in the background, and after the Quiet Revolution peaked in 1968, Quebec was to secularize in a radical way, not leaving much time for adaptation or preparation.

Micheline Milot argues that Quebec today is experiencing issues with laicity, as a neutral-state process of determining the space allowed to religious institutions and groups of faith in the public sphere, notably in schools, in the government, in military forces, in medical facilities and more. She also suggests that laicity, as a process, started before secularization in Quebec. If laicity can be measured in terms of legislative and juridic changes in Canadian State and laws, secularization is usually a slower process qualified by the waning force of the Church's grip and religious morals on society as a whole (Bruce 2006, 419). With that said, French Canada, by the end of the eighteenth century, was freed from the Protestant and Anglican religious pull at the political level, but Quebec's mindset remained quite dominated by the Catholic Church's pressures to conform to a pious lifestyle. As such, the rise of Paganism and New Age practices in Quebec can be counted as one of the many changes resulting from Quebec's secularization process.

In her paper "Gendering Secularization Theory" (Woodhead 2008), Linda Woodhead, looking at power relations in terms of gender, class, ethnicity, and sexuality, to which we should add physical abilities, age, language, and so on, suggests that 1960s sexual revolution did not have the magnitude certain scholars have wanted to show. It is interesting to mention here that women only received the right to vote in 1940 in Quebec, showing somewhat of a twenty-year delay behind the United States in terms of women and sexual minorities' rights. Echoing Vacante's claim (2005), Woodhead states that women in Britain did not experience the same kind of disaffiliation from the Church and religion as men did. Their relationship to "traditional" domestic roles and work opportunities vary greatly from those that men have to face, creating different pressures to distance themselves from religious commitment. This can certainly be applied to non-heterosexual and queer individuals back then and to this day in Quebec. Moreover, Woodhead argues that Pagan religiosities are particularly adapted to respond to women's needs, to create meaning or foster healing in times of hardship.

Following Charles Taylor's notion of an ethics of authenticity (1991), religion is mediated today through individual experience mostly, and has largely become a matter of identity (Beauchemin 2005). Instead of coming from a transcendent source of power and authority, religious experience occurs through a horizontal immanent sacrality which has different value for everyone and comes from no specific areas of culture and society (Lombo de León and van Leeuwen 2003, 81). In a context where multi-culturalism or interculturalism (Bouchard 1995), alongside globalization and the pervasiveness of the Internet, redefine social networks and identities, modern individualism can only be organized on a larger scale by a neat separation between people's untouched freedom of faith and the effect of people's faiths on common social arenas.

This chapter aims to show how Pagan spiritualities are understood by my informants in regard to Quebec's attitudes toward religion as a social nor-mative system, and as an important part of public everyday life. It will take into account the complex meaning coming out of their life narratives around their gender and sexual identities. It will also show how certain negotiations with Pagan religiosities reflect on their perception of categories such as reli-gion, spirituality, and identity. The next sections will give a brief description of contemporary Paganism and how LGBTQ (lesbian, gay, bisexual, trans-gender, and queer) Pagans I have met challenge gendered representations and practices inside and outside the Pagan community.

Paganisms and queer identities

Contemporary Paganism is an umbrella term used to characterize several sub-traditions like Wicca, Goddess spiritualities, Druidry, Heathenism, and various ethnic and Romanticism-inspired religiosities focused on the sacredness of Nature (Davy 2007; Harvey 1997). These traditions, as most Pagans call their religion or spirituality, are often rooted in the revival of ancient and pre-Christian mytholo-gies and religious cultures. Wicca, for one, the most influential Pagan movement in Quebec (Gagnon 2003), is based on the idea that contemporary witchcraft is ulti-mately inherited from magical practices having survived the Christianization of Europe, all heir to an ancient pan-Indoeuropean fertility worship to an encom-passing Great Goddess and Horned God (Clifton 2006; Hutton 1996, 1999).

Since religious authority is very loose in Pagan traditions, leaders being guides more than rulers, there are no strong boundaries between traditions, as individuals mix inspirations, rituals, and symbolic systems according to their preferences. Eclectic Wicca, or what some adepts call neo-Wicca, is very much present in Montreal, where Pagan traditions merge for different reasons. Much effort is put toward teaching new generations of Wiccans and Pagans in Montreal, but teaching generally allows for a great deal of freedom when it comes to practice and belief. Furthermore, lack of religious authority has resulted, over the decades, in the prevalence of experience when it comes to authenticity (Ezzy 2014). People join Pagan traditions and groups because it works for them.

Wicca in Quebec is very much the result of different Pagan and New Age trends coming from Great Britain and the United States from the 1960s on (Clifton 2006). After Gerald B. Gardner's impact on the revival of contemporary Paganism in Great Britain, Wicca, which he had invented inspired by Romantic poets like Robert Graves, occultists like Aleister Crowley and Helena Blavatsky, and the famous anthropologist Margaret Murray, met the American melting pot, West Coast second-wave feminism and the psychedelic hippie counterculture of the 1960s. In the absence of data on that convergence in Quebec, it is reasonable to think that all those influences did not meet very much outside of urban Montreal context before the end of the 1970s, largely due to their prominence specifically in English and among non-religious milieus.

Today, Pagans enjoy some recognition in the public sphere, but nothing in Quebec and in Canada has been officialized or instituted. Certain Pagan-identified characters and symbols, like the pentacle or pentagram, and the triquatra, have wildly been used in popular television shows and movies. Conversely, there has been some recognition in the military, especially in the United States where soldiers can hold Pagan rituals on base (Davy 2007). In Toronto, the Wiccan Church of Canada has sought governmental recognition and tax exemptions as an official religious organization for years, to no avail. In Montreal groups like the Greenwood coven or the Crescent Moon School of Magic and Paganism are mostly focused on teaching and social events, rather than institutionalization. Wiccan priesthood, at its most codified and traditional, is still not recognized as an official religious position. And although Wicca is part of the many other sub-denominations comprised within the Unitarian Church of Montreal, for instance, Unitarian Universalism itself remains a very alternative denomination with very few religious identity markers.

Most Pagan traditions follow a liturgical and ritual calendar inspired by the cyclical movement of the sun and the moon. Specifically, the Wheel of the Year puts the world into a narrative of birth and rebirth prescribing agricultural and seasonal rites for each of the eight sabbats and thirteen esbats which happen on full moons. Some sabbats, like the ones generally known as Halloween or May Day are often portrayed by Pagans on television as ancient pre-Christian feasts (respectively Samhain and Beltane), but they remain more of a romantic narrative than they convey historical facts. They are the most notable Pagan events in popular culture and on social media, whereas other rituals like Wiccannings or Handfastings, Wiccan baptisms and weddings, hardly ever get attention in the public sphere.

Because my research focused on LGBTQ (lesbian, gay, bisexual, transgender, and queer) individuals and groups, traditions and participation were greatly divergent from traditional or more dualistic Wicca, which revolves around the sexual relationship between the Triple Goddess as an ideal of femininity and the Horned God as an ideal of masculinity. During my four-year fieldwork research, I have partaken in different types of groups' gatherings and meetings, private, public, and on festival locations, and all of them tried to recognize everybody's sensibility in terms of religious preference. This translates into a variety of configurations of gender representation. Masculinity and femininity, the realms of manhood and womanhood as divine essences, are perceived in more or less rigid ways depending on the specific tradition or even on the individual who joins them. For instance, when I was invited to join esbat rituals among a Montreal coven called Silverwheel, a small private group of practitioners, the Goddess and the God were very much influential, the Goddess being the most important part of their divinity. In comparison, when they invited me to a more populated semi-public ritual for Beltane, the symbolism of the Goddess and the God loomed over everything, even if they were not mentioned explicitly. During New Moon Drums circles, organized by members of the Montreal Pagan community who identified with the Pagan tradition Reclaiming Witchcraft, which portrays gender in a more fluid way, the Goddess was prominent and often used as an archetypal figure on which every participant could rely no matter their gender or sexual identity. Other meetings arranged by members of another part of the Pagan movement, the Radical Faeries, enacted a great deal of awareness of non-binary gender issues, as did a small number of rituals during the most popular Pagan festival in Canada, Kaleidoscope Gathering (Lepage 2013).

In order to understand the normative underpinnings of LGBTQ Pagans identities, I conducted semi-directive interviews, which allowed me to draw on the "meaning itineraries" of my informants. Meaning itineraries refer to a project of construction of the self aiming to make the person whole and to put into a coherent narrative different contradictions of existence and singular events (Lemieux 2003). These itineraries show the ways in which Pagan people deal with discrepancies between ritual symbolics and their gender or sexual identity, what we call queer negotiations. They also show how LGBTQ Pagan people position themselves in regard to, mainly, the Catholic Church, as well as religion more generally, as they encounter it in the public sphere.

In this respect, performance and ritual studies developed by British anthropologist Victor Turner (1969, 1986), inspired by French ethnologist Arnold Van Gennep (1909), suggest that every ritual act works to perform an identity validated by the community after it has been internalized through the force of experience (Grimes 1982; Houseman 2012; Schechner 2006). This applies, to different degrees, to other aspects of identities like gender, social status, class, and so on. Rituals, in that sense, can be shared, transposed, and transformed through multiple communities to which individuals belong (McGuire 2008). The next section will examine more closely the relationship between contemporary Paganism and the emergence of sexual diversity in

Quebec, as well as the ways in which my informants position themselves and their practices in this network of power relations.

Religion and the LGBTQ movement in Quebec

Montreal Pagans I met certainly identified with some *queerer* factions of the Montreal LGBTQ community, which remains, despite (or because of?) a Gay Village, very fragmented (Higgins 1999). In the same way, the LGBTQ community is, in general, very much disconnected as a whole from religious affiliations and devoid of explicit rituals. This phenomenon is largely due to the general discourse of religious institutions against LGBTQ identities and, more precisely in Quebec, to an earlier more complex relation between gender and sexuality since the Quiet Revolution.

Jeffery Vacante (2005) argues that the narrative of the alleged sexual revolution of the 1960s in Quebec was constructed in a very heterocentric way. Aimed at heterosexual men in order to rebuild national identity, as they would become "Masters in their own homes" again, this project put forward the notion of a "normal" Quebec. This was mainly in response to the emasculating of men by the Church, but also by English conquests which put French-Canadian men in a position of inferiority. Instead of a revolution, Quebec ended up with a new set of unspoken rules designed to control women and sexual deviants, which widely mistakenly included rapists, pedophiles, as well as those charged with incest and bestiality. Vacante states:

> Some of the loudest calls for an activist and secular state during these years came from those people who argued that the Church was instilling "feminine" values in boys and standing in the way of Quebec's virile destiny. The centralization of social services and education in the state during the 1960s, therefore, became the means to reverse the "effeminizing" influence of the Catholic Church and transformed the state into the primary instrument for men's empowerment.
>
> (Vacante 2005, 36)

Still moved by the strong climate of sexual anxiety and a male identity crisis that occurred during the Quiet Revolution, the LGBTQ community is witnessing, like the rest of society, more and more occurrences of gay, lesbian, and transgender public personalities and characters in Quebec media. In addition, more and more Christian denominations are accepting of LGBTQ individuals and families, and a certain shift in discourse is occurring as certain main events within the gay or queer communities pertain to spiritual experiences and certain new types of religiosities (self-discovery, self-growth, healing, and drug-induced spiritual experiences, etc.).

Nevertheless, some Pagans who identify more specifically as queer chose to create a safe and friendly space outside of the Pagan community in which to practice rituals and organize spiritual activities (Lepage and Gauthier 2016;

Lepage 2013, 2015). As a matter of fact, some of my informants are very much engaged in leading different kinds of rituals during queer events, offering tarot card readings, yoga classes for heavier people, advice services, and teaching those techniques as well. Others are part of performative art groups in which they express non-binary gender roles, experienced as rites of passage for themselves and for their community. My paper "A Lokian Family" (Lepage 2013) gives a detailed description of an all-queer Norse-inspired group of Montreal Pagans.

Through a close examination of life narratives and meaning itineraries, the next section will help determine whether or not the non-binary way in which some of my informants define identity and sexuality is reflected in a less exclusive separation between religion, synonym for an oppressed Quebec, and spirituality, as a way to gain power individually and collectively.

Pagans choose to practice and live by certain rites and ideas that imbue their lives with a sense of community, which Quebec society, as a sexually and spiritually normative society, has failed to provide. They (not all of them, as this chapter shows), choose to go against a certain national project and general Quebec identity by returning to religion or to spirituality which, even if very popular among youths and the general public, is still frowned upon by secular society as irrational.

Even if they generally position themselves against Christianity and Catholicism, a number of my informants don't see a real distinction between different religions, whether Christianity, Buddhism, Judaism, and so on, as they understand them to originate from the same Ancient religions. As an example, one of them, Sarabee, speaks of religions and differences between them in this way:

"I'm gonna give to you so that you'll give back to me": that's the Christian way. But the Buddhist is like: "Don't punch this guy if you don't want to get punched". That makes more sense to me. I got that at a pretty early age and I never really renounced Christianity. When I read the Bible I see a story in my head that is beautiful. I see the lessons of Jesus and how they bastardized it and masculinized it and ruined so much richness, like the richness of a mother who would give up everything and watch her son die... All these different symbolisms, I see it as rich and powerful lessons to learn, and I can integrate them to all the religions that I've read about. I get the picture... the Bhagavad Gita... They all seem to be telling the same story just about two thousand years apart and I kind of don't understand how the rest of the world doesn't see it. I don't care if I don't believe what you believe, I want to know and be able to state what I believe in. I don't see religion as a burden. Church is pretty, it smells nice, it has candles, and it has art. There is a traditionalist in me, a big part that respects tradition and things that are old, that have been said and been written down. Even if I realize the Bible has been *man-anized*. As women, we don't have a written history, it's *his-story*. So I see religion, I do feel kind of missing from it... all the religions that are structural, I see that as restrictive, but I can also see through it what the beauty is, what they hold in the ritual and the having of a communal get together at a certain time and place.

Sarabee's words speak loud and clear of the distinctions she makes about religion. All religions have a common core of moral values which should help anyone belonging to any religion to become a better person. Religions, as they become instituted, use their narratives to separate between cultures, races, men, and women. But being Pagan, Sarabee insists that she understands the beauty and the artistry behind them, the love that comes out of their narratives, which allows her to develop an open spirituality welcoming of different beliefs and practices. This is the general consensus among Pagans I have met as to how religion can be double-edged and spirituality, all-encompassing.

This perspective on these categories needs to be further problematized. On the one hand, contemporary Pagans often draw parallels between non-traditional and alternative rituals and beliefs adjacent to dominant religious institutions, as well as certain Indigenous and Aboriginal traditions, as they would be sort of cousin-traditions (York 2003). Just as they create communities in which heterosexuality is more or less understood as a standard or criteria for the recognition of one's identity, their practices are typical of a liberal multicultural project aiming at the integration of several cultures into one.

On the other hand, certain similarities arise when it comes to issues of authenticity around Pagan identity. If Quebec national identity is torn between Canadian multiculturalism and a *pure laine* or "pure wool" French-Canadian imagery, Pagans understand their ancestry as generally mixed culturally. Montreal Pagans claim ancestry stretching out to Irish, Scottish, Italian, and Celtic cultures, but rarely use the *Québecois de souche* or "Quebecer at the root" identity as a pointer for their religiosities. Not all with the same attention to cultural appropriation, they look at Indigenous traditions when it comes to Ancient and pre-Christian pre-colonized Quebec territory (Lepage, 2018).

The last portion of this chapter will examine, through case studies, the complex networks of meaning within which two of my informants position themselves in regard to Quebec's negative perception of religion and to gender representations and practices within the Pagan community and in society in general. It will then compare the lines of their life narratives to show the extent to which gender and sexual identity impact their relationship to their religiosities.

Maria

Maria is a forty-year-old divorced woman who works as an administrative assistant. Six years ago, she quit a promising job in information technology, feeling the need to regain contact with her spiritual life. Her strict Italian Catholic education had never quite reached her heart, and she chose to study yoga in order to teach it. She explains:

> Once I got a bit older, I thought, "Well, these are really not my values, so why would I go to church?" I ended up looking up… well Pagan would be something that makes sense to me, so when I started researching stuff on Paganism, I saw still a whole bunch of things about worship, worshiping Gods and Goddesses, and that's not any better. Okay, it's fine, they have a male and female figure, but there is still this idea of worship, and I still have a problem with that. So I just got the whole thing and I said, "Forget it, I'm just not religious, not into this worship stuff." Well into my 30s, I started doing my yoga certification which is much more spiritual. But then too there is like a certain level of other values that were not personal to me. I said, "Okay, this is still an interesting concept, but it's not something I follow every day." I just feel I'm making my own way, and my own path and just the past couple of years, I've been really fleshing that out more and see exactly what my spirituality means to me.

Maria qualifies her gender as queer, refusing to limit her sexual orientation to a fixed identity. She also identifies as bisexual and she is in a polyamorous relationship with two transgender persons. Consequently, when Maria found Paganism, she did not feel very attracted to Wicca or to other gendered spiritualities. However, she was rapidly inspired by practices of ancestor worship and by the symbolics surrounding the elements (water, earth, air, fire, and spirit), which she considers to be the oldest of ancestors. Maria identifies herself as a spiritualist or a Pagan pantheist. She says, talking about the influence of a Catholic education on her present spiritual practice:

> The only concept that was kept, and it's just a concept, I got from my childhood, in terms of them calling it God… God is in everybody, and that is a concept that I still believe in. I expanded it to not just people, but plants, animals… everything that is embodied has this spirit within them. I guess the other thing which was one of the childhood lessons I learned from Jesus, is that he would often talk about love, and that kind of universal love, this is what I try to do in my life. Things I do are manifestations of love. This is something I hold on to, that I believe comes from that, even if they are very general concepts anyway.

Moreover, telling her story, Maria specifies that her experience with her polyamorous relationship has a great influence on her diverse interests in

Pagan religiosities. Although she takes part in the Montreal all-queer group
Lokabrenna Kindred, Maria strongly indicated to me that her affiliation with
this group was only as a guest. She rather emphasizes her solitary religious
practice which includes a learning journey toward mediumship, in order to
communicate with the spirits of the dead and to gain sensibility over the
living and the elements. Furthermore, Maria frequently uses the aromather-
apy technique called Bach Flower Remedies to yield the energies within the
spirits of plants. Through these practices, Maria experiences a spirituality that
focuses less on gender and sex and more on the immaterial and the invisible.

On the other hand, Maria's relationship with her other transgender
boyfriend allows her to put forward her interest in social activism. With her
boyfriend, she practices commemoration rites for the ancestors, inspired by
his direct knowledge of First Nations spiritualities. She explains, "I try to
honor the land I currently live on, that was colonized by our ancestors, and to
respect it. If there's things I could do in a native American tradition, that, I
would do it, in respect for where I am, where I live." In addition, both are
members of a drag king group with which they personify and parody the
gender binary. Maria is also one of the organizers of the third-gender ritual
given at Kaleidoscope Gathering in 2012, during which they tended to suf-
ferings caused by homophobia and transphobia.

Maria's spiritual practices, even though she perceives them to be solitary,
have an effect on her community. She says,

> I've gotten so much within the past years on the type of spirituality that
> is important to me: talking to spirits, being able to be open, to speak
> messages whether they are for me or someone else, being able to be open
> enough to speak messages. It's a way of living. Spirituality is intertwined
> with art, with sex and sexuality, in a tantric way but also just in the
> sharing of intimate space.

Maria's contribution to Lokkabrenna Kindred does more than just emphasize
the value of energies or the spirit of things, instead of the gendered materiality
of the body. In addition to revealing the nature of Maria's view of the world,
of her actions on the world, and of her relationships with her dear ones, the
openness she talks about reflects her queer identity as well as how she wants
to put it out in the world. In fact, the love and respect she values so much
within her spirituality also go hand in hand with her social activism against
cultural appropriation and with her lifestyle. She feels the need to respect
First Nations people by trying to understand them and pay homage to their
ancestors, and she tries to evacuate from her practice any reference to the
gender binary. This certainly demonstrates, contrary to her religious education, how important individual and consensual autonomy is to her. For
Maria, this autonomy can ensure her agency and her power to influence the
meaning and the value of her actions in every sphere of her life.

Callum

Callum, 24, is a preschool teacher, a conceptual and visual artist, an author, a director, and a diviner. He is single and lives with roommates in Montreal. Raised by a Presbyterian family from Toronto, he came to Montreal after high school, speaking both English and French, in order to study to become a teacher. Callum was raised in a very liberal household and, with the advent of the Internet, he was able, at a young age, to satisfy his interest for other cultures from around the world, like those of Egypt, China, and Scotland, the country of his ancestors. He describes his religious education as such:

> I was brought up Presbyterian, I was baptized when I was a child, and my parents decided to take us to church on Sundays when I was six. Very close to my house, it was the United Church and they had Sunday school. The kids would go to the front of the church and sit in front of the altar and the priest would tell a bad story and the parents would beam and be happy and the kids would be shipped off to Sunday school. The teachers there were rad... it wasn't bad, despite the play every year at Christmas. But we had to memorize a song for a certain age, and I did memorize the Lord's prayers, and I got a Bible as a present because they thought I was gonna be a minister. It was a really great present to my very inquiring mind and I started marking the stuff that I knew my parents didn't follow. They were not very religious, but they felt it was their duty. After the age of six, my life would start to take a different turn. I would mark the stuff, including gay stuff. I was not into it anymore, I told my parents and they respected that. It kinda felt like a punishment, me staying home alone. But they would go the three of them and I would stay home and read about Ancient Egypt, wishing that my parents worshiped Thoth instead of the Christian god.

In his teenage years, he had already explored different spiritualities like Buddhism and Wicca, which he quickly gave up for a much more chaotic spirituality inspired by the Radical Faeries and LaVey's Satanism. He then immersed himself in punk culture, alcohol, and drugs, leaving aside his interest for spirituality until he got to college and took anthropology classes about magic.

Today, Callum identifies as a queer man, because he has no problem identifying with a masculine gender, but he refuses to be categorized by his sexual orientation. He says: "I have an issue with masculinity, but not with being masculine. [...] I feel like a man, like, I'm masculine, but I'm my own masculine, which is not aggressive and domineering and all of those things that identify with patriarchy." By the age of four or five, he already suspected he was queer, but it is only when he discovered Pagan religiosities that he was able to express and fully assume his queer sexual identity. He talks about his coming out in this way:

When I swallowed my pride and told one of my best friends... I was so excited to speak to him... I remembered that recently... it was a secret place we would meet, behind my parents' house... I would smoke a cigarette and offer the smoke to him... thinking back that gave me strength and something exciting to kinda look back on, like "Here's what I'm doing with this project of telling people and coming out", and it was like immensely helpful and powerful. I felt myself doing a complete 180. I felt like a complete different person, at school and with my friends, I absorbed the message of valuing yourself and knowing yourself to be divine, even though there is no divinity, you being the godhead. It was great, I didn't leave myself behind, I just absorbed this huge lesson... even my walk changed. I was, like, a confident fucker.

The act of coming out, for him, was then a project to put forward this connection to the divine element within himself, certainly a very common narrative for LGBTQ Pagans. In accordance with that, Callum describes himself as a magician, as in a practitioner of magic, and only joins the Pagan movement because it gives a more familiar voice to his solitary practice. More specifically, after the death of his grandfather, he started building small altars dedicated to his deceased grandparents and to his ancestors in general. Very moved by the symbolism surrounding death, the passing of time and the cycles of life, he also maintains on these altars the image of the Mexican goddess of death, Santa Muerte, which he sees as a multicultural archetype of healing and magic. He says: "She protects queers, the sex workers, people who ride motorcycles, drug dealers, people who cross the border, the things that institutions are against." He also believes in respecting and honoring the spirit of the place, in his case the spirits of the city who inhabit urban spaces and fill them with life. Callum thus advocates a spiritual or religious experience that is rooted in the physical world and the material but also devoid of gendered or, at least, heteronormative content.

In the same way, his job as a preschool teacher allows him to teach children some general knowledge, also present in contemporary Paganism, that is seen as universal, such as the changing of the seasons, the celebration of cultural diversity, basic astronomy, elements like fire and water, as well as energy-raising techniques. Outside of work, Callum also started to gather, for Halloween or the summer solstice for example, a small group of friends and acquaintances, to commemorate the dead and promote diverse transitions of life with people who are not used to that kind of practices. Identifying more and more publicly as being Pagan, Callum encourages people in his life even more easily to come to him for advice or perspective. Through divination, like tarot, dream interpretation or I-Ching, he often talks about very intimate matters with his "clients," like death, family problems, identity problems or illness. He also encourages members of his family to ritualize even more their multiple family celebrations by promoting a spiritual experience through the pleasures of the senses (meals, chants, music).

Callum's religious and magical practices allow him to express a "deep-seated need for something, which is mystical and divine and magical that re-imbues life with something of power and mystery." This is also the need of many LGBTQ people who want to open up the limits of the sexual binary. By promoting diversity, he opts for a symbolic and physical performance functioning without referring to gender or sexual identity. In defining himself as a solitary practitioner of magic, Callum, distanced from the general Pagan community, carries on his de-compartmentalizing or queering efforts in his relationship with his family, friends, work and magical practices. In fact, Callum describes his practices as a kind of "internal alchemy" that can transform a situation of domination into one of empowerment, and that allows people to connect more deeply with the world around them.

Conclusion

This chapter has shed light on some of the negotiations that Montreal LGBTQ Pagans perform in order to make sense of gender representations and practices in the Pagan community. With practices they claim to be spiritual and separated from religious institutions, Pagans who have different views on gender are able to make sense of their own experiences, and deal in their own way with gender norms. Moreover, most of them also agree in their critique of how masculinity and femininity, as social constructs, should be perceived on more equal grounds. For that reason, they choose to adopt different practices that appeal to the physical and spiritual aspects of their non-binary gender and sexual identities. Being less normative than what usually occurs in Wicca or mainstream Paganism or in Western culture in general, they convey different attitudes toward religion and the religious context in Quebec.

Their practices, which they consider as being separate from religion, touch the public sphere, to some degree, outside of their respective communities, or at least, imbue people with enough power to change the boundaries between those communities. Maria, through the lens of her non-binary gender and sexual orientation, takes her spirituality to a political level. Even if religion remains somewhat of a normative institution for her, she also still feels connected to Catholicism as it taught her, first and foremost, the values of love and respect. In that sense, spirituality, instead of being understood only as separated from the Church, becomes a tool for peaceful action outside of religious contexts and within a larger queer community. For Callum, whose queer identity allows him to develop a critique of heteronormativity in society, spirituality goes beyond a distinction between communities, whether religious, sexual, or connected to family ties or friends. It also reaches out to more public milieus in his professional life, which instills in them a need for connection between people, their worldviews and their actions.

The life narratives of my informants Maria and Callum, and the discourse of most LGBTQ Pagans I met, show a strong reaction against Quebec religious history in terms of how the Catholic Church impacted women and LGBTQ people negatively. With that said, there is somewhat of a gap between that preconceived perception of religion and how Catholic rites and beliefs actually had a negative effect on their lives. Those who have deconstructed power relations in society, starting with gender, tend to have a more comprehensive notion of religion in Quebec, in coherence with the ways in which they open up gender identities. But those individuals actually often started out with a more liberal and tolerant religious education. This certainly pertains to secularization and laicity issues in the Canadian province, inasmuch as such attitudes toward diversity, be it religious, sexual, ethnic, and so on, are very much prized in Quebec as a multiplicity of identities come in contact with each other. They recognize individual experiences as specific to certain areas of the population, and they allow for their worldviews to have an equal meeting ground, and for their practices to be freely expressed, passed on, and valued for their authenticity.

In sum, this chapter and the experiences it portrays point to the urgency of understanding social power relations in dynamics with several loci of normativity and agency. Having focused on two of them, religious norms and gender, this chapter also reminds of the socio-scientific potential contained in comparing and combining social norms (Dorlin 2009) in the study of new identities and religious practices.

Note

1 As of March 2020, this curriculum has been abolished in Quebec by Prime Minister François Legault's administration

References

Adler, Margot. 1986. *Drawing Down the Moon: Witches, Druids, Goddess-Worshippers and Other Pagans in America Today.* Boston: Beacon Press.
Beauchemin, Jacques. 2005. *La société des identités: éthique et politique dans le monde contemporain.* Montréal: Athéna Éditions.
Bouchard, Gérard. 1995. "Le Québec comme collectivité neuve. Le refus de l'américanité dans le discours de la survivance." In *Québécois et Américains. La culture québécoise aux XIXe et XXe siècles,* edited by Yvan Lamonde and Gérard Bouchard, 15–60. Montréal: Fides.
Bruce, Steve. 2006. "Secularization." In *The Blackwell Companion to the Study of Religion,* edited by Robert A. Segal, 413–429. Blackwell: Oxford.
Butler, Judith. 1990. *Trouble dans le genre: Le féminisme et la subversion de l'identité.* Paris: La Découverte.
Butler, Judith. 1993. *Bodies that Matter: On the Discursive Limits of "Sex".* New York: Routledge.
Chamberland, Line, Blye W. Frank and Janice Ristock. 2009. *Diversité sexuelle et construction de genre.* Québec: Presses de l'Université du Québec.
Charbonneau, Marisol. 2001. "Mother Earth, Father Sky? The Sexual Politics of Contemporary Wicca and Paganism." In *Stories from Montreal 2: Ethnographic*

Accounts of Life in North America's Francophone Metropolis, edited by Tammy Saxton, Crystal Léger and Karoline Truchon, 1–19. Montréal: Armchair Academic Publications/Concordia.

Charbonneau, Marisol. 2008. "A Distinct Paganism: The Contemporary Pagan Revival in Montreal at the Turn of the Millennium." Master's diss., University of Ottawa.

Clifton, Chas. 2006. *Her Hidden Children: The Rise of Wicca and Paganism in America*. Lanham, MD: AltaMira Press.

Davy, Barbara Jane. 2007. *Introduction to Pagan Studies*. Lanham, MD: AltaMira Press.

de Beauvoir, Simone. 1949. *Le Deuxième Sexe*. Paris: Gallimard.

de Lauretis, Teresa. 2007. *Théorie queer et cultures populaires: De Foucault à Cronenberg*. Translated by Marie-Hélène Bourcier. Paris: La dispute.

Dorlin, Elsa. 2008. *Sexe, genre et sexualités: Introduction à la théorie féministe*. Paris: Presses Universitaires de France.

Dorlin, Elsa, ed. 2009. *Sexe, race, classe: pour une épistémologie de la domination*. Paris: Presses Universitaires de France.

Dufresne, Lucie. 2004. "The Goddess Incarnate: A Discourse on the Body Within One Community of Contemporary North American Goddess Worshippers." PhD diss., University of Ottawa.

Estivalèzes, Mireille, and Solange Lefebvre. 2012. *Le programme d'éthique et culture religieuse: l'exigeante conciliation entre le soi, l'autre et le nous*. Québec: Presses de l'Université Laval.

Ezzy, Douglas. 2014. *Sex, Death, and Witchcraft: A Contemporary Pagan Festival*. New York: Bloomsbury.

Foucault, Michel. 1976. *Histoire de la sexualité, tome 1, La volonté de savoir*. Paris: Gallimard.

Gagnon, Mireille. 2003. "La mouvance wiccanne au Québec: un portrait de la sorcellerie contemporaine". Master's diss., Université Laval.

Gauthier, François and Jean-Philippe Perreault. 2008. "Jeunes et religion dans la société de consommation: état des lieux et prospective." In *Jeunes et religion au Québec*, edited by François Gauthier and Jean-Philippe Perreault, 9–28. Québec: Presses de l'Université Laval.

Griffin, Wendy. 1999. *Daughters of the Goddess. Studies in Healing, Identity, and Empowerment*, Walnut Creek, CA: AltaMira Press.

Grimes, Ronald. L., 1982, "Defining Nascent Ritual." *Journal of the American Academy of Religion* 50(4): 539–555.

Guilhaumou, Jacques. 2013. "Autour du concept d'agentivité." *Rives méditerranéennes* 41: 25–34.

Harvey, Graham. 1997. *Listening People, Speaking Earth*. New York: New York University Press.

Heelas, Paul. 2008. *Spiritualities of Life: New Age Romanticism and Consumptive Capitalism*. Malden, MA: Blackwell Publishing.

Heelas, Paul and Linda Woodhead. 2005. *Spiritual Revolution: Why Religion is Giving Way to Spirituality*. Oxford: Blackwell.

Higgins, Ross. 1999. *De la clandestinité à l'affirmation: Pour une histoire de la communauté gaie montréalaise*. Montreal: Comeau & Nadeau.

Houseman, Michel. 2012. *Le rouge est le noir: Essais sur le rituel*. Toulouse: Presses universitaires du Mirail.

Hurteau, Pierre. 1993. "L'homosexualité masculine et les discours sur le sexe en con-texte montréalais de la fin du XIXe siècle à la Révolution tranquille." *Histoire sociale/Social History* 26(51): 41–66.

Hutton, Ronald. 1996. *The Stations of the Sun: A History of the Ritual Year in Brit-ain.* New York: Oxford University Press.

Hutton, Ronald. 1999. *The Triumph of the Moon: A History of Modern Pagan Witchcraft.* New York: Oxford University Press.

Kraemer, Christine Hoff. 2012. "Gender and Sexuality in Contemporary Paganism." *Religion Compass* 6(8): 390–401.

Lamoureux, Diane, ed. 1998. *Les limites de l'identité sexuelle.* Montréal: Remue-ménage.

Lemieux, Raymond. 2003. "Bricolage et itinéraires de sens." *Religiologiques* 26: 11–34.

Lepage, Martin. 2013. "A Lokian Family: Queer and Pagan Agency in Montreal." *The Pomegranate,* 15(1–2): 79–101.

Lepage, Martin. 2015. "Ritualités queer et performativité du genre: le cas du néo-paganisme à Montréal." In *La fabrication des rites,* edited by Denis Jeffrey and Angelo Cardita, 157–177. Québec: Presses de l'Université Laval.

Lepage, Martin. 2018. "Religiosités queer néo-païennes et la question de l'authenticité dans la Wicca." *Religiologiques.* 36: 1–27.

Lepage, Martin and François Gauthier. 2016. "Les fées dansent autour du Mont-Royal: Magie et négociations queer chez les néo-païens de Montréal." *Anthro-pologica* 58(2): 264–276.

Lombo de León, Francisco and Bart van Leeuwen. 2003. "Charles Taylor on Secu-larization. Introduction and Interview." *Ethical Perspectives* 10(1): 78–86.

Luhrmann, Tanya M. 1989. *Persuasions of the Witch's Craft: Ritual Magic in Con-temporary England.* Cambridge, MA: Harvard University Press.

Magliocco, Sabina. 2004. *Witching Culture: Folklore and Neo-Paganism in America.* Philadelphia: University of Pennsylvania Press.

McGuire, Meredith. 2008. *Lived Religion: Faith and Practice in Everyday Life.* New York: Oxford University Press.

Milot, Micheline. 2004. "Laïcisation au Canada et au Québec: un processus tran-quille." *Studies in Religion / Sciences Religieuses* 33(1): 27–49.

Schechner, Richard. 2006. *Performance Studies: An Introduction.* New York: Routledge.

Sedgwick, Eve Kosofsky. 1990. *Epistemology of the Closet.* Berkeley, CA: University of California Press.

Taylor, Charles. 1991. *The Ethics of Authenticity.* Cambridge, MA: Harvard University.

Turner, Victor W., 1969. *Le phénomène rituel: Structure et contre-structure.* Paris: Presses Universitaires de France.

Turner, Victor W. 1986. *The Anthropology of Performance.* New York: PAJ Publications.

Vacante, Jeffery. 2005. "Writing the History of Sexuality and 'National' History in Quebec." *Journal of Canadian Studies/Revue d'études canadiennes* 39(2): 31–55.

Van Gennep, Arnold. 1909. *Les rites de passage.* Paris: Émile Nourry.

Woodhead, Linda. 2008. "Gendering Secularization theory." *Social Compass* 55(2): 187–193.

York, Michael. 2003. *Pagan Theology: Paganism as a World Religion.* New York: New York University Press.

Afterword

To the vagina triangle and beyond!

Linda Woodhead

Consider the religious landscape of a city in Brazil, China, Nigeria, India or Singapore today. It is rich, bustling and competitive. Large historic temples, churches, mosques and cathedrals occupy dominant spaces; their almost exclusively male priests, pastors, bishops and imams have a high status. Most are thronged with ordinary people doing their own thing: meeting, praying, making offerings at shrines, venerating sacred beings, asking for good fortune, divining the future, purifying body and mind. In other nooks and crannies of these cities one stumbles across a plethora of local shrines covered in offerings to local deities; some to high gods and goddesses too. Look a bit deeper, and you will find networks of spiritual practitioners operating from homes and shops proffering various kinds of healing, magic, deliverance, contact with the dead, removal of curses, and so on. Even though they may never tell their clerics, many people – especially but not exclusively women – move skilfully through this rich landscape, seeking out the services they need for themselves and loved ones or enemies. They judge astutely how to filter that information for the enquiring priest, pollster or secular authority, if asked.

Turn next to a city in a relatively affluent liberal democracy like Canada, Britain, Greece, Sweden or Spain today. As the twenty-first century matures, we are beginning to see something not dissimilar. Even though the religious landscape has thinned out, churches continue to have a dominant place, albeit one of legacy rather than vitality. Waves of post-war migration have brought much greater religious pluralism, with mosques being particularly visible indicators. But the rapidly waning influence of the churches and the gradual de-stigmatization of popular forms of spiritual practice – even by secular authorities – have led to an increasingly lively marketplace of spiritual alternatives. Cathedrals, holy wells and other historic sacred sites draw people for a wide range of reasons; ancient festivals are revived; tarot, astrology and belief in angels are on the rise; alternative spiritual practices are increasingly influential in once 'secular' spaces like the leisure and wellbeing domain, schools and hospitals.

The gender revolution in the study of religion has played a very important part in helping bring these changes into clearer relief, as contributions to this volume confirm. The creative upheaval it precipitated has challenged overconcentration on Olympian, male-founded, male-led religions, and reversed the scholarly dismissal of alternative practices as 'primitive', 'superstitious' or inconsequential. No longer are terms like 'magic' deployed to disqualify such phenomena from consideration. It is now normal to take female religious leaders and practitioners seriously and to appreciate their innovative and entrepreneurial role. It is normal and mainstream to research female-dominated or 'queer' forms of modern spirituality and to assess their competition with older forms of religion. It is also possible to question existing theories and approaches and to forge new concepts like 'lived' or 'everyday' religion to guide enquiry.

As this revolution has got under way, and as today's super-diverse religious landscapes have come into clearer focus, we have arrived at the point where our existing theoretical and conceptual categories are clearly failing us. This is the situation that this volume grasps and illuminates so clearly, both in its empirical contributions and its wider reflections. The editors take us through the step-wise progress that has been made so far. First there was 'religion', understood according to a very particular model imprinted by churches and other male-dominated institutions. Then there was 'spirituality' which, once it started to be taken seriously, opened up a new, creative phase of study. Attention was then given to the 'religion/spirituality' binary and the various ways in which the two might relate: 'spiritual not religious', 'spiritual and religious', and so on. Next, as exemplified by this volume, comes a situation where the category of the 'secular' or nonreligious is introduced as a substantive term and subject of study in its own right. As the editors say, it is not that the study of religion was ever unaware of 'secularization', but turning the secular into a field of study in its own right is a recent step. It represents a shift from treating the secular as a negative – the decline and absence of religion – to a positive: sets of practices, values and attitudes that compete with religion or ignore it altogether. This volume works with the full conceptual triad of the religious, the spiritual and the secular: what the editors delightfully label the 'vagina triangle'. The results, in terms of enhanced understanding, speak for themselves.

Yet the reflections in the book also show that these categories are breaking down. That is even clearer when we add a fourth category of 'no religion'. An artefact of surveys that ask people whether they belong to a particular religion or to 'none', the number of people identifying as nonreligious has been swelling recently, especially in many Christian-heritage liberal democracies. The move to take the category of 'no religion' more seriously in the study of contemporary culture and society is creating both greater illumination and deeper confusion. For 'non religion' is an even murkier term than 'religion' or 'secularism'. In some ways it is a mere placeholder rather than something substantive. Yet it is starting to be claimed as an identity-marker by individuals and institutions: the rise of 'non-religious' funerals and weddings is one example, as is the way that a society like the British Humanist Association has rebranded itself as Humanists UK with the express intention of representing not just self-identified 'humanists' but all 'nones'.

This piling up of categories – religious, secular, spiritual, non-religious – is problematic. We can end up spending so much time debating how to define them and where the boundaries between them lie that it becomes a distraction and an end-in-itself. That way madness lies, because these are tools of enquiry forged in different theoretical, empirical and research settings, with different strengths and vulnerabilities. Definitional clarity is a chimera. They can't be made to sit neatly side by side without overlap or confusion. Once we add 'lived religion' and 'everyday religion' to the mix the situation gets even worse. Our conceptual apparatus is creaking and groaning – and women are to blame!

One option now is to proceed pragmatically. Many chapters in this volume illustrate how the existing concepts and their associated theories can be used like a toolbox: open the box and select the tools that fit your data. That is a perfectly sensible strategy that can yield great insight. Having a fuller toolbox means that there is a better chance of finding appropriate tools for more nuanced analysis. The danger, however, for the study of religion and non-religion as a field, is that such eclecticism can lead to an accumulation of case studies that make sense on their own terms, but are incommensurable. What we gain in detailed understanding we lose in overall comprehension: a case of not being able to see the wood for the trees. An alternative option is innovation through the invention of new categories. Faced by the growing supply of operative concepts, the priority becomes not so much critique and supplement, but innovation and re-creation. Prompted by this book and wider reflection, I see at least two ways in which that can start to happen. I am enthusiastic about them both, though they are very different.

The first strategy is to go back to basics in the study of lived religion by looking for foundational building-blocks. This is partly how the field was forged in the first place, as categories like myth and ritual, church, sect and cult came into circulation. This time, however, we have a broader outlook, due in no small part to the way in which gendered and intersectional approaches have reworked the field. So, a rethink of foundational concepts needs to encompass not just the conventionally religious and secular, but those activities, beliefs and institutions that are occluded by both but are nonetheless oriented towards the sacred and/or supernatural. We thereby take lived practices and beliefs more seriously than ever: not merely as 'folk', 'vernacular' or 'popular' religion – somehow secondary to 'real' religion – but as equally, if not more, important. This approach, in the context of the contemporary religious landscapes that opened this Afterword, offers an exciting opportunity to rethink and refocus. For example, it may be that close attention to real-world categories that are widely shared across different cultures and societies will bring to the fore neglected but important common categories like ancestors, healing, witchcraft and divination/fortune-telling. The rich case studies that have been accumulating lately, combined with over a century of ethnographic and other research, directly resource such work.

The second, very different, approach is to go wider and become more abstract rather than more concrete. This will involve not so much the consolidation of a new suite of concepts, but the creation of new meta-theoretical approaches. The sociology of religion was dominated for over a century by the theory of secularization. Whatever its drawbacks, it gave coherence to the field, even when people were arguing strongly against it. Now that secularization theory has lost its ability to function in this way, the ground is clear for other frameworks to be constructed. In a seminal article, Stephen Warner (1993) argued that a growing focus on pluralization would play this role, and to some extent he has been proved right, especially if one includes under this heading a concern with crossings and boundaries. Francois Gauthier (2019) suggests that 'marketization' offers the most promising theoretical approach. Scott Draper (2019) presents 'religious interaction ritual' as a new meta-theoretical approach.

We can appreciate these suggestions but remain unconvinced that any single process – any '-ization' – can ever do justice to the dynamics of the religious and non-religious. My personal hunch is that there are a number of less all-encompassing theories – middle-level theories – that can be formulated to guide us through new territory. For example, reading this volume encourages me to revisit a framework that posits a permanent tension and interplay between two very different impulses. Drawing on the work of Michel de Certeau, I have called these the 'strategic' and the 'tactical' (Woodhead, 2013). The 'strategic' covers those forms and agents of religion and secularity that operate from a position of structural and institutional power. They look outward, plan, set the rules and try to dictate the future. The 'tactical' encompasses how people act in relation to strategic power, with different aims and ends, and using the tools to hand: reactively and subtly, often at the level of the personal, familial or small-group. Tactical religion does not merely operate through passive acts of resistance: it is creative and subversive in its own right. The tactical and the strategic always work together, in a dance or conflict of continuous interplay. In this volume we are introduced to many examples of this interplay between powerful, strategic forms of religion, and women and men who take from them what they want, use them, subvert them and play with them. We see also how such pragmatic, tactical action can impact back upon the strategy of the powerful. These dynamics can be glimpsed not only in relation to religion, but spirituality and secularism too.

This volume suggests to me that these power dynamics can also be thought of in terms of a dialectic between purifiers and pragmatists. Some of its contributions reveal a tension in contemporary global societies between strong 'fundamentalist' dynamics of purification and simplification (ideological, moral, regulatory, religious, secular and spiritual, gendered and sexed), and opposing movements towards 'lived', 'everyday' individual choice, pragmatic solutions, pluralization, post-rationalism and deregulation. The purificatory drive can be seen at work in several domains, including official religion, organized secularism, the law and politics. Religious officials and institutions have a natural tendency to want to purify, simplify and regulate. That tendency has intensified since the 1980s – as we see, for example, in the vast outpouring of catechisms, confessions, encyclicals and moral strictures by the magisterium of the Roman Catholic Church. We see the same tendency in the rise and growing influence of fundamentalism in all parts of the world. By definition, fundamentalists seek to reduce religion to a small number of clear and timeless principles, including patriarchal control. Modern media increase the propensity to communicate in easily digestible formulae. Institutionalized kinds of secularism display similar dynamics: the 'new atheism' of the post-9/11 period offers simplified and simplistic accounts of religion, pitting against them the vision of societies purified of all religious elements in public life.

Law and politics reinforce these purifying tendencies, often unwittingly. Clarity and simplification make things easier to operationalize for those in these domains who have to make difficult adjudications with weighty consequences. Moreover, legal and political elites are likely to be removed from the lived practices of religion and to encounter representatives of strategic religion and secularism, not representatives of its more tactical and pragmatic forms. So, for example, the concept of 'religious freedom' has been mobilized to reinforce the privileges of existing religious powers, to defend proselytization by mission-oriented faiths, to argue against state 'interference' in religious bodies, and to argue for exemptions from legal duties and obligations that are binding on other public bodies – such as those involving equality on the basis of gender and sexuality.

But the purificatory drive has been matched by the opposite dynamic on the ground: increasing fragmentation, pluralization, blurring of boundaries, refusal to accept traditional religious and secular expertise and privileges. Britain, for example, has moved in the space of my single lifespan from being a Christian-majority country to having a 'no-religion' majority. But some 'nones' say they are spiritual, and only a minority of them are atheist. Even within the 'spiritual' category there has been rapid change and a proliferation of different groups and activities. Most people no longer fit the old categories of religious, spiritual or secular very well. We draw eclectically on what works and what is personally meaningful. Traditional symbols float free, ancient practices are revived and modified, and new media connect people with like-minded others.

There is no escape from the push–pull of these competing dynamics, and no neutral ground between the different concepts that structure the study of religion. As scholars and as citizens, we inevitably get drawn into the battles and take sides, even if we don't like to admit it. If we treat church-based Christianity or mosque-based Islam as more real and important than private forms of spirituality, for example, then we give support to the strategic and purificatory enterprises; if, on the other hand, we question the judgement that solitary or 'privatized' forms of religion or spirituality are inferior and less important, we give support to more tactical, pragmatic approaches. There is no escape from the wider power struggles that this volume deals with, not even in ivory towers. But there has never been a better time to be self-critical and creative about the approaches we use, and in the process to bring to light aspects of religion and culture that deserve greater attention.

References

Draper, Scott (2019), *Religious Interaction Ritual: The Microsociology of the Spirit.* Lanham: Lexington Books.

Gauthier, François (2019), *Religion, Modernity, Globalisation: From Nation-State to Market.* Abingdon: Routledge.

Warner, Stephen (1993), Work in Progress towards a New Paradigm for the Sociological Study of Religion in the United States, *American Journal of Sociology*, 98, 1044–1093.

Woodhead, Linda (2013), Tactical and Strategic Religion. In Nathal Dessing, Nadia Jeldtoft, Jørgen Nielsen and Linda Woodhead (eds), *Everyday Lived Islam in Europe*, pp. 1–14. Aldershot: Ashgate.

Index